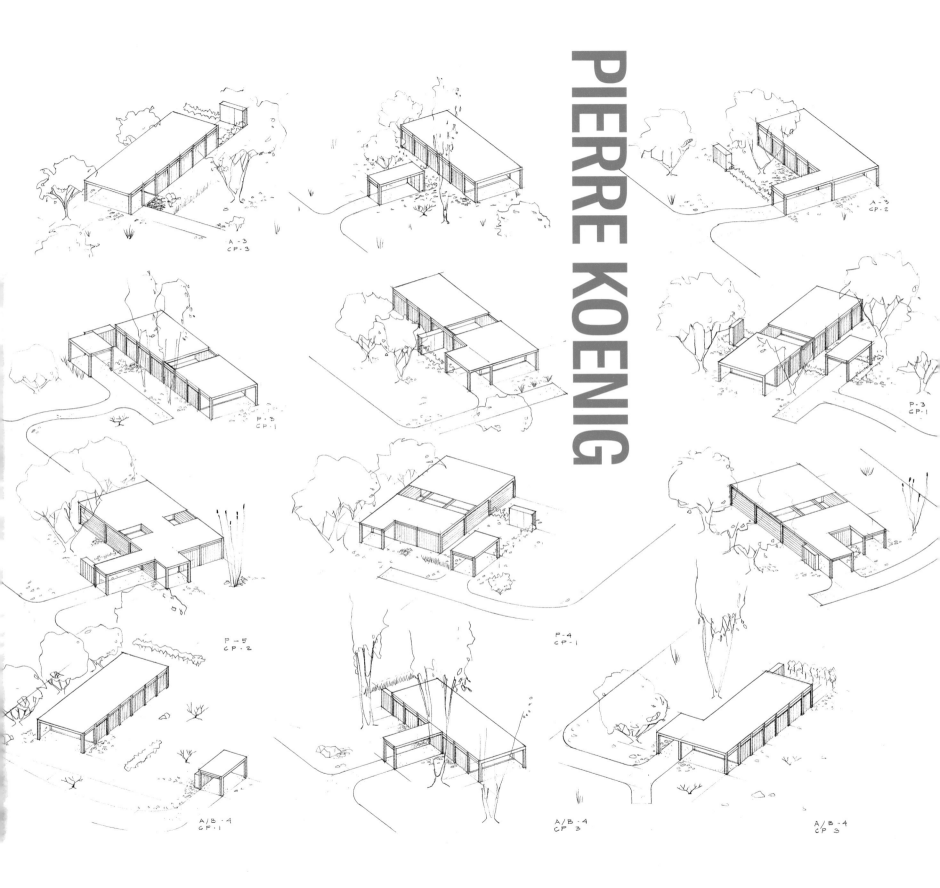

PIERRE KOENIG

A · 3
CP · 3

A · 3
CP · 2

P · 3
CP · 1

P · 3
CP · 1

P → 5
CP · 2

P · 4
CP · 1

A/B · 4
CP · 1

A/B · 4
CP 3

A/B · 4
CP 3

Stahl House (Case Study House 22), 1960. Photo by Julius Shulman.

NEIL JACKSON

# PIERRE KOENIG
## A VIEW FROM THE ARCHIVE

PUBLISHED BY THE GETTY RESEARCH INSTITUTE | LOS ANGELES

# CONTENTS

Pierre Koenig and George Foy at Koenig House 1,
Glendale, 1952. Photo by Julius Shulman.

# A VIEW FROM THE ARCHIVE

What does one know about architects after they die? There are the articles and interviews, sometimes the books, but always the buildings. The buildings are, above all, the lasting memory, the heritage, the inheritance. Yet for every building an architect completes, there are many they do not. So it was with Pierre Koenig, who died in Los Angeles in 2004. For most observers, his lasting memory now resides, perhaps more than anywhere else, in one nighttime photograph taken by Julius Shulman in 1960 of Case Study House 22. The building was unfinished when that photograph was taken, and, in any case, Koenig did not think it was his best work. That was Case Study House 21.

In 2006, the Getty Research Institute took possession of Pierre Koenig's archive from his widow, Gloria. It is an extensive collection containing over one hundred box files of correspondence, documents, drawings, photographs, and other material, both professional and private, as well as over 250 flat files of drawings, and rolled drawings too. It is a comprehensive yet an inevitably incomplete record of his life, but one that brings to light much that was unknown or forgotten and corrects many of the misunderstandings that have accumulated over the years. The purpose of this book is to explore the work of Pierre Koenig through the medium of his archive, for there his architectural development can be best understood, and from there, the best composite picture constructed. Yet unavoidably, other sources—including contemporaneous publications, later research, recorded interviews, and informal conversations—have been drawn upon to help assemble a more complete narrative.

Writing in *The Aspern Papers* (1888), Henry James commented that "the historian, essentially, wants more documents than he can really use." Considering the extent of the Koenig archive, such an observation might well be applied to this present interrogation. Consequently, the *view* that this book offers, whether an examination or a vista, is just one interpretation. □

Pierre Koenig, architect and general contractor, at the Bailey House (Case Study House 21), ca. 1958. Photo: Bethlehem Steel contact prints.

PROJECTED PERSPECTIVE OF B-25 MEDIUM BOMBER                    AERONAUTICAL DRAFTING

# BEGINNINGS

In a lecture given in 1990 at the San Francisco Museum of Modern Art, Pierre Koenig recalled his early life in that great port city: "I was born and raised here . . . and grew up around Golden Gate Park and the Marina and Ft. Mason."[1] The French Hospital, where he was born on 17 October 1925, was a large chateâuesque building on Geary Street, between Fifth and Sixth Avenues. His birth certificate describes his mother, Blanche Jeanne Chigé, as a housewife, and his father, Harold Rudolph Koenig, as a salesman with the Woods Lorry Company.[2] Young Pierre Francis Koenig was brought up at 2575 Washington Street, a four-story, bay-windowed apartment just two minutes' walk from Alta Plaza Park in Pacific Heights. The Marina District was only a few blocks to the north, and there, along the dockside, in what he called an "enriched environment,"[3] he would draw, ships, cranes, and whatever else caught his eye. "I feel the varied experience S.F. offers enriches a child' life," he told his San Francisco audience. "My later professional life was certainly influenced by the orient and its culture including the architecture and the ships and the music I experienced as a child. . . . I think Los Angeles is alright too. . . . The weather and the population explosion in L.A. gave me the chance to do a lot of experimenting."[4]

In 1939, the family moved to San Gabriel, east of Los Angeles, where Koenig attended Alhambra City High School, graduating in the summer of 1943. There was little in the yearbook, *The Alhambran,* to suggest what he wanted to do—for his future plans, he put "General"—but his friend Warren Rapelje inscribed the book, "Good luck to a super draftsman and good fellow."[5]

While still in elementary school, Rapelje had set up a shop selling parts for miniature airplanes and had been invited, at the age of ten, to join the San Gabriel Chamber of Commerce.[6] Perhaps it was Koenig's friendship with Rapelje that gave Koenig the impetus to start drawing planes. He soon showed a great aptitude for it. In high school, where he was excused from mechanical drawing classes, his pen-and-ink illustrations of military aircraft were put on show (fig. 1.1).[7] It could have been this interest in mechanical drawing or the "enriched environment" of the San Francisco dockside that encouraged him to enroll, in the autumn of 1943, at the School of Engineering at the University of Utah.[8] However, his time there was brief, for that December he was ordered to report for military service.

On 13 August 1943, soon after graduating from high school, Koenig joined the Enlisted Reserve Corps.[9] After receiving a high score in excess of 110 on the Army General Classification Test, Koenig was selected for the Army Specialized Training Program (ASTP), intended for men of high intelligence.[10] The US Army, in collaboration with a number of universities, ran the ASTP to train junior officers in areas such as engineering, medicine, and foreign languages. Among its alumni were Henry Kissinger, Ed Koch, and Kurt Vonnegut. The program, which was considered more demanding than West Point, offered a four-year college education in eighteen months before sending the students to Officer Training Candidate School.[11]

Fig. 1.1.
A B-25 medium bomber above a tropical coastline, aeronautical drawing, ca. 1942–43.

Koenig reported to the infantry school at Fort Benning, outside of Columbus, Georgia, for his ASTP basic training on 16 December 1943 (fig. 1.2). He took out National Service Life Insurance from the Veterans Administration two days later. At Fort Benning, he would have lived like a soldier, wearing a military uniform, receiving army pay, marching to class, and eating in the mess hall in his barracks. The weekly timetable included twenty-four hours each of classroom work and self-directed study, as well as six hours of physical training and five hours of military instruction. However, in February 1944, with increased manpower required in the long lead-up to D-day, Koenig was told that, along with about 110,000 other ASTP students, he would be transferred to a combat unit with the rank of private. He was sent to join the 86th Infantry Division (also known as the Black Hawk Division), at Camp Livingston, near Alexandria, Louisiana. There, he later said, he "endured" another basic training and became an expert rifleman.[12] His next posting was to Camp Bowie, at Brownwood, Texas, where he joined the 292nd Field Artillery Observation Battalion (FAOB), which had been formed there that February. It was with this battalion that, on 23 November 1944, he sailed from New York for England on the HMS *Carnarvon Castle* as part of a large convoy of some one hundred ships (fig. 1.3). After fifteen days at sea in the North Atlantic, during which they endured U-boat attacks and a huge storm, they docked safely at Southampton.[13]

For almost two months, the 292nd FAOB was bivouacked at the Grand Hotel in Swanage, Dorset, a large, turn-of-the-century, red-brick seaside hotel overlooking Swanage Bay and the English Channel. Although today a colorful seaside resort, in the winter of 1944–45, Swanage would have been dark and cold. Observation posts and dragon's-teeth tank traps littered the surrounding hills, and concrete pillboxes flanked the sides of Swanage Bay, where sea mines were deployed to prevent enemy landings. The town had been damaged by German bombing in 1942, and twenty people were killed. More recently, the area, and particularly Studland Bay to the north, had been used for practice landings in anticipation of D-day. It was, for Koenig, a gentle introduction to a continent at war. Worse was to come.

In his "Combat Diary," Koenig wrote, "Sailed from Weymouth, U.K. on L.S.T. 307, 3 feb '45. Crossed Channel Landed at La Harve, France, 4 feb. '45, on Beach. City Destroyed."[14] From Le

Fig. 1.2.
Pierre Koenig in military uniform at 626 North Alhambra Road, ca. 1943. Photographer unknown.

Fig. 1.3.
*H.M.S. Carnovan Castle* [*sic*], sketch from Koenig's "Combat Diary," 1944–45.

Havre, the 292nd was taken by motor convoy to Camp Twenty Grand, a tent city between Duclair and Hénouville, near Rouen.[15] From Camp Twenty Grand, they moved through Reims (staying there a night), Nancy, and Luneville to Betting, south of Saarbrücken and deep into the German annexed territories of northeast France. They were attacked by Messerschmitt Bf 109s and Junkers Ju 87s (the fearsome Stuka dive-bombers), as well as by two Heinkel He 219 night fighters, which they downed with their "50 mm machine guns." When taking classes in aeronautical drafting, Koenig had drawn the Stuka dive-bombers in action (fig. 1.4).

Koenig's ability to recognize these planes was probably the result of his training with the 292nd FAOB, whose job it was to pinpoint the location of enemy guns. Using direct eyesight, the Flash Section would spot muzzle blasts while the Sound Section, with the help of microphones placed in the ground, would listen for them. So fast and accurate was their detection of enemy guns, the US counter-battery could return fire within about forty-five seconds of the first flash being spotted. Working from four observation posts spread out along a ten-mile (sixteen kilometer) section of the front line, they were very much in the thick of it and sometimes found themselves behind the German front line.[16]

Fig. 1.4.
A Stuka attacking a seaport, aeronautical drawing,
ca. 1942–43.

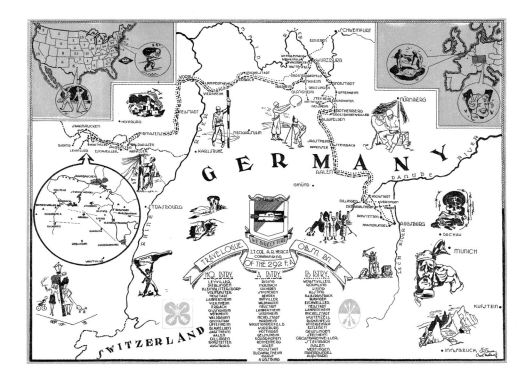

There is, in the archive, an illustrated map titled *Travelogue of the 292 F.A. OSBN. BN.*, which shows the route the 292nd took from Saarbrücken to Augsburg (fig. 1.5).[17] Although the map does not include the German front line, it does show how the three parts of the battalion—HQ Battery, A Battery, and B Battery—took separate positions around Saarbrücken, Würzburg, and Augsburg. From Betting (shown on the map as "Biding"), A Battery, which was Koenig's outfit, set up four observation posts around Forbach and Morsbach. Koenig's observation post at Morsbach was number 3; his "Combat Diary" records that posts 1 and 4 were knocked out.[18] On his hand-drawn map illustrating the "Disposition of Enemy Troops the first week of March '45," the observation posts are indicated by three small triangles positioned around Forbach; Morsbach is just to the south (fig. 1.6).[19] Forbach fell on 6 March, and A Battery moved about five miles (eight kilometers) north to Spicheren. Saarbrücken was the next target, and A Battery placed their four observation posts on a hill overlooking the south bank of the Saar River (fig. 1.7).[20] They were subjected to "much '88' shelling" until Saarbrücken fell on 20 March.[21]

From there, A Battery pulled back to Behren-lès-Forbach and then, for a short rest, to Hanweiler on the Siegfried Line, before regrouping with the other batteries and moving northeast to Neustadt and eventually crossing the Rhine at Worms. Lampertheim, Viernheim, and Michelstadt followed, where "beaucoupe wine was found," and then it was on to Hardheim: "good food ... and a few Gerry strafers, one JU 87 and eleven me 109 G's on 31 March '45."[22] Grossrinderfeld was reached on 2 April, and A Battery set up observation posts around Würzburg, which had suffered appalling bombing by the Royal Air Force, who, on 16 March, had generated a firestorm in the town. Koenig records that Würzburg fell on 5 April and that there was "Much champaigne. Much loot."[23]

The battalion now split up, A Battery made slow progress over the next few days. On 6 April, they returned to Grossrinderfeld before moving to Gützingen the next day. Three days later, they were in Neuses, followed by a stop in Röttingen on Friday the thirteenth. It was an inauspicious date:

Fig. 1.5.
*Travelogue of the 292 F.A. OBSN. BN.,* ca. 1946.

Fig. 1.6.
*Disposition of Enemy Troops the First Week of March '45,* sketch from Koenig's "Combat Diary," 1944–45.

Fig. 1.7.
*Disposition of Enemy Troops the Second Week of March '45,* sketch from Koenig's "Combat Diary," 1944–45.

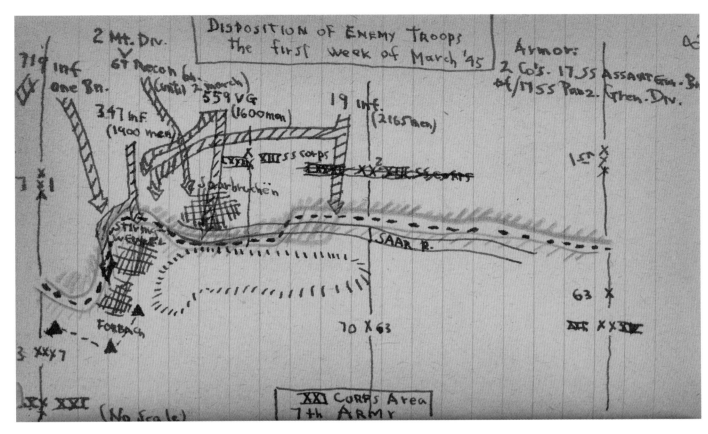

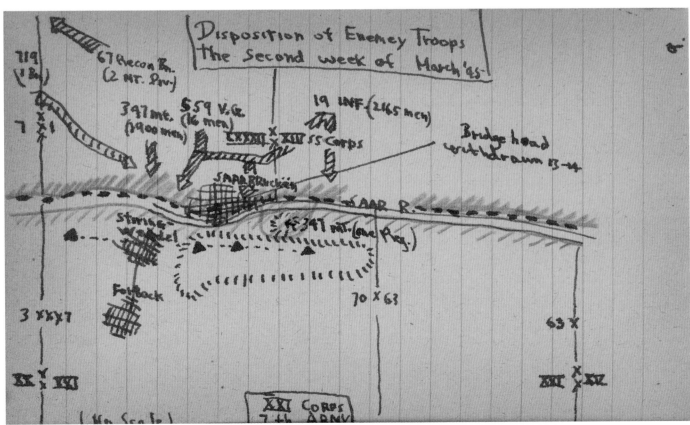

"Truck accident," Koenig wrote in his diary, "sent to clearing sta. Two casualties."[24] He rejoined his unit, now at Gelchsheim, later the same day or the next.[25] They were still only about nineteen miles (thirty kilometers) south of Würzburg.

Koenig was more badly injured than previously thought, for on 16 April, he was sent back to the casualty clearing station with a fever and then flown to Reims General Hospital in a C-47 transport plane. Recovery must have taken a few days, because the next entry in the diary reads, "Out of hospital, trip to Paris for Pass on VE day (May 8 1945) Rode on civilian train. Very Crowded."[26] Apart from a sketch in his diary, there is no indication of what he got up to in Paris, but, judging from the illustration, he must have had a good time (fig. 1.8).

Koenig writes that he rejoined his unit on 5 June at Schwäbisch-Gmünd, about seventy miles (113 kilometers) south of Würzburg. In the seven weeks during which he had been absent, they had not moved very far. The task now, but not for long, was the guarding of a displaced persons camp for Russians. Four days later, they were in Neckarsulm, thirty-seven miles (sixty kilometers) northwest. Despite the discomfort of "many bed bugs," they were "On way home."[27] From there, the 292nd passed through Heidelberg, Mannheim ("complete Destruction"), and Metz, arriving at the tent city of Camp Brooklyn near Reims on 15 June.[28] After two weeks, they were transported to Camp Lucky Strike, a tent city of about 1500 acres for 58,000 GIs at Saint-Sylvain, between Saint-Valery-en-Caux and Cany-Barville, on the Normandy coast. Arriving there on 1 July, they would have been reminded that personnel were allowed only one souvenir pistol, and that anyone found to possess more than one would be court-martialed and sentenced to six months hard labor in the European Theater of Operations.[29] Koenig might have evaded this rule, for a filing card in the archive states that he owned both a 9mm Mauser and a 9mm Luger.[30] After five days, they were shipped to Southampton and taken to a camp at Barton Stacey, to the east of Andover. "Good Camp (British)," Koenig wrote in his diary.[31] During the three-week stay, a leave must have been granted, for Koenig's "Combat Diary" shows a drawing of Piccadilly Circus in London with three heavily made-up "tarts" waiting to rough-up an inebriated GI (fig. 1.9). On 26 July, the soldiers took a train from Andover to Scotland. After traveling overnight, they arrived at Clydebank, where, with 15,999 other returning GIs, Koenig embarked the HMT *Queen Mary*.[32] They weighed anchor the following day, and, five days later, he wrote, "Arrived New York harbor 2 Aug. 1945 amid wild celebration. Home again to good 'ole' U.S.A.!"[33] Koenig's war, or at least one version of it, was now over. On 1 May 1946, he was given an honorable discharge at Camp Beale, in the Sacramento Valley, near Marysville, California. Already promoted to corporal, he was awarded the American Campaign Medal, the Army of Occupation Medal, the Good Conduct Medal, the European African Middle Eastern Campaign Medal, and the World War II Victory Medal. He had served for two years, four months, and sixteen days.[34]

There is a cleanliness and consistency about Koenig's "Combat Diary" that suggests it was assembled after the fact. Both the text, all written in the same ink pen, and the hand-drawn maps fall neatly into the first ten numbered pages. Next come the cartoonlike illustrations on unnumbered pages. There are no smudges, stains, muddy marks, or other suggestions that it was prepared in the field. Indeed, a rubber stamp imprinting his name on the cover indicates a later production. Yet there is no reason to doubt what it contains. The places mentioned, whether towns or small villages, are all identifiable, even if the spellings are incorrect, and they correlate to a confined and sometimes circulatory pattern of movement, which is understandable in a war.[35] There is also some documentary evidence to support this. On 6 July 1997, an old army buddy, Joe Knipps, now living in Alamogordo, New Mexico, wrote to Koenig:

Fig. 1.8.
*Paris* (Victory in Europe Day), sketch from Koenig's "Combat Diary," 1944–45.

Fig. 1.9.
*London* (Piccadilly Circus), sketch from Koenig's "Combat Diary," 1944–45.

Thanks for the video tape. Nice job!

Familiar names, but hard to recognize the faces. Names—Beck, Felt, Gay, Green, Koenig, Tygret, Ziegler. Faces—only Felt and Koenig.

A picture shown toward the end of the tape—of faces—waving from window of troop train (heading for home) recognized Felt and (I think) myself. . . . Won't be able to make the reunion in Florida.[36]

On 2 September 1997, Knipps wrote again:

Do remember climbing stairs to an OP in a church steeple.

From the picture you sent, I remember being in the same section with Maury & Bill Tygret. Also remember that it was a very exciting time in my life—WOULDN'T want to do it over, but I'm glad we were there.

Remember Jim Clark with that chaw of tobacco, Maury always up to some practical job. Wrestling Bill Tygret in the Mess Hall. . . . The picture (and also the audio) brought back many memories.[37]

The videotape that Knipps mentions had been prepared by Koenig in anticipation of a 292nd FAOB reunion in Orlando, Florida, in December 1997. Although referred to on the box as *292 at War,* the typescript bore the long title *A Computer Generated Presentation about the 292 Field Artillery Observation Battalion in Combat during World War II.*[38] It was ultimately intended for distribution to former members of his unit and anyone else interested. It ran a little over twenty-one minutes and comprised 450 still frames, with sound effects and a voice-over. The introduction to the printed script reads,

An historical account based on the experiences of Pierre Koenig during World War II. A computerized slide show with narration. All the images are snapshots taken by Koenig and other members of the 292nd. In the Atlantic/European combat zone from 1944 to 1945. A few photos were shot during subsequent trips to the battlefields. Factual information was taken from notes prepared by Koenig at the time. Places and events were researched in books and interviews with colleagues to assure historical accuracy. Some of this historical background material was used to augment the presentation.[39]

There is much in the videotape that corresponds to Koenig's diary or that can be independently confirmed. His expert rifleman status is borne out by his discharge papers, which designate him as "Expert M1 Rifle Mar 44."[40] Knipps's second letter recalled the moment, also described by Koenig, when "we arrived at the church at Morsback, what was to be my first Flash outpost. I found it to be under attack. After waiting awhile for the shelling to subside, we set up O.P. number three in the church tower."[41] We are told that, during training, Koenig learned how to drive a ten-wheeler truck at the driving school at Fort Sill at Lawton, Oklahoma,[42] and that the accident that later sent him to the hospital occurred when "one of our Flash trucks was blown up."[43] There is, nevertheless, some confusion or perhaps elaboration. According to the diary, his unit left Neckarsulm for Metz, via Heidelberg and Mannheim, on 9 June; while in the videotape, he claims they pulled out of Germany on 8 June. Similarly, the diary has him outside Saarbrücken enduring shelling from 88s for two weeks, but the videotape has him there for three weeks—"while we got the CRAP pounded out of us."[44]

The big anomaly occurs after the Flash truck accident. Rather than being flown to Paris, Koenig, according to the videotape, continued advancing with his unit.

> We crossed the Danube OK but after we were on the other side, way ahead of the main body of the 7th. army, the 12th SS Panzer Division and the 1st Panzer "Leibstandarte" Division closed the river in back of us. We spent a couple of days traveling alone on the road to Munich when we had the shock of our lives. We accidently ran into Dachau. We did not know what we had discovered. After a while it sunk in—a concentration camp! After shooting off the lock on the gates, we had to wait helplessly for the main body to arrive. We had very little to offer these thousands of helpless sick and starving victims. This was the worst thing I have ever seen in my life. The inmates killed some of the guards when they saw us coming.[45]

The US 7th Army did indeed liberate Dachau on 29 April 1945. However, contrary to what Koenig implies, the 12th SS Panzer Division and the 1st Panzer Division "Leibstandarte" were not in that area. As part of the 6th SS Panzer Army, both divisions were involved in Operation Spring Awakening (or the Plattensee Offensive) in Hungary during the first half of March 1945.[46] This was the last great offensive of the war.

After Koenig's unit, A Battery, crossed the Danube at Höchstädt an der Donau, the *Travelogue* map shows that they moved southeast to Zusamaltheim before turning east to Markt and then following the Schmutter River south to Augsburg, where they met up again with the other two batteries. There the routes on the *Travelogue* map end.

When Koenig says, "We spent a couple of days traveling alone on the road to Munich" before accidentally running into Dachau, that is wholly possible. Augsburg is a little over twenty-five miles (forty kilometers) northwest of Dachau, and, if they went there, the 292nd FAOB might have followed the Reichsautobahn (now Bundesautobahn 8) from Augsburg toward Munich or, more likely, what is now the St2051, which joins the St2047 near Schwabhausen before arriving at Dachau. But that is all speculation. Another explanation could be in the fact that Dachau was not one large site. There were over one hundred Dachau subcamps—mostly work camps, or *Arbeitskommandos.* A number of these were located around Augsburg, one specifically to provide forced labor for the Messerschmitt factory there. Perhaps it was one of these that they found.

Whatever the accuracy of this part of Koenig's war story, one who did question it was a former member of the FAOB's HQ Battery radio unit, William C. Hudelson, who, on 2 September 1997, wrote from Annapolis, Maryland, expressing his disgust at Koenig's effort:

> On my first viewing of your video clip which apparently purports to chronicle the participation of the 292nd FAOB in World War II, I was inclined to simply mail it back to you. However on a second viewing I decided it wasn't worth the postage. If that clip was supposed to represent the activities of the 292nd I will defer to the remark Col. Hercz made to me while you were making your presentation at Detroit "I'm not sure we were in the same war."[47] Your video clip appears to me to be a "Hollywood" version of your participation, with very little pretensions of accuracy. Your attempt to finance it under the guise of a contribution to the reunion fund, I find most reprehensible.[48]

The big problem for Hudelson was the mention by Koenig of Dachau. In his letter, he said that he had obtained some three hundred pages of historical data from the National Archives, which did not support Koenig's reference.

> Nowhere in the Historical Records [Hudelson wrote] is there any mention of Dachau. Therefore as far as the Battalion is concerned Dachau did not exist until information became public. However, I, too, have pictures of Dachau, and proof of dates. Until Detroit I had *never* shared those pictures and information with anyone other than my immediate family. From some of the comments in the newsletter apparently you have been discussing the Dachau incident with what I consider "outsiders." . . . I cannot of course stop you from talking to anyone. But if there is an attempt by you, or anyone, to involve outsiders in our reunion there is apt to be embarrassing consequences.[49]

Then, almost as an afterthought, Hudelson enclosed with his letter a *History of the 292nd Field Observation Battalion,* which he thought "might be of interest."[50]

Koenig's videotape raises some interesting questions. Why did it tell a different story from his "Combat Diary"? It was made more than fifty years after the events that it recalls: did it present a false memory, an adjusted memory, or a previously suppressed memory?[51] Koenig's diary, which is usually so accurate about dates and places, says nothing about the time between 16 April, when he was sent back to the casualty clearing station with a fever, and 8 May 1945 (VE Day), when he left the hospital to go to Paris.[52] It was during this three-week hiatus that Dachau was liberated. If the diary, being written after the event, is in this part a construct that, by omitting any reference to Dachau, reflects the official version of the 292nd FAOB's history, as contained in the National Archives, then so too is the videotape, which not only misplaces the two German Panzer Divisions but also tells a story that neither Colonel Arthur Raster Hercz nor his radio operator, Hudelson, recognized. From Hudelson's comments regarding the sharing of information on *"the Dachau incident"* with *"outsiders,"* it seems likely that, despite whatever the National Archives' historical records say, the 292nd FAOB was involved in the relief of the main camp or one of the many subcamps. But was Koenig actually there, or did he, through the videotape, simply place himself there after the event?

The trajectory of Koenig's career as an architect will become clear as this book develops, but, at this stage, it would be worth observing that in 1997, when he made the videotape, he had recently finished building what was to be his last new house, and, despite various approaches from potential clients, he had no new work on the horizon. Although being increasingly fêted for his past successes and in demand for lectures and exhibitions, his more recent work was not receiving any great recognition. Perhaps he thought that the reunion in Orlando of the 292nd FAOB would give him the opportunity to take center stage once again. □

# EDUCATION

If the experience of the war had given Pierre Koenig anything, it was an inner strength and the courage to take risks. In the script for his video presentation on the 292nd Field Artillery Observation Battalion (FAOB), Koenig wrote about army boot camp and being at war in Europe: "We had fights, got drunk together, took chances together and as it turned out almost got killed together. All this will never be forgotten."[1]

When interviewed close to the end of his life, he explained how the war had changed him:

A lot of us that came out of the War plunged into all these crazy things, 'cos you come out the War feeling different about things. I mean, nothing is really that important any more. 'Cos after that, you know, it is not important. You know what things are important after that. And you take chances. You do things you wouldn't ordinarily. . . . So if you look at all the people who were in the service during the War, it was a very bad thing but on the other hand you came out stronger. Either that or you break. . . . In World War II men weren't allowed to cry. You weren't allowed to have any feelings. You had to be strong. That's important. That thing's an important aspect. . . . It's a significant thing, I think.[2]

In the same interview, he stated that, as a child, he had never wanted to be an architect, yet he felt that it was his early experiences that eventually determined the type and character of his architecture.[3] Those experiences can probably be identified as two things: a growing awareness of industrial processes—first appreciated in the docklands of San Francisco and later manifest in his facility at drawing—and his ability to take risks, which he learned during the war.

As he told his audience at the San Francisco Museum of Modern Art in 1990:

When I came out of the War there was a great impetus to change. The War had developed many new materials and processes. Industrialization and mass production had reached their zenith during the War (right across the Bay Henry Kaiser was building a ship a day) and there was great need to provide homes and all types of buildings. Many architects started experimenting with new methods and different materials of building to replace the old methods. There was a certain excitement in the air, a feeling any problem could be solved.[4]

Then, one day, in the San Gabriel public library, he picked up a copy of *Arts & Architecture:* "I remember vividly those beautiful pen and ink drawings by Paul Rudolph and Ralph Rapson in *Arts and Architecture* magazine. I had never seen anything like it before."[5]

Koenig was most likely referring to Ralph Rapson's Greenbelt House, Case Study House 4, which had been published in *Arts & Architecture* in August and September 1945.[6] Rapson's evocative perspective drawings with a helicopter hovering above the building must have appealed to Koenig. It is ironic that it was this building, together with Koenig's own Case Study House 22, that was re-created for the *Blueprints for Modern Living: History and Legacy of the Case Study Houses* exhibition held at the Museum of Contemporary Art's Temporary Contemporary in Los Angeles in 1989.

Paul Rudolph was, at the time these drawings appeared, still completing his education at Harvard University while working during vacations with Ralph Twitchell in Sarasota, Florida. Although Rudolph left to tour Europe from mid-1948 to mid-1949, *Arts & Architecture* published the Miller Boat House and the Shute House in his absence and the Leavengood House following his return.[7] If Rapson's perspectives were a little whimsical, Rudolph's were rich and full and suggested to Koenig what he could do. In almost the same words as he had used for his San Francisco audience the previous year, he told students at Harvard in 1991 of the great impression these drawings had made on him: "I remember vividly, right after the war, those beautiful pen and ink drawings of Paul Rudolph and Ralph Rapson in *Arts and Architecture* magazine. I had never seen anything like it before. Suddenly the future became bright."[8]

Koenig's brief time studying engineering at the University of Utah did not help him gain immediate entrance to the architecture program at the University of Southern California (USC) following his demobilization in 1946. There was such a demand for university enrollment by returning GIs that his entry to USC was delayed for two years, during which time he attended Pasadena City College to

Fig. 2.1.
Drawing exercise, 11 December 1947.

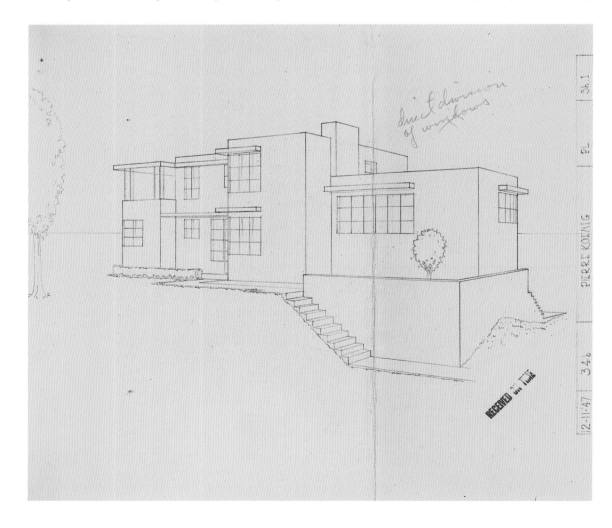

learn basic architecture skills. There is little in the work he produced there to suggest the direction his architecture was soon to take. For a graphics class in September 1947, Koenig drew the perspective of a modern block, on which his instructor, Mr. Annis, wrote in red, "poor weight of line Keep pencil sharp."[9] The modernist house Koenig drew that December came back annotated "direct division of windows" (fig. 2.1).[10] There was a lack of depth to the mullions and the window reveals, as if the external features were printed on the building's facade. For the course in interior decoration, he drew the five classical orders of architecture and an early American living room complete with leaded-light windows, Bristol glass, toby jugs, and pewterware. It was clearly a very traditional architectural education but one not untypical of the time. (figs. 2.2, 2.3).[11]

Desperate to gain admission to USC, Koenig and his friend George Foy sat in the dean's office for a week until they were finally accepted into the second year of the architecture program in the fall of 1948.[12] Here, Koenig was to receive a very different architectural education from what Pasadena City College had given him. In the 1930s, in an attempt to break away from the traditional education system derived from the École des Beaux-Arts, Arthur Clason Weatherhead, the dean of architecture at USC, had revolutionized the architecture program. His successor, Arthur Gallion, continued the process of modernization, turning the still quite young department into the leading West Coast architecture school, where the instructors taught not just architecture but also landscape design, industrial design, and textile technology.[13] The program continued to be characterized by Weatherhead's

Fig. 2.2.
*The Five Orders of Architecture,* 1948.

Fig. 2.3.
*Details—Early American Living Room,* 1948.

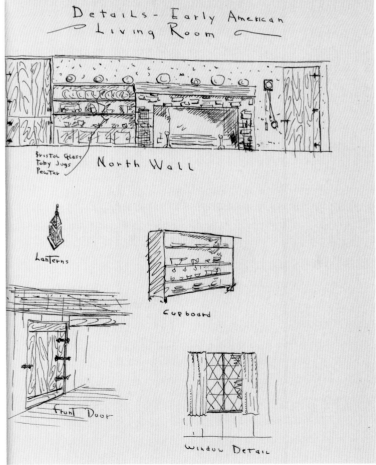

four main pedagogic aims: contemporary design and regional identity, technical proficiency, social responsiveness, and the involvement of cognate disciplines.[14]

Two pieces of coursework from Koenig's time at USC remain in the Getty Research Institute archive. One is a design for a branch library—a simple, asymmetrical, timber-frame building that, with its diagrammatic plan analysis, appears to be a second-year project (see pl. 1). The other is his third-year project, "Housing, Wood, and the Community: An Analysis," completed in January 1950. To head the third year, Gallion appointed one of Weatherhead's graduates, Calvin Straub, with whom he also practiced as an architect.[15] Straub's third-year studio was central to both the curriculum and the ethos of USC. Another contemporaneous student, Frank Gehry, later wrote of Straub's studio, "My third year was a turning point."[16] Teaching in the studio alongside the landscape designer Garrett Eckbo, Straub continued Weatherhead's pedagogical approach, promoting, as Ken Breisch observed, "a wooden post-and-beam structural system that allowed free-flowing interior spaces to open generously onto the surrounding landscape."[17] The architecture critic Esther McCoy, who knew many of the architects involved, attributed this approach to what she termed the USC-Pasadena School:

> Post-and-beam was popularized during the late forties and the fifties by the USC-Pasadena school—so called because many of its practitioners taught architecture at USC or lived in Pasadena. Theirs was mainly a panel-post system on a four-foot module, panels of solid or transparent materials filling the spaces between four-by-four posts. Post-and-beam reduced the number, or eliminated altogether, interior bearing walls, and was a more direct approach to achieving a flexible plan.[18]

When Koenig entered the program in the fall of 1948, those practitioners to whom McCoy referred were listed in the annual *Bulletin,* mostly as visiting critics for architecture: Gregory Ain, Gordon Drake, Harwell Hamilton Harris, Richard Neutra, Rudolph Schindler—all of Los Angeles—and Whitney Smith of Pasadena.[19] By the time Koenig entered the third year of the program in 1949, Drake had moved to Northern California, and another of Weatherhead's graduates, Raphael Soriano, had joined the school.[20] This slight change in pedagogic emphasis, from Drake's timber-based architecture to Soriano's steel-based architecture, at what was a crucial point in Koenig's education, was to prove significant. Also significant for Koenig were the appointments of Kenneth Lind in 1950 and A. (Archibald) Quincy Jones the following year.[21] Koenig credited Lind with teaching him how to create and organize space.[22] Jones, the fifth-year design critic, saw him through to his graduation in August 1952; and later, when building the all-steel Eichler Homes X-100 in San Mateo, California, he employed Koenig in his office.

Koenig's third-year project, "Housing, Wood, and the Community: An Analysis"—which was marked "good" and "pass+" and given a B grade—reflects all of the school's pedagogic aims.[23] Here, in a gesture of social responsiveness, Koenig asks, "Does a housing problem exist?," to which he answers, "Very definitely." He deplores the unsanitary and chaotic conditions of one-quarter of the nation's housing and cites the need to build 1.5 million new homes a year for the next fifteen years. Beneath a small photograph of a shantytown development within Los Angeles, he writes, "Coherence and order is just as important as sanitary conveniences for two reasons: they facilitate physical movement and provide the eye and mind impressions that influence living habits."[24] In a response that is symptomatic of his Los Angeleno context and a reflection of what he would have been reading in *Arts & Architecture* and the architectural press in general, Koenig argued, "The single family detached dwelling is the only type of unit that offers all the advantages of maximum living needs."[25] What then follows is no less than a manifesto for the modern house and a description of what was to be his own architectural direction:

> In order to produce a house that will serve the maximum types of people with the minimum of cost and effort it will be necessary to turn to the efficiency of American mass-production methods without sacrificing any human needs by paralysis of a static design. In order to do this I think a modular system of parts should be established so as to dispense with expensive cutting on the job that costs time and wastes material. While labor salaries are rising the efficiency of industry is also rising which leaves us to believe that the fabrication of parts at the factory is less expensive than the high-priced rather awkward mode of fabricating on site.[26]

Koenig then cites the inefficiency of building a house in situ, where differences of an inch or two in the structural timber frame leads to both unnecessary cuttings and wastage as well as an increase in the chances of error. To avoid the "paralysis" that a regular, repetitive architecture might induce, he argues for a system of identical measurements that allow modular units to be added or subtracted as needed.

To demonstrate these ideas, Koenig included in the submission a number of alternative plans for a small house. Using a concrete slab measuring 26 by 48 feet, he showed how the same foundations and services could be adapted on a modular basis to accommodate one or two adults or a family of three or four (fig. 2.4). At one end of the slab, the gas, water, and sewer pipes rose to service the kitchen, while about halfway along the slab's length, another set of water and sewer pipes serves the bathroom(s) and utility space. If the house did not cover the whole of the slab, as in *Variation IV,* a carport could be located alongside it (fig. 2.5). Where this plan shows spaces for entertainment and sleeping, Koenig wrote "good studio" in red and marked the separation between the two as flexible. This became the basis, if not the exact diagram, of the steel-frame house that he was to build for himself in Glendale later in 1950.

Fig. 2.4.
*Variation III,* house for a family of three or four, 1950.

Fig. 2.5.
*Variation IV,* house for one or two adults, 1950.

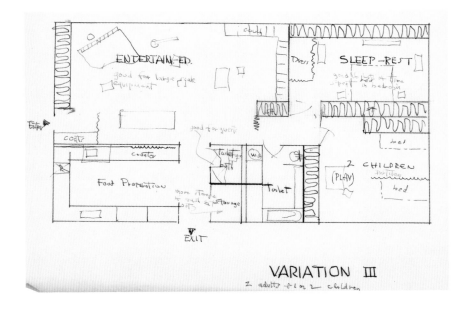

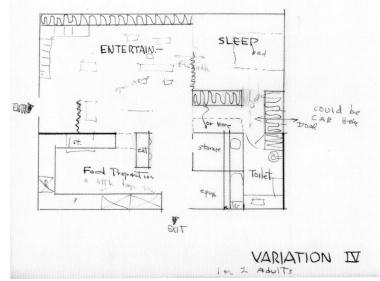

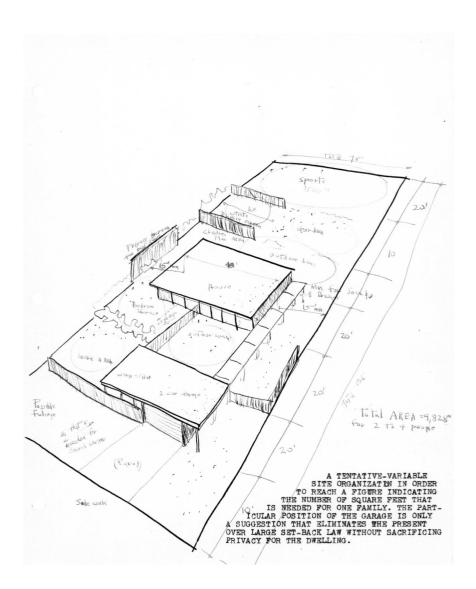

The handwritten labels on the drawing include: Total 78', Sports 1560'', Utility, privacy screen, Garden, Children play area, outdoor living, 10', 20', House, 48', Bedroom terrace, Min. for South to of Beach, 15' min, 26', outdoor living, Work area, 20', Work/Hot, 2 car garage, Possible foliage, All that is needed to extend comfort, (Paved), Side walk, 10', 20', Total AREA = 9,828'' for 2 to 4 people

A TENTATIVE-VARIABLE
SITE ORGANIZATION IN ORDER
TO REACH A FIGURE INDICATING
THE NUMBER OF SQUARE FEET THAT
IS NEEDED FOR ONE FAMILY. THE PART-
ICULAR POSITION OF THE GARAGE IS ONLY
A SUGGESTION THAT ELIMINATES THE PRESENT
OVER LARGE SET-BACK LAW WITHOUT SACRIFICING
PRIVACY FOR THE DWELLING.

What is noticeable from these early drawings is the emphasis in the planning on flexibility and the use of modular, factory-made furniture units to separate the spaces. With the exception of the service wall next to the bathroom, there is no single full-height internal wall anywhere. Curiously, neither the structure nor the external envelope plays any part in these rudimentary plans. Either they have been ignored or, as an arrangement of slim timber columns and glass, they are regarded as so thin as to be unnoticeable. Whereas, architecturally, this is nonsense, it does suggest nevertheless the transparency and ephemerality of the glass-and-steel frame he was soon to use in his own first house.

The one perspective drawing in the set shows the standardized (26 by 48 feet) plan developed into a house for two to four people on a site measuring 78 by 116 feet (fig. 2.6). Described as a "tentative-variable site organizati(o)n," it shows the house screened from the street by a two-car garage/workshop connected to a covered walkway. Carefully placed fencing or "privacy screens" shield the house and garden from both the street and the neighbors. The positioning of the house and garage/workshop serve to create a series of usable external spaces: a work area outside the workshop; a terrace outside the bedroom; outdoor living areas between the garage/workshop and house and

Fig. 2.6.
*A Tentative-Variable Site Organizati(o)n . . .*, 1950.

again at the rear of the house; a contained children's play area behind the house; a screened utility space (for hanging out the washing); a garden area (for vegetables, perhaps); and, beyond that, a sports area. It is a highly ordered and structured arrangement designed for indoor-outdoor living and suggestive of the good life of the young postwar suburban family.

Because wood was the subject of "Housing, Wood, and the Community," Koenig sought to justify its use. He wrote, "Our technology is basically wood technology. While great strides have been made with the use and production of other materials the fullest advantages of wood, together with new techniques of application have not yet been fully explored. If for no other reason the great demand and supply of wood as a basic commodity has made wood the most inexpensive material we can procure." He then expresses his reservations: "The present mode of construction prevailent in this section of the country—the diligent use of myrads of two by four's—has, I believe, reached the maximum of limitation and exhausted it's potentialities. Because of the above reasons I will attempt investigate some new (sic) possibilities of construction with wood that will conform to the needs listed on the previous page."[27]

The result was a series of perspective sketches of timber-construction details headed *A Simple Post & Beam Type* (fig. 2.7). Using 4-by-4-inch posts and 4-by-12-inch joists, Koenig envisioned a simple structure with a flat roof and overhanging eaves; paneled wall construction (plastered or sheathed externally); full-frame glass windows; and, where necessary due to seismic conditions,

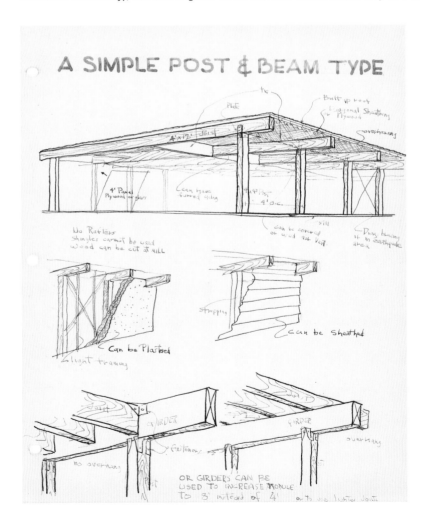

Fig. 2.7.
*A Simple Post & Beam Type,* construction details, 1950.

diagonal cross-bracing. Variations were available: deeper beams, or what he called "girders," could be used to increase the module span from 4 to 8 feet or to allow for lighter joists. But in all cases, the post-and-beam junctions were achieved with nailed metal straps or plates that, being unsightly, would have to be hidden within the lining of the walls or ceiling.

When he entered Calvin Straub's third-year class in the fall of 1949, Koenig must have felt unsettled. "As a student at the USC School of Architecture," he later wrote, "I learned to ask questions. A major question occupied my mind that seemed to have no ready answer: If architecture was a social study and our aim was to improve the quality of life for people through better housing, why weren't we as investigators pursuing more efficient means to produce this much needed product?"[28] Although there was to be a lot in "Housing, Wood, and the Community" to suggest a factory-based, modular approach to design, it was still timber-frame architecture that he was designing. A more efficient solution, he thought, would be to use steel, but that was an industrial, not a residential, material, and he was told housewives would not like it. "I don't agree with what you are doing," Straub said, "but I'll let you do it."[29] Koenig tried it, but, probably due to his ignorance of steel construction, his grades plummeted, and he failed the year.[30] Although he later credited Straub with making him aware of notions of social space in architecture and the need for low-cost housing, both of which remained with him throughout his career, the post-and-beam USC-Pasadena approach to house construction offered him little comfort.[31] Realizing, as he put it, "that no-one had approached the problem of the steel house, I thought the best way to learn this lesson was to build one, which I did."[32]

So it was that during his third year at USC, Koenig bought a foreclosed north-facing lot on Los Encinos Avenue in Glendale, and that August, with the help of his friend George Foy, he drew up plans for the building.[33] It was then that he approached Raphael Soriano. As Koenig later explained,

> I was interested in the same things he was interested in. Soriano, of course, had been doing the steel-framed buildings for a long time, and when I was starting to do mine, the first one in Glendale, I needed a summer job. So I naturally went to him because I had something to offer him and he to me. I worked for him that summer. And, of course, it was terribly educational and a lot of fun and most interesting, and it contributed toward my apprenticeship. So I'm grateful for Soriano for giving me that time.[34]

By the summer of 1950, Soriano had four steel-frame houses on the go: the Shulman House (for the photographer Julius Shulman) in the Hollywood Hills; the Curtis (or Noyes) House in Bel Air; the Krause House in Whittier; and the Olds House (the *Arts & Architecture* Case Study House for 1950) in Pacific Palisades. Although it is likely that the Shulman House, where construction had started in 1949, was the first to be designed,[35] it is more probable that it was the Curtis House, which Soriano described as the "Experimental House,"[36] that caught Koenig's attention. As Soriano later explained, "To me, the Shulman House is not really the real all-metal home, the way I did the Curtis House. That was the only house where I tried my system of not only metal structure but also all the cabinets and walls. Everything else was prefabricated assembly method. That was the first one where it was tried like that."[37] *Architectural Forum* described the Curtis House as a "flexible space under a steel umbrella—a further step toward the industrialization of home building."[38] The frame had gone up in a day, or thirty-two man-hours; the roof decking then went on in less than a day, just twenty man-hours. Next came the sandwich floor and the ceiling finish, followed by the preassembled storage walls, and, finally, the glass sliding windows and external wall panels. By the end of

1951, *Architectural Forum* announced that "the Curtis House is probably the finest industrial product the American home can boast."[39] This, surely, was what Koenig was looking for.

With the exception of the two perspective drawings of the Olds House that appeared in *Arts & Architecture* in August 1950, it is hard to tell what Koenig's contribution to that building might have been.[40] It has to be admitted, though, that these perspectives were a great advancement on Soriano's part, as shown in *Arts & Architecture* in April 1948.[41] Koenig's initial contribution could have been in the development of the scheme, for although the house was first announced in the December 1949 issue of *Arts & Architecture,* the February 1950 issue contained a "Diagrammatic Analysis of Site Plan" showing three different versions of the layout.[42] "The major problem," the journal commented, "now consists, after all these studies, of analyzing and adapting the most practical overall solution from the best elements of all three schemes."[43]

Koenig was going through the same analytic process in the development of his house in Glendale (see pl. 2). What he had thought would be a $5,000 bid had come in at $12,000, so, to lower the price, he studied the manufacturing and assembly processes of the various elements involved in the making of his house.[44] Realizing that what he had designed was a steel version of a timber house, he revised the design to reduce site work to a minimum, and he used long-span steel beams instead of short ones and single rather than double sliding glass windows. This process of reduction and factory-based manufacture successfully decreased the cost, and the building came in on budget (fig. 2.8).

Fig. 2.8.
Koenig House 1, Glendale, 1951.
Photographer unknown.

Where Koenig's house corresponded with Soriano's Case Study House was not just in the structure but also in the interior fittings, although Koenig's was done on a much smaller budget. Both houses used 3½-inch tubular-steel lally columns set on a 10-by-20-foot grid.[45] Whereas Soriano used a Holorib metal roof decking with a 10-inch structural-steel U-section fascia, Koenig used a Truscon metal roof decking with a 6-inch fascia.[46] In both instances, the metal decking bridged the short span and was tack-welded in place. And between the columns, both houses had 20-foot sliding glass doors comprising two 10-foot sections to fit the module. Internally, Soriano fitted-out the house with factory-made space-dividing storage units, while Koenig used unwanted cabinets that he had found in a cabinetmaker's workshop. But the principle was the same.

Although Koenig still had the better part of two years of schooling ahead of him when he designed his house in Glendale, he was already looking ahead to private practice. The rubber-stamp

Fig. 2.9.
Pierre Koenig at his drawing board in Koenig House 1, Glendale, 1952. Photo by Julius Shulman.

title panel on the drawings in the archive describe him as a designer, and soon he had a commission for another house on Los Encinos Avenue. In 1952, John Entenza, owner and editor of *Arts & Architecture,* sent Julius Shulman to look at Koenig's recently finished house in Glendale. Shulman was impressed with what he saw and took a handful of pictures.[47] It was, however, *Living for Young Homemakers* that, under the title "The Pioneering Urge in Action," first published the house, in February 1953.[48] *Arts & Architecture* followed eight months later, describing the building as "a simple, light and spacious structure."[49] To the side of the text is a photograph of Koenig at his drawing board in the house's living area (fig. 2.9).[50] It is both a demonstration and a confirmation of what Koenig knew, deep down, was possible and what *Arts & Architecture* promoted simply in boldfaced lowercase lettering as "steel frame house" (see p. iv).

Koenig's evolution as an architect of steel houses had had its genesis in both the design studios at USC and his experiences in the army. The timber post-and-beam approach of the USC-Pasadena School was, to Koenig, equally valid when interpreted in steel. His development, for example, of alternative plans for a small house as part of his third-year project, "Housing, Wood, and the Community," demonstrated much of the generic and modular thinking necessary for industrialized steel-house construction. Although, at USC, Calvin Straub and others disagreed with what he was doing, Raphael Soriano and A. Quincy Jones understood him, and both gave him work. The army had taught Koenig the value of order, process, and efficiency: this he recognized in the "American mass-production methods" that had helped to win the war. When training for the 292nd FAOB at Camp Bowie, Texas, Koenig "had to know Algebra, Geometry, Trigonometry, and ballistics. Everyone had to have experience with every technique used in the battalion: Sound equipment, Flash scopes, communications, Surveying. In addition we learned how to drive a truck."[51] This was an education far in excess of what a school of architecture might offer, although the opportunities for its application were considerably more dangerous. In rejecting the timber-frame ethos of USC for steel, Koenig took a risk, and, as a result, his grades plummeted. He might have learned a lesson from this, but instead he persisted, and, as if to prove the point, he went and built a steel house for himself. As he later said, "They put it up in one day."[52] □

# GLENDALE

In April 1953, soon after the first publication of his own house in Glendale in *Living for Young Home-makers,* Pierre Koenig began work on the first of three steel houses he designed that year.[1] This house was for Jacqueline and Edward Lamel and was located on Los Encinos Avenue, just down the road from where Koenig lived.[2] The next two houses Koenig designed, coincident with the second publication of his own house in *Arts & Architecture,* were for Edwin M. Scott in Tujunga and for William Squire in La Cañada.[3] The Scott House was on the drawing board in late September and the Squire House by the start of October. Located within a few miles of each other and within easy reach of Foothill Boulevard, which runs along the north edge of the San Gabriel Valley, these houses were in an area that was rapidly changing in the 1940s and 1950s from farmland into a bedroom community for Los Angeles.[4] The opportunities this location offered, combined with his early success in gaining commissions, must have seemed to Koenig like a promising start to a career.

The ground on the south side of Los Encinos Avenue rose steeply from the road, requiring both Koenig's own house and the later Lamel House to be cut into the hillside. But unlike Koenig's house, which sat parallel to the road and had a long concrete retaining wall along the east end holding back the hillside, the Lamel House was set perpendicular to the road, with its living accommodation raised one story to the rear. Only 20 feet wide but 80 feet deep, the house is approached through the carport and up a flight of twelve steps contained between concrete-block retaining walls (see pl. 3). Once reached, the living level is raised only 7 feet, 6 inches and aligns with the underside of the carport roof, making the scale surprisingly small. The house, which from the street appears closed and almost uninviting, opens up to the west in a manner only suggested in Koenig's own house (fig. 3.1). The variety and complexity of space this provides accounted for the price of $12,000, for although the covered livable area was, at 1,000 square feet, only 200 square feet greater than Koenig's house, the Lamel House cost more than twice as much.

Here Koenig's belief in "process" was put to the test and came off second best. The steel framing of the Lamel House proved to be much more difficult to conceive than it had been for his own house. This was due to the articulation of the plan and the need to attach wall panels and sliding-window sections to the circular columns, often at right angles to each other. In his own house, Koenig had butt-welded the jambs of the sliding windows to the circular columns and welded L-sections to the columns in order to attach the wall panels.[5] Neither was a perfect solution. Raphael Soriano, who had similarly used circular columns in his Case Study House for 1950, largely avoided the problem by positioning the sliding windows back from the columns. The archive retains a number of drawings showing how Koenig struggled to resolve this problem—one analogous to that cliché of fitting a square peg into a round hole. Sheet 3, dated 6 April 1953, shows 2½-inch-diameter columns supporting 6-inch I-section beams and C-section channels.[6] Sheet 4, bearing the same date and titled "HALF-FULL SIZE STEEL PLAN," shows 4-inch pipe columns with a variety of steel angles, either

Fig. 3.1.
Lamel House, 1955. Photo by Julius Shulman.

T- or L-shaped, welded on.[7] In the end, it became obvious that the answer lay in the use of 3½-inch square pipe columns in combination with similarly sized circular pipe columns.[8] Where any two walls came together, a square column was used; where the column was freestanding, as in the carport or along the open walkway to the west, it was circular. It was a pragmatic solution in which practicality won over uniformity.

Koenig's own house in Glendale was a simple contained box measuring 20 by 40 feet, with the open carport to one side. At the far end of the carport, the kitchen wall was withdrawn 3 feet behind the building's roofline to provide a shallow entranceway to the house, but this was not part of the living space. At the Lamel House, in a manner that immediately recalls Soriano's Krause House, the walls are pulled back within the confines of the framework to create not just an entranceway but a deep central patio open to the sky, from which a continuous brick-paved terrace reaches out among the oak trees that surround the building. The effect of openness is accentuated by the use of full-height glazing along most of the garden elevation, with the result that as one approaches the top of the entrance steps one is already beneath the roof and within the framework of the building (fig. 3.2). In a way that the tight envelope of his own house never allowed, Koenig here success-fully dematerialized the building so that the barrier between indoors and outdoors becomes totally ambiguous. To maintain this conceit, a vertical modesty panel of white corrugated plastic set in a

Fig. 3.2.
Lamel House, entranceway, 1955. Photo by Julius Shulman.

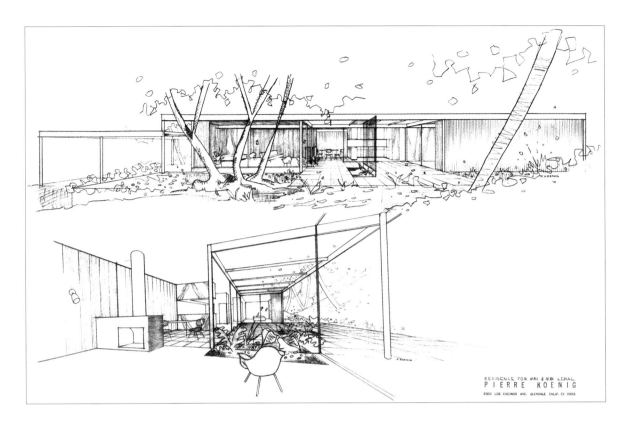

Fig. 3.3.
Lamel House, view from west and living/dining room, 1953.

shallow, rectangular lily pond shields the view of the glazed inner-bedroom wall from the top of the entrance steps.

In this early house, Koenig came as close as he ever did to the loose, additive nature of Case Study House 8, by Charles and Ray Eames, which had been published upon completion in *Arts & Architecture* in 1949.[9] In 1966, the British architect and critic Michael Brawne wrote that "the Eames House, however, differs from its nearest predecessors, the steel-framed buildings of Soriano, and also its possible successors, the houses of Koenig, Craig Ellwood and others in the Los Angeles area, in that its composition is wholly additive, with frame and cladding not separated, but working together, and that it possesses wit, a quality extremely rare in architecture. Its wit is, of course, largely the result of the additive process, of the seemingly casual juxtaposition of different elements."[10] Compared with the rather po-faced appearance of Koenig's later Case Study Houses, which presumably Brawne had in mind, there is much about the Lamel House, from the entrance steps that penetrate the enclosure to the white corrugated plastic modesty panel and the cross-views within and beyond the building, that is unexpected. Koenig was too serious to have thought of this as witty, but the apparently additive appearance of the building and its fragmentary form, where the central patio simultaneously bifurcates the house and opens up to the garden, owes more than a little to the Eameses' earlier example.

In the archive, there are two perspective drawings of the Lamel House drawn on a single sheet: one is of the house seen from the garden, and the other is an interior view from the living room toward the central patio (fig. 3.3). Curiously, as on the pencil plan that must have accompanied them, Koenig spelled the client's name as "Lemal." Could these drawings have been by his friend George Foy? In the foreground of the interior view, there is an Eames 1948 molded-fiberglass-shell LAX chair with a solid-rod X-base. Two such chairs are visible in the exterior view, which also shows what appear to be Eames 1946 molded-plywood DCM dining chairs clustered around the dining table. The sofa, which is also visible in the external view, is based on a daybed by George Nelson. All these items were shown in the 1952 Herman Miller catalog that Koenig must have had beside his (or Foy's) drawing board.[11] As later correspondence with other clients shows, the choice of the right furniture for his houses was important to him.[12] It was mostly with Eames furniture that he had populated his own house, at least for Julius Shulman's photographs. But, as other pictures show, he ended up living with something much more mundane.[13] For the publicity shots, the living room of the Lamel House appeared very much as it did on the perspective drawings, whereas in the dining room, a white laminated table with hairpin legs was introduced and the Eames chairs were replaced with something more generic.[14] Above the table hung a George Nelson Saucer Bubble Pendant light, first marketed by Herman Miller in 1952 (fig. 3.4).

Nine months after Koenig first started work on the design of the Lamel House, *Arts & Architecture* published the plan and the two perspective drawings, observing that "the structure is all steel frame," confirming the use of 2½-inch square columns.[15] But it was another eighteen months until the magazine published the finished house in June 1955. Once more, the use of steel was emphasized: "Steel is used in the construction in such a way as to achieve maximum use and economy."[16] The exposed internal steelwork and roof deck were painted blue gray, but the external beams and fascia, which on his own house had been red, were here kept white. Three months later, it became apparent that the emphasis on steel had not been wasted on Barbara East, who, writing in the *San Francisco Examiner* under the headline "There May Be a Steel House...In Your Very Near Future," claimed that "As a material steel is about as American as apple pie."[17] To make the point, she discusses two developers' prototype houses designed by architects for whom Koenig had worked or was to do so: A. Quincy Jones's US Gypsum Research Village House in Barrington, Illinois (1955), and Raphael Soriano's Eichler House in Palo Alto, California (1955), which she illustrates together with Soriano's Curtis House (1950) in Bel Air. Koenig is the only other architect mentioned, and while the article leads with three pictures of the Lamel House, East fails to mention it by name in the text.

It was clearly the Lamel House to which Koenig was referring when he was quoted by Esther McCoy in the Pictorial Living section of the *Los Angeles Examiner* the following February: "It's neutral, but not cold, says Koenig of steel, pointing out that it's a means to open our houses to wooded sites and to bring the sun into intimate patios."[18] Almost eighteen months later, in an article for the *Los Angeles Times Home Magazine* titled "What I Believe...A Statement of Architectural Principles by Pierre Koenig," McCoy returns to the Lamel House: "Koenig prefers exposing the structure because it reduces cost and is also aesthetically acceptable." Once again, she quotes him: "Good living arrangement does not come from steel construction, but this material makes better solutions possible."[19] It was a philosophy with which Koenig was now, four years after designing the Lamel House, increasingly comfortable, and one on which McCoy allowed him to expound:

> The steel house is considered new, although it's been with us for three decades. . . .
>
> The steel house is out of the pioneering stage, but radically new technologies are long past due. Any large-scale experiment of this nature must be conducted by industry, for the architect cannot afford it. Once it is undertaken, the steel house will cost less than the wood house. The architects have carried the ball for a long time and now it's industry's turn.[20]

The interim had seen the building of two more steel houses, the Scott House and the Squire House; and a fourth, the Burwash House, was already on site. By the time Barbara Stovall featured the Lamel House as "Home of the Week" in the *Independent Star News* in August 1958, Koenig's career was well on its way. With the patriotic, apple-pie enthusiasm of Barbara East, Stovall wrote, "The 1,000-square-foot structure fits into its oak-studded site with all the adaptability of a log cabin, providing an indoor-outdoor way of life its pioneer ancestor could never have achieved. . . . Despite its steel and glass construction, there is nothing cold and uninviting about the contemporary home designed by Architect Pierre Koenig, AIA."[21]

It was homemaking magazines such as *Living for Young Homemakers,* which published the house as early as February 1956, and *Sunset,* which carried it three years later, that promoted Koenig's work.[22] With the exception of *Arts & Architecture,* the architectural press was remarkably quiet on the subject, although in France, *L'architecture d'aujourd'hui* gave Koenig his first international

**Fig. 3.4.**
Lamel House, patio, 1955. Photo by Julius Shulman.

exposure in September 1957.[23] The reluctance of the architectural press and the building world in general to engage with Koenig's vision of a steel-frame, component-based, modular architecture would frequently frustrate him throughout his career. However, in the fall of 1953, with the Lamel House near completion and the Scott and Squire Houses on the drawing board, the future looked good. As if to compound his immediate success, Koenig married Merry Sue Thompson, and their son, Randall Francis, was born early the following year.[24]

Compared with the longitudinal form of Koenig's two houses in Glendale, the Scott and Squire Houses were more or less square on plan (see pls. 4, 7). To give himself more flexibility, Koenig moved away from the rigorously enforced 20-by-10-foot linear grid, running the spans in two directions: north-south and east-west. The use of a 20-foot clear span, as at the Lamel House, had allowed the provision of a carport for two vehicles. Once that was established within the plans of the Scott and Squire Houses, the adjacent 20-by-10-foot bays could run in either direction. In both cases, the living accommodation wrapped itself around two sides of the carport and adjacent entranceway, allowing access to the building to be made close to the center of the plan. Although the ensemble was tightly configured, Koenig was able to provide indoor-outdoor dining spaces, as at the Lamel House, by incorporating internal patios into both plans while, at the Squire House, also accommodating olive trees already established on the site.

In both the Scott and the Squire Houses, Koenig used $3\frac{1}{2}$-inch-diameter steel pipe columns in preference to square columns to support the I-section beams and C-section channels. The beams sat on top of the round columns and were attached with a fillet weld, and the fascia channels, where not butt-welded to the ends of the beams, were notched to fit around the columns and fixed with a fillet weld on the inside of the channel (see pl. 5). Although the structural engineer William Porush is credited with these buildings, Koenig did his own structural calculations, including bearings on concrete and foundation beams, buckling calculations, and welding instructions. With these small buildings, Porush's role was probably no more than to sign off the calculations.

Where both of these buildings differed noticeably from Koenig's first two steel houses was in the use of fireplaces. In the Lamel House, there had been a small masonry fireplace with a steel-encased concrete flue, while in the Scott and Squire Houses, Koenig introduced full-height fireplace walls with concealed terracotta flues. Yet the walls were not structural. At the Scott House, there were two fireplaces set into the common wall separating the living and dining rooms from the entrance hall: one was recessed deep into a stone-veneered wall, and the other, with exposed copper hood, formed part of a built-in seat (see pl. 6). At the Squire House, the fireplace wall was more modest. Faced with Flagcrete veneer, it divided the living room from the study and second bedroom (see pl. 8). Such masonry construction, although apparently at odds with the prefabricated intentions of the steel frame, had its advantages, for it would create a heat sink, which, during cold nights, would provide some stability for temperature swings within these lightweight houses.

Although structurally similar, the Scott and Squire Houses took on rather different external appearances. The Scott House was to be clad with corrugated Transite, whereas for the solid walls of the Squire House, Koenig specified stucco. Alongside the carport and entranceway of both houses, Koenig softened the appearance by specifying birch-faced plywood at the Scott House and redwood siding at the Squire House. Elsewhere, the buildings' envelopes comprised fixed or sliding windows with clear glass. Where privacy was required, such as in the guest bathroom at the Scott House or around the bedroom patio at the Squire House, translucent or frosted glass was used. In accordance with the prefabricated, modular approach to the architecture, these walling elements were full-height units, with the exception of the rather incongruous small, horizontal, sliding-sash window inserted into the bathroom corner of the east-facing Transite wall at the Scott House.

Both houses were built with the owners acting as general contractors, as Koenig and Lamel had done for their own houses. Therefore, the finishes, when they were eventually applied, were not quite what Koenig had in mind. It was the Scott House that probably diverged the most from Koenig's original intentions. The stone veneer specified on the construction drawings was never applied to the concrete-block walls around the fireplaces, even though a perspective drawing shows the blockwork as exposed (fig. 3.5). The three-quarter-height storage units adjacent to the entrance were never finished with the beech-faced plywood, as intended, nor were the walls flanking the dining room and adjacent external terrace clad in plywood, as Koenig's perspective sketch suggests (fig. 3.6). At the Squire House, the rear perspective view, which is populated with a Weber barbecue and a collection of Eames LAX chairs, shows the study wall lined in plywood, as specified on the construction drawings (fig. 3.7). In the end, this wall was finished with plaster.

There are no other drawings in the archive originating from Koenig's Los Encinos Avenue address, but there is one that can be attributed to that address, by both its presumed date and its verifiable location. This is the perspective drawing of the Paola Oldsmobile Showroom (fig. 3.8). Displayed in the showroom is a recognizable 1955 Oldsmobile 98, which would date the drawing to 1954 or 1955, depending on when the 1955 model of Oldsmobile was delivered to the dealer. Koenig, with his particular drawing skill and interest in cars, would not have drawn an old model in the showroom.[25] The Williamson Oldsmobile dealership, which Lincoln "Link" Paola and his brother, Pete, bought in 1951, was located in La Crescenta, near Glendale, at the junction of Foothill Boulevard and Glenwood Avenue. Link Paola, who was well known for customizing cars, had an auto-body workshop in Glendale and was just the sort of person Koenig would have befriended, for both his skills and his equipment, when building his own steel house nearby. Within a few years, the Paolas had added a showroom next door to the dealership. A 1956 photograph clearly shows this to be the building in Koenig's drawing.[26] But the purpose of the drawing remains a mystery. Did Koenig design the building and hand over all the construction drawings to the Paolas or did they just ask him for

**Fig. 3.5.**
Scott House, living room, 1953.

**Fig. 3.6.**
Scott House, dining room and patio, 1953.

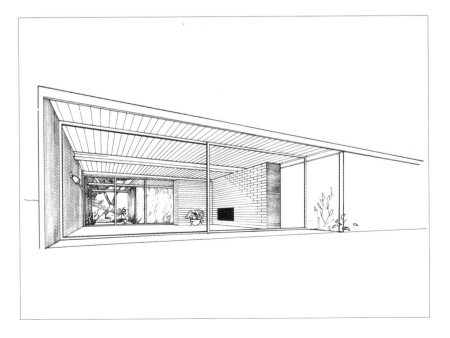

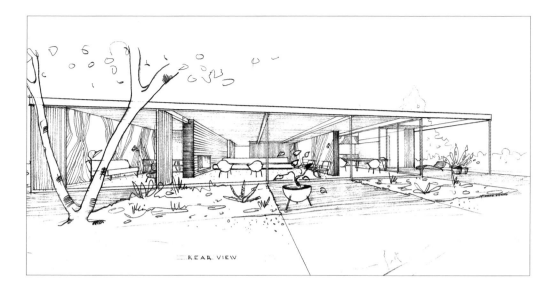

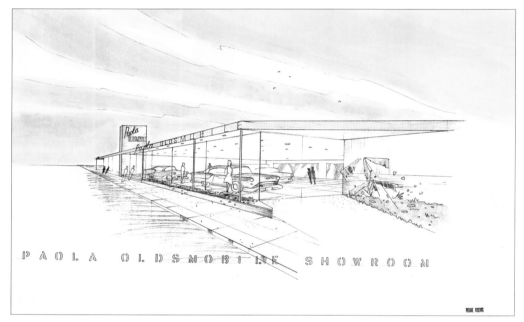

a sketch, which they then had a contractor develop into a building? Or were the construction drawings simply lost and the project forgotten? Whatever the answer, the building, which still stands on Foothill Boulevard, could well be the earliest commercial building by Pierre Koenig.

What is apparent in these early buildings is the hands-on nature of the architecture. Koenig built his own house, learning welding techniques from local steel suppliers, although it is tempting to think that Link Paola might have lent a hand somewhere.[27] Lamel, Scott, and Squire were their own general contractors, hiring skilled workers for certain jobs and probably doing much of the labor themselves. By the use of carefully selected, factory-made components, these small steel-frame houses could be assembled more quickly and easily than their traditional timber-frame counterparts. It was a validation of the ideas that Koenig had first developed at the University of Southern California. □

Fig. 3.7.
Squire House, view from north, 1953.

Fig. 3.8.
Paola Oldsmobile Showroom, view from east, 1954–55.

## CHAPTER 4

# SANTA MONICA AND SAN VICENTE

In the early years of his practice, Pierre Koenig worked from home—first from his house in Glendale, and later, after he sold it in 1956, from a rented apartment on Twenty-Sixth Street in Santa Monica, where the family stayed only briefly.[1] With a small child and the need, perhaps, for greater space and a more professional appearance, he rented an office in a small shopping center on San Vicente Boulevard, in January 1957.[2] During the three years that he spent there, he designed his two Case Study Houses and established himself within the Los Angeles architectural community. There was a string of commissions that allowed him to explore the possibilities of steel construction, but very few, as is often the way in architecture, were actually realized. However, at the end of 1959, even before Case Study House 22 was completed, Koenig bought an old house at 12221 Dorothy Street in Brentwood and moved his small office into the garage. It was, in a way, a defensive move to protect himself from corporate clients who, doing the rounds of Los Angeles architects, would come knocking at the door. Believing, perhaps rightly, that these corporate clients would not seek out an architect who worked from a garage in a residential suburb, he thought that the move would allow him to keep his practice small—one secretary and an assistant or two—and leave him the time he needed to design new projects and supervise ongoing ones, thus retaining total control over the office's output. It was a successful strategy that enabled him to maintain the high standard of design he demanded of himself, as evidenced by the prizewinning Oberman House of 1960, but one that, at the same time, had the effect of limiting his output.

During this time, as James Steele and David Jenkins have said, Koenig supplemented his income by working for other architects, such as the firm of Kistner, Wright and Wright, who in 1958 completed the slick, curtain-walled IBM Building in Riverside, Califorina.[3] In 1956, Koenig took his knowledge of steel-house construction to his former USC fifth-year design critic, A. Quincy Jones, who was then working on the Eichler Homes X-100, a steel-frame exhibition house in San Mateo, California, for the developer Joseph Eichler.[4] Jones was not a newcomer to steel houses, having built one for himself in Bel Air in 1954 and contributed another to the US Gypsum Research Village in Barrington, Illinois, in 1955,[5] yet Koenig already had more experience than Jones with steel houses and, as he said with regard to Raphael Soriano, had something to offer him. Koenig also assisted Candreva and Jarrett, the architects of the building on San Vicente Boulevard that housed both their offices and Koenig's. Koenig remembers that there must have been a dozen architectural practices within a four-block radius, with Frank Gehry right across the street.[6] Peter Jack Candreva and William Carlton Jarrett were, like Koenig and Gehry, University of Southern California (USC) alumni—Candreva had graduated with Koenig in 1952. In the spring of 1957, while helping out Candreva and Jarrett, Koenig was called for jury service but was excused following a letter from Candreva claiming that "the pressure of work here is too great at this time to go without his services."[7]

At the time he took the office on San Vicente Boulevard, Koenig still termed himself an architectural draftsman as opposed to an architect, a distinction of which he was conscious.[8] When, in February 1956, the New York–based magazine *Living for Young Homemakers* featured the Lamel House, they referred to him as an architect.[9] Koenig quickly responded with a telegram to the editor, Edith Evans, dated 23 January 1956: "Many thanks for the fine article on Lamel House. May I correct two errors? I am not a licensed architect. House cost $12,000 without owner's work."[10] It was not until 2 October 1957 that he received his architectural license for the state of California. On 23 December that year, he was elected a member of the American Institute of Architects (AIA) and, on 11 February the next year, a member of the Southern California Chapter of the AIA. As he later explained when talking about the architecture program at USC, it was not unusual to be running an architectural drafting business long before qualifying as an architect:

> The students themselves in 1948 were different from the students today, however. Since most of them were World War II veterans, they were older, and most of them were married and some had children. Half of the class had design-drafting businesses and the other half was working for the first half. Conrad Bluff III and Don Hensmen, as students, were already working together for Calvin Straub. . . . Buff, Straub and Hensmen designed Case Study House no. 20.[11]

Less than two months after Koenig had qualified, the Santa Monica–based the *Roberts News* carried a front-page feature on the young architect and his "associate," Boris Marks, under the headline "Redesigning Venice Is Koenig Mission."[12] As Toni Edgerton reported, a group of real estate agents from the Venice Development Company was seeking "big money" to redevelop the Venice oceanfront area. Koenig, she wrote, had been retained to design the master plan and the individual buildings, with the hope that "new buildings will rise where shacks now stand."[13] Apart from saying that "older buildings suitable for remodeling will emerge with new lines and a new look," the article gave nothing away about the proposed plans, but it did provide a fairly clear statement of his architectural philosophy. Under the topical subheading "Sputnik-Like Career," she wrote, "Koenig's star has shot up like a Sputnik since he graduated as an architecture major from USC in 1952."[14] Believing (because she had read it in a schoolbook) that the Taj Mahal was the most beautiful building in the world, Edgerton asked Koenig what he thought the second most beautiful building was. She was, perhaps, not prepared for the answer: "I don't agree about the Taj Mahal. It was built in a decadent period and is too ornate and scattered. When a period grows too luxurious decadence follows. In architecture too much ornamentation is plastered on. The simplicity of our modern houses may have been partially inspired by the Japanese, but I believe it is largely coincidental. Japanese houses have been the same for 800 years."[15]

Did Koenig have Candreva and Jarrett's very Japanese-looking swimming pool cabana at the Brown House in mind? "Coincidental," it was probably not. At this time, only five years after the end of the American occupation, there were many architects on the West Coast looking toward Japan for inspiration. In addition, there was the building of Junzō Yoshimura's well-publicized Japanese house in the garden of the Museum of Modern Art in New York in 1954 and Arthur Drexler's accompanying book of 1955.[16]

Despite the promises of Edgerton's article, there is little evidence in the archive of the "big money" redevelopment of Venice. Nevertheless, some work was carried out at 1500 Pacific Avenue, apparently without permission, for on 9 April 1959, the Venice Development Company was

Fig. 4.1.
Sidewalker Cafe, view from Windward Avenue, ca. 1959.

served with a Notice to Comply by the City of Los Angeles Department of Building and Safety, which resulted in Koenig submitting drawings for a plan check four days later.[17] The following July, he invoiced the Venice Development Company for forty-five dollars for drawings for an ice-cream parlor.[18] In addition, there were a number of other remodeling jobs proposed: in the archive, there are drawings of 30 Dudley Avenue (for the Venice Development Company) and the Waldorf Hotel, both dated 1958; the Casa Loma Apartments of 1958–59; and Saint Mark's Hotel and the Knickerbocker Building, both of 1959. The address 1500 Pacific Avenue was, by 1962, that of the Seidel Investment Company, perhaps synonymous with or a successor to the Venice Development Company. In 1959, Koenig provided the Seidel Investment Company with designs for the rear elevation of an apartment building on Brooks Avenue.[19] He also drew a perspective drawing of the Sidewalker Cafe set in an old arcaded corner building with views of the beach and passersby. This was Saint Mark's Hotel at the junction of Windward Avenue and Ocean Front Walk (fig. 4.1).

The archive contains only one set of drawings that date from the time between the completion of the Squire and Scott Houses in, respectively, 1954 and 1955, and the move to the San Vicente office in 1957. These are for a house commissioned by Walter and Mary Bailey on Wonderland Park Avenue in the Hollywood Hills—what was to become, two years later, Case Study House 21. But the drawings, which Koenig was developing in Santa Monica in April 1956, were to go through considerable changes before that building was realized.[20]

The house for Henry Burwash and his wife must have been in preparation during this time: both the drawings, which are dated February 1957, and the promotional statement bear the San Vicente address, and preliminary pencil sketches for the two houses can be found in a spiral-bound

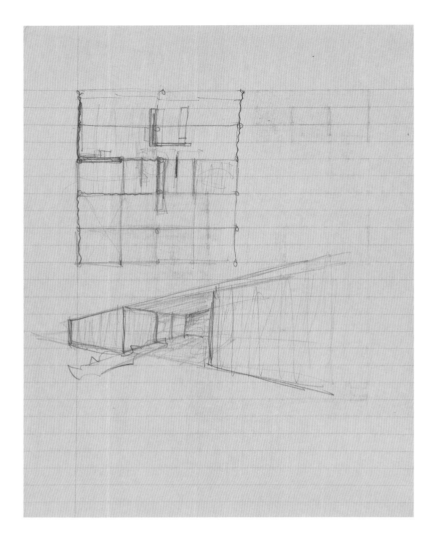

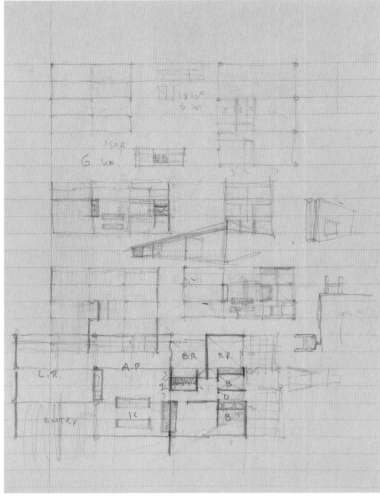

notebook of the time (figs. 4.2, 4.3).[21] Although only a short distance from the Scott House in Tujunga, the Burwash House was very different in its conception. What it demonstrated for the first time in built form had already been thought through on paper in the 1956 designs for the Bailey and Beidleman Houses.[22] It was in these designs, drawn up ten months or so before the Burwash House, that Koenig specified for the first time 4-inch H-section columns in place of the more familiar 3½-inch pipe columns. This decision meant that the beams could run in only one direction without the columns being turned; whereas, with a circular column, they could run in any direction. This innovation would have coincided with or followed very soon after the time in 1956 that Koenig spent working for Jones on the Eichler Homes X-100, which used H-section columns, rather than the Soriano-type pipe columns.

The choice of the H-section column had the effect of rationalizing the structural grid, which, at the Scott and Squire Houses, appeared to go in two directions. Although the Bailey, Beidleman, and Burwash Houses were all set out on the familiar 10-foot grid, Koenig varied his use of the beam as a structural component. The design for the Bailey House shows I-section steel beams supported midway and at the ends (see pl. 10).[23] Meanwhile, at the Beidleman House and then later at the Burwash House, he reduced the length of the span but extended the beams beyond the columns, using the cantilever to counterbalance the beam's weight and consequently reduce its depth (see pl. 20).[24]

Fig. 4.2.
Bailey House, version 1, preliminary pencil sketches, 1956.

Fig. 4.3.
Burwash House, preliminary pencil sketches, 1957.

What had been, in April 1956, a published sketch design for the Beidleman House developed into working drawings in April 1957, barely two months after those for the Burwash House, thus making the detailed development of these schemes more or less concurrent.[25]

At the Bailey House, the restricted nature of the hillside site required the building to be positioned north-south, while at the Burwash House, where the hot west sun was to be avoided, the building was set east-west. If the preferred south view was to be achieved in each case, then the windows at the Bailey House had to be set on the short side, parallel to the steel beams; while at the Burwash House, they had to be on the long side, perpendicular to the beams. As a result, the Bailey House could use two 20-foot sliding glass doors across its 40-foot width, but at the Burwash House, the glazing was limited to a series of 10-foot sliders corresponding to the width of the bays (see pls. 11, 21).

It is difficult to say whether it was more innovative for Koenig to use, in a domestic situation, 40-foot steel beams (albeit supported midway), as at the Bailey House, or 30-foot steel beams incorporating a 5-foot cantilever, as at the Burwash House. He was still finding his way but, in doing so, was rationalizing his use of steel. In any event, the Burwash House was completed first, and the Bailey House went through further design modifications before it came to site.

In the earliest surviving publicity statement that Koenig prepared for any of his houses, he describes the Burwash House as follows:

> The site for this house is a pre-leveled hilltop with a 180 degree view of hills and mountains. The "rear" of the house, almost all glass, faces the predominate north view. The entrance elevation faces south and is protected by a 5-foot overhang. It was decided to forego the western view due to the almost uncontrollable afternoon sun and blank the elevation completely.
>
> Designed for a family without children, this exposed steel frame house contains 1250 sq. ft. of inside living space and 442 sq. ft. of carport and outside storage. The 10" steel I beams span 25' and cantilever 5' on one side. There are no columns or bearing walls within the perimeter. The columns are 4 WF 13#. Exposed steel decking spans 10'–0." All the component parts are cut and partially fabricated in a shop and assembled on site by means of arc-welding. Joints will be ground smooth and all large areas shall be spray-painted.[26]

This description suggests both an industrial-looking building and an industrial building process. Yet the exterior of the house was not to be clad in the ribbed-steel decking and galvanized, corrugated iron siding, which he had already selected for the Bailey House; rather, it was clad in a variety of plywood. The 30-foot-long west elevation, which was exposed to the afternoon and evening sun, was finished in Texture 111 (called "tee-one-eleven"), vertically scored plywood sheeting commonly used to clad barns, while the shorter east elevation, which was less exposed to the sun, was to be painted ³⁄₈-inch exterior-grade Douglas fir plywood.[27] Such a wooden finish might appear to be somewhat at odds with the factory-made aesthetic promoted in the publicity statement, which would account for its exclusion. Yet plywood, whether Texture 111 or exterior-grade Douglas fir sheets, was undeniably a factory-made, modular product, and one that fitted with his architectural philosophy (fig. 4.4).

When the Burwash House first appeared in *Arts & Architecture* in March 1957, it was under the headline "Low-Cost Production House."[28] Illustrated with a plan and three perspective drawings, the article emphasized the benefits of the structure-free interior and the prefabricated construction

process, both of which Koenig referenced in his publicity statement: "The entire interior is free to allow for variations in floor plans without change of the steel frame or roof. To combat today's high cost of building and to produce a competitive home with features not ordinarily found in mass-produced houses, every up-to-date building method will be used."[29] The steel frame, the steel roof decking, the steel-frame sliding glass doors, and the louvered and fixed-glass windows were all to be prefabricated and assembled or fitted on site. All dimensions were to be checked in advance, and there was to be no on-site cutting. The only wet work was to be the concrete slab and the low, concrete-block fireplace (see pl. 22). The construction process was described in *Arts & Architecture:* "After the steel is up, all work will be done under cover and after the doors, windows, plumbing, heating, and electric work are in place the slab will be poured. The concrete slab is then adjusted for ceiling height and type of floor covering whether it be polished, or covered with tile or carpet; the steel never changes."[30]

The notion that theirs was a production house might have come as a surprise to Mr. and Mrs. Burwash, but, by promoting his architecture in this way, Koenig was searching for other possibilities and outlets. Both the Case Study House for 1950 and the Eichler Homes X-100, on which he had worked, were, in theory, mass-production prototypes, and this is how he would have seen this house. Nevertheless, despite the use of factory-made Glide-all sliding doors for all the closets, there was a considerable amount of on-site joinery that had to be done, and this Koenig detailed with infinite care (see pl. 23).

The three years spent in the San Vicente office saw both the consolidation of Koenig's practice and the exploration of a range of building types. Whereas the two Case Study Houses made him architecturally famous, the Burwash, Seidel, and Dzur Houses allowed him to investigate further the idea of the production house and the house as pavilion, whereas the Beidleman, Dowden, and Metcalf Houses allowed him to explore the use of steel for hillside sites.[31] The commercial work, which he soon came to avoid, is evidenced only in the studio building for the KYOR radio station in Blythe, California. This was published in *Arts & Architecture* in July 1958, together with a project for a speculative, steel-frame shopping center in Playa del Rey, of which there is no record in the archive.[32]

Fig. 4.4.
Burwash House, view from southwest, 1957.

To these years can probably be attributed the working drawings that Koenig provided for a small, two-story addition to Markel's Auto Upholstery Shop on Melrose Avenue (see pl. 134)[33] and the extension that he added to Mr. and Mrs. Sol Stern's house in Santa Monica (see pl. 135).[34] Smaller still was the kitchen remodel he designed in May 1957 for Mr. and Mrs. Frank K. Danzig in Beverly Hills.[35] Koenig's client index card shows that Danzig was involved at this time with the KYOR radio station project, the preliminary drawings for which are dated August 1957. Although the client index card lists the radio station under both Danzig's name and that of J. E. Mason, only Mason's name appears on the drawings.[36] Much of this was bread-and-butter work, but sometimes, in these small projects, a sense of proselytizing comes through. In the scheme for two rental units that he designed at the San Vicente office for Bob Fujioka, he provides alternative steel and timber versions. However, the drawing of the steel version is so much more dominant than the timber one that Fujioka could have been left with no doubt as to which was Koenig's preference (see pl. 133).

Koenig's practice as a commercial architect, first in Santa Monica and then in the San Vicente office, was short-lived. His subsequent retreat to the garage on Dorothy Street denied him many possibilities, and although he would still accept the occasional commercial commission, it allowed him to concentrate on domestic architecture, whether in steel or timber, and to promote the values of technical efficiency and social responsiveness he had first learned at USC. This opportunity came with the two Case Study Houses. □

# CASE STUDY HOUSES

The Case Study House Program was announced by John Entenza, owner and editor of *Arts & Architecture,* in January 1945. The intention was to promote what the magazine called "house—post war" by "giving some direction to the creative thinking on housing being done by good architects and good manufacturers whose joint objective is good housing."[1] Between 1945 and 1958, when *Arts & Architecture* published Pierre Koenig's Case Study House 21, there were twenty-five houses designed and published by the magazine, although not all were built.[2] Beginning with the construction of the Eames House (Case Study House 8) and the Entenza House (Case Study House 9) in Pacific Palisades in 1949, all the subsequent houses promoted by the program had steel frames. These were Raphael Soriano's Case Study House for 1950 in Pacific Palisades, on which Koenig worked, and the three Case Study Houses (16, 17, and 18) by Craig Ellwood: the Salzman House (1953), in Bel Air, and the Hoffman and Fields Houses (1955, 1958), in Beverly Hills. "One of the purposes of this house," *Arts & Architecture* wrote of Case Study House 18, "is to show how good design can be applied to prefabrication."[3] It was, perhaps, not surprising that Entenza next turned to Koenig, whose work, following his inclusion in the São Paulo Biennale of 1957, was beginning to be noticed. When interviewed forty years later, Koenig recalled the moment: "John asked me to come in one day and...said, 'If you ever have a good house with some good clients tell me and we'll make it a Case Study House.' Well, I did, and that was Case Study House 21."[4]

The "good clients" were a Los Angeles psychologist, Walter Bailey, and his wife, Mary, a social worker. The "good house" had been on the drawing board for over two years by the time *Arts & Architecture* announced it as Case Study House 21 in May 1958.[5] The changes in Koenig's approach to structure apparent in the first design have already been discussed, but the plan form, which was to represent a way of thinking often repeated in his work, was new. Although this was a one-off commission for a private house on a specific site, Koenig always saw it as a prototype that could be developed as a production house and located on any site anywhere. It had, as he always said, "Two details—one north/south and one east/west. One material for the roof, same one for the walls. Minimal house, maximum space."[6]

By spanning the steel beams at the first version of the Bailey House along an east-west axis, this prototypical building could be extended or reduced in length to accommodate however many functions were needed. Since the side walls were always to be windowless and the glazing restricted to the north and south ends, the building, as it lengthened, could be opened up in the middle to allow in light and ventilation. Therefore, it was in the center of the east elevation that Koenig located the entrance, dividing the house into two parts separated by a paved walkway and a screened patio. To the left, on entering, was the living room, kitchen, and all-purpose room; to the right, the bedrooms (one of which, opening onto the patio, could be used as a study), bathrooms, and carport (see pl. 11).

Fig. 5.1.
Bailey House, version 1, entranceway with stone wall, 1956.

Fig. 5.2.
Bailey House, version 1, entranceway with brick wall, 1956.

For all the rhetoric about prefabrication that accompanied the later design, the first version of the house included a masonry fireplace wall much like those of the earlier Scott and Squire Houses. While one side of the fireplace wall opened onto the living room, the other protruded into the 10-foot-wide entrance bay, reducing its width and providing a comfortably scaled and welcoming opening where the sliding glass doors could be positioned. Two designs for this entrance survive in the archive. One shows the masonry wall faced with brick to the exterior but with stone internally, thus delineating between indoors and outdoors; the other shows the use of brick throughout, which the working drawings indicate was the eventual choice (figs. 5.1, 5.2).[7] Unlike the masonry fireplace, which is located off-grid to control the entrance, there is no clear reason for the off-grid positioning of the bathrooms, laundry, and storage area separated by stud-wall partitions. These appear to be packed in with little reference to the structure—neither the I-section beams above nor the H-section columns that penetrate the space. It is the same solution proposed for the Burwash House, but there it seemed to matter less, for, as Koenig said in the publicity statement for that house, "There are no columns or bearing walls within the perimeter."[8] This is no more noticeable at the Bailey House than in the introduction of an off-grid external wall along the west side of the carport that extends 10 feet beyond the flat roof to its own otherwise unconnected H-section column. Although this extension is visible from both east and west, the wall, clad with 20-gauge ribbed steel, appears nevertheless to be part of the east elevation, which is similarly finished with 20-gauge ribbed steel (except for one bay, flanking the entrance, where tongue-and-groove birch siding is used). However, the ribbed steel's double-sided finish leaves it rather at odds with the west elevation, where a cheaper 22-gauge galvanized-iron corrugated siding is specified. It is an awkward solution to an awkward problem.

The two perspective drawings that Koenig prepared of the first version of the Bailey House show the relationship between the frame and the walls. In the east perspective, the wall along the back of the carport can be seen to protrude beyond the building's framework, breaking the sense of containment that the structural frame provides (fig. 5.3). In the south perspective, the glazed south wall is recessed slightly behind the framework, the roof and side walls extending to provide shade from the south and west sun (fig. 5.4). Beyond the glass, the living accommodation is clearly exposed, a tall dividing wall positioned on-grid separating the living room from the kitchen and all-purpose room. Here, there is a sense of order, but deeper within the building, beyond the internal patio, the formal relationship between the walls and the structure is less clear. Neither these perspective drawings nor the presentation plan was published. The cost of the building turned out to be too high, and the design was shelved. The revised design, which emerged two years later, was much reduced in form and consequently more affordable but also more coherent in plan.

In May 1958, when the new design for the Bailey House appeared in *Arts & Architecture* as Case Study House 21, the practicalities of the design were well advanced. At the start of the month, Converse Foundation Engineers had reported to Koenig on the condition of the site. A series of test holes dug at the proposed location of the steel columns showed that the southeast corner of the site, where the living room would be, was made up of organic fill to a depth of $11\frac{1}{2}$ feet to $13\frac{1}{2}$ feet, requiring piers numbered one to five to extend down 33 feet. On the opposite side of the building, where piers numbered fifteen to eighteen were to be, there was no organic fill, and piers would need to be no deeper than 7 feet. The working drawings for the foundations, which the piles were to support, had been completed toward the end of April and show the infinite (and necessary) care to which Koenig went. Even the formwork for the concrete pads, which were to sit on top of the

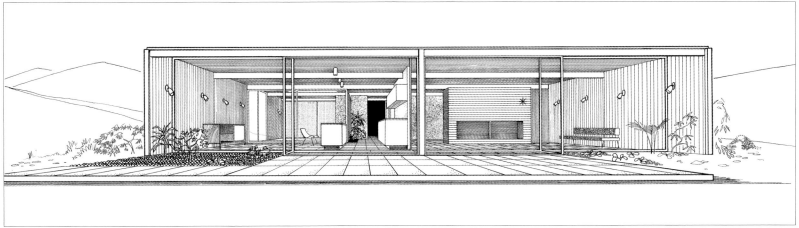

Fig. 5.3.
Bailey House, version 1, view from east, 1956.

Fig. 5.4.
Bailey House, version 1, view from south, 1956.

foundations, was detailed: 5½-inch-deep wooden boxes with lap joints—a square one for an interior column and a rectangular one for an exterior column, where the pad, emerging from the lily ponds that surrounded the building, would fuse with the thickened edge of the floor slab (see pls. 13, 15).[9] Similar details for the first version of the Bailey House, prepared exactly two years earlier, had been as carefully drawn but were simpler in construction: both the external and internal column foundations, as well as the slab edge, were shallower. Only the extraneous H-section column at the end of the protruding wall required a deeper and independent foundation (see pl. 12).

The construction details for the second version of the Bailey House also show a number of changes due to both Koenig's greater experience and the availability of new building products and materials. The steel-frame sliders, for example, were neither welded nor screwed in place but held by Thiokol polymer, a structural sealant.[10] The building would now be externally clad with 20-gauge Stran-steel roof decking, rather than a combination of materials, and finished internally with adhesive-fixed, laminated Kaiser gypsum board with metal edging strips. In the first design, plaster on metal laths and 1-by-4-inch tongue-and-groove birch had been specified. Stran-steel studs were used within the wall construction where previously timber studs had been shown, while, along the eaves, a C-section channel replaced the Z-bar to give a crisper and more consistent finish on all elevations.[11] Finally, the fireplace was dispensed with and, consequently, there was to be no masonry work. These changes in the construction of what was still, conceptually, a very similar building suggests a process of rationalization and simplification that was developed further in the plan.

With a total span of 44 feet, the new design for the Bailey House—let us now call it Case Study House 21—was wider than its predecessor, where the span was only 40 feet, 2 inches. The length was still the same, six bays of 10 feet each, but now the entranceway split the plan, placing the front door at the end of the carport, three bays (as opposed to four) from the north end of the building (see pl. 14). By reducing the accommodation from three bedrooms (or two plus an office) to two, Koenig could now locate all the living spaces to south of the entranceway, thus condensing and clarifying the plan. A bedroom and a study, separated from the living room and kitchen by a freestanding bathroom zone, were now where the all-purpose room and kitchen had been. Unconnected to the external walls in what Koenig referred to as a "discrete plan," the twinned bath and shower rooms (and the boiler room) opened onto a small open-air court with a fountain, thus allowing ventilation and natural daylight into the center of the building.[12] The L-shaped kitchen, suited to the informal entertaining that the Baileys enjoyed, contained the dining area while at the same time forming the entry hall and leading visitors into the living room, where the two 10-foot, 10-inch Bellevue glass sliders pulled back to open the room to the terrace beyond.[13] This time, there was no overhang on the south elevation for sun protection; instead, in its place, Koenig inserted removable louvered Koolshade sunscreens. Additional air-cooling was supplied by the water that coursed through the shallow lily ponds, flowing beneath the terraces and jetting out of waterspouts along the eaves. It was a remarkably compact, effective, and efficient design that far surpassed the hesitations and irregularities of his earlier effort. The house was, of course, smaller, but it was now within Walter and Mary Bailey's budget (fig. 5.5).

The fact that Koenig had been able to so revise the plan without essentially changing the form and structure of the building reflected his intention for this house to be a prototype for a production house. His notion that the exterior and interior walls should be entirely different things reduced the building, conceptually, to a container and its contents. But Koenig also conceived it as an industrial product, manufactured in a factory and assembled on site. Nevertheless, the application of the final finish was an on-site industrial process. First, the whole house was sprayed inside and outside with black Permabar coal-tar epoxy for rust protection, and then, once the columns and beams had been masked, the exposed surfaces were sprayed again with a light-gray polyvinyl acrylic. When the masking was removed, the dark-frame and light-wall composition was revealed. There had been no hand painting in the whole process.[14]

After publishing progress reports in August and November 1958, *Arts & Architecture* announced, in January 1959, that the house was ready to be opened to the public.[15] And over seven successive weekends, from Saturday, 3 January, the public came. In all, 608 people signed the visitors' book. On 10 January, Koenig's father, Harold, came to see the building, and the following weekend, George Hasslein, head of the Department of Architectural Engineering at California Polytechnic State University, San Luis Obispo, brought fifty-seven of his students. In February, Koenig's former instructor from the University of Southern California, Garrett Eckbo, who lived on the same street and over

the months would have seen the house progress, came with his wife, Arline, as did Philo Jacobsen (who later worked for Craig Ellwood) and Ellwood's associate, Jerrold Lomax.[16] Two of Koenig's clients were among the February visitors: Arnold Metcalf, whose three-story steel house had been on Koenig's drawing board since the previous August, and Carlotta Stahl, who with her husband, Buck, had already commissioned Case Study House 22.[17] That month, *Arts & Architecture* celebrated the opening of the house with eight pages of photographs and text, promoting it as a "finished product comparable to any other luxury home…minus the excessive cost usually associated with quality and originality."[18]

To help contain costs on the building, Koenig had drawn all the steel construction drawings himself and had also acted as the general contractor for the building process, an experience that, at the end of the job, had left him exhausted. Nevertheless, Case Study House 21 was probably the most expensive house, per square foot, Koenig ever did due as much as anything to its size, there being an inverse relationship between the size of a building and its cost per square foot. Had the design gone into mass production, as he would have liked, it would have been his most inexpensive house due to the simplicity of the structure.[19]

Case Study House 21 was not site specific, so it could have been built anywhere, whereas the Stahl House, which followed close on its heels, was specifically designed for its hilltop site at 1635 Woods Drive, high above Hollywood Boulevard. Here, at the top of a precipitous drop, Buck Stahl envisioned a modern, low-budget, southwest-facing house with a butterfly roof and an unobstructed 270-degree view. He had already built up the site by hand with waste concrete to provide a level base.[20] For this job, which presented obvious challenges, Stahl interviewed seven Los Angeles architects: five could not do it, and the sixth did not want to.[21] Koenig, however, saw it as a challenge and agreed to take it on. Although busy supervising Case Study House 21 on site, he completed a

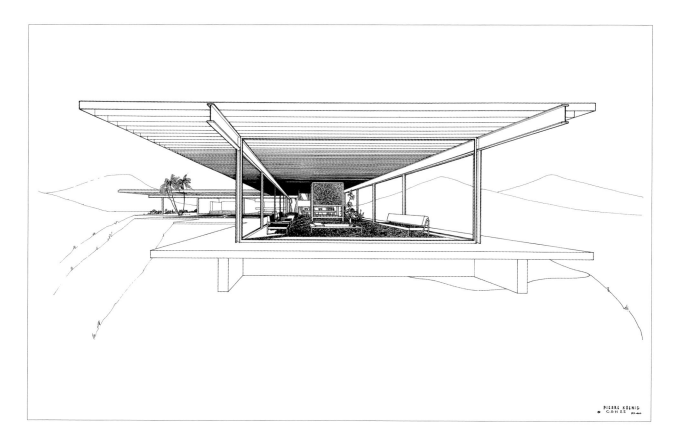

set of eight working drawings by the beginning of July 1958.[22] Ten months later, *Arts & Architecture* introduced it to their readership as Case Study House 22 (fig. 5.6).[23]

The site that Buck Stahl had bought in 1954 was 125 feet above Marlay Drive, and parts of the escarpment to the south were more than 45 degrees steep. On the east side, the drop was almost vertical (see pl. 31).[24] Although Koenig affirmed that "the ground conditions are excellent with no extraneous water problems and without fill," the buildable area was limited, so rather than placing his house where the ground was most firm, he pushed it to the side, forming an L-shaped plan, and allocated the secure, central space to the swimming pool (see pl. 32).[25] As he later explained, "The house, in a sense, is off on the space. There might be some dirt under it but it is tentative. The house is on piers and cantilevers, and with big overhangs. A little different approach for me."[26] In a typewritten statement prepared for *Arts & Architecture* and retained in the archive, Koenig extolled the virtues of the site: "This is a concept of a pavilion-type house related to a most ideal setting. By understanding the structure a balanced relationship has been established between house, pool, sky and view. In this project a happy combination of site, soil, height and location combined to suggest a solution in which it was possible to take advantage of all elements without the necessity of compromising the design."[27]

Julius Shulman's nighttime view of the south end of Case Study House 22, taken without the distraction of the two young women in the famous photograph of the house, shows why the positioning of the building, on its hilltop site, was so effective (fig. 5.7). By aligning the living accommodation with the grid of the city below, while using the bedrooms to close off the street behind, Koenig tied in his design firmly with both the site and the view. This worked not only in terms of the extended roof beams that picked up the lines of the north-south streets—specifically North Harper and North

Fig. 5.6.
Stahl House (Case Study House 22), view from south, 1959.

Sweetzer Avenues as they reached south beyond Sunset Boulevard—but also in the way the pro-filed roof decking, which extended out beyond the building's envelope, corresponded to the cross streets receding into the distance.

There has been some dispute about whether or not Stahl provided Koenig with the idea for the building. Writing in the *Los Angeles Times* in 2009, Barbara Thornburg recounts how a photograph in a Stahl family album, taken in July 1956, shows a large-scale model of a steel-and-glass house with a butterfly roof and a curved wing containing two bedrooms and a carport in between.[28] The article also states that Koenig was hired in 1957, the date repeated by Jeffrey Head in his 2017 article in *Long-form,* but there is no evidence in the archive to support this.[29] The first working drawings, as already noted, are dated July 1958, and Koenig's client index card for Clarence "Buck" and Carlotta Stahl and their two children, prepared at that time or soon after, gives the date 1959–60.[30] The similarities between Buck Stahl's proposal and Koenig's solution should not be unexpected, for Stahl's require-ments, when applied to the site, offered few other options. The swimming pool, however, seems to have been very much part of Koenig's conception, although it was forced upon the Stahls by the loan company. Writing in *Longform,* Head suggests that the Stahls' original intention had been to have an open yard or garden rather than a pool, but that Broadway Federal, who had loaned them $34,000 to build the house, required them to obtain a further $3,800 from another company with which to build a swimming pool. Although this would increase the overall building cost, it would make the property more valuable and thus help secure the initial loan.[31] Koenig's positioning of the house to the back and side of the site—"off on the space," as he said—rather than on the more solid ground in the center, was intended to accommodate the pool.[32] The development of the L-shaped plan, as opposed to one that was rectangular or curved, was predetermined by the pool, as the sketch in his notebook of 1958 shows (see pl. 33).[33] Without the pool, the house would have had little of the drama and presence that Koenig consequently gave it.

Whereas Case Study House 21 is a neat essay in prefabrication expressed in the allocation of the materials and the reduction of the details, Case Study House 22 is a bold demonstration of expansive space. At its most minimal, it is little more than a steel frame beneath an oversailing roof, the glass walls dematerializing any sense of barrier or containment. Where Case Study House 21 appears almost delicate, Case Study House 22 is hefty, using mostly a 20-by-20-foot grid rather than the smaller 10-by-20-foot grid. The 12-inch steel I-sections are of inordinate length: those with a north-south orientation above the living spaces are 78 feet long, while the one fronting the bedrooms measures 58 feet, 2 inches. The steel beam along the back of the site facing the street is, at 80 feet, 4 inches, the longest. But since that one elevation is almost wholly clad, the effect of the beam is less apparent (fig. 5.8). The profiled roof decking, which at Case Study House 21 wrapped the building, here floats above the space. The 5-inch T-steel sheets, which are almost 30 feet in length, span the 20-foot bays and cantilever out on either side. The sense of openness that pervades the living space is further emphasized by the manner in which the two fixed items, the kitchen and the fireplace, are aedicules within the space. Each is defined by a steel frame of its own—a small building set on an open plateau high above the city (fig. 5.9). As if to emphasize its independence, the fireplace was originally intended to be faced with a Palos Verdes stone veneer, as Buck Stahl had imagined in his own conception of the house. To save money, the stonework was not, at first, applied but it has since been added (see pl. 34). Because the building codes would have required the steel fireplace to be supported by caisson foundations, thus increasing the cost of the substructure considerably, Koenig welded it to the roof deck so that it was suspended above the concrete slab.[34] Only when the floor screed was poured was the fireplace secured in position. The roof of the kitchen is similarly attached to the roof deck, but now by steel tension wires, for stability during earthquakes.

As built, Case Study House 22 is a slightly modified version of what was initially intended. The plan first dated 3 July 1958 (sheet 2 of 8) shows the north-south wing of the building comprising four 20-foot bays and extending to a total length of 85 feet, including the overhanging roof.[35] This brought the end of that wing very close to the edge of the usable site, as the site section dated 6 September 1958 demonstrates.[36] Here, the last 10 feet of the living room cantilever out beyond the final caisson foundation, and, as the plan shows, a diagonal ground beam is inserted to help strengthen the southwest corner of the structure. However, a later version of this plan drawing—now with revisions dated 14 July 1958, 25 November 1958, and 5 January 1959—shows the end bay of that wing reduced from 20 feet to 10 feet, as eventually built.[37] The east-west wing was similarly reduced from 75 feet to 70 feet, the saving being made in the carport. It is likely that these changes were the revisions made on 14 July, for this is the most consistent revision date throughout the set of drawings. The note dated 16 July on the sheet of elevations that reads "add formed pier—remove st'l column" would seem to confirm this.[38]

Fig. 5.8.
Stahl House (Case Study House 22), street facade, with a 1955 Ford Country Sedan, 1960. Photo by Julius Shulman.

Fig. 5.9.
Stahl House (Case Study House 22), interior view showing kitchen unit, 1959.

What brought about these changes is suggested in Head's article in *Longform.* "The Building Department," Head quotes Koenig as saying, "thought I was crazy.... I can remember one of the engineers saying, 'Why are you going to all this trouble? All you have to do is open up the code book and put down what's in the code book. You could have a permit tomorrow.' I asked myself, *Why am I doing this?!* I was motivated by some subconscious thing."[39] To expedite the proposals through the approval process, Head writes, Koenig reduced the living room's length by 10 feet and the drawings finally received approval in January 1959.

The same plan, originally dated 3 July 1958, shows that the deep foundations for the living-room wing were not to be set directly beneath the columns but arranged in pairs down the center of the floor plan with cantilevered ground beams reaching out, as the site section shows, to support the columns on either side. As Koenig explained in a written statement contained in the archive, "The piers are not under the columns in this case but are set back from five to seven feet. In this way any possibility of damaging erosive action is eliminated. The columns are bearing at the ends of the concrete beams and are encased with twelve inches of concrete for resistance to seismic forces. With glass on all exterior walls except the street side, all horizontal forces can be resisted in this manner."[40]

What made Case Study House 22 affordable was both the application of new technologies and the use of off-site construction. Manufacturers of new products, who anticipated the publicity the house could offer, came to Koenig's office to encourage him to specify their materials or components. Bethlehem Steel, who supplied the steel frame, gave the Stahls a five-hundred-dollar rebate on the cost of the steel.[41] Nothing, it seems, was too difficult for them. The 4-inch H-section steel columns were attached to the beams in the workshop and the 78-foot sections were delivered complete to the site, despite the hairpin bends in the steep access road. As a result, there were only a few welded connections to be made on-site, and the frame was assembled in one day, thus saving on-site costs. Once again, the building was sealed with Permabar coal-tar epoxy for rust protection, and then a topcoat of light-gray polyvinyl acrylic was applied. As Koenig later admitted, he put everything he knew into that building, allowing him to build the house, including the pool, for the $35,000 budget. In the end, it came in one hundred dollars or so over budget, which Stahl withheld from Koenig's fee.[42]

The finished quality of both this house and Case Study House 21 was due as much as anything to Koenig's constant, almost daily site visits, for it was only through continuous supervision that problems could be resolved and the standard of finish he demanded be maintained. Despite this, or perhaps because of it, the date for completion of the house began to slip. On Easter Monday, 18 April 1960, Koenig was at the site again, and the following day, he fired off a strongly worded letter, typed in uppercase, to Bob Brady, the contractor.

WHEN I WENT TO THE JOB MON. I WAS SHOCKED TO SEE NO ONE THERE AND MANY THINGS TO BE DONE YET. AS YOU KNOW WE WERE SUPPOSED TO SHOOT MONDAY. THE DEADLINE HAS BEEN CHANGED ONCE BUT IT IS IMPOSSIBLE TO CHANGE IT AGAIN. THE DYE IS SET. MR. VAN KEPPLE IS WAITING TO MOVE FURNITURE IN. SHULMAN COMES BY THE JOB EVERY DAY TO SEE WHEN HE CAN SHOOT. MR. ENTENZA IS SHOUTING FOR PHOTOS SO HE CAN PRINT THE NEXT ISSUE. THE PRESIDENT OF BETHLEHEM IS SUPPOSED TO VISIT THE FINISHED HOUSE THIS FRIDAY. THERE IS TO BE A CONFERENCE THIS WEEK-END. NOT TO MENTION MR. STAHL. THIS WILL GIVE YOU SOME IDEA OF THE PRESSURE BEING PUT ON. I HOPE YOU CAN ACT IN ACCORDANCE.[43]

The house was still unfinished when Julius Shulman came to take his photographs on 9 May 1960.[44] It was unfurnished and full of plaster dust. Koenig brought in his own pottery to place on the borrowed Van Keppel furniture. To provide the semblance of a planted landscape outside, cut branches were held in place by clamps or by hand. In the nighttime photograph that later became so well known, two young women, one an undergraduate at the University of California, Los Angeles, and the other a senior at Pasadena High School, sit poised in conversation. To bring out the distant city lights, Shulman used a seven-minute exposure and then popped a flash bulb to capture the two women, with the result that the lights of the city are visible through their white dresses. The photograph, which first appeared five weeks later on the front cover of the "Sunday Pictorial" section of the *Los Angeles Times,* probably did more for Shulman's career than it ever did for Koenig's.[45] Although Koenig later resented the injustice, he returned to the house on the fortieth anniversary of the shoot and shared with Shulman a laugh over the photograph (fig. 5.10). In the June issue, *Arts & Architecture* published the house in an eight-page spread, using sixteen of Shulman's photographs but with little of the editorial hyperbole that might have been expected for such a design and without the now famous photograph.[46]

Although Shulman's photograph—which was later rediscovered by Reyner Banham and used in his book *Los Angeles: The Architecture of Four Ecologies* (1971)[47]—has made Case Study House 22 the most well known of Koenig's houses, it was the earlier Case Study House 21 that he always thought his best.[48] This was probably for two reasons: first, as a design, it had improved immeasurably from its original iteration, a development that client pressure and shortage of time (as at Case Study House 22) rarely afforded; and second, because it was conceived, like the Burwash House before it, as a production house. Although it never actually achieved this status, its extendable longitudinal plan form and central courtyard space provided the parti for many of the Chemehuevi project houses. Case Study House 22 was, by comparison, much more of a custom design. When asked by John Entenza if he would do another Case Study House, Koenig declined. It was just too much work, and, in any case, he already had other jobs on the drawing board, including a steel house in Mandeville Canyon.[49] ☐

Fig. 5.10.
Julius Shulman and Pierre Koenig at Stahl House (Case Study House 22), 2000. Photographer unknown.

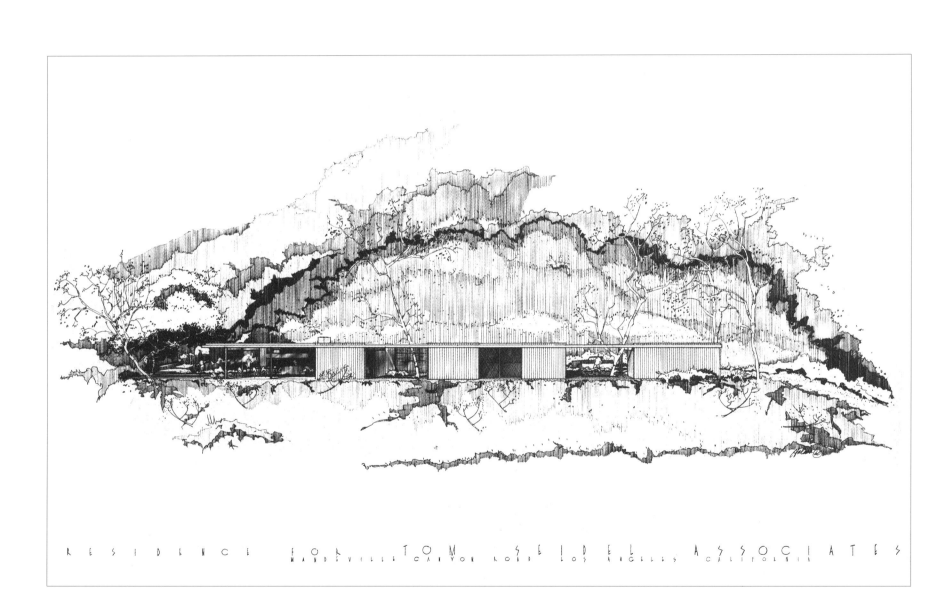

RESIDENCE FOR TOM SEIDEL ASSOCIATES
MANDEVILLE CANYON ROAD LOS ANGELES CALIFORNIA

# STEEL PAVILIONS

The site that Tom Seidel and his associates owned on Mandeville Canyon Road was, like that of Case Study House 21, a long, thin shelf of land above and parallel to the west side of the road. Excavation work at the rear of the site had resulted in a steep, nonconforming slope. In 1957, Seidel applied for permission to maintain the slope and build next to it, and although the application was approved with conditions in May and June 1957, no work was carried out.[1] In January 1959, W. E. Milburn, the chief of the Grading Division at the Department of Building and Safety, wrote to Seidel, extending the permission until 1 July 1959.[2] It was probably a case of now or never, so, as it would seem, Seidel asked Pierre Koenig to help him. By the middle of June, Koenig had prepared working drawings for a steel house on the site and submitted them to the city for a plan check.[3] Koenig and Seidel then completed an Appeal for Modification of Building Ordinance to request a further extension of the permission.[4] The hearing of the request was on 2 July, and the variation was duly approved, allowing the building to go ahead.[5]

The house that Koenig designed for Tom Seidel Associates was long and low, fitting the narrow site snugly. The perspective drawing held in the archive shows its hillside location perfectly (fig. 6.1). The body of the house was 24 feet wide and 116 feet long; the frame and roof decking extended to 32 feet by 121 feet. The living accommodation to the south comprised two linked blocks separated by a 16-foot patio, with a second 16-foot patio separating the carport to the north (see pl. 39). This had to be kept open to allow for the runoff of water, as requested by the Grading Division.[6] A covered walkway ran along the west side of the house, from the carport to the centrally positioned entrance—an arrangement similar to that for Case Study House 21. The diagram of the house shows a series of separate pavilions, each with its own and distinct function, linked by the external walkway. The pavilion to the south contained the living room, kitchen, and all-purpose room; the one in the center held the master bedroom (which could be subdivided), a second bedroom, and two bathrooms; and that to the north provided space enough for two cars. Both the bedrooms and the living room opened onto the two patios, each planted with small trees, while the kitchen and all-purpose room opened onto a terrace and the garden to the south. Although, as in both versions of the Bailey House (Case Study House 21), the two patios served to bring light and air into the center of the building, Koenig introduced glass into both the east and west sides, something that he had not done in the two earlier designs. No longer could he describe the design as "two details—one north/south and one east/west," nor could he say it was a minimal house with maximum space. It was an advance from a simple yet highly effective solution to something more complex and diffracted.

The body of the house was defined by six pairs of 4-inch H-section columns, between which Koenig set 10-inch I-section beams; five of these beams were extended an additional 8 feet to support the covered walkway. For the roof decking over the living accommodation, he specified 8-inch,

Fig. 6.1.

Seidel Associates House, view from east, 1959.

16-gauge galvanized-steel T-deck; whereas, over the carport, he thought 5-inch, 18-gauge T-deck would be sufficient. Why there should have been a difference in the depth of the profile is unclear: maybe it came down to cost. The walls, however, were clad in the heavier 20-gauge galvanized-steel decking, it being more resilient to knocks (see pl. 40). The roof decking, which was shipped on 6 August by the T-Steel Corporation in Kirkland, Washington, was arranged into five "bundles": four bundles of 16-gauge decking cut to specified lengths and one of 18-gauge decking, along with various accessories (such as starter channels, shear plates) and a quart of paint.[7] The order cost $3,191.00. The 20-gauge decking came later, once the roof was on and the concrete floor was cast.

Building work continued for ten months, into the spring of 1960, but by May, Koenig was able to calculate a final cost for the house.[8] Including everything from the site survey to the asphalt drive, the total came to $33,307.65.[9] The T-deck roof had cost less than 10 percent of the total price. With this house, perhaps more than with either of the Case Study Houses, Koenig established an approach to his use of steel that he followed thereafter, so much so that over thirty years later, in 1993, he could look back and comment on this consistency of his architecture:

> Most of my work in the aspect of steel design can be characterized by my use of hot-rolled structural steel in combination with cold-formed light-gauge steel. For the supporting structure, hot-rolled wide flange or I-beams are generally used, with WF shapes or round pipe used as columns....
>
> I like to differentiate between hot-rolled and cold-formed steel as each one serves a different purpose and each one has it's own unique appearance. Hot-rolled is a primary load-supporting material while cold-formed is a secondary material that supports it's own weight only. Hot rolled has a very rough appearance while cold-formed or cold-rolled exhibits a very smooth surface. While hot-rolled is linear in its geometry, cold formed is planar and covers large surfaces. I do not sand-blast hot rolled surfaces as I prefer to accentuate the differences.[10]

When, in the 1980s and 1990s, Koenig came to extend the house for Della and Gary Rollé by inserting a new structural frame around and within the existing structure, these differences, of which he wrote, were very apparent. Here the steel has not been sandblasted and the welded joints are clearly visible.

In his promotion of the Mandeville Canyon house, Koenig drew attention to both the use of steel and how it was colored: "To increase the privacy where needed and also to define the house clearly in its rustic setting a 20 ga. steel decking was used for the exterior walls, laid vertically against purlins. Painted light blue, the deck'g accentuates the house's clean lines and blends with the wooded and rocky terrain. The olive drab trim provides a transition between house and site."[11] Another statement, which was repeated almost verbatim in *Arts & Architecture,* said:

> The bold and imaginative use of color on the exterior of the structure is carried through the interior. The light blue color is repeated on the exposed ceiling flanges of the steel deck, producing a striped effect. The olive drab trim is repeated on the steel-framed fireplace—contrasted against the natural red brick. The steel kitchen cabinets are yellow, supported on slim olive drab tube-framing.[12]

This was very different from the black-and-gray palette he had used on the Case Study Houses.

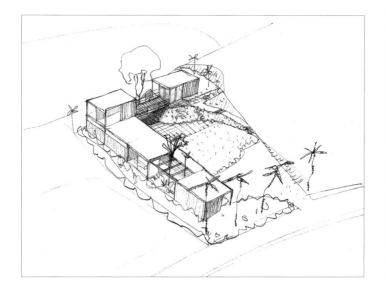

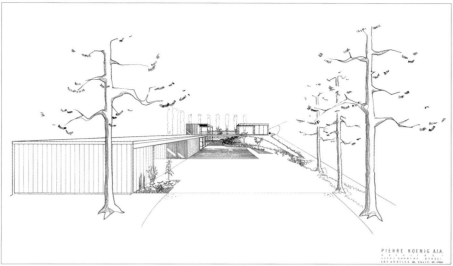

Koenig's publicity efforts paid off. The Seidel Associates House was published in *Arts & Architecture* in April 1961[13] and, like Case Study House 21,[14] won an American Institute of Architects (AIA) and *Sunset* magazine award the following year. In October 1961, *Arts & Architecture* published it again, but now as an advertisement.[15] The house, which had been built as a speculation, was for sale.

A similarly long, thin plan was adopted for the house designed in 1959 for Albert A. Dzur on an oceanfront site in San Pedro.[16] Dzur, an independent contractor who, at the time, was building geodesic domes, had first gone to Craig Ellwood for a design, but Ellwood, being too busy, recommended Koenig. Like the Seidel Associates House, the job was begun in the San Vicente office and continued in the Dorothy Street office. Although the house was never built, the drawings in the archive show two things. First, when taken together, they show a scheme developing from the roughest sketches to scaled plans: the only other early set of drawings in the archive to do so is for the Willheim House of 1962. Second, they demonstrate how one idea, in this case the spiral staircase, could be the genesis of an element realized many years later in another quite unconnected building.

The project was for a family house to accommodate the Dzurs' three children, with an attached guest house on an adjacent knoll for Albert Dzur's parents-in-law. The drawings proceed through the design process from rough space allocation diagrams to floor plans with dimensions and corrections marked in red (see pls. 44, 45). There is a small aerial perspective showing the buildings grouped together on the site, as well as two finished perspective drawings, the last stamped with the Dorothy Street address (figs. 6.2, 6.3). Dzur's signature appears on a couple of the plans, and his surname has been scribbled onto a number of the other drawings in the archive. One sheet, dated 29 September 1959, is labeled "Guest House Dzur Residence."[17] There are, however, no working drawings. The project was canceled before that stage when, in 1960, the Dzurs decided to move to Santa Barbara.

Although the design went through various configurations, the parti was always the same: a long, thin, steel-frame rectangle running north-south that comprised five 20-by-20-foot bays linked by a bridge at the north end to the guest house on the raised ground to the east (see pl. 46). One earlier arrangement, as shown in the aerial perspective drawing, has the carport separated from the house by a contained patio onto which the family room opens, much as in the Seidel Associates House.

Fig. 6.2.
Dzur House and guest house, aerial view, 1959.

Fig. 6.3.
Dzur House and guest house, view from south, 1959.

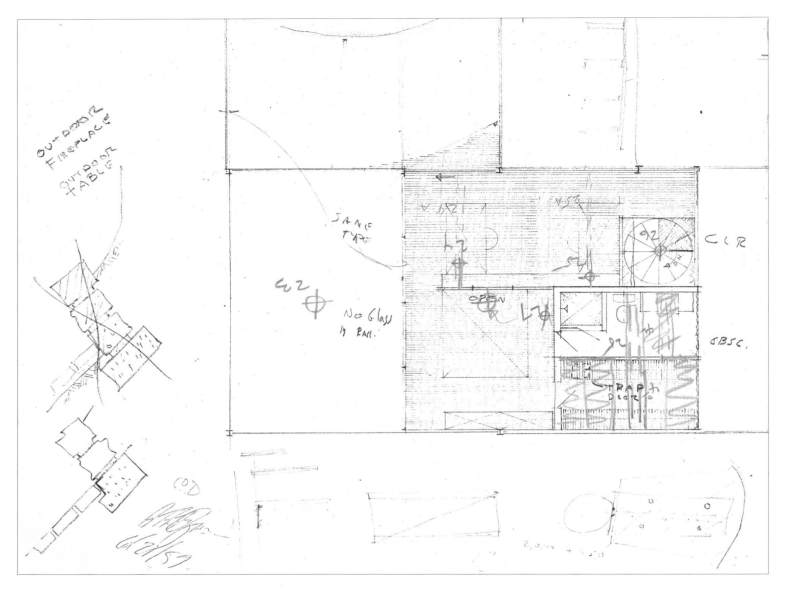

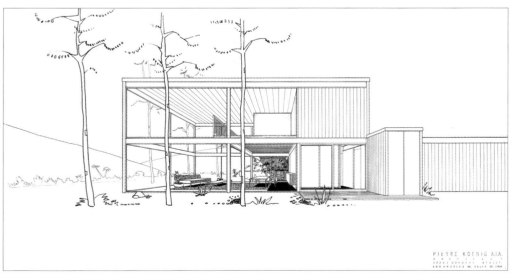

Fig. 6.4.
Dzur House and guest house, final upper-floor plan, detail,
signed by Dzur and dated 21 June 1959.

Fig. 6.5.
Dzur House, view from west, 1959.

Another, marked "DZUR," shows a large storage room in this position with the family room beyond separated by a range of three children's bedrooms with retractable or folding walls between them (see pl. 47). The final configuration, at least for the house, was arrived at by 21 June 1959, when Dzur signed the drawings, although these two sheets, one for the lower floor and one for the upper floor, are heavily marked up in red (fig. 6.4). Now the storage room has moved to the south end of the house, beyond the carport, and the three children's rooms are oriented east-west, providing a passageway from the family room to the carport (see pl. 44) and obviating the need for the covered external walkway shown on an earlier arrangement (see pl. 47). The perspective drawing viewed from the south shows what must be the final configuration (see fig. 6.3).

The guest house also went through many configurations, as did the related space at the west end of the linking bridge that contained the master bedroom. Here, the stairs changed from a dogleg to a spiral, which, in turn, changed position (see pls. 48, 49). The final arrangement, as seen on the signed drawings, relates to the perspective drawing showing the house from the west (fig. 6.5). Here, the master bedroom on the upper level overlooks the living room below. This is the first example in Koenig's work of the exploitation of vertical space.

At the house Koenig designed for Mayer Oberman in early 1960, the plan conformed very much to the pavilion type that he had developed at the Seidel Associates and Dzur Houses the previous year. Although the hilltop site in Rancho Palos Verdes was largely unrestricted by high ground, as had been the case in the two earlier buildings, there was now the need to accommodate an 18-by-60-foot swimming pool, thus confining the house to the long, eastern side of the site (see pl. 51). The Obermans' son, Bill, aspired to be a competitive swimmer, and the house, with its pool, was built to accommodate this goal (fig. 6.6). As in those earlier buildings and the two versions of the Bailey House before them, Koenig broke up the length of the building by using an enclosed patio to separate the carport from the domestic accommodation, which took up less than half of the floor plan. In doing so, he stretched the steel structure farther than he had done before, taking advantage of the increased length of steelwork now readily available. Thirty-five-foot sections of 18-gauge galvanized-steel T-roof decking were supported on four parallel, 12-inch I-section steel beams, each 95 feet, 8 inches long, that ran the full length of the house (fig. 6.7). The middle two beams, positioned slightly off-center and set 7 feet apart, supported the covered walkway that connected the carport and the house and defined the position of the kitchen and bathrooms, which were lit and ventilated by raised roof lights. On the east side of this divide were the dining room and the two bedrooms, while on the west side, overlooking the pool, were the breakfast room, living room, and study or music room where Mayer Oberman, a former violinist for the Chicago Symphony Orchestra, could practice, and his wife, Janet, a piano instructor, had her grand piano.[18] Here, for the first time, Koenig glazed all four walls of the domestic accommodation. In the absence of overhangs that might have been lifted by the wind coming in off the ocean, he used blue Koolshade louvered screens on the south and west sides to protect against solar penetration. The result was as Oberman wanted it: a clean, crisp building with no extraneous projections other than the water spouts along the roofline.

Koenig's detailing for steel houses was now becoming standardized, allowing him to develop a series of numbered construction detail sheets that could be applied to any of his houses. Some of these were used for the Oberman House, including the sheets for a column baseplate (no. 100), stud wall (no. 185), fascia with capping channel (no. 187) (see pl. 52), roof canopy (no. 191), fascia with capping channel and beam (no. 300), and beam-to-column connection (no. 316). Many other examples can be found throughout the archive; they indicate the production-house attitude that

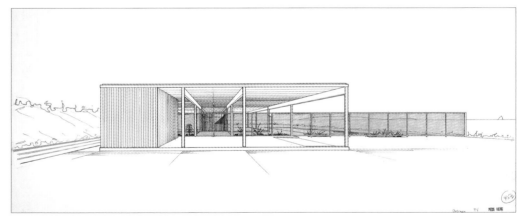

Koenig applied to steel-house construction. On each detail sheet, he would write the name of the building and apply a date stamp. Although some, until they appeared on another building, were customized for a particular job (for example, nos. 187 and 300, which cross-reference each other), many were designed to be universal in their application. Koenig similarly produced standard notes and specifications, making changes where necessary to suit the specific job—such as substituting "LA County" for, presumably, "LA City."[19] There was nothing in these requirements that was neither sensible nor expected.

Unlike the Seidel Associates House, which was colored to blend with its wooded-canyon location, the Oberman House, on its exposed site overlooking the ocean, was made to stand out. Koenig's publicity statement, which informed the first article on the house in *Arts & Architecture*,[20] states, "The color scheme, interior and exterior, is white with white on white Terazzo floors throughout."[21] He later added a handwritten note: "white drapes–white rug–gray couches." To this, he could have added the two black Ludwig Mies van der Rohe Barcelona chairs that he ordered from Knoll Associates in New York on behalf of the Obermans, at a cost of $990.[22] "All furnishings," as *Arts &*

Fig. 6.6.
Mayer, Janet, and Bill Oberman at home, ca. 1962. Photographer unknown.

Fig. 6.7.
Oberman House, view from north, 1960.

Fig. 6.8.
The Oberman House with Catalina Island in the
distance, 1962. Photo by Leland Y. Lee. Courtesy the
Leland Y. Lee Estate.

*Architecture* pointed out, "were selected by the architect."[23] Despite the monochromatic specification, color was allowed. "Blue enameled steel cabinets, and areas of walnut," as well as red side chairs would, according to the draft publicity statement, "add contrast to the interior."[24] At the bottom of the statement is another handwritten note: "Color achieved from mood of sky–sunsets etc."

When it came to the publicity shots, things did not bode well. In his absence from the office, an assistant made these notes in Koenig's logbook for 9 July 1962: "Janet Oberman called—raised Hell about having a model (she was calling model)! Also about man bringing furniture."[25] And, on 13 July: "Jan Oberman: Doesn't want to feed pool people—never talked to her about pictures. Salazar brought friend! (Also wants construction shots). I asked her if she wanted to call off picture taking! She said no—she wanted the photos—great prestige for her."[26] Janet Oberman got her construction shots, taken by Modernage Photo Service, showing the steel frame, decking, and footings. For *Arts & Architecture,* Leland Y. Lee went to the house twice. On one occasion he photographed a male model, perhaps Salazar or his friend, standing in his swimwear at the far end of the pool. It was a foggy day with almost no visibility, but by using infrared film, Lee cut through the haze to reveal Santa Catalina Island clearly in the distance (fig. 6.8).

On 26 July 1967, Kurt Meyer, of the Southern California Chapter of the American Institute of Architects' Los Angeles Fiesta Committee, wrote to Koenig to say that the "Palos Verde House has been honored with an Award."[27] This was on the occasion of the 186th birthday of the City of Los Angeles, and the Oberman House was named, along with the Eames House and Craig Ellwood's Rosen House, on the list of Architectural Grand Prix awardees.[28] The five judges—who included the architect John Merrill of Skidmore, Owings & Merrill; Samuel Hurst, dean of architecture at the University of Southern California (USC); George Dudley, dean of architecture at the University of California, Los Angeles; and the *Los Angeles Times* architecture critic Art Seidenbaum—declared the Oberman House to be a "fine example of industrial materials imaginatively employed to a well-organized, well-detailed residence. Indoor–outdoor functions are directly related and the over-all result suggests a richness of living possibilities."[29] The awards, which represented the thirty-six most significant buildings built in Los Angeles since 1947, were announced at a dinner at the Century Plaza Hotel on 1 September.[30] However, the house had already been recognized in 1963 by the American Iron and Steel Institute for "Excellence for Use of Structural Steel," and the chairman of the senate at USC had written to Koenig, who was now teaching at the School of Architecture, saying, "Your recognition in this way reflects not only on your own position but also the stature of the University as a whole."[31] Whatever the success of the house, in the year following the Architectural Grand Prix award, it was put on the market with Coldwell Banker & Company for $118,500.[32]

The vacation house that Koenig drew up for Dr. and Mrs. Jules Plaut in February 1961 took the idea of the simple steel-frame pavilion to the extreme, but, as a vacation house, it had fairly straightforward requirements (see pl. 58). Comprising seven 10-by-20-foot bays, with the kitchen and children's bathroom units floating as space dividers within the long rectangle, the house had the master bedroom at one end and the three children's bedrooms at the other, with the living room positioned as a buffer in between. This basic parti of a long, glazed rectangle with discrete service units set within it had been the arrangement at Case Study House 22. There, in the north-south wing, the fireplace and kitchen units both subdivided the living functions and separated them from the enclosed utility spaces beyond. This arrangement was repeated at the Plaut Vacation House, where it was now the children's bedrooms that were set at one end; but, here, the positioning of the children's bathroom unit off-grid makes for uncomfortable alignments.

The same parti was employed at the house Koenig designed later that year for Cyrus and Elizabeth Johnson in Carmel Valley in central California. The working drawings, dated 9 September 1961, show a T-shaped steel house set on a 20-by-20-foot grid (see pl. 59). Five bays at the top of the T, situated nearer the road, contain the bedrooms, a service core (comprising a dressing room, bathroom, and laundry), entranceway, workshop, and carport. The three bays that make up the leg of the T extend southward from the centrally positioned service core and contain the kitchen, dining, and living areas. Almost fully glazed on three sides and set beneath a broad overhang, this wing replicates the north-south wing of Case Study House 22 in more ways than one. It not only is set up on artificially raised ground (into which Koenig inserted a hidden basement), thus projecting the living area out above the reconstructed landscape, but also, in adjoining the bedroom wing, forms an L-shaped plan that both mirrors Case Study House 22 and contains, within its angle, the swimming pool (fig. 6.9). Although the working drawings show the two 12-inch I-section steel beams flanking the south wing to be supported at their ends by H-section columns, in the event, the columns were withdrawn 10 feet to where the glazing ended and the beam ends were allowed to cantilever beyond, tapering as they did so. It was a more elegant solution than at Case Study House 22, and, by reducing the weight of the beams, it was structurally more economical. The 12-inch I-section beams flanking the top of the T-plan, if installed in one piece, would have reached 100 feet—longer even than at the Oberman House—and those flanking the living areas would have been 60 feet. The windows were the now standard 20-foot glass sliders.

Cyrus and Elizabeth Johnson had visited Case Study House 22 and, wanting a modern house, had contacted Koenig. It is perhaps not surprising, therefore, that there are similarities between the two houses: the L-shaped arrangement of living and sleeping accommodation within the Johnson

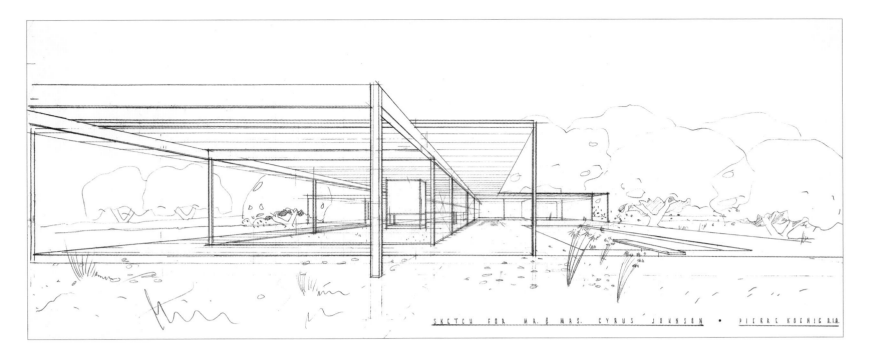

SKETCH FOR MR. & MRS. CYRUS JOHNSON • PIERRE KOENIG R.I.A.

Fig. 6.9.
Johnson House, view from south, 1961.

House replicates closely, but in mirror fashion, what Koenig had designed at Case Study House 22. The Johnsons, nevertheless, had their own requirements. The rural site that they owned in Carmel Valley was over an acre in area, south sloping, and dotted with California oak trees. Unlike Koenig's other houses, this one was to occupy an unconfined rural site unencumbered by adjacent properties. The Johnsons, consequently, asked for an open-plan house that would take advantage of the environment.[33] They also asked for a 20-foot section of the west wall along part of the living-room elevation to be solid so as to shelter their piano and other fine furniture from the low evening sun. Koenig finished the internal wall with natural teak and the external expanse with vertically hung 20-gauge galvanized-steel decking. The living room, as a result, was not an all-glass box as it might have been, but, being raised some 6 feet above the natural grade, it offered a commanding view.

The pure geometry emerging in Koenig's designs at this time began to find expression in symmetry. The hillside house Koenig drew up in December 1960 for Andrew Whittlesey on the north side of Hyperion Avenue, a busy street in the Silver Lake neighborhood, was arranged, at least on the upper level, symmetrically (see pls. 56, 57). Here, the pedestrian walkway is set on axis between the two parking spaces, with the front door recessed deep into the plan alongside the guest bathroom. As a result, the internal space takes on an H shape, with the kitchen and dining room to one side and the living room to the other. The stairs and a terrace infill the other central recess of the H but, in doing so, imbalance the otherwise symmetrical rear elevation. Similarly, the symmetry of the upper-floor plan is lost on the lower level, where three bedrooms cluster informally around the shared bathroom and utility area.

The working drawings for the De Winter House, drawn up thirteen months later in January 1962, show another hillside house where the level platform of the upper floor is arranged symmetrically. Intended for a sloping site on Deep Dell Place in the hills above the Hollywood Freeway (US 101), the upper floor was arranged much as at the Plaut Vacation House: a centrally positioned kitchen and bathroom unit separate the living room from the two bedrooms (see pl. 62). Although the plan of the upper floor, down to the positioning (if not the size) of the external decks, was symmetrical, the variation between solid and glazed wall sections made it appear far more informal than might be expected (see pl. 63). Had the house been set on a flat site, as at Case Study House 21, this contrast between the intention of the plan (symmetry) and result of the elevation (asymmetry) might have been uncomfortable. But the need to raise the building above the sloping site allowed a freedom of approach that Koenig was already exploiting in a number of other hillside houses at the beginning of the 1960s. As hillside houses, the Whittlesey House and the De Winter House will be explored further in the following chapter.

It is interesting to note how Koenig's use of axial symmetry as an organizing principle on plan became the modus operandi in his domestic architecture at this time. Although there was a degree of symmetry in the arrangement of the bedrooms and bathroom in the preliminary design of the second Biedleman House in January 1960, Koenig's first fully symmetrical plan would be for the Seidel Beach House (see chapter 8) later the same month. Axiality, if not symmetry, was then used at the Oberman House the following June. In the fourteen-month period between December 1960 and February 1962, axial symmetry was the organizing principle behind the Whittlesey, Plaut, Johnson, De Winter, and Beidleman Houses. Only with the Willheim House (see chapter 8) of March 1962 and the Beagles House (see chapter 7) eight months later did Koenig return to informal planning. These dates coincide almost exactly with the two years or so during which Koenig worked alone from the garage at Dorothy Street. His retreat to Brentwood at the end of 1959 removed him from the architectural environment that existed within that four-block radius of the San Vicente office and the critical challenges that working in such a context would have brought. His friend Peter Candreva, for example, would not suddenly walk in and start commenting on his drawings, nor could he turn to another architect when needing quick advice. At Dorothy Street, he was on his own, and the attraction of the symmetrical plan, as an easy but not always suitable way of arranging spaces, was perhaps too tempting. His rejection of axial symmetry in 1962 was made as quickly as his adoption of it had been two years earlier and coincides with his accepting the position of instructor in the School of Architecture at USC. It is likely that in that learning environment, he found himself challenged, once more, to think critically.

When Koenig designed his last steel-frame pavilion house in 1966, there was conscious effort to break the symmetry, and the plan reverted almost to the linear informality of the Seidel Associates House. The house commissioned by the horticulturalist Richard W. Bosley is more unusual, however, for being located out of state, in Mentor, Ohio. The Mentor Avenue address on the drawings was that for Bosley's nursery business on the edge of a busy highway,[34] and the site plan suggests that the house was to be located at the far end of his land, farthest from the highway. Although a horticulturist by trade, Bosley became famous in the 1950s for building a sleek sports car called the Bosley Mark I, which was mostly culled from parts of other cars. Then, in the mid-1960s, he built a follow-up called the Bosley Mark II Interstate. How he knew Koenig one can only guess, but Koenig liked sports cars and owned a 1965 Porsche 356 C Coupe.[35]

Two different positions for the Bosley House were tried. A preliminary study, dated August 1966, has the house facing due south across a large rectangular pond; the other, which accompanied the working drawings seven months later, has the pond, now larger, positioned to the southwest and the vehicular access is different. The steel-frame house, however, remains the same in both the preliminary design and the working drawings (see pl. 80). Arranged over almost four and a half bays, it measures 80 by 30 feet, with the living room, dining room, and entrance at one end and a large three-car garage at the other. In the two central bays are the three bedrooms, the kitchen, and the bathrooms.

The plan could have been symmetrical had it not been for the asymmetrical corridor connecting each end of the building. Positioned carefully off-axis and lit by a raised roof light, the corridor cuts through the building beneath the 30-foot crossbeams that clearly define the different zones. A broad overhang to the south is designed to permit only winter sunlight to penetrate the living spaces, while another at the west end, in combination with two screen walls, is designed to block the setting sun (see pl. 81). The house, with full-height sliding glass doors and clad in steel decking, offered as sleek and modern an image as the prototype Mark II Interstate that might have been parked in the garage. However, the house, like the car, never went into production.

Although, following his involvement with the Case Study House Program, Koenig continued to design and build steel-frame houses, few architects in the 1960s took up the challenge. In the dry heat of Palm Springs, where steel would not corrode, William Cody built steel houses as did Albert Frey.[36] But in Los Angeles, it was really only Craig Ellwood, the architect of three steel-frame Case Study Houses in the 1950s, who remained faithful to the material; Raphael Soriano was now building in aluminum.[37]

The early 1960s saw the adoption of axial symmetry, not just in Koenig's plans—and possibly for the reasons suggested—but also in the designs coming from Ellwood's office, where the change of personnel often brought about a shift in architectural output. Whereas Ellwood's Case Study Houses had been loosely planned affairs, his pavilion houses of the 1960s, whether steel or timber frame, adopted the same partis as Koenig had done at the Plaut and Johnson Houses (already examined), and the Seidel Beach House. The common source for this pavilion plan was Mies van der Rohe's Farnsworth House at Plano, Illinois, completed in 1951. It had been published in *Arts & Architecture* as early as March 1952.[38] □

PIERRE KOENIG A.I.A.
ARCHITECT
11681 SAN VICENTE BLVD.
LOS ANGELES 49, CALIF. GR. 37634

# HILLSIDE HOUSES

There is a perspective drawing in the Pierre Koenig archive, dating from the San Vicente years, of an unidentified hillside house built with a timber frame and wraparound siding (fig. 7.1). Perched on a steep escarpment overlooking the ocean, it is monodirectional in its arrangement, with all the windows opening to the view. There are also two plans of the same time, one with a balcony longer than the other. Although neither plan corresponds perfectly with the hillside house, they can be for no other building (see pls. 136, 137). Both plans clearly reflect the house's six-bay linear arrangement, in which one end bay is given over to the carport. In both versions, the bathroom and kitchen units, positioned centrally within the remaining five bays, divide the living area from the sleeping area in a manner not unlike that at the Plaut Vacation House, for this is clearly a vacation house too. Whether this was a commissioned design or simply speculative cannot be said, but the idea was not altogether new.

Ever since the 1930s, when Richard Neutra and Rudolph Schindler started building modern houses in the hills around Silver Lake, hillside houses have been very much a part of the output of many Los Angeles architects. Calvin Straub, Koenig's third-year tutor at the University of Southern California (USC), working with Arthur Gallion, the dean of architecture, had built just such a house in Beverly Glen in 1949, as had Koenig's fifth-year tutor, A. Quincy Jones, in Brentwood, the following year.[1] At the same time, hillside houses were also coming off the drawing boards of the architecture school's visiting critics, Gregory Ain, Gordon Drake, and Whitney Smith.[2]

As early as April 1956, *Arts & Architecture* had published a design by Koenig for a linear hillside house with a steel frame and a lower story inserted beneath.[3] With three bedrooms and a utility room, this was not a vacation house but a family home commissioned by Larry and Francis Beidleman (see pl. 25). The steep, north-facing site on Hanley Avenue, in the Crestwood Hills area, suggested the use of a steel frame. Koenig therefore raised the living accommodation to the level of the road, placing the third bedroom, intended for an adult, together with the utility room and carport, below.[4] The initial publication in *Arts & Architecture,* under the title "Steel House," comprised photographs of the model and two floor plans, although it was not until a year later that Koenig produced the working drawings.[5] The innovative nature of this design was described in the published article: "The upper floor is a 3½" concrete slab poured over inverted steel decking which locks together and no additional reinforcing steel is needed. Also, forms are eliminated and a finished surface is produced on the ceiling below. The roof will be exposed steel deck, reverted, the same as is used on the floor but with insulation and composition roofing over."[6]

This method of using steel decking to provide both permanent formwork and tensile reinforcement for the concrete slabs became a standard feature of Koenig's multistory steel houses, so much so that when *Arts & Architecture* published the design for the Metcalf House in January 1959, it was under the heading "Steel and Concrete Hillside House."[7]

Fig. 7.1.
Hillside house with timber frame, ca. 1957–59.

Although the text of the article does not mention it, the other innovation at the Beidleman House was the adoption of the H-section column. Hitherto, all Koenig's steel houses had had circular pipe columns, as he had learned from Soriano. This preliminary design for the Beidleman House was published in the same month as he dated the working drawings for the first version of the Bailey House, so it is likely that the two houses were developed concurrently. This was, as mentioned in chapter 4, around the time that he was working for A. Quincy Jones on the Eichler Homes X-100.

The working drawings for the Beidleman House, which were produced in April 1957, show clearly how Koenig used the steel frame to greatest advantage on the steeply sloping site. Arranged in seven bays at 10-foot centers, the H-section columns were set 15 feet apart, allowing the 12-inch I-section floor beams and the 6-inch I-section roof beams to cantilever out on either side, albeit unevenly, using the counterweight principle recently employed at the Burwash House (see pl. 26).[8] Glazed toward the northern valley view and clad with 20-gauge steel decking on the opposite, road side, except where the protruding stair bay was faced in brick, this was Koenig's first fully developed multistory house (see pl. 27). But it was never to be built. When, five years later, the Beidlemans returned for another design for the same site, Koenig provided a very different solution.

The idea behind the first Beidleman House, however, was not lost. The Dowden House of 1958 was for a very similar hillside site, and although three versions of this building remain in the archive, none of them progressed as far as working drawings. One solution, surviving only in an aerial perspective, was for an L-shaped plan with the living accommodation, apparently, on the lower level, set around a swimming pool (fig. 7.2). Another design, closer to the Beidleman solution, had a structural grid enlarged to five 20-by-20-foot bays, with the main living accommodation, the master bedroom, and the bathroom all together at road level, where there was parking for three cars, and the guest and ancillary spaces located below. This, it would appear, was superseded by another design, now drawn up in plan and perspective, and date-stamped August 1958 (see pl. 35). Here, a clearer sense of domestic separation was achieved with the bedrooms being placed below and the kitchen, dining, and living areas above, at the level of the entrance and the two-car carport. Drawn as a dramatic perspective that emphasizes the steel structure, this house, which was also never built, suggests much of what Koenig was to achieve, given the right site and the right client, over the next twenty-five years (fig. 7.3).

That client might have been his old friend from USC, Arnold Metcalf, who had a hillside site on Moreno Drive overlooking the Silver Lake reservoir. When Arnold Metcalf and his wife visited Case Study House 21 on 10 January 1959, they noted "T-Steel" parenthetically after their name in the visitors' book.[9] Metcalf was in the steel business,[10] and the new house in Silver Lake was to make good use of the product: Koenig specified 16-gauge galvanized-steel T-deck for the roof and, inverted, for the floors,[11] while the walls were to be clad with either Robertson #3 18-gauge wall deck (wide rib out) or American steel deck Type R 20-gauge.[12]

The Metcalfs' site was very similar to that of the Dowden House, and both houses were developed simultaneously, the working drawings for the Metcalf House, like the third version of the Dowden House, being dated August 1958. The street elevation for both houses and the positioning of the carport and entrance walkway are also very similar (fig. 7.4). Beyond the carport, however, the plans are different (see pls. 36, 37). For whereas the rectangular plan of the Dowden House looks back to that of the Beidleman House, the square plan of the Metcalf House offers a much more compact arrangement. On the top and middle floors, the living accommodation is gathered tightly around a centrally positioned dogleg stair beside which a chimney core rises through the building. On the north side,

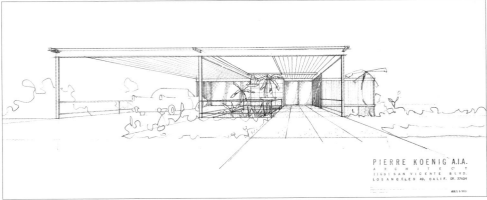

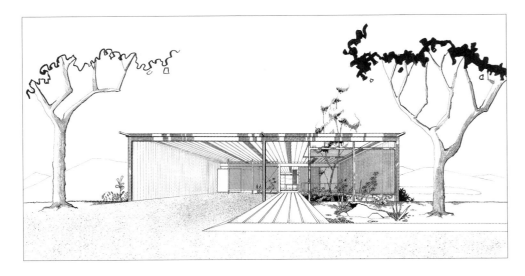

Fig. 7.2.
Dowden House, aerial view, 1958.

Fig. 7.3.
Dowden House, view from west, 15 August 1958.

Fig. 7.4.
Metcalf House, view from west, 1958.

overlooking the valley, the balconies at the upper and middle level are offset, the former outside the living area and the latter outside the kitchen. On the south side, beneath the carport, a deck is inserted between the son's bedroom and the hillside (see pl. 38). The lowest level is left open as a shaded play area accessed by a spiral stair from a balcony outside the kitchen. This stair, conceived in the same manner as he was to do at the Dzur House, offered a unique method of construction. Each tread, supported on a triangular bracket, was to be welded onto the circular central shaft. Although never realized here or at the Dzur House, Koenig's idea for a spiral stair did eventually emerge at the Schwartz House over thirty years later.

Of the early multistory houses Koenig designed while at the San Vicente office, the Metcalf House came nearest to being built. A building application was lodged with the City of Los Angeles in September 1958,[13] but the Metcalfs' imminent divorce brought the project to an early end.[14]

Fifteen months later, just at the time when Koenig moved his office from San Vicente to Dorothy Street, the Beidleman project was reactivated. There are, in the archive, three preliminary plans for the principal living floor of the new version of the Beidleman House. These drawings, which show variations on the same basic idea, are referred to, rather confusingly, as "Upper Level," "Upper Floor," and "First Floor."[15] It was the one called "First Floor" that was agreed upon and signed "L. Beidleman" on 7 January 1960 (see pl. 28). The principle behind all three schemes was the same: a raised box measuring 48 by 35 feet with a centrally positioned open-air patio, around which the domestic accommodation is arranged. Apart from a few vertical cladding panels, the external walls are exclusively glass with the entrance on the long, south side. From here, a spiral stair, positioned slightly differently in all three iterations, leads down to the lower floor. Other differences between the schemes are few: a variation in the position of the cladding panels, in the arrangement of the bathroom, or its relationship to the two adjacent bedrooms. There are no preliminary plans for the lower floor remaining, but the working drawings, dated February 1962, show two additional bedrooms, a bathroom, and a utility room arranged in a tight block with a two-car carport alongside. The two-year delay between the preliminary plans and the working drawings resulted in further changes and modifications to the upper-floor plan, such as the repositioning, once again, of the spiral stair, but nothing to substantially change the design.

With the second version of the Beidleman House, Koenig completely rethought the problem of how to build a steel-frame house on a hill. What, in 1957, had been a long rectangle supported on no fewer than fifteen columns was now a much tighter rectangle supported on just four. To provide a platform for the house, Koenig conceived a system of two-way cantilevers comprising two 44-foot-long steel I-section beams tapered at the ends, as at the Johnson House, on which sat five I-section crossbeams measuring 35 feet, 4 inches (see pl. 29). Whereas the four supporting columns, arranged on a 27-by-18-foot grid, were centered beneath this platform, the lower-level domestic accommodation was pushed to one side in order to provide space on the east side for the carport. The result was that, in the working drawings, one column broke through a bedroom wall while another stood alone in the corner of the bathroom (see pl. 30). It was not an altogether tidy arrangement, but it was rectified by the time the drawings were published in James Steele and David Jenkins's book thirty-six years later.[16] Those drawings are also in the archive.[17]

In the two years between Beidleman's signing of the drawings for his house in January 1960, and the preparation of the working drawings in February 1962, Koenig produced designs for both the Whittlesey House and the De Winter House, taking the latter to working drawing stage. Being positioned on sloping ground, both houses adopted the four-point structural system developed for

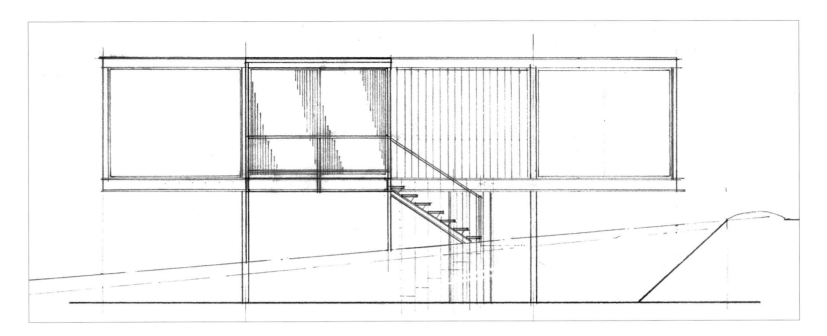

the Beidleman House to raise the main living accommodation to or above the level of the road. At the Whittlesey House, the columns formed a 20-by-24-foot grid from which the upper level cantilevered 7 feet on either side. This was connected to the road by a 20-foot access bridge (see pl. 55). The De Winter House was raised above the road that swept around the site and was approached by stairs from below, where the cars were parked and a small guest suite was located. Supported on a 20-by-20-foot grid of columns, the upper level cantilevered out 20 feet, east and west, and supported balconies on either side (fig. 7.5). In all three of these designs, the use of the double, counterbalancing cantilever allowed Koenig to minimize the depth of the main beams and reduce the number of columns and the associated foundation work.

Although it was a divorce that prevented the Metcalf House from being built, what put an end to the proposals for the Dowden, Beidleman, Whittlesey, and De Winter Houses is not known. Maybe it was the cost or the difficulty of the hillside sites, although in the cases of the latter two, Koenig seems to have resolved that well. The only steel-frame hillside house to be built at this time was the one designed for Robert and Alice Beagles on a cliff-top site on Revello Drive overlooking the ocean in Pacific Palisades.

The working drawings in the archive provide a clear explanation of how, based upon the soil engineer's report, Koenig had first intended to support the house on the steep slope of the site (see pls. 68, 69). For this, William Porush, his engineer, had devised a 60-by-40-foot grid of reinforced-concrete ground beams, each 2 feet, 6 inches deep, to be laid across the 33-degree incline.[18] This was to be retained by reinforced-concrete caissons, measuring 2 feet, 4 inches in diameter, sunk deep into the hillside. Due to the steepness of the gradient, the house met the ground beams at just three points. At the top level, the upper story of the house was raised on four rectangular reinforced-concrete piers that were 2 feet deep, 18 inches wide, and 4 feet, 4 inches tall. In the center, the rear wall of the lower story of the house rested on an 18-inch-wide seat formed into the ground beams. And at the lowest level, another row of reinforced-concrete piers, measuring 5 feet, 10 inches tall, supported the center of the lower story, which then cantilevered 10 feet beyond. Above this reinforced-concrete substructure, the superstructure was all steel frame (fig. 7.6). When

Fig. 7.5.
De Winter House 2, north elevation, ca. 1960.

he took the drawings down to City Hall to obtain the building permit, Koenig discovered, by chance, that the site for the house was in what had been designated an active landslide area. This sudden realization required the redesign by Porush of the whole substructure and the increase in depth of the piers to some 6 feet. Nevertheless, it proved expedient, for in May 1965, less than a year after the house was completed, the Los Liones landslide (named after the street below Revello Drive) washed away the road and three homes alongside the Beagles House, as well as a new apartment building and some tennis courts below, dumping them all at the bottom of the hill.[19] The Beagles House was undamaged.

The appearance of the Beagles House from the street is one of a low, long pavilion, leaving the visitor unprepared for the explosion of space inside (fig. 7.7). The arrangement of the house on plan is very similar to that of the hillside house with which this chapter started: a rectangle of six 10-foot bays opening to the ocean, with the garage inserted on the upper level at one end. The distribution of the living spaces over the two floors tended to separate the children—at this time, two young girls—from the adults. The upper level comprised the children's bedrooms and family room as well as the kitchen and dining room, while the lower level was centered around a large living room that separated the master bedroom and bathroom from the guest suite. All rooms, except for the family room, faced the long balcony, which, at each level, overlooked the ocean. The family room opened onto a small screened patio and garden set against the road. Apart from its sleek black metal trim and crisp aluminum sliders, there was little about the house to suggest the industrial processes that were so much a part of Koenig's vocabulary. The external walls, where not glazed, were finished in a light-gray cement render, and the internal walls and ceilings were plastered. Only the four steel I-section columns that penetrated the living room bore any witness to the structure that held this building to its hillside site. The main feature of the house, apart from the view, was the centrally positioned fireplace with its black steel canopy and flue rising up through the stairwell in front of

Fig. 7.6.
Beagles House under construction, ca. 1963.

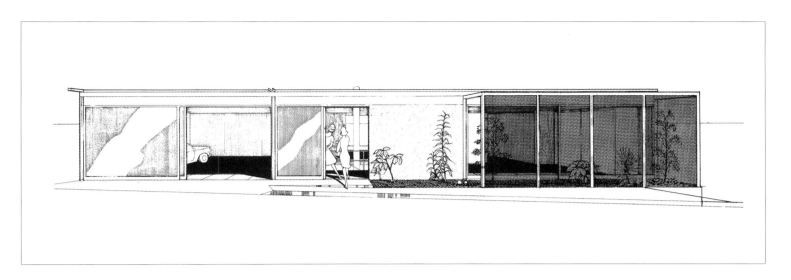

the open-tread dogleg stairs. As with all Koenig's working drawings, it was meticulously detailed and drawn up.

The Beagles House was finished in 1963, and it was two years before Koenig designed any more hillside houses. The delay, or perhaps change of pace, reflects the change in his architectural practice, for by 1963 he was already teaching at USC, and in 1964 he was appointed an assistant professor. Therefore, the need to pursue independent work was not so pressing. What might be seen as the last in this sequence of steel-frame hillside houses was the one designed for Richard and Vickie Iwata on Summit Place in Monterey Park in 1965. However, due to its scale and arrangement, it represented a departure from the pattern that had been established in his hillside houses of the late 1950s. Its design was driven less by structure or materials than by environmental controls, but, due to the demands of a large family, the drama of the exterior was lost internally.

The Iwata House was much bigger than any house Koenig had built before and was intended to accommodate what he described as a "very active family of two adults and five children with many interests and needs."[20] This was achieved by dividing the house into three separate, horizontal layers of increasing size and complexity, the middle level acting as a sound buffer between the other two (fig. 7.8). The triangular site faced southeast over a steep escarpment; its narrow end, where the pool and pool house were located, faced northwest. Rather than having what might have been a three-story building perched on the edge of the site, Koenig cut a shelf into the escarpment to take the lowest floor so that the house could be entered at its middle level from a bridge, thus reducing the amount of vertical circulation once inside the house (see pl. 72). The three levels of the house were treated as independent elements supported by what Koenig called a "tree-like cantilevered steel frame."[21] In his structural notes on the house, he wrote,

This three story cantilevered house is supported by a steel structural "tree" composed of 27WF 84# girders under the second floor and 21WF 55# girders under the third floor with 16WF 26# beams spanning across the girders. The 8" × 8" × ³⁄₈" steel tube columns are designed to resist lateral loads and are cantilevered from concrete footings. The first floor is on a concrete slab. The two walls on the first floor are designed to stiffen the structure slightly under light lateral loads but are calculated to fail under severe horizontal forces thus allowing the steel frame to resist the heavy loads during a severe earthquake.[22]

Fig. 7.7.
Beagles House, view from north, 1962.

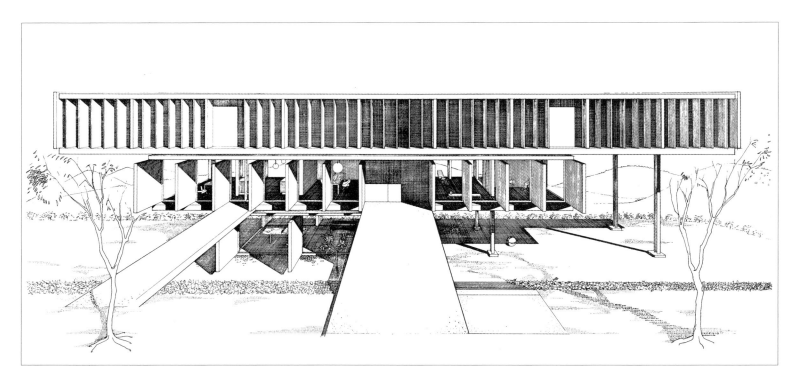

This is what might be called a dynamic structure, designed both to absorb light shocks and to resist strong lateral movement. The independent floors could react differently to seismic movement without affecting each other. The structural system reads very clearly in the construction-site photographs, which show each story supported on steel but framed out in timber (fig. 7.9). This layered structural system also allowed for the inclusion of all the services within the almost 4-foot gap between the floors. Services were then brought to and taken away from the building beneath the access bridge.

The other area in which the Iwata House was innovative was in the control of solar penetration, which was achieved with vertical fins along both long elevations. In his publicity statement, Koenig wrote,

> The size and spacing of the sun control fins reflect the sizes of the spaces they control. The efficiency of the fins in terms of controlling direct sunlight is equalized at each floor by decreasing the spacing and decreasing the width at the same time as we move upward. The progression upwards is: 1–2–6. The visual response from the interior varies at each floor, providing a systematic change. The horizontal plane formed by the overhanging floor above each level aids in controlling the difficult east-west sun condition.[23]

A model was made to test, on a heliodon, the shading effect of the fins, the result demonstrating the benefit of their close spacing (fig. 7.10). The manner in which the upper stories effectively shaded the levels below is shown in Koenig's perspective view of the building from the southwest

Fig. 7.8.
Iwata House, view from northwest, 1965.

Fig. 7.9.
Iwata House under construction, ca. 1966. Photographer unknown.

Fig. 7.10.
Iwata House, heliodon test model, 1965.

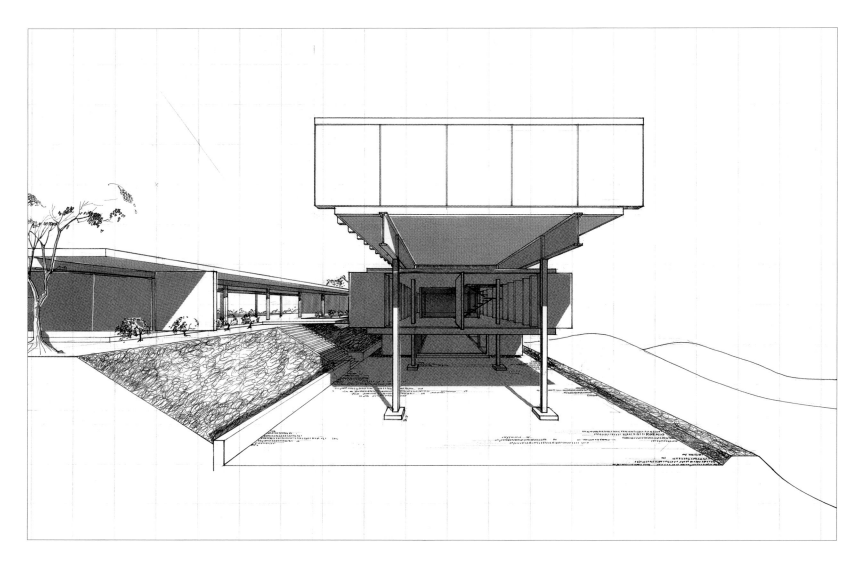

(fig. 7.11). These precautions must have worked, because, in his publicity statement, Koenig noted that although there was provision for future air-conditioning, "So far there is no need for artificial cooling."[24]

The fins visually unified each level of the building yet also removed any indication of how the spaces inside might be arranged. On each successive level, the floor plan grew larger and the internal arrangement more complex. At the lowest level, in an area defined by six H-section steel columns, the stairs and a single bathroom divided the playroom from the outdoor play area, which was well shaded, as shown in the southwest perspective drawing. At the middle level, approached directly from the access bridge, the quieter living rooms, to the south, were separated from the dining room, kitchen, and family room by the stairs and a sliding screen partition set between flanking columns. Beyond the partition, a freestanding washroom and a protruding pantry (positioned between the fins of the southeast wall) further subdivided the space, pushing the family room and kitchen to the far end, where a second, smaller access bridge provided a backdoor for children and kitchen deliveries. Due to these various intrusions, there was, in this arrangement, little of the clarity that characterized, for example, the Plaut Vacation House or the De Winter House, both similarly open-plan spaces. Finally, the top floor was the largest and in many ways the most disappointing:

Fig. 7.11.
Iwata House, view from southwest, 1965.

here, six bedrooms, a library, a radio room, a sewing room, and three bathrooms had to be accommodated. The result is not unlike a hotel plan, with the long corridor, set off-center, running from the master bedroom at one end to the library at the other. The children's bedrooms and the radio room are to one side, facing southeast, and the service rooms are to the other, facing northwest. The disappointment of this plan might be blamed on the repetitive nature of the requirements, suggesting that the pavilion plan, which is really the basis of each of these three floors, works only up to a certain size. Beyond that, it loses coherence.

Nevertheless, the house served the different demands of the Iwata family for over forty years. In 2002, Koenig received this email:[25]

> Dear Mr Koenig
> Congratulations on your architectural works and professional achievements. I am the daughter of Richard and Vickie. I have a daughter who will be attending UCS, School of Engineering this fall and she finds my parents home most interesting. We are now living with my mother since the passing of my father. You are a legendary name in our home and this "white house" has touched many people for over 35 years in our lives and in the community.
> Respectfully Yours,
> Elizabeth Morinaka

From the mid-1970s, all the new steel houses built by Koenig, with the exception of his own house in Brentwood, were to be on hillside sites. Both the material and the method of construction lent itself well to the situation. But he also explored the use of timber for hillside construction, as in the Colwes House (1968) and the later Burton House (1978). However, the nature of the material, as will be shown, led to rather different solutions. □

# TIMBER HOUSES

Timber is the material of choice for almost all California architects, and it was timber buildings that Pierre Koenig was taught to design at the University of Southern California. Although he quickly converted to steel construction, he did not totally reject timber construction. Indeed, as a young architect trying to make his way with house extensions and conversions, he could not afford to. And he often incorporated timber into his steel-frame houses; the Iwata House is but one example. Yet timber construction, when compared to steel, leads to different results, for both the properties and the strengths of the materials are different. The archive contains no evidence of timber-frame buildings for about the first ten years of Koenig's career. Even the addition he proposed in 1960 for the rear of the Philbrick House in Santa Monica, a traditional timber-frame and stucco building in the Italianate style, was to be steel and glass.[1] Most architects would have done it in timber.

A few months earlier, in January 1960, just after he moved his office from San Vicente to the garage on Dorothy Street, Koenig had designed a timber beach house for Tom Seidel and his wife, the Oscar-nominated actress Jean Hagen (fig. 8.1).[2] The house's location on the ocean's edge in Malibu precluded any use of steel, and it is reasonable to assume that the challenge of this simple timber structure reminded Koenig of the material's possibilities. The house, which faced southwest over the ocean, was a simple rectangle, measuring 20 feet, 6 inches by 46 feet, 6 inches, supported on six 12-inch-diameter timber posts driven into the sand (see pl. 50). The pile caps (the two long beams on top of the piles that supported the house) were 12-by-14-inch structural-grade treated timber (probably redwood), on which the 2-by-12-inch floor joists sat. Rather than using a shear wall to provide lateral restraint, as is common in timber-frame construction, Koenig used ½-inch galvanized-steel rods, tightened with turnbuckles, as diagonal cross bracing in one bay of the open, seaward end of the building. He had proposed this method of restraint previously, in the design for the first Beidleman House, of 1957, and the Metcalf House of the following year, but here it gave an edge or, quite literally, a tension to the timber structure. The house is otherwise unremarkable, the external walls being standard 4-by-8-foot asbestos sheets on 2-by-4-inch studs with 2-inch vertical battens covering the joints. The only windows, apart from the 20-foot glass slider at the ocean end, were two slim louvers facing the road, one to each bedroom. By separating the side and end elevations, these louvres served to accentuate the building envelope's panel construction.

The plan, as the positioning of the louvers would suggest, is symmetrical, with the two bedrooms at one end, the bathroom and kitchen island in the middle, and a large living area at the other end opening onto a deck with steps (albeit set asymmetrically at one side) to the beach beyond. This was Koenig's first fully symmetrical plan, predating both the Whittlesey House, designed in December that year, and the Plaut Vacation House of February 1961, his earliest symmetrical designs in steel. As Koenig's first design from the new office on Dorothy Street, the Seidel Beach House could not have been more different from the buildings that preceded it.

Fig. 8.1.
Seidel Beach House, view from southwest, 1960.

Eighteen months later, in June 1961, Koenig designed a two-car carport to be positioned at road level behind the beach house, its platform reaching out above the sloping foreshore.[3] Half-inch-diameter steel tie rods tightened with turnbuckles, as before, would brace the 4-by-4-inch timber frame across the open sides and the end elevation, where the long supports dropped down to the beach. Here, a four-panel glass screen would shelter the cars from the salt wind coming off the ocean. Had it been built, the carport would have been linked by steps to the deck at the rear of the beach house, but this never happened.

When the Bel Air/Brentwood fire of 5–8 November 1961 destroyed Robert Willheim's timber house on North Bundy Drive, Koenig was asked to design a replacement. In the archive, there is an undated Application to Alter–Repair–Demolish, made to the City of Los Angeles, that requests permission to "Rebuild fire-damaged dwelling (100%) on existing footings & 2nd story addition on the footings."[4] Tom Seidel is shown as the contractor. The new house is documented in the archive, and the drawings, like those for the earlier Dzur House, show how it evolved from sketches to preliminary designs and then to working drawings (see pls. 65, 66). What resulted was a long, rectangular form beneath an overhanging roof raised to two stories at the north end (see pl. 67). The east elevation to the road gave little away, but to the rear, the house opened up around the swimming pool. Here, tall windows lit the stairs, and a pergola shaded the terrace (fig. 8.2). The palette of materials varied from vertical cedar boarding and cement render on the front to exterior-quality plywood and cement render on the sides and rear. There was nowhere a sense of modular design or an industrial process. It was, in both its arrangement and use of materials, a quite different type of building from either the Seidel Beach House or the steel houses that had preceded it.

In 1962 and 1963, Koenig designed two different houses for David Herrington on adjacent plots on North Beverly Drive in Beverly Hills. It is likely that these were both speculative developments,

Fig. 8.2.
Willheim House, garden and patio, 1962. Photo by Carlos von Frankenberg.

for the two sets of drawings have the same Santa Monica address. In other words, it would appear that Herrington did not move into the first house when it was finished but proceeded to build the other, this one with his wife. Both houses, the first single story and the second two story, clearly show how free and informal the planning can be when timber construction is used (see pls. 64, 70). Located on either side of a common driveway, both plans comprise a cluster of irregular, often trapezoidal spaces cut through by a diagonal line. In the first, this would appear to correspond with the bend in the road, and in the second with the apparently self-imposed site boundary, for the lot is much larger.[5] But neither plan is a design solution that Koenig would have allowed himself when building with steel.

What was lacking in the two Herrington Houses, and to a lesser extent the Willheim House, was a rigorous response on Koenig's part to the nature of the material with which he was building. In his steel houses, he had shown this in exemplary fashion. Whereas the Seidel Beach House was, in many ways, a steel house executed in wood, these other early timber houses failed to use the material for its best qualities: a linear, structural material, strong (up to a point) in both compression and tension. With the house he built for Harold and Martha Henbest on Crest Road in Palos Verdes, he demonstrated how timber really could be used.

In one of Koenig's spiral-bound notebooks in the archive, there is an early sketch, dated 31 May 1965, for the Henbest House (fig. 8.3).[6] At this point, Koenig was playing with the concept of a folded-plate roof structure, an idea perhaps derived from the San Diego architects Frederick Liebhardt and

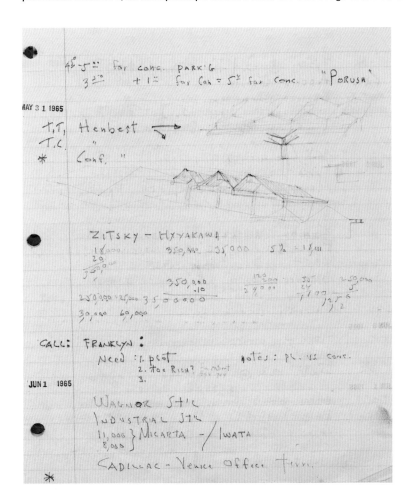

Fig. 8.3.
Henbest House on Crest Road, preliminary pencil sketches, 1965.

Eugene Weston's recently completed DuPont House (1962) in Del Mar, published the previous year.[7] When the working drawings emerged on 11 August, this was the dominant idea behind the scheme (see pl. 73). Set on a delicate framework of 4-by-4-inch wooden posts and 4-by-12-inch wooden beams, the four central bays of the six-bay folded-plate roof appeared to float like a billowing canopy between the two projecting side wings. The plan, balanced if not symmetrical, thus addressed the front garden with its centrally positioned lawn (see pl. 74). So far, so good. However, the two projecting side wings, comprising the master bedroom and bedroom 3, were set beneath flat roofs that appeared to emerge from under the folded-plate roof. It is a curious solution, when the folded-plate roof could so easily have been extended forward over the side wings. As it is, there is no relationship on plan between the folded-plate roof and these two bedrooms—a rather jarring solution that is further compromised by the covered walkway and garage/workshop, which are connected by more flat roofs to bedroom 3. The primacy of the folded-plate roof and the delicate framework that supports it is also lost internally; rather than allowing it to extend uninterrupted across the whole width of the building, from where, at the rear, a clear view of the ocean would have been available, Koenig broke up the space by inserting the utility and furnace rooms close to the long, glazed wall, and by closing off one end bay to make bedroom 2. As a result, the rear elevation is not a continuous wall of glass beneath a folded-plate roof but instead a series of pitched-roof elements, sometimes glazed, sometimes boarded, and sometimes, perhaps, rendered—for the plan and elevation drawings are inconsistent when describing the wall finishes.[8]

Yet what the Henbest House achieves, for all its inconsistencies, is a demonstration of how expressive lightweight framing can be when done in timber. Combined with the domestic idiom of pitched roofs, the result is perhaps more immediately homely, even when used in conjunction with great quantities of glass, than the flat-roofed steel-and-glass boxes for which Koenig has become known. This is conceivably most apparent in the small pavilion, one of two buildings that he designed at this time for Evelyn Heller. Intended for a site at Makawao, Maui, in the Hawaiian Islands, but apparently never built, its square plan, open walls, and pyramidal roof almost recall Marc-Antoine Laugier's primitive hut (fig. 8.4).[9]

Maybe the glazing made Harold Henbest's house in Palos Verdes too exposed, for in 1971, he asked Koenig to design another house nearby on Avenida de Calma. Two versions of the house were provided, one in July and the other in September, and the Koenig client index cards show that he was paid $598 for work done between 12 July and 16 November 1971.[10] Both versions were in timber, and it was the second scheme, combining an elongated pitched roof with solid walls in an almost Scandinavian manner, that was built. There is, in the archive, a small, bird's-eye view of the house as well as a few working drawings (fig. 8.5). Most surprisingly, both versions of the new house almost perfectly replicate the plan of the original house on Crest Road. And not only that, but the plan for the first version of the Avenida de Calma house is clearly a reworking of a copy negative of the plan of the Crest Road house. The stenciled lettering is in exactly the same place on both sheets and the scratched-out lines on the later drawing correspond to the pencil lines on the earlier one.[11] Yet for all the similarities of the plans, the appearance of the house, as built, is quite different.

What Koenig had achieved with an expressive roof form on the flat site of Crest Road, he did again on a hillside site with the house he designed for Matthew Colwes in 1968.[12] The effect was in the use of a repeating monopitch roof that stepped down the hillside in five easy stages (see pl. 84). The frame could, of course, have been done in steel, but there would have been little economy and, indeed, little point in this, when the timber could be handled so much more easily on a sloping site.

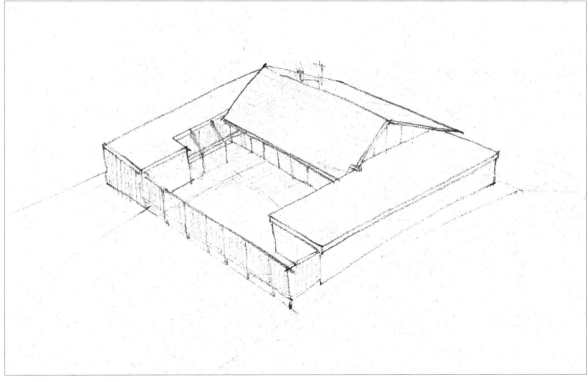

**Fig. 8.4.**
Heller House, view of pavilion, ca. 1970.

**Fig. 8.5.**
Henbest House on Avenida de Calma, aerial view, 1971.

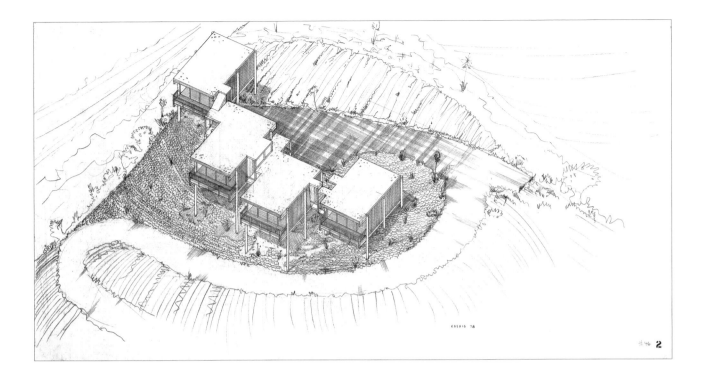

Here, and in the roof of the first Henbest House, Koenig was at last using timber in an expressive and purposeful way.

There was, by contrast, little that was remarkable about the duplex apartment building on Vista del Rey in Playa del Rey that Koenig designed for Josef and Rozanna Korzeniowski in 1971. However, as a demonstration of Koenig's meticulous attention to construction detailing, the drawings in the archive are instructive. Drawn, as always, in pencil, dimensioned and heavily annotated, they show a command of the timber construction as confident and sure as that of his steel construction (see pl. 98).

The Burton House, or "pole house," marked a departure in almost every way from Koenig's normal modus operandi. First, it was for a client who wished to build the house himself and to do it in stages. Second, although it was a hillside house, it was to be built with heavy timbers and solid if not actually crude construction. Thus, it had none of the fragility of Koenig's steel hillside houses, such as the Metcalf House, or his timber flatland houses, such as the first Henbest House. It was, in Koenig's oeuvre, quite unique.

The house, which overlooked the ocean in Malibu, was built for Ferrell Burton III and his wife, Christine, the daughter of Tom and Jean Seidel. The idea was to create a framework of timber poles—hence the name—around which the living accommodation could be built in stages. Although, in the archive, there are no letters or documents relating to the house, Koenig's client index cards show that the Burtons engaged him on 4 July 1978 and later made a payment of $1,500 for work done between 6 July 1978 and November 1979.[13] Since the agreement was made on Independence Day, it is wholly possible that the Koenigs had got together that day with Tom Seidel (Jean, divorced from Tom, had died the previous August) and the Burtons, perhaps for a barbecue, and this was the outcome.

Although Koenig provided working drawings for both plans and elevations, the built form of the house deviated from them and has been altered and modified in subsequent years. The only drawing

Fig. 8.6.
Burton House, aerial view, 1978.

Fig. 8.7.
Burton House under construction, ca. 1979. Photographer unknown.

in the archive to show a date is the aerial view marked "Koenig 78"; it also bears the sheet number 2, which would make it part of the set of plans, elevations, and details that originally comprised at least ten sheets (fig. 8.6).[14] In this drawing, four loosely interconnected boxlike structures are each shown supported on six poles at the top of a winding driveway. Although the boxes are shown in some detail, what the drawing does not indicate is the steepness of the site and the robust nature of the timber framework. This can be understood from the construction photographs in the archive (fig. 8.7). As designed, each box provided an enclosed space measuring 20 by 24 feet opening onto a 5-foot-6-inch-deep balcony along the west side. The side walls of the boxes were to be clad, perhaps surprisingly, in 18-gauge galvanized, corrugated steel,[15] which somewhat constrained the view, but windows in the rear or east side opened onto the rising ground beyond. The rear walls and soffit of each box were also to be clad in galvanized, corrugated steel (see pl. 103). Each box was connected to the next by an exposed, stepped walkway described as an "unheated space," and an additional walkway, rising from ground level, linked them at the rear (see pl. 104). The boxes provided, respectively from the south, the studio, recreation room, living room, and master bedroom. But as they were built incrementally, their functions as well as their physical relationship to each other changed. Each box was supported by six 12-inch timber poles set at 12-foot centers that rose from 24-inch reinforced-concrete caisson foundations set deep into the hillside and secured laterally by reinforced-concrete ground beams (see pl. 105). The poles were braced with diagonal tension wires attached to the caisson foundations and secured to the beams with large bolts, while shear panels, set beneath the windows, strengthened the east elevations. True to his modular approach to design, Koenig specified 20-foot sliding glass doors for the west elevations, while employing a solar-shade analysis to determine the extent of the overhang on the balcony roofs. By testing the sun angle at different times of the day on 21 June and 21 December, Koenig could adjust both the walls and the roof to ensure that, after nine o'clock in the morning, there was no sun penetration in June, but that in December, the warming morning sun could be allowed into the building (see pl. 106).

The archive holds what appear to be the last two designs Koenig made for new timber houses. They are not dissimilar in plan; neither, however, was built. The first was a sketch scheme for Milt and Mildred Holland drawn up in May 1979. The Hollands lived on Wonderland Park Avenue, about four doors away from the Bailey House (Case Study House 21), which is probably why they approached Koenig. The building he offered them, however, was quite different. It was a long rectangle measuring 96 by 27 feet divided into eight 12-foot bays. Each bay was defined by a simple post-and-beam double cantilever frame that extended out 5 feet, 6 inches on either side of a central 16-foot span (see pl. 107). In this long central core, described by Koenig as zone 1, were the dining room, living room, and kitchen. The end three bays, which accommodated the bedrooms and were described as zone 2, extended under the cantilever roof on one side. On the other side, presumably the south, the external wall was pulled back to the line of the columns for the whole length of the building. What the elevations show, and this is developed in some sketch details, is what appears to be a warm-air ventilation system set above the flat roof and running the whole length of the building. Served by the furnace, which was set beneath the cantilever, this would discharge warm air from a ceiling vent into the 6 or 8 inches between the glass and the drapes. This scheme progressed no further than a preliminary proposal, and even this contained uncertainties. One bay has been reduced to 10 feet, which would have compromised the regularity of the elevation, and the three external walls of the dining room all appear to be solid, a decision that surely was questionable.

In the same way that the Hollands lived a stone's throw from the Bailey House, Shirley Bayer lived just along Mandeville Canyon Road from the house Koenig had built for Tom Seidel Associates. Drawings in the archive indicate that the house on the site had been previously owned by Dr. and Mrs. Robert Bayer, for a garage conversion had been carried out there in 1957.[16] However, it was now Shirley Bayer who, in March 1980, commissioned Koenig, and between 12 July 1980 and 29 August 1984 paid him $6,875.[17] That sum suggests a substantial amount of work on Koenig's part, yet the evidence in the archive is very sparse. The one surviving sheet of drawings, dated February 1982, shows a rectangular house not dissimilar to the Holland House, measuring 84 by 24 feet (see pl. 108). Rather than using close-set double cantilever frames, as at the Holland House, Koenig divided the length of the house into three equal 28-foot bays separated by post-and-beam frames, each comprising two 12-foot spans. Within these bays, the subdivisions are irregular, providing three bedrooms, a kitchen, dining room, and living room, all of varying sizes. It is a compact plan, with an edge corridor lit by a long, south-facing clerestory roof light running down one side and rooms opening out to the garden along the other. The house, which is set on a slope, is supported on long legs on the downhill side, where there is a raised entrance porch with an access ramp at one end and a protruding balcony outside the master bathroom at the other. How the building was to be finished externally is not known, but, judging from the small perspective drawing and the experience of the Burton House four years earlier, it is likely to have been clad in galvanized, corrugated steel.

Timber, rather than steel, was the material of choice if not necessity for the many small additions, conversions, and remodels that, as Koenig's bread-and-butter work, filled the gaps between the larger projects. One of the largest of these was the studio and laundry that he designed in 1961 for the rear of Leon and Felicia Papernow's house on Corsica Drive in Pacific Palisades.[18] Taking up the space between the existing house and the garage, it was a simple, timber-frame, pitched-roof structure finished externally with 1-by-3-inch vertical battens over 1-by-12-inch boards to match the existing building. However, the long garden-front elevation to the south allowed Koenig to insert three pairs of 10-foot glass sliding windows. When remodeling a house, such opportunities were rare. Usually, as in the case of the bay window addition of 1985 for Pam Wayne on Thirty-Second Street in Manhattan Beach[19] or the new upper-story addition of 1986 for Carol May and Robert van der Linde, which he made to the house he had built twenty-two years earlier for Ira Lawrence on Meier Street in Mar Vista, it was a case of working within the confines of the existing structure and palette of materials.[20] Such were the various interior remodeling jobs: a major internal refit with external decks and stairs for Bruce and Laurie Rozet in Santa Monica (1969)[21] and new kitchens for both Michael Nemo in Los Angeles (1975)[22] and Rose Peterson in Venice (1976).[23] Although the flat-roofed carport he added in 1976 to the front of Hubert and Sibylle Grebe's house in Mar Vista[24] was supported on 4-by-4-inch timber posts, the one he designed in 1988 for the rear of Arlette Mosher's house in Brentwood used steel H-columns.[25] Mosher, a neighbor who commissioned a studio in 1986 and a kitchen remodel in 1987,[26] would have watched Koenig's own house on Dorothy Street being erected and, in commissioning a new carport from him, must have known what to expect.

The bread-and-butter work notwithstanding, Koenig's timber houses largely lacked the rigor so often seen in his steel houses. Due to their site conditions, the choice of timber for the Seidel Beach House and the Colwes House was understandable, as it was for the do-it-yourself nature of the Burton House. However, the Holland and Bayer Houses were conceptually steel pavilions, the former conceivably derived from Raphael Soriano's Eichler House (1955) in Palo Alto, California, and there is no obvious reason apart from, perhaps, client preference why they should have been executed in timber. A steel frame and, consequently, a more modular or component-based approach to their construction might have introduced greater rigor to the planning of both houses. □

## CHAPTER 9

# MIDCAREER STEEL HOUSES

On 21 June 1971, Pierre Koenig was elected a member of the College of Fellows of the American Institute of Architects.[1] In as much as this gave him recognition as a senior member of the profession, it also implied that there was a younger and perhaps more forceful generation of architects emerging in Los Angeles. The Case Study House architects, as Reyner Banham later noted, were fast becoming yesterday's heroes,[2] and a new generation, led by Frank Gehry, was starting to make its mark. Inspired by artists such as Jasper Johns and Robert Rauschenberg, Gehry's use of common or found materials eventually manifested itself in 1978 in the fragmented architecture of his own house in Santa Monica. Here, Koenig's favored material, profiled metal decking, found itself used in a context wholly unimaginable to him. Such fragmentation became, in the 1980s, the mise-en-scène of Los Angeles architecture, although sometimes, as at the Kate Mantilini restaurant in Beverly Hills designed by Morphosis and opened in 1986, it was hidden behind an elegant colonnaded steel facade that could easily have been attributed to Koenig.[3]

Meanwhile, Koenig continued working in practice and as an associate professor at the University of Southern California. The period signified, to some extent, the start of a consolidation in his work that came to a conclusion, in the late 1980s, with the building at 12221 Dorothy Street of his second house and the rebuilding of Case Study House 22 at the Temporary Contemporary Museum in Los Angeles. With these two buildings, his career was to take off again.

The house and garage on Dorothy Street, into which he had moved both his family and his office at the end of 1959, must never have been quite satisfactory. Even before he demolished it to build a new steel house on the site in 1985, he made a number of attempts to improve it. In 1966, he drew up two schemes for a small addition fronting the alleyway at the rear of the site. Both schemes were to provide a carport at street level with the possibility of one floor of accommodation above. The first scheme, dated 19 January 1966, was for a simple steel-frame structure measuring 30 by 20 feet made up of three parallel frames, comprising 5-inch H-section columns and 12-inch I-section beams, spanning the longer distance.[4] An upper story is shown in dotted line on the elevations and annotated "future 2nd story."

The second attempt at designing the carport came six months later, in July 1966, and suggested a much more sophisticated building (see pl. 75). Using the same site and the same overall dimensions, Koenig now proposed a two-story, six-bay structure made up of what he called "basic units," using "L" (for lower) and "U" (for upper). Each unit was framed by 2-by-2-inch square-section hollow pipe columns, so that when four units came together, there was a cluster of four columns at the meeting point. A laminated-timber floor, supported on 6-inch C-section steel beams, separated the lower and upper units, and the roof was finished with an 18-gauge galvanized-steel deck. The frames were not welded but bolted together, one bay on each level on each side tensioned with steel cross-bracing rods a half inch in diameter. What this represented was an experiment,

Fig. 9.1.
West House, view from southwest, 1969.

85

in his own backyard, to test lightweight modular frame construction. Was this intended to inform the design of the Electronics Enclosures building, which he drew up as a preliminary study that September? As a large building on an awkward triangular site, Koenig's usual long-span steel construction might not have worked too well, and a modular approach, using smaller units, could have been more applicable.

In the event, it was the January design for the carport that was built, but the possibility of an upper floor was not forgotten. In 1975, Koenig asked his structural engineer, William Porush, to provide calculations for a new roof deck and beams for what would be a den.[5] The intention was to build on top of the existing carport and provide a dogleg stair at the rear for access. Although two variations of this scheme survive in the archive, neither was built.[6] In one, the stairs run parallel to the rear wall of the building, resulting in an L-shaped plan; in the other, they are positioned perpendicular to the building, forming a T-shaped plan. In both cases, the stairs and half-landing are supported by H-section columns and enclosed by vertical cladding. Koenig returned to the problem years later following the rebuilding of his own house in 1985. The drawings, which were now computer-generated, show an upstairs recreation room fitted with a workbench and a stainless-steel sink.[7] Once again, the stairs are set perpendicular to the building, but now they are neither supported by H-section columns nor enclosed by vertical cladding. Instead, they are left open to the elements and the half landing is, apparently, suspended 6 feet, 8 inches above the ground by a steel cable attached at a 45-degree angle to the steel frame at roof level (see pl. 76). This scheme was not realized either.

The preliminary drawings for the garage and den or recreation room are, at first glance, so similar to the house that Koenig designed in 1969 for Dr. Samuel West that when the archive was first catalogued, these drawings were thought to be of that building. However, where the West House differs is that it was three stories, not two, and measured 50 feet by 26 feet, 6 inches on plan. West, a dental surgeon in Oakland, California, is one of the very few clients outside Los Angeles for whom Koenig actually built a building, although there were a number of schemes that never came to fruition. Located on the high ground of Carquinez Heights, Vallejo, overlooking the confluence of the Napa River and San Pablo Bay, the house was intended to be a showroom for West's artworks, but he died before the house could be completed. What remained on the exposed hilltop for a while was an intentionally rusty skeleton of Cor-ten steel, the first of a colony of houses that West had envisioned on the site.

For its size, the house offered very little accommodation (see pl. 85). There was no living space on the lowest floor, just a small, centrally positioned equipment room measuring 10 feet by 15 feet, 6 inches, with a large forced-air and air-conditioning unit. To one side, the remainder of the space was given over to car parking and access to the floor above by an external stair; to the other side, the land fell away. On the middle floor, the accommodation was larger, measuring 40 by 20 feet, and comprised an all-purpose room, a bedroom, and a bathroom. From here, internal stairs led to the top floor, where, within the same dimensions, there was the kitchen and the living room. Where the house was interesting, however, was in the way in which Koenig conceived it as almost one building within another: the main external frame was 50 feet by 26 feet, 6 inches, but the rectangular building that rose within it was only 40 by 20 feet, with the remaining space given over to external decks or void spaces (fig. 9.1). It was an idea to which he would return at the Schwartz House.

As at the Burton House, Koenig carried out a series of sun analyses to test the shadow-spread across the top floor of the house at different hours of the day on both of the solstices and equinoxes (see pl. 86). In March and September, the living room remained in shade until late afternoon, while the kitchen got the benefit of the morning sun. In June, due to the height of the sun, there was generally more shade throughout the day, while in December the sun reached into the living room throughout the day. An external deck surrounded three sides of the top floor, but the east end, beyond the kitchen, was left void; this allowed sunlight through to the level below, as the sun analysis showed. However, the elevations show that the bedroom at the east end of the middle level had no windows, so it would not have benefited from this gesture. Why the room had no windows is unknown, but perhaps it was seen as an extension of the all-purpose room to be used for the display of West's art collection. The intention, however, was not to hang the pictures on the walls but to suspend them from the steel decking that formed the ceiling. In contrast to the enclosed middle floor, the top floor was glazed on all sides but shaded, as has been described, by the overhanging roof. The detailing was sparse and pragmatic, the hand rail for the external stairs, for example, being a 2½-by-2½-inch steel L-section welded at one end to an 8-by-8-inch H-section column and to a 4-by-4-inch H-section post at the other. The external walls were equally functional—16-gauge steel mesh on the lower floor, 18-gauge weathering steel decking on the middle floor, and tinted gray glass surrounding the top floor.

With the house that John and Patricia Dye requested in 1972, Koenig returned to more familiar territory.[8] This was to be a small steel-frame building set on high ground above the Pacific Coast Highway in Newport Beach, with views of Newport Bay and the Balboa Peninsula. The design of the house offered a similar solution to that at the Whittlesey House, but it was restricted to just one floor approached by a short bridge. This superstructure was a simple box raised on four H-section columns, with cross braces, set on 20-foot reinforced-concrete caisson foundations connected by 18-by-18-inch ground beams (see pl. 99). As at the Beagles House, Koenig used 18-inch open-web structural floor joists, rather than much heavier I-section beams, to reduce the weight of the building. But in contrast to the Beagles House, where the joists were hidden by steel edge beams, here they were left exposed on all sides, giving the building a sense of lightness that was echoed in the 18-gauge steel decking used on the walls. Measuring just 46 by 40 feet, the accommodation was tightly planned, with almost one-quarter of the space devoted to the two-car garage. The living room and master bedroom, separated by a small kitchen, were set along the rear of the building overlooking the ocean, and a second bedroom was squeezed in adjacent to the entrance. Although there was a small outdoor terrace set into one corner of the living room, there was no balcony, as might be expected—just a 2-foot-wide window-washing deck cantilevered along the glazed south elevation.

Whereas at the Dye House, Koenig stepped the building out over the falling ground, at the house he designed for Alex and Therona Whittemore, he leveled the sloping hillside. Although the working drawings in the archive are not dated, there is a three-page specification dated 1 June 1973 and a docket from the Building and Safety Division of the County of Los Angeles Engineer's Department showing that the drawings were either submitted or approved in July 1973.[9] Located on Coast View Drive, above the Pacific Coast Highway in Malibu, the Whittemore House, which formed a T-shape on plan, comprised a long, low pavilion cut into the hillside with a carport set on higher ground behind (see pl. 100). This, in a way, was classic steel pavilion architecture and Koenig's last throw of that particular die. It was also a building that offered remarkably little accommodation. Although the house measured 76 feet, 7 inches by 23 feet, 6 inches, a comfortable 1,800 square feet, it contained only one bedroom and the utility room was located between the house and the carport (see pl. 101). The uniformity of the long south elevation was impressive, but the positioning of the two intermediate columns that divided the elevation into three sets of five bays (or windows) bore little relationship to the interior arrangement. One column did align with the kitchen counter, but the other was located midway along the study wall, while the one bay at the east end of the elevation was actually outside the building envelope and enclosed by only a metal fly screen (see pl. 102). Internally, there was little rigor in the positioning of the bathrooms, entrance, and other space dividers, which is at odds with the formality and symmetry implied by the T-shaped plan and the apparently balanced elevations. The economy achieved by the use of continuous 12-inch I-section steel beams along the south and north elevations and 8-inch crossbeams above to form the room and cantilevers, as well as the repetitive use of 5-foot sliding glass doors combined with 18-gauge galvanized-steel decking on the walls, implied a precision that the internal arrangement, and to some extent the elevations, did not meet.

The West House was never completed, and neither the Dye House nor the Whittemore House progressed further than the drawing board. It had been ten years since Koenig had built a new steel house, the Beagles House of 1963, and it was to be another ten years before he would see a steel house through to completion. This was to be the house he designed for Michael Gantert, a general contractor, on a precipitous site overlooking the US 101 Freeway on La Punta Drive in the Hollywood Hills. "The lot," Koenig wrote in his description of the house, "has a slope steeper than one to one and was originally thought to be unbuildable by most people, including the Building Department."[10] However, working with Dimitry Vergun, now his engineer of choice, he devised what he called "a very intricate system of two-way cantilevers"[11] and supported the entire two-story house and carport on only four columns, with a bridge connecting the carport to the street. The Gantert House, like his other hillside houses, was entered at the upper level, where the living room was divided from the dining room, kitchen, and laundry by a central core containing the dogleg stair, which, at the lower level, separated the master bedroom from the two smaller bedrooms (see pl. 109). A raised roof above the stairwell provided clerestory lighting to the center of the house, while a single window in the west wall lit the space between the living and dining areas. This window was the subject of some uncertainty, appearing and then disappearing from the perspective drawings for the house, only to emerge again at the end. On the south side, which was wholly glazed, a 3-foot-wide balcony fronted both the living room and, below it, the master bedroom and bathroom.

In the archive, there is an axonometric drawing of the steel frame that best shows how the intricate system of two-way cantilevers formed the framework for the building (fig. 9.2). The central core, where the stairs were located, was defined by two levels of staggered columns, their displaced load taken by beams to the level below and ultimately to the four columns that were set on reinforced-concrete foundations in the hillside. From either side of this central core, the floor and roof plates were cantilevered equally. The middle "plate"—that is, the upper floor of the house—extended back toward the road, where it rested on a reinforced-concrete retaining wall, thereby providing a structural bridge that also supported the entrance facade of the building. Thus, the Gantert House might be seen not only as "a very intricate system of two-way cantilevers" but also, perhaps, as a tree whose branches formed smaller branches, reaching out and up until they eventually touched the hillside.

The two perspective drawings of the Gantert House in the archive tell a little about the development of the design. The first is dated 1979 and shows the house with a pencil line through the west window, an opening about 6 feet wide, and the word "OUT" scribbled above (fig. 9.3). To the right, there is the rough penciled outline of an external flue and the word "STACK." The second perspec-

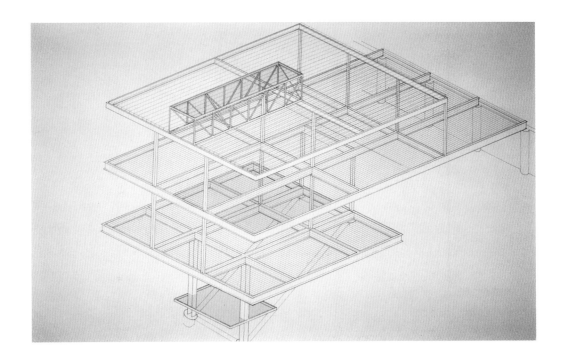

Fig. 9.2.
Gantert House, frame construction, 1980.

tive drawing, which is not dated, shows the stack, but the window has been removed (fig. 9.4). And so it might have stayed, except that when the working drawings were produced in August 1980, a 12-foot-wide window appeared on the west elevation together with the stack, complete with chimney brackets and spark arrestor (see pl. 110). Rather than serving a log-burning stove in the living room, the stack served one in the master bedroom. However, when the house was built, the stack was omitted but the window was retained.

There is something about the tall central space at the Gantert House, where the light comes in from the clerestory above, that hints at the house Koenig built next, for himself, on Dorothy Street. It had been almost thirty-five years since he had built his first house in Glendale, and those many years of experience, and a somewhat larger budget, were to come into play here.

In December 1981, Koenig drew up a site plan for 12221 Dorothy Street that showed the footprint of the proposed house set against that of the existing one. Although the building line for all the other houses along Dorothy Street was set back 40 feet from the curb, the encroachment over the line of the porches at 12249 and 12221 by some 6 feet reduced the average setback distance a little. This gave Koenig some leeway and the excuse to move his new house forward. The site-plan drawing, which was to go through plan checks on 30 December 1981 and 22 June 1982, anticipated the proposed setback from the curb at 33 feet.[12] On 20 December 1982, he applied for a zoning modification, requesting an extra 5 feet, 6 inches, so that "the one story portion and a 6 foot fence of a proposed single family residence be allowed a 33 foot front yard set back where the average set back is now 38.5 feet."[13] And, in support of this, he had his neighbors on either side, at 12217 and 12225 Dorothy Street, sign a letter stating that they had no objection to "a 6 foot projection into the front yard."[14] The reason given was "to have a minimum rear yard between the proposed residence and the existing car-port and to maintain a one-story elevation at the front."[15] As he noted on the draft copy of the application, "a 34 foot front yard set back was recently granted to 12249 Dorothy Street."[16] Even before the application was approved on 3 February 1983, "subject to one year utilization clause as in the case of variances," Koenig had set about preparing the working drawings.[17]

Although the basic form of the house—a three-story central section stepping down to two stories front and back and then down again to a single story at the front—must have been established early on, the arrangement of the front part, which gave pedestrian access off the street and provided an office wing, went through some changes. The earlier version split the front yard evenly between garden space and office (fig. 9.5). The later version, as shown on the approved site plan, provided less garden space and a larger L-shaped office (fig. 9.6).[18] On both drawings, Koenig showed the shadows at two o'clock in the afternoon on the summer solstice, indicating that after about noon, there would be no sun penetration into the office from the garden windows. The inclusion of an office in the house plan was possible only because of the precedent established by his continuous use for over twenty-one years of the garage located at the rear of the old house as an office. This was to be demolished.

The story of Koenig House 2 is very much that of the steel frame, which was implicit in the building's stepped form. Exactly how this was first intended to be is unknown, but there must have been a series of drawings of a preliminary version of the house—perhaps the one shown in the earlier scheme for the front yard—for there is a letter in the archive from Weld-Rite Welding Services, dated 12 June 1981, which costed out the job, based on drawings dated 11 March 1981, at $19,464.[19] No such drawings remain. The design must then have changed, for the archive contains Dimitry Vergun's steelwork calculation, first dated February 1982 and revised that June,[20] which would have been done prior to a price being established.

Although there is not a full set of working drawings in the archive, those dated (with the exception of the site plan) from 5 January 1983 to 26 April 1983 and sometimes to 5 January 1985 give enough detail about the form and construction of the house for it to be understood.[21] The main body of the house, which measured 30 by 45 feet, was conceived in three parts, each measuring 30 by 15 feet. These were framed by eight 6-inch H-section columns and, at each level and running in both directions, by 16-inch I-section beams (see pl. 77). The outer two-thirds of the house, each two stories, contained the bedrooms and bathrooms above and the kitchen, dining, and other living spaces below. They were linked by a bridge that spanned the central three-story atrium at bedroom level. Stairs ran from the atrium floor to the bridge and then from the bridge to the clerestory level, with access to the roof. The expanse of this central space was shown in a downward-looking perspective that Koenig drew up after the house was occupied. It captures both the emptiness and the spaciousness of the central volume (fig. 9.7). At the street end of the main body of the house, the single-story office wing was framed in 6-inch H-section columns and 10-inch I-section beams. The whole, where not glazed, was clad with 18-gauge galvanized-steel decking (see pl. 78).

On 6 April 1983, while the drawings were still being revised, the steelwork was costed out by Brace Engineering at $34,255.[22] This price was agreed upon, and Koenig countersigned the letter, thus making it a contract. For the general contractor, Koenig engaged Robert D. Anderson, a steel fabricator and erector with whom he had previously worked. Indeed, Anderson was keen to retain this relationship, and, in January 1983, he wrote to Koenig:

It has been a pleasure doing business for you and I would like to thank you for the opportunity to serve you.

As I take a very real and personal interest in your satisfaction, I should greatly appreciate your letting me know—by mail—how you liked our handling of the House project.

More than that, I want you to know my interest does not stop with this project. If at any time

Fig. 9.3.
Gantert House, view from southwest, without stack, 1979.

Fig. 9.4.
Gantert House, view from southwest, with stack, ca. 1979.

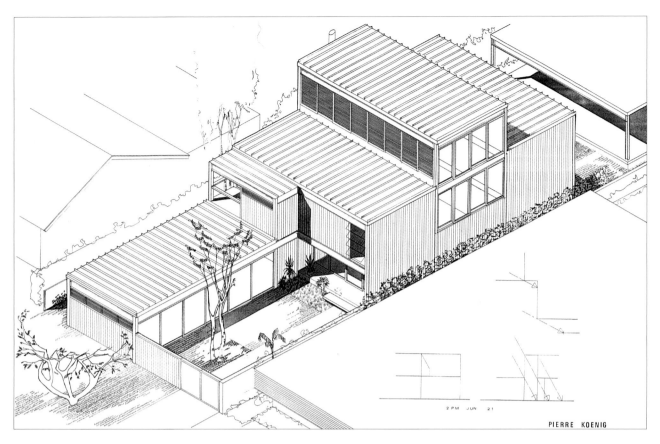

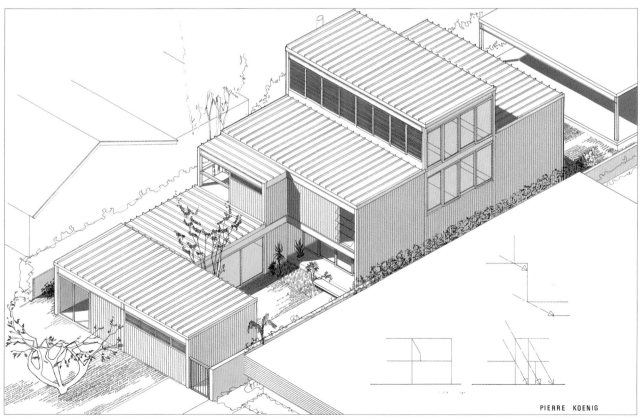

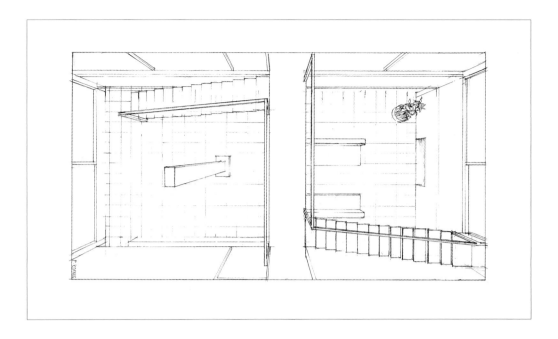

our workmanship should not merit your approval, I should consider it a favor if you would call on me at once.

I am looking forward to being of service to you in the future.[23]

The Standard Form of Agreement between Owner and Contractor was signed with Anderson on 22 November 1983 for $34,255, which was later revised to $25,541.[24] In later years, Koenig often spoke of his $10,000 drawing, a twelve-stage, step-by-step series of axonometric projections that explained the assembly process for the frame (see pl. 79).[25] This, he would say, resulted in the reduction of the contract by $10,000, but whether this was with Brace Engineering or with Anderson is hard to say because no documentary evidence remains. But it is a salutary lesson in the benefits of good communication and a reminder that what might be straightforward to the architect is not necessarily so to the builder, who, because of his ignorance of the process, raises his bid to safeguard his position.

In the event, and due no doubt to the $10,000 drawing, the assembly of the building progressed rapidly. A 100-foot crane erected the steel frame in one day. A delivery truck then drove into the building carrying the prefabricated stairs and railings, which were lifted into place and welded.[26] On 12 December, less than three weeks after engaging Anderson as the general contractor, Koenig requested the California Federal Savings and Loan Association make two payments to Brace Engineering: the first of $17,128 was for "steel frames in place on site. 50% of contract less material cost," and the second of $1,562, for "80% of contract, less materials cost."[27] Two days later, Anderson sent Koenig an invoice for $18,690, confirming the position on-site: "fabrication and erection of steel, 80% complete."[28] Another for $5,573 followed two weeks later.[29] The steelwork was now 95 percent complete. The 22-gauge galvanized-steel decking for the roof came on-site in the New Year, with Besteel quoting $1,725 on 17 February 1984[30] and invoicing Koenig just eleven days later.[31] By mid-May, the interior must have been almost finished, for, on the eleventh of that month, Anderson invoiced Koenig $695.57 for the handrail[32] and $750 for the rental equipment.[33] A week earlier,

Fig. 9.5.
Koenig House 2, aerial view, with rectangular office, 1983.

Fig. 9.6.
Koenig House 2, aerial view, with L-shaped office, 1983.

Fig. 9.7.
Koenig House 2, interior view, atrium from above, 1983.

Koenig had sent drawings to St. Charles of Southern California (more correctly, of Los Angeles) for the manufacture and supply of the stainless-steel kitchen units, writing,

> After all these years of specifying your cabinets for other people I am now going to have a chance to use them in my own home. The kitchen is open to a 26' high atrium framed with 30' steel beams which should be quite spectacular, I hope.
>
> Please give these plans your special attention. I am enclosing a floor plan and the interior elevations.[34]

A month later, Dana Clarrissimeaux of St. Charles wrote back with a quote for $16,097.39, noting, somewhat unnecessarily, that "the flush smooth surfaces of St. Charles enameled steel exteriors are the choice of those who appreciate the beauty and sophistication of straight lines." Then, perhaps aware of the company's slow response, she added, "Pierre, I appreciate the patience you have had."[35] The price seems to have been renegotiated, because a contract for $8,273 was drawn up by Clarrissimeaux on 3 August 1984[36] and another for $1,065 eleven days later.[37] The final invoices for both contracts came through on 1 November, but as late as 19 December, Clarrissimeaux wrote to Koenig requesting payment for the second.[38] "In the event there may be a problem with your cabinetry," she wrote, "please advise me and I will certainly rectify the problem."[39] Had there been a problem, there is no indication in the archive of what it might have been. Perhaps Koenig had been waiting for the Formica and brushed-aluminum kitchen countertop, which were to be supplied by Elkan Custom Made Furniture; Elkan's final invoice was dated 30 November 1984.[40]

In August 1983, in anticipation of the work to be done, Koenig produced a cost breakdown for the California Federal Savings and Loan Association, which was financing the building. The estimated total was $182,786. An earlier breakdown in May had estimated $183,874; as quotes came in, he could more accurately estimate the final cost. What the August breakdown forecast was that the foundations and concrete slab would cost, cumulatively, $22,800; the structural steelwork, $42,000; the roof, $1,300; the siding, $12,109; and the sliding glass doors, $9,875. Although there is no documentation in the archive indicating what the final cost of the house might have been, these estimates do show that Koenig predicted that the foundations, structural frame, and building envelope were less than half the total cost.

While he was dealing with Clarrissimeaux, Koenig started the working drawings for his first building outside the continental United States. This was to be a house for Frank Steven Stuermer, a systems specialist in the Los Angeles Department of City Planning who, in November 1983, had paid Koenig a retainer of $2,000 for the design of a house on the Hawaiian island of Oahu.[41] Located on steeply sloping ground at the end of Alina Place, Kaneohe, the site offered spectacular views across Kaneohe Bay to the Mokapu Peninsula. Rather than adopting hillside strategies familiar from earlier designs, Koenig proposed building up a concrete blockwork base, containing the garage, and erecting an uncharacteristic four-story towerlike house on top (fig. 9.8). There were various versions of this. The preliminary design of 24 June 1984 was of a duplex, a two-story apartment below and a single-story apartment above, all accessed from a stair tower at the rear and finished with a pyramidal roof.[42] The preliminary design of 8 July 1984 inverted the arrangement, placing the single-story apartment at the lower level and the two-story apartment above, with the living room at the top.[43] This version had a pitched roof. Retained in the archive is a marked-up print of the 24 June drawing showing, in red, the changes being worked through.[44] By 9 November, Koenig appears to

have returned to the original arrangement with the single-story apartment at the top, but now with a mezzanine level set beneath a monopitch tiled roof. The elevations for this version of the house,[45] framed in exposed steel and clad in galvanized-steel decking, remained incomplete, suggesting that at this point the project was put on hold.

When the Stuermer House plans did emerge again, in February 1985, they were for a very different building. The name of Mrs. Stuermer was now included in the title panel, which might explain the change. What was planned was a single-story two-bedroom house with a balcony on three sides beneath a broad overhanging roof (see pl. 111). The building was raised off the ground on six 8-inch H-section steel columns, which supported, at floor and eaves level, two parallel 12-inch I-section steel beams. These, in turn, supported the floor and roof, which were built up in timber. Despite the presence of what Koenig called "architecturally exposed structural steel"[46] and the cladding of the side and rear walls with 18-gauge galvanized-steel decking, the elevated building, with its surrounding balcony and overhanging eaves, timber fasciae, and pitched roof with blue "oriental glazed roofing tile," gave every impression of being a subtropical bungalow.[47] What Koenig had arrived at was, effectively, a hybrid between a Los Angeleno hillside house and the popular conception of a Polynesian homestead. Stuermer made another payment of $11,500 to Koenig in September 1986,[48] but, despite the fact that Koenig continued to amend the drawings for yet another year, the project did not appear to go ahead.[49]

Koenig's midcareer years were not as lean as this chapter might suggest. His teaching at the University of Southern California kept him busy, as did the additions to the remodeling of the Bailey, Seidel Associates, Squire, and Johnson Houses. But perhaps the largest and certainly the longest-running project was for the development of the Chemehuevi Reservation at Lake Havasu. Here, Koenig had a real opportunity to achieve his ambition of building production houses. □

Fig. 9.8.
Stuermer House, version 1, view from southeast, 1984.

## CHAPTER 10

# PRODUCTION HOUSES

In 1959, Theodore "Ted" Weitzel, of the Venice Development Company, engaged Koenig to develop an area of land in Saint-Jean-sur-Richelieu, Quebec, referred to in the archive as St. Jean.[1] The plot plan, dated September 1959, shows a roughly triangular site marked out with over two hundred plots designated as either bungalows or residences and set around a small "parc pour jeux d'enfants" (children's play park).[2] The intention, as Koenig's early perspective drawing shows, was to build a leafy suburb populated with production houses (fig. 10.1). As *Arts & Architecture* observed, "While the idea of mass producing a house made of metal in a factory on a production basis is not new, no one has actually produced a design on this basis that reflects its origin or utilizes contemporary design techniques. This is not an experimental house but an actual production model that is now being manufactured in Detroit. The components are prefabricated and will be shipped to the site in Canada."[3] It was the intention to ship the houses, quite literally, by water from Detroit, across Lake Erie and Lake Ontario to the Saint Lawrence River, and thence, from Sorel, up the Richelieu River to St. Jean.

The basis of the design for the production houses was the arctic panel developed in the 1950s by the R. C. Mahon Company of Torrance, California, for the United States Distant Early Warning (DEW) Line defensive system, which, in anticipation of Soviet air strikes across the North Pole, required the building of radar stations in the far northern Arctic regions of Alaska and Canada. These panels were, therefore, well suited for the comparatively mild Canadian winters and, when used in association with lightweight steel frames, offered a great variety of modular applications. The system is described in an incomplete set of blueprints from Mahon dated August 1960 that are retained in the archive.[4]

Another set of drawings, titled "Venice Development Co., St Jean, Quebec" and dated 8 August 1960, shows a prototypical steel house using the Mahon panels. Unlike Koenig's more familiar use of 10-foot or, later, 20-foot modules, this one is based on a 3-foot-4-inch module, the equivalent of one meter. Yet, even so, Koenig conspired to use the metric module in groups of three or six to achieve the familiar 10- or 20-foot dimensions. Thus, the house and garage both have a depth, front to rear, of 20 feet, and the garage a width of 10 feet, the same as the covered walkway between the two. Only the longitudinal dimension of the house, at 26 feet, 8 inches, is irregular; one extra bay would have rounded it up to 30 feet. Cognizant that the weather in Canada can be as hot in summer as it is cold in winter, Koenig provided a covered and screened patio at one corner of the house and two covered walkways connecting the house and the garage and left a small garden space in between. The house has a pinwheel plan: the patio, kitchen, and dining and living rooms are arranged around the centrally placed, open-tread dogleg stairs (see pl. 54). On the upper floor, three bedrooms and a bathroom open off the tightly planned landing. It is a most economical design, and nothing is left to chance: closets and cupboards, all neatly shown on another drawing, fill out the void spaces,

Fig. 10.1.
Production Houses, St. Jean, Quebec, street view, 1960.

and planters bring color to the patio.[5] Externally, beneath the overhanging flat roof composed of Arctic panels, vertically hung Mahon panels alternate with full-height windows, many with top-hung vents at both ceiling and floor level, and sliding glass doors (see pl. 53). As *Arts & Architecture* commented, "No attempt was made to make the houses comply with any regional styles nor were any native materials used. The owners did not wish to compromise on the basis of nebulous public acceptance theories."[6]

One house was transported to St. Jean by road and erected on site (fig. 10.2). But to have imported the full complement of houses by water from the United States, as Koenig later explained, would have incurred a tariff of 40 percent, which, for a $1,200 house, was not economical.[7] As a result, the project failed.

It was eight years before Koenig became involved in another scheme for production houses: this was a project for a development of eighteen steel-frame holiday cabins called El Campo Turistico "Manuel's." Located on the Rio Hardy, south of Mexicali in Baja California, the scheme had originated in diagrammatic sketches, presumably by Manuel, on the back of a menu card from Manuel's Carnitas on West Olympic Boulevard. Arranged as a chevron plan around a central garden and fountain, each unit provided a sheltered outdoor sitting area to the front, overlooking the river, and domestic accommodation and car parking behind. Although the production-line approach was explicit in the repetitive nature of the concept, it was not enough to see the project into working drawings: only the aerial view remains in the archive (fig. 10.3).[8]

Koenig's most ambitious attempt to develop production houses began two years later: it was for the Chemehuevi Indians at Lake Havasu in the California desert. It was to be a deep involvement that lasted six years, but, as Wim de Wit observed in the *Getty Research Journal,* "It is a story of frustrated dreams that reveals the limits of the political potential of modernist architecture."[9] But its greater success was in the role it played in enabling the Chemehuevi, who as a tribe had become widely dispersed, to reclaim their tribal identity and, to some extent, their land.

The Chemehuevi, a branch of the Southern Paiute people, came from the Chemehuevi Valley on the California side of the Colorado River. However, following the building in 1934–38 of the Parker

Fig. 10.2.
Production Houses, St. Jean, Quebec, dry assembly of production house, 1960. Photographer unknown.

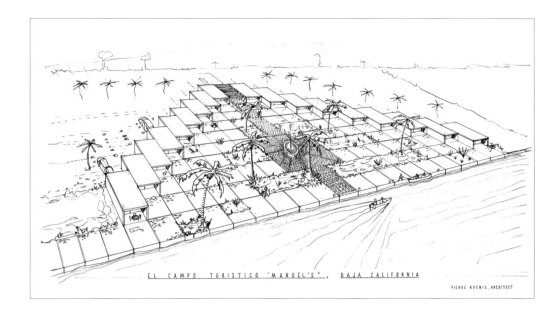

EL CAMPO TURISTICO "MANUEL'S", BAJA CALIFORNIA

PIERRE KOENIG, ARCHITECT

Dam by the United States Bureau of Reclamation and the creation of Lake Havasu (the Mojave word for "blue"), they were forced off their land. Only when, in the 1960s, the government moved to declare the tribe extinct and give their land to the adjacent Mojave reservation did they regroup and in 1970, following the writing of a constitution and the democratic election of a tribal chief, achieve federal recognition. This allowed them to return to their reservation alongside Lake Havasu, but there was nothing there for them. They had to start from the beginning and build a settlement. For this, they needed professional designers to develop the site.

De Wit speculates that it might have been Terry Tombs, a University of Southern California (USC) student who was working as an intern for the Chemehuevi during the summer of 1970, who set up the first contact between the tribe and the USC School of Architecture.[10] However the connection came about—and there is no documentation in the archive regarding this—it was Koenig who picked up the challenge.

By now he was assistant director, under Konrad Wachsmann, of the Institute of Building Research at USC.[11] Wachsmann had even said to him, "I want you to do my house when I'm ready." To which Koenig had replied, "Me, little me, do a house for Konrad Wachsmann? No!"[12] The prospect of promoting a prefabricated building solution to a very real problem must have been appealing. So, working with colleagues Keith Grey and Peter Rodemeier, and his third-year architecture design students (a group that changed every year[13]), Koenig set about the task of providing the Chemehuevi with the housing and public facilities they desired. As a result, the archive contains a number of drawings related to the project that are not in Koenig's hand, but the buildings that emerged clearly have done so under his tutelage.

Koenig and his colleagues took on a big task not only because there was no basic infrastructure such as roads or services on the site but also because a great deal of negotiating had to be done with the Department of Housing and Urban Development (HUD) and other public agencies if anything was to be achieved. It was a job that expanded far beyond anything the Chemehuevi initially imagined. Koenig later told a general tribal meeting, "We have been developing an interdisciplinary team using various departments of the University, we've gone to other universities to bring in specialists where we need them. . . . We were trying to put together a complete package of

Fig. 10.3.
El Campo Turistico "Manuel's," Baja California, aerial view, 1968.

architecture, economics, law, medicine, you name it, whatever is necessary to plan the reservation."[14] On-site, Koenig's team had to deal with a great variety of urgent matters ranging from road planning to the planting of jojoba beans.[15]

In October 1971, the tribal council, under the chairmanship of Herbert Pencille, resolved to dedicate four acres of land to be used for a Chemehuevi Indian Tribal Neighborhood Center.[16] The tribe had already applied for a grant from HUD in the belief that "such a center is necessary to the welfare of the Tribe, to promote cohesiveness in the community and to develop responsibility among tribal members."[17] The preliminary design for what is called the Chemehuevi Community Facility, which bears Koenig's name stamp and the date 16 August 1972, shows a 3,780-square-foot, steel-frame, single-story building set out on a nominal 10-by-20-foot grid (see pl. 87). The planning, which comprised blank walls to the west and north and extensive shaded areas to the east and south, was designed to shelter the interior from the heat of the sun. Within the enclosed space, which measured 2,100 square feet, there was, set to the front, an assembly hall for ninety-nine people with a conference table; and, to the rear, behind a bank of storage cupboards, there were offices, a coffee room, a kitchen, toilets, and an overnight accommodation.

A similar plan is retained in the archive for what is called the Chemehuevi Tribal Council House (see pl. 88). The design principles are the same: a low, steel-frame building with far-extending roofs, but now measuring 60 by 40 feet, with an enclosed area of just 40 by 20 feet. Internally, the assembly hall seated only thirty-five people; there was no conference table. The back-of-house accommodation was reduced to a single room and a separate bathroom. A perspective drawing in Koenig's hand shows a fashionably attired figure striding toward the building. The sign in the foreground reads, rather ambiguously, "Chemehuevi Center" (fig. 10.4). Whether or not this second scheme is actually a reduced version of the first but under a different name is hard to say, even though the north point on the plans varies by a few degrees. Neither scheme is shown with any context or other locating factors.

There is, however, a site plan for yet another version of what must be the Tribal Neighborhood Center showing a much larger and more sophisticated building close to the road running along the west bank of Lake Havasu.[18] Since the road layout had to be established as part of the rehabilitation scheme, this clearly represents a much later development of the project. This building is a large single-story, steel-frame structure set out on a 20-by-25-foot grid (see pl. 89).[19] Facing due south, its 80-foot glazed frontage is shielded from the sun by a deep portico, whereas its side walls are left completely blank. The accommodation is laid out in much the same way as in the earlier Tribal Neighborhood Center design: a long storage wall separating the assembly hall, now seating about 150, from the smaller rooms, all of which look out to the desert through the long glazed north wall. In the foreground, a paved and planted terrace extends from beneath the portico toward a grassy area with shade structures for outdoor sitting, shown clearly in an early sketch section (fig. 10.5). In its formality and simplicity, this was very much a building and landscape conceived in the manner of Koenig's earlier pavilion-type houses.

Shade structures were an important part of the scheme and featured in a number of iterations throughout the Chemehuevi project. With average summer temperatures recorded at nearby Parker, Arizona, in excess of 100°F (37.7°C) from June to September, with the highest on record peaking at 124°F (51.1°C), shade was essential.[20] The shade structures were to be located not only at the Tribal Neighborhood Center but also in the trailer park and, as sketches in the archive indicate, in the parking lot. In July 1973, as part of the Chemehuevi Project III, a shade structure measuring 12

Fig. 10.4.
Chemehuevi Housing Project, Chemehuevi Center, view from south, ca. 1972.

Fig. 10.5.
Chemehuevi Housing Project, sketch section through meeting hall, landscape garden, and shade structures, ca. 1972.

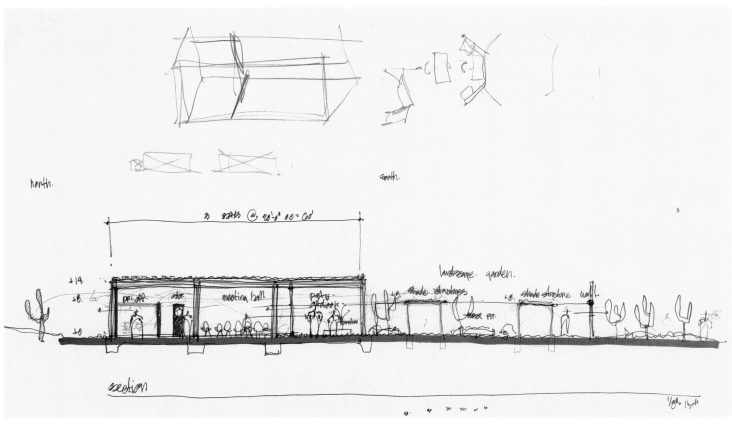

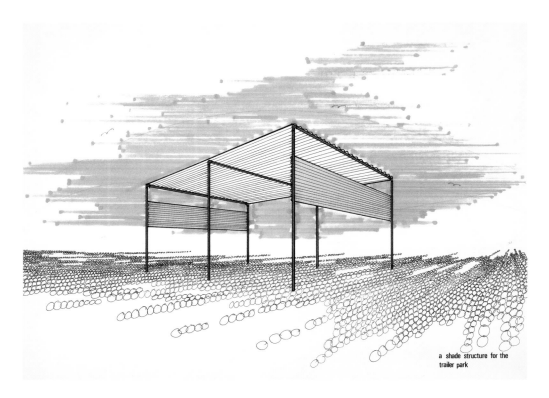

a shade structure for the
trailer park

Fig. 10.6.
Chemehuevi Housing Project, shade structure, 1973.

Fig. 10.7.
Chemehuevi Housing Project, shade structure, ca. 1973.
Photographer unknown.

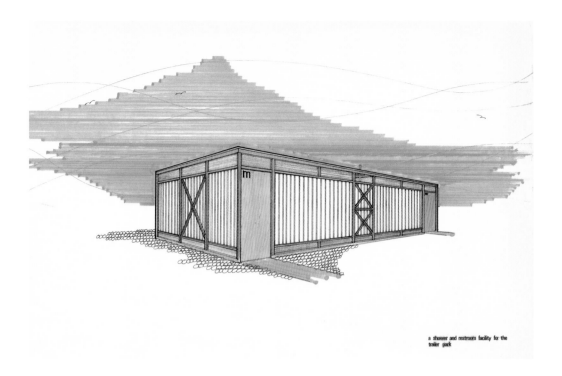

a shower and restroom facility for the
trailer park

Fig. 10.8.
Chemehuevi Housing Project, shower and toilet building,
1973.

feet long, 8 feet, 9 inches wide, and 7 feet, 6 inches tall was designed. Constructed of 1-inch galvanized-steel pipes and clad, on the roof and part of the east and west walls, with sheets of 20-gauge galvanized, corrugated steel, it gave the appearance of a fragile structure (fig. 10.6). A study was carried out to determine the position of the shadows cast at three different times of day, not only at the equinoxes but also on 21 May and 24 July, one month on either side of midsummer (see pl. 90). Depending on the structure's orientation, the horizontal shading panels could be applied to either the long or the short side, but their effect appears not to have been recorded in this study (fig. 10.7).

The first Chemehuevi to return to the tribal reservation had done so in their trailers and mobile homes, so a very early requirement was for the provision of suitable bathroom and toilet facilities. Yet it was not until July 1973, as part of the Chemehuevi Project III, that designs were produced for a trailer park with forty-two parking bays and a public toilet and shower facility, with a water reservoir on higher ground behind.[21] Although the toilet/shower building was clad in metal roof decking, the frame was made out of 4-by-4-inch timber posts and beams (fig. 10.8; see pl. 91). Given that, in the desert climate, timber would be prone to shrinkage and insect infestation, this was a surprising choice. Steel, as used in the shade structures, would have been far more suitable. When eventually built, modesty screens were added around each of the two entrances.

As early as June 1971, Koenig's first cohort of third-year students had produced an extensive portfolio of house designs, which continued to be refined until Koenig submitted them to HUD in 1976. These were incorporated into a report, *The Chemehuevi Project: An Exploratory Land Use, Planning, and Housing Study,* published in July 1971.[22] The report was divided into three main parts, each one prepared by students under the direction of one of the USC staff leading the project.[23] Koenig's contribution, "Low Cost Tribal Housing Study for the Chemehuevi Reservation," was the shortest. The original intention, as the report explains, was to provide thirty low-cost, detached, single-family units. Due to the great expense of on-site labor (including transportation and accommodation), a semi-industrialized building system was to be employed: the units would be made off-site using existing hardware and then transported to the site for assembly.[24] The units were to be constructed of 20-foot clear-span steel frames set 10 feet apart (making bays of 200 square feet) and bolted to the concrete-slab foundation. The cladding, for both the walls and the roof, was to be 40-inch-wide, prefabricated, insulated panels faced externally with 18-gauge steel decking, filled with polyurethane foam, and finished internally with gypsum board.[25] Windows and doors were to fit the 40-inch module of the cladding panels while larger openings were to be aluminum-frame sliding glass doors or fixed windows. It was, in many ways, a familiar specification.

Despite their shared heritage, the Chemehuevi had been dispersed for so long that there was no common demographic. As at St. Jean, where a totally neutral approach was taken in the provision of the housing, the project design team developed a standardized prefabricated building type that could be adapted to suit individual needs and preferences. "The building," the report stated, "was designed specifically in response to the desert and input from members of the tribe."[26] A wide variety of plan types was created, ranging from a two-bay, one-bedroom dwelling with a carport (400 square feet) to a six-bay, four-bedroom dwelling with two carports and an interior patio (1,200 square feet) (see pls. 92, 93). The designs were flexible: bays could be added on at any time, and solid panels could be changed to glass or vice versa. And there was also an economic benefit, as the report said: "Owing to the limited number of different parts, the cost per bay will decrease as the number of bays increases. Therefore, by using the same parts for all aspects of establishing an initial population on the reservation, the maximum amount of bays can be used, which will minimize the unit cost."[27] The report provided a ten-point construction sequence and, in addition to a great number of plan arrangements, detailed drawings of things such as foundations, interior wall panels, plumbing, and electrical wiring assemblies (see pl. 94).

Whereas Koenig's section of the report concentrated on the various configurations possible with the individual house and its detailed design, Peter Rodemeier's contribution, "Study of Planning Alternatives for Section 19 of the Chemehuevi Reservation," investigated the grouping of the units, means of access, and the location of common facilities. Here, in contrast to Koenig's plans, the housing units were based on a 12-foot-square grid and were often positioned in short staggered rows, sometimes without a carport but with a separate, shared garage a little distance from the houses. If there was a lack of coordination across the report, it showed up here.

In February 1973, David Brindle, a British architect and systems design and production consultant, produced the first part of a "Study to Determine the Roof and Wall Components for the Chemehuevi Project."[28] "This task," he wrote, "identifies features of the wall and roof elements which the USC Project Team has expressed, either in the Chemehuevi Report or at meetings, as requirements for the exterior skin." These requirements fell into one of two groups: mandatory requirements central to the appearance, construction, and/or operation of the buildings as a whole, and nonmandatory requirements, usually relating to product types, that were reversible if a suitable alternative product could be found.[29] The mandatory requirements suggested these basic design principles:

a. All roofs and walls should be panelized and all outside and inside surfaces, insulation, and structural parts should be preassembled before delivery to the site.
b. Panels for the east and west sides should be solid, but small, fully glazed panels may be inserted.
c. Panels for the north and south sides should be fully glazed, but solid panels may be inserted.

d. The solid walls should contain a chase for electrical distribution. No electrical distribution should be located in the roof panels.

It was, however, the nonmandatory requirements that most reflected Koenig's design preferences:

a. All roof and wall panels should be similar in construction and width.
b. All panels should be 40 inches wide.
c. All panels should have steel exterior surface.
d. Wall panels should be prewired for electrical distribution.
e. Walls should be located on the inside surface of the structural column.
f. The roof should be located on top of the structural beams.

Two of the attributes or qualities that Brindle recognized in his report were that the exterior skin should be visually pleasing outside and inside (as determined "pleasing" by the project design team) and that it should establish and maintain an indoor comfort level throughout the twenty-four hours of the day without recourse to mechanical heating or cooling. However, he took exception to the proposed aluminum finish for the wall and roof decking on the grounds of heat transfer. "Aluminum," he wrote, "will reflect 85% of the sun's heat, but loss of the remaining heat by emissivity is only 2%, whereas white panels will reflect only 71% but loss by emissivity is 89%. This accounts for white painted metals being cooler to touch when exposed to the sun than aluminum."[30] Furthermore, he recommended that the exterior skin be positioned inside the structure so as to avoid thermal bridging.[31] Brindle also commented that "the site layouts, as developed by the Project Team, as shown in the Chemehuevi Report, do not group dwellings in such a way as to reduce the solar gain."[32] Traditionally, he pointed out, this would have been achieved by the use of thick walls and roofs in combination with close-together planning around courtyards containing water and vegetables. Although Koenig proposed courtyard spaces within the individual dwellings, the dispersed nature of the site planning and the use of thin albeit insulated aluminum-clad wall panels ran against conventional wisdom.

Four months later, Brindle, now working with Anne Vernez, issued the second part of his study. This time, he concentrated on the availability of suitable products and methods of manufacture that met the criteria previously established. His recommendations ran from alternative subframe configurations for wall and roof panels to directions for the erection sequence and preferred design details. "It is likely," he wrote, "that 'away from home' labor will be sent to the site from Los Angeles and that work on site will proceed at night on an overtime basis due to high daytime temperatures. To avoid excessive on-site construction costs, it is important to maximize labor productivity."[33]

A year later, in June 1974, Brindle returned with an "Evaluation of Dwelling Plans to Meet the FHA Minimum Property Standards for the Chemehuevi Project."[34] The Federal Housing Authority's (FHA) minimum property standards had to be met if HUD were to finance the construction of the houses, although the standards could be flexible in order to meet the social background of the tribe. However, certain design preferences, such as the use of external sliding glass doors, were "not allowed in sandy desert regions due to sand fouling the siding action."[35]

Koenig and his USC students returned to the drawing board to bring the scheme into line with the requirements of HUD and the FHA. This was the third iteration of the scheme: the Chemehuevi Project III. A comparison between Brindle's proposal for an A-400:B-600 housing unit with a central patio and end carport and the USC drawing of the same configuration dated July 1974 indicates the close extent to which the recommendations were followed (see pls. 95, 96). That summer, a large composite sheet of drawings was prepared showing sixteen different variations of the Chemehuevi housing. Titled "Variations," it offered the complete range of house types that Koenig intended to put forward to HUD (see pl. 97).

In July 1976, Joseph W. Janick, western Arizona district engineer, wrote to Jack Turner, chairman of the All Mission Indian Housing Authority, confirming that the Chemehuevi housing development comprised thirty-five housing units.[36] Koenig subsequently submitted his schematic design to HUD on 22 November, receiving corrections a month later, on 23 December.[37] Koenig's "Outline Specification," which probably formed part of that package,[38] listed David Brindle as an associate and William Porush as the consultant structural engineer, and it stated that Koenig himself had designed and built "over two dozen similar prototypes over a period of 23 years." As evidence, he listed twelve of his own houses as representative examples, describing their climatic conditions and locations, which ranged from "Cool" (coast, Beagles House) to "Cool-Hot" (mountain, Lamel House) to "Hot" (desert, Burwash House). The specification promoted the benefits of his design approach:

> Each of these houses is an adaptation to the site, need, and climatic conditions of the specific problem. Variations of the system allow for a wide range of adaptation to plan and climate. Interior plan changes can be easily accomplished after construction as the walls are non-bearing. . . .
>
> A high level of quality control can be achieved through the maximum use of plant fabrication. Not all the components can be pre-fabricated (foundations, finish, some painting) but by reducing the number of these on-site operations we can raise the level of over-all quality control and reduce the changes for error.[39]

In December, Koenig, in a statement to the All Mission Indian Housing Authority, estimated that construction costs would range from $27,000 to $36,000 for each housing unit, which was over budget.[40] With the advice of the Housing Authority, Koenig therefore urged HUD for a cost analysis to be done. This raised certain objections to which he responded in February 1977, while, at the same time, acting upon their request to obtain quotations from contractors.[41] Jayne Hulbert, director of housing in the Office of Indian Programs at HUD, wrote to ask that these bids be in their San Francisco office by 3 March, but Koenig did not receive her letter until three days after the due date. His response was immediate:

> I received an undated letter from you today (Mar. 7, 1977) that represents the facts in such a distorted manner that I feel a strong response is definitely in order. The tone of the letter is destructive and does nothing to encourage the success of the project.
>
> In an attempt to discredit me the letter states I did not have the estimates with me at the Feb. 24 meeting and that H.U.D. could not prepare an analysis. The fact is that the estimates were already at the H.U.D. office and the analysis was indeed prepared.

The letter continues in a similar tone, listing disagreements and corrections, but there are conciliatory moments:

The meeting with your cost analyst was cordial and mutually informative. A genuine attempt to resolve differences was put forth by both parties. I don't understand why three items of the whole package are picked out of context to discredit the whole. I could turn it around and pick out three errors your office made but I see no useful purpose in pursuing this. . . .

This office has responded in good faith to all your requests and we have met all deadlines set by your office although we were never consulted before hand about these dates (except for the Nov. 22, 1976 deadline) and then only at the last minute. Your letter states that you would like to see these units proceed as expeditiously as possible. The facts do not reflect this philosophy.

If you cancel this project it won't be because of this Architects actions.[42]

As Wim de Wit observes in his essay in the *Getty Research Journal,* Koenig was unwilling to relinquish his fundamental architectural concept, and HUD's demands would have hurt the essence of his design.[43] There was to be no meeting of the ways and the project was canceled.

There is, in the same box as Koenig's client index cards, a single filing card with a handwritten note. It shows an extract from a report on Indian affairs from Secretary of War Henry Knox to George Washington, dated 7 July 1789, that summarizes Koenig's feelings and frustrations about the whole Chemehuevi debacle:

That the civilization of the Indians would be an operation of complicated difficulty. That it would require the highest knowledge of the human character, & steady perseverance in a wise system for a series of years, cannot be doubted. While it is contended that the object is practicable, under a proper system, it is admitted in the fullest force, to *be impractible* [*sic*] according to the ordinary course of things, & that it could not be effected in a short period.[44]

Koenig never managed to achieve his dream of the production house, although there were later possibilities. In the archive, there are letters from Ted Weitzel, his old contact from the Venice Development Company who was now in Miami, Florida, regarding a housing project in Israel and another in Dade County. The first, however, appears to have been a nonstarter—"We have not given up on the Israel housing project but are having a very hard time getting the information we need to proceed," Weitzel wrote on 4 October 1991, before adding, "Israel right now is on our back burner."[45] Later that month, Weitzel wrote again with a proposition:

We have been approached by a company that owns over 100 scattered lots in Dade County. Some are duplex but most are single family. . . . I thought of steel because it could be fabricated in a shop and then erected quickly on a foundation to avoid the costly security of protecting a conventional project. . . . Do you have any low cost designs on hand that could be a starting point?[46]

It was a long while and at least one phone call before Koenig offered a reply:

Sorry I took so long in answering your phone call regarding steel houses in Florida. . . .

My experience is that these buildings don't get done unless I'm there. I'm not looking for travel these days, it's a fact General Contractors cannot handle them alone. . . .

The other problem is style. Modern doesn't do well these days except in certain sophisti-cated areas and I don't know Florida that well although I was there a couple of times for a small job I designed for Disneyworld.

There is one big advantage to my designs: strength. They are superb in earthquakes and could be designed for hurricanes just as well. Especially good if the house were on "stilts" to avoid flooding, which, I understand, is the big problem. I don't know if people are willing to pay for protection. They aren't here but then again we haven't had our "big one" yet either.

I hope this answers your question.[47]

Since some of the sites were in flood areas, the suggestion of "stilts" appealed to Weitzel, who thought them more practical than raising the whole foundation should the houses on these sites be rebuilt.[48] However, uncertainty about the flood sites remained, and on 11 December he wrote again, enclosing two newspaper cuttings regarding the flood rules.[49] "Things are still in limbo," he said, "so I am going to wait a little longer before I send you the information that is geared to this area."[50] There is no further information in the archive, and the project, about which Koenig, in any case, did not seem too enthusiastic, never developed.

The dream of the factory-made house was not Koenig's alone. In 1946, the General Panel Cor-poration opened a factory in Burbank for the production of prefabricated modern homes.[51] Founded in New York in 1942 by Konrad Wachsmann and Walter Gropius, the company produced fewer than two hundred houses before closing down in 1952. The fact that Wachsmann and Gropius had set up their production plant in a former aircraft factory was not coincidental. The use of redundant wartime factories for peacetime house production was an obvious opportunity for the use of both the space and the existing technology. In 1947, Henry Dreyfuss (designer of the Polaroid camera) and the architect Edward Larrabee Barnes collaborated with aircraft engineers at the Consolidated Vultee Aircraft Factory in Los Angeles to make the prefabricated modular "House in a Factory," but it never went into production.[52] And in 1957, Koenig himself had approached Bethlehem Steel, sug-gesting that following the spring rush for the automobile industry, they might turn their factories to house production. But the company rejected the designs, thinking them too individualistic and not suited to a mass market.[53]

Once *Arts & Architecture* had published its special issue on prefabrication in July 1944, the underlying direction of the Case Study House Program was set. "My intention," Koenig later observed, "was to be part of a mechanism that could produce billions of homes like sausages or cars in a factory. In the end the programme failed because it addressed clients and architects, rather than contractors, who do 95% of all housing."[54] □

# CHAPTER 11
# "I'M YOUR ARCHITECT"

Della Rollé remembers how, soon after she and her husband, Gary, moved into the Seidel Associates House on Mandeville Canyon Road, a white 365 Porsche coupe drove up the driveway. Pierre Koenig got out of the car and introduced himself, saying, in an almost proprietorial way, "I'm your architect."[1]

Koenig always maintained a sense of ownership over his houses. "These were his children," Della Rollé said.[2] He even kept a set of keys for each one in a cabinet in his office. If one of his houses was going to be extended or restored, he would want to do it. It was in the nature of their modular, steel-frame construction to be altered or extended. Second-story additions were made to the house on Mandeville Canyon Road on two different occasions. Alterations and extensions were also made to the Burwash and Squire Houses, and the Gantert House was remodeled internally. The Bailey House was renovated to award-winning condition, while the Johnson House, which had suffered the most awful abuse, was restored to its original appearance and given a new wing.

The Burwash House, as the publicity statement had said, was designed for a married couple without children.[3] Dr. and Mrs. Bruce Whitehead, the new owners, presumably did have children, because the extension that Koenig designed for them in February 1965 included two new bedrooms, a bathroom, and a laundry (see pl. 24). The two bedrooms in the existing part of the house remained untouched, but the two bathrooms were combined into one, and the kitchen was remodeled and extended. The new accommodation was fitted into the three bays of the carport that extended 30 feet to the south; a further two bays were added on for a new carport. A new hallway, with external doors to both the front and the rear, now separated the new bedroom wing from the older part of the house.

The new bedroom wing was clad, as was the existing building, with Texture 111 vertically scored plywood sheeting. It had narrow top-opening clerestory windows on the west side, where the evening sun was fierce, and a 10-foot sliding glass door and two smaller horizontal sliding windows (for the bathroom and laundry) on the east side. There were no windows on the south wall, although the carport roof would have shaded them. Perhaps Koenig wished to guard against the headlights of approaching cars or the smell of their exhaust fumes.

Beyond the old south wall, the new bedroom, which measured 12 by 20 feet, was to be occupied by two children. This can be judged from the two small built-in writing desks and the large wardrobe that separated them. The other new bedroom, about half the size and with a single desk and a smaller wardrobe, was perhaps for an older child. As in the existing house, the internal stud-work partitions separating the rooms were positioned independently of the steel frame, aligning with neither the columns nor the beams above. And the internal corridors were reduced 3 feet in width, which is not a natural subdivision of a 10-by-20-foot module. Only on the east wall was the rhythm of the structural frame acknowledged. Here, where the 10-foot sliding glass door occupies one bay, the positioning of the bathroom and laundry windows in relation to the columns is not shown on the working drawings by measured dimensions but rather by the word "equal"—indicating that the width of each window and the distance between them would be the same. This apparent disparity between the interior, where the partitions are independent of the frame, and the exterior, where the openings are regularly positioned on the grid, demonstrates the advantage of this type of building, where the load-bearing steel frame allows total flexibility within.[4]

Koenig took a similar approach when designing an extension to the Squire House for Frank and Margaret South in 1987 (see pl. 9). The intention here was to add a master bedroom to the north side of the house that would look out onto rising ground, with a series of raised terraces and planters culminating in a lap pool and hot tub. Within the existing house, nothing was to change except for the addition of a skylight over the patio that separated the carport from the kitchen. The Squire House, designed in 1953 and therefore one of Koenig's earliest buildings, had been built with 3½-inch-diameter steel columns, which he intended to reemploy in the new design. In the same way that the spans of the old house ran in two directions, north-south and east-west, so they did in the proposed wing. Consequently, the master bedroom and dressing room were contained within two 10-by-20-foot bays set north-south, while the transitional space, with twin bathrooms that separated the bedroom from the house, was treated as a single 10-by-20-foot bay running east-west. Structurally, it was a response totally in keeping with the earlier building. Yet, the external walls, where not glazed, were clad in anodized-aluminum panels, whereas in the original building, they had been stuccoed. In the end, the works were not carried out.

One difficulty that emerges when examining the drawings of the Squire/South House is that, between the two sets of drawings, the north point varies by 90 degrees. The original drawings of 1953 have the rear of the house facing north, whereas those dated 1987 have it facing west. Thus, the caption on the elevations for the 1987 addition that read "right (north) elevation" should actually read "right (east) elevation."[5] In reality, the house is aligned a little north of northwest.

Koenig returned to the Squire House for a third time in May 2000, when he drew up an American Institute of Architects (AIA) contract for the restoration, addition, landscaping, and interiors for the new owners, Alan and Denise Schier.[6] However, there is no further evidence of this work in the archive, so it was likely never done.

There is little in the archive regarding Koenig's relationships with his clients. Many contracts, such as those mentioned above with Frank South and Alan Schier, were never fulfilled. When it came to renovating or restoring a house that he had built earlier, there was clearly a need for Koenig to have a good rapport with the new owner. With the restorations of the Bailey and Johnson Houses, this was the case, as it was with the additions he made to the Seidel Associates House on Mandeville Canyon Road.

Tom Seidel and his associates had built the house as a speculation. When it was put on the market in October 1961 by Ken Kremith, Realtors,[7] who were located on San Vicente Boulevard near where Koenig had had his office a couple of years before, it was bought by Seidel's own lawyer, Steven Valensi. Within a year, the house must have felt too small for the family of three and the mother-in-law who lived there, for there are preliminary designs in the archive for the extension of the house on the east side, above the road. Dated 27 December 1962, these sketches show the addition of a dining room and a den set on a 16-foot-square grid to correspond with the existing structure. A perspective sketch shows the two bays, supported on thin legs, reaching out above the

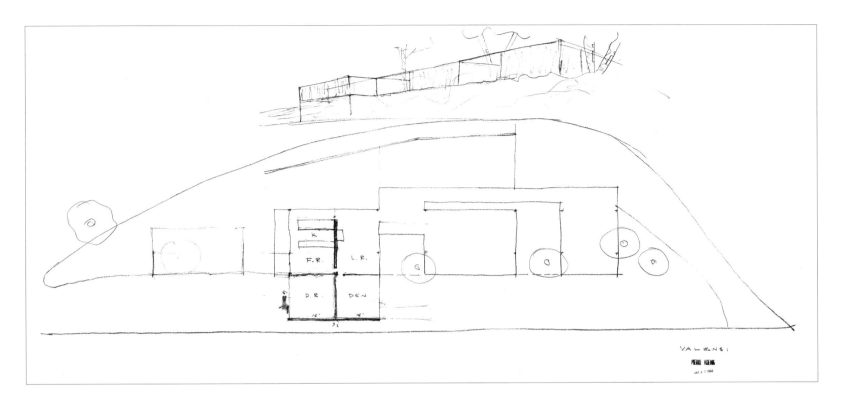

Fig. 11.1.
Valensi Addition to Seidel Associates House, view from
east, plan, 1962.

slope (fig. 11.1). Although the project was not carried out, it demonstrates immediately the ease at which such modular buildings can develop.

It was almost three years before Koenig did extend the Valensi House, but now the additions were much more modest; they involved only the introduction or relocation of walls beneath the roof overhangs. A preliminary study drawing of 7 August 1965 shows the enclosure and subdivision of the space beneath the entrance canopy for a small hallway and study, beyond which a new carport was extended out toward the hillside. At the far end of the house, the glass sliding doors to the kitchen were to be moved out 5 feet to the end of the roof overhang.[8] The working drawings, dated 1 September, largely follow these proposals, but the entrance hallway is reduced in size, and what was the study is now larger and described as the "new den"; the two were separated from each other by floor-to-ceiling double-sided shelf units. The new space is enclosed, externally, by vertical steel decking, and the original sliding glass doors are reused for the entrance. Although the proposed carport has been rejected, the extension of the kitchen through the repositioning of the sliding glass doors remains (see pl. 41). This time, the work was done.

Della and Gary Rollé bought the house in 1972 and, in 1980, asked Koenig to extend it.[9] "I didn't really want to do it," he told an audience at the San Francisco Museum of Modern Art many years later. "At first I was reticent about it. But after having done it, I like it better now, because it puts the people up into the trees, into the leaves, rather than down in the branches."[10] In fact, he had little choice in the solution. In a handwritten statement in the archive, Koenig wrote:

When the owners needed to expand the house the only way/direction to add on was up. In order to preserve the integrity of the existing space (and to allow the owner use of the house during construction) a completely independent second story was designed to drop over the existing 32' × 37' living area.[11]

This new structure was to have its own roof and floor system supported by steel columns positioned on the outside of the existing frame. Thus, one building, quite literally, straddled the other. Set above the kitchen, living room, and all-purpose room, this new floor was to accommodate a master bedroom and bathroom, a large walk-through closet, and a dressing room, in addition to a study and storage space (see pl. 42).

The new structure employed a combination of 4-by-4-inch square-section and 4-inch H-section steel columns supporting I-section steel beams for the first floor and the roof. The steel-work calculations by Koenig's engineer, Dimitry Vergun, show the complexity of some of the joints. At the south end, beyond the kitchen and the repositioned sliding glass doors, the two supporting square-section steel columns aligned with the existing frame, one on the southwest corner and the other 16 feet away, leaving an 8-foot cantilever on the east side (fig. 11.2). Extending as far back as the central patio, the new upper story incorporated the entrance hall and den that Valensi had enclosed, turning it into a double-height space to accommodate the stairs. The adjacent central patio was left open to the sky. In the entrance hall, the new square-section columns were placed in line with the external wall. They butted up against the existing H-section columns and supported the cantilevered 18-inch and 14-inch steel I-section beams that reached out, respectively, at the upper floor and roof levels to enclose the new stairwell. The roof deck was 4½-inch 8-gauge LS1 (long-span) decking from H. H. Robertson Co., and the new upper floor was plywood on timber joists set between the steel beams. The walls were finished externally with 1½-inch 18-gauge galvanized-steel siding.

There was a delay of almost eighteen months between Vergun completing the steel calculations in June 1981 and the City of Los Angeles Department of Building and Safety doing the plan check in December 1982.[12] Whatever the cause of the delay, Koenig returned to the job in the summer of 1982, redrawing the plans "per mutual agreement."[13] His subsequent statement for $1,000 for professional services, submitted on 1 August, was followed with drip-feed regularity by further statements over the next four months: 1 September, $2,000 due; 4 October, $1,000 due; 3 November, $1,000 due; and 1 December, $2,000 due.[14] Sometimes the monthly charge of $1,000 was unpaid, resulting in that sum being carried over to the following month. Aware of this difficulty, Gary Rollé wrote to Koenig on 20 December:

> In reviewing my files, I note that we have paid $7,500 for architectural services, $2,000 for costs incurred by you for the redrawing of the plans plus various fees for filings over the last two years. Are these amounts correct, and are future payments to be considered payments made in the bidding and negotiating phase? Please estimate total fees that need to be paid through bidding and construction phase so that I can have monies for you when necessary.
>     We appreciate your help.[15]

Koenig replied the following day, saying that to date $8,500 had been paid on professional fees and services and $915.95 on city fees and blueprints, and that a further $1,100 was now due for professional service.[16]

After another hiatus, the monthly statements, now for the construction phase, resumed on 1 June 1983 and continued until 1 September.[17] Although the archive holds no further statements showing the progression of work, there is one small drawing for repair to a corroded steel column dated 30 March 1984.[18] A year later, the building now complete, Koenig prepared for publication his

statement quoted above. In June, John Mutlow, the editor of the AIA journal, *LA Architect,* returned, with thanks, Koenig's original copy, adding that three thousand copies of that month's issue had been distributed at the national convention in San Francisco.[19]

Six years later, the Rollés commissioned from Koenig their second addition, and the contract for a "Phase two second story addition and patio enclosure" was signed on 1 July 1991.[20] This took the same form as the earlier addition—one building straddling the other. The new work encompassed the remaining single-story part of the house, excluding the carport and adjacent patio, and turned the central patio into a three-story atrium (see pl. 43). Once again, 4-by-4-inch square-section steel columns, placed in advance of the existing H-section columns, supported the 18-inch and 14-inch steel I-section beams that spanned the upper floor and the roof, while 8-inch I-section steel beams were introduced above the atrium (fig. 11.3). Glazing now enclosed the east end of the atrium, the north and south clerestory, and the roof. The sliding glass doors between the living room and the central patio were removed, and the boiler, which had previously separated the central patio from the entrance hall, was pushed to one side to open up the entrance. Upstairs, the new addition comprised one large all-purpose room with a long, thin bathroom ranged along the east wall. Eighteen-gauge galvanized-steel decking was used externally to match the original, but, as Koenig noted, it would "have to be custom formed, as it was last time, because it hasn't been manufactured for years."[21]

Work on the second addition started in September 1993. As with the first addition, the new steel frame required caisson foundations, which were to go down about 37 feet. The concrete had just been poured and the steel reinforcement bars set in place when, on 17 January 1994, the Northridge earthquake struck with a Richter force of 6.7. The epicenter was in Reseda, in the San Fernando Valley, just a few miles north of Mandeville Canyon. The damage across Los Angeles was extensive: 57 people were killed and over 8,500 injured. However, the laterally stiff "moment frame"

Fig. 11.2.
First Rollé Addition to Seidel Associates House under construction, 1983. Photographer unknown.

Fig. 11.3.
Second Rollé Addition to Seidel Associates House, atrium, 1994. Photographer unknown.

of the Rollés' house withstood the initial shake and the strong aftershocks, as did the new foundations; their specification had been upgraded at the request of the civil engineer shortly before the earthquake struck.[22]

The building of the new addition saw the introduction of Kemal Ramezani of the contractor R. G. West Corporation, who was soon to work with Koenig on the Schwartz House. The cost estimate for the addition, drawn up on 9 July 1993, had been $195,428,[23] but when R. G. West submitted a final account eighteen months later, it was for $284,539.[24] There had been changes and thus extra costs. On 21 February 1994, for example, R. G. West had submitted, in addition to the fourth payment request for $25,004.70, an additional charge of $17,233.04 constituting "the final [account] on change of casons and grade beams and adds 36 days to contract period in addition to rainy days that will be calculated at the end of the project."[25] It was, as it turned out, money well spent.

For help with the interior, Koenig turned to Joe Bavaro of Bavaro Design Studio in Reseda, setting out the terms of his engagement in a letter of 12 October 1992: "You will participate in discussions with the client and myself, visit the job site when necessary, assist in selecting materials, products and items needed to complete the design. Provide samples. You will prepare interior drawings, according to my format, write specifications and otherwise assist in the preparation of the interior drawings."[26] For the new work, Bavaro was to receive 1.5 percent of the construction costs and, for the necessary work on the two lower-floor bathrooms, a flat fee of $1,500.[27]

Much of Bavaro's work, done in Koenig's name, was in the selection and ordering of furniture for the house. In October 1994, he sent Koenig a fax itemizing a Nelson sling sofa, a Minotti Piacere sofa, two Wassily chairs, and an Eames lounge chair and ottoman—all in black leather—for a price, which included a Megaron floor lamp, of almost $19,000.[28] When Koenig eventually placed the orders with Jules Seltzer Associates of Beverly Boulevard, they comprised four Eames lounge chairs and ottomans in black and one lounge chair and ottoman in gray, and a Nelson sling sofa in black.[29] The cost was almost $16,000. In addition, an order for over $8,500 was placed with Knoll for other furniture.[30] It was a fit-out intended by Koenig to complement his architecture.

The restoration of the Gantert House was the last job Koenig took on. In August 2003, Billy Rose of Billy Rose Design & Development had written to Sotheby's International Realty of Beverly Hills making (under cover) his all-cash offer for the house and declaring his enthusiasm for the architecture:

> I love this property and am emotional about it. I have long been a fan of mid-century modern architecture, generally, and of Pierre Koenig's, specifically. It is from this perspective that I come to make this offer.
>
> I believe most would agree that I should not expect to make much of a profit from the renovation of this icon. Indeed, I am expecting, merely, to break even. It is enough for me to have worked on a Koenig project (and that is even enhanced by the prospect of working with the master himself).[31]

His business, Rose explained, was property renovation, and he had a great deal of experience in that, adding that he was "not scared off by items and problems that would be major concerns of others."[32] Unlike other clients who wished to live in a Koenig house, it was Rose's intention to take on the house as a short-term investment that he would soon sell. There was, as it happened, little about the house that might cause major concern, but previous owners had certainly compromised its modernist appearance. A paneled oak bar (and adjacent cupboard door) had been installed between the kitchen and the stairwell, and wooden baseboards, doors, and architraves had been fitted elsewhere.

Rose's offer, which must have been near the asking price of $950,000,[33] was accepted, and less than three weeks later, on 12 September 2003, he signed an AIA contract with Koenig.[34] From the beginning, Rose saw himself being very involved with the renovation of the building. "I am very excited about transforming this property into something of which we can all be very proud," he wrote to Koenig on 20 September, adding, "As my hope is to absorb as much as possible from you and Joe in this process, it is my true desire that I will be able to participate (and, hopefully, contribute) in an integral fashion."[35] He initially saw his contribution to be in the procurement of products and materials at a reduced price, if not actually free, "by virtue," as he told Koenig, "of the fact that the master himself (you) is remodeling one of his previous works."[36] By promoting the renovation in various architectural and design publications, he hoped to obtain discounts from suppliers. The choice of magazines, which he sent to Koenig, ranged from *Wallpaper* to *Architectural Digest* and *Elle Décor.* The titles were noticeably distinct from the more professional architectural press.[37]

For interior work—specifically, the provision of drawings, the selection of materials, and site management—Koenig engaged Joe Bavaro. For this, Bavaro would charge between $4,000 and $5,000, depending on the amount of work involved.[38] An early site inspection he made with Koenig listed over thirty items in need of attention or consideration, many of which, such as the removal of all oak trim and the restoration of black vinyl baseboards, were intended to return the house to its original appearance. But the list also included possible changes to the master bedroom, kitchen, and laundry room—items that Koenig was quick to address.[39]

In response to Rose's letter of 20 September, in which he laid out his initial design considerations, Koenig had started, by the end of the month, to send Rose sketch designs indicating how the interior of the house might be rearranged. The first was a proposal for the kitchen island: "Tell me what you think and consider materials," Koenig wrote. To this, he added a postscript: "All systems are go. I am holding email and FAX lines open for you."[40] Next came two ideas involving the bedrooms: the expansion of the bathroom into the master bedroom, a proposal that shaved some space off the master bedroom and removed a door, and the combining of the second and third bedrooms into one. "I think both schemes have turned out nice," Koenig wrote, "I hope you agree."[41] Finally, a week later, Koenig sent by fax a design showing how the laundry room might be rearranged to accommodate the refrigerator on the kitchen side. His cover note reads, "We tried all other alternatives and this is the only scheme that works."[42] The archive contains no responses from Rose to these proposals, but a later suggestion, sent on 22 December, for a new handrail was faxed back to Koenig the same day with the comment "Pierre—Great! That's the 6530 moulding in Aluminum (not the colorail) right? Billy."[43]

There are no further dated communications in the archive until the letter of 12 January 2004, which Rose sent to Koenig.[44] It is the first and, indeed, only evidence that things were not going well. "I have to confess that, after our meeting on Friday," the letter starts, "I was very disappointed." On that day, Rose had arrived a few minutes late only to discover that the meeting between Koenig and the contractor had started early, and that the business was now concluded. He clearly felt excluded and expressed this in his letter:

I know you are one of the world's (indeed, one of history's) foremost architects. This is the very reason I bought the house—it was designed by you and you wanted to be involved in the remodel. However, as you know, I undertook this project to further my career as a designer and as a developer and to have the opportunity to work with the "grand master" himself. Consequently, as I mentioned to you and Joe at the outset, it was my expectation that this would be a collaborative process.

Rose was frustrated that Koenig had resisted or flatly refused some of his requests concerning the house, such as the enlargement of the master bathroom to incorporate the balcony to the south or the patio to the east. "With regard to the former," he wrote, "you have told me you will not, and, with regard to the latter, you have told me that you cannot." Another disagreement concerned the insertion of a new window into the west wall of the reconfigured guest bedroom, which for reasons initially of expense and later of heat gain and the dangers of installation, Koenig rejected. However, he eventually acceded both to this and to the extension of the master bathroom to incorporate the south balcony.[45]

Rose, however, was not to be dissuaded, and the final two paragraphs of his letter declared, once again, his belief not only in his architect but also in the value of his own contribution:

Pierre, I remain your biggest fan. I worship your accomplishments and your abilities. However, although you clearly know more than I do, I believe that I can make an important contribution to this project. When I decided to undertake this project, it was my hope that, being different people, from different eras, with (sometimes) different beliefs, we would educate each other as to our respective opinions and perspectives on design, architecture and the desires and lifestyles of today's homeowners. In my idealistic world, that exchange would have a synergistic effect, yielding a better product than either of us could have achieved without the other.

Perhaps I am being naïve, and maybe my hopes are quixotic. But, in any event, hopefully you will receive this letter in the spirit in which it was intended—a plea to be treated as a partner and not a patron by someone who wants to accomplish the same thing as you: to turn the Gantert House into something of which we can all be proud.

It was Rose's misfortune that Koenig was now seriously ill with leukemia and had only a few weeks left to live. Had it been another time, the renovation might have gone more as Rose had wished. Koenig had never been adverse to working with his clients, particularly when restoring one of his earlier houses, for the houses were, in his heart, as much his as the owner's, whomever that might now be. □

# RESTORATION

When Cyrus Johnson asked Pierre Koenig to build him a version of Case Study House 22 in Carmel Valley, he sought to bring, perhaps unintentionally, the crisp forms of modern urban architecture to the rural outback of coastal California. It is perhaps no surprise, but a shame nevertheless, that in 1967 the next owner, James Murphy, commissioned the Monterey architect Donald Wald to remodel the house to better reflect neighboring properties on La Rancheria.[1] So the house was refaced on the street front with vertical timber boarding; two bay windows with internal window seats were brought out and two porthole windows were set in; and a pitched-roof porch with a wooden pergola was added (fig. 12.1). Internally, a molded mantelpiece on carved wooden brackets was fixed above the living-room fireplace, which was itself refaced with large square tiles, and the exposed metal decking of the ceiling was hidden beneath unwrought redwood boarding (fig. 12.2). Elsewhere, paneled doors with bullnose wooden architraves and round brass handles were substituted.[2] Writing later of the house in the *New York Times,* the architecture critic Joseph Giovannini described it as being "reminiscent of a trailer park on a bad-tire day."[3] No one who knew a Koenig house by sight would ever have recognized it.

When, in late 1987, Cynthia and Fred Riebe went to see 54 La Rancheria during a Realtor's open house, it looked so unappealing that Fred refused to get out of the car.[4] Cynthia went inside and then out into the back garden, where she saw the great glass windows still remained. Curious, she returned inside to look at the drawings for the house that had been laid out on the piano. She did not recognize Koenig's name, but, as she later said, "I recognized the futura font he used on his drawings and thought he must be a modernist."[5] The Riebes made an offer for the house but were unsuccessful, and the house was sold to John R. Meyer. Soon after Meyer moved in, he held a garage sale, and the Riebes, then living in a rented cottage in Carmel, attended. During a conversation, it transpired that they were all from Minnesota, and Fred told Meyer how they had also been interested in the house and had made an offer. A few months later, Meyer, who was spending much of his time out of the area, telephoned Fred to ask if the Riebes might still be interested in buying it. They were, and they did, paying the price Meyer had paid less than a year before, minus the cost of the paneled mahogany front door with an integral beveled-glass fanlight that Meyer had installed.

If they were to buy the house, the Riebes wanted the original architect to help them restore it. Fred located Koenig in Los Angeles and telephoned him. "Most people think I am dead," Koenig remarked.[6] Fred followed up the phone call with a letter dated 21 September 1988, with which he sent some pictures of the house and copies of the remodel drawings. "Don't cry when you see them!," he wrote, adding, as if to give encouragement, "My wife is an ASID Designer I work in the field of mergers and acquisitions; we have spent most of our married life living abroad, much of it in Japan. We are great admirers of your work."[7]

Koenig flew to Monterey on 13 October, and Cynthia and Fred took him to see the house, then in escrow. He was devastated. "No one has ever done this to one of my houses. We have to restore this house!," he said.[8] Seven weeks later, they completed the purchase and a great friendship began.[9]

Koenig—or Mr. Conehead, as the Riebes' children, Uli and Ilse, then aged six and four, thought he was called[10]—returned that October evening to Los Angeles and soon sent Fred and Cynthia a note: "Enjoyed the time with you both Thurs. I have ideas already. We will discuss when I finalize. Cheers, Pierre ps: both wines were good."[11] The day after his return to Los Angeles, Koenig added the Riebes' name to a client index card and drew up an American Institute of Architects (AIA) agreement.[12] On a Post-it note attached to the agreement, beneath Koenig's handwritten instruction "SIGN & RETURN TO ARCHITECT," Fred wrote, "look forward to getting started, we should close just before Thanksgiving, everything all set, survey next week."[13] On 4 November, the Riebes paid Koenig a retainer of $1,500,[14] and two weeks later, Koenig completed the first preliminary drawing.[15]

Fig. 12.1.
Johnson House, before restoration, porch and pergola, 1988. Photographer unknown.

Fig. 12.2.
Johnson House, before restoration, living room, 1988. Photographer unknown.

It was decided early on that the best approach to restoring the house was to strip it back to its bare bones.[16] The Riebes wanted two bedrooms and two bathrooms for the children, as well as a study for themselves, and these were to be located in the top of the T-shaped plan, where the master bedroom was.[17] This involved converting the workshop (now a bay-windowed bedroom) and relocating the carport. Koenig's first drawings, dated 18 November, show the new carport extending to the north of the house, making a cruciform plan.

On 28 November, the Monday after Thanksgiving, Cynthia wrote to Koenig, "We were happy to receive the first drawings and liked very much your proposed changes to the driveway, carport & entry. I like the opening up of the office wall—it will be a wonderful room. Can we recover storage where possible, both inside & out? (I have a 'Put things away' obsession). Enclosed are a few notes I made."[18] Cynthia had sketched out their thoughts on a piece of tracing paper overlaid on Koenig's drawing (fig. 12.3). Inscribed in red ink, her preference for an uncluttered, minimal aesthetic came through clearly: "would like to keep this wall space clear, no openings; like very much this space opened up; carve out storage wherever possible; need more utility space . . . good-bye to powder room?"[19]

The next set of drawings, dated 8 December 1988, arrived a week before Christmas,[20] and these too Cynthia worked over, noting in red against the elevations on her trace overlay, "I am going to like this!"[21] The first problem was with the new carport. Koenig initially proposed separating the house from the garage and storage area by a vehicular drive-through. This solution, which placed the garage four steps higher than the house, would have required raising the roofline and sacrificing a fine oak tree. The idea was subsequently abandoned and the original roofline maintained.

In the days after Christmas, Cynthia worked on the bedroom and bathroom designs, and, on a long strip plan dated 26 December and marked up in red, she raised various concerns: "Some way to get powder room & shared bath for kids," indicating with an arrow where Koenig might "relocate powder for larger utility room" (fig. 12.4).[22] The conversion of the west wing into the children's bedrooms raised problems: "afraid rooms too narrow if overhang restored," she noted, and "need inside access to kids rooms." Cynthia drew another red arrow pointing to the fireplace and wrote, "restore orig. fireplace profile? surface?"

The layout of the kitchen and laundry/utility space also created problems. One early diagrammatic plan shows an arrow looping through what would be the kitchen, linking the study (now opened up) to the first west-wing bedroom (also opened up). The danger this posed was clear, as Cynthia noted in her red ink: "DILEMMA: racetrack for Kindergarteners."[23] On the 26 December strip plan, she wrote, "would *like* visual privacy through here not a corridor." Cynthia worked on the layout of the kitchen and utility room, trying out a variety of arrangements until, one evening, she was too tired to think. "Late," she wrote, "mostly junk. a circle feels good but I can't make it work. enclosed for what it's worth. I struggle" (fig. 12.5).[24] On 28 December, she sent Koenig her ideas, writing,

Sorry for the delay in returning the drawings. The children are on school break and the only chance I get to think is after their bedtime. The light is dim and so are the cerebral impulses.

Let's talk by phone after you've had a chance to look at our notes. In general all looks good, clean, straightforward. Spots that trouble me are just our own peculiar way of living and using the spaces ie. The kitchen & utility area. . . . The kitchen/workspace has such potential and I don't want to rush it. It simply hasn't gestated long enough for me yet.[25]

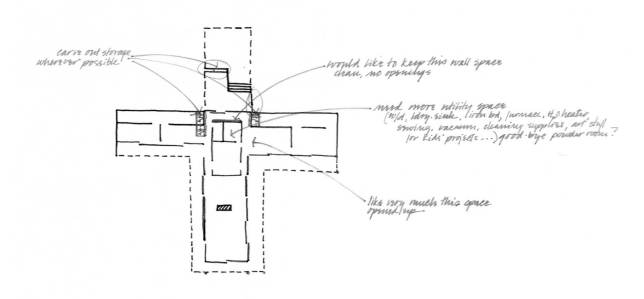

*11/28*

The solution, when it came, was provided by a photograph that Fred had seen in the magazine *Designers' Kitchens and Baths,* as Cynthia explained in a note to Koenig: "Fred saw this kitchen with 'east/west' open & 'south' wall closed as a compromise—still deliberating this, but do like opening up to both directions & bedroom wings. Kitchen too kitcheny."[26] This was the basis of a series of plans that Cynthia then drew up. These were then offered to Fred for his opinion, and version C came out on top, with A second (fig. 12.6). Each provided a U-shaped kitchen-counter arrangement, but the one that best contained the space while not restricting the views out to either side was chosen. Koenig's drawing of 8 December was subsequently altered on 13 January 1989 to show the kitchen and utility room more as Fred's photograph had suggested. It also showed the end of the new carport stepping up over the higher ground to the north of the house. And, in the southeast corner of the garden, there was a lap pool that was first featured on the Johnson drawings.

Later in January 1989, Koenig sent the Riebes the final set of preliminary drawings, which they approved and duly returned.[27] On 23 March, he wrote to them acknowledging the receipt of the drawings and stating his readiness to start on the working drawings. To avoid any difficulty in obtaining the necessary permissions, he explained, "I am going in to the building dept's as a restoration so permit cannot be denied. To this end I will provide drawings showing original plans."[28] This perhaps clarifies one of the contradictions apparent in the drawings held in the archive. The elevation drawing dated 15 May 1989 shows the two main roof beams of the living-room wing of the house extending out beyond the south end of the roof to where they are linked by a crossbeam and

Fig. 12.3.
Riebe Addition to Johnson House, sketch plan with Cynthia Riebe's annotations, 28 November 1988.

Fig. 12.4.
Riebe Addition to Johnson House, bedroom and bathroom plans with Cynthia Riebe's annotations, 26 December 1988.

Fig. 12.5.
Riebe Addition to Johnson House, kitchen and utility-room plans with Cynthia Riebe's annotations, 1988.

Fig. 12.6.
Riebe Addition to Johnson House, kitchen and utility-room plans with Cynthia Riebe's annotations, 1988.

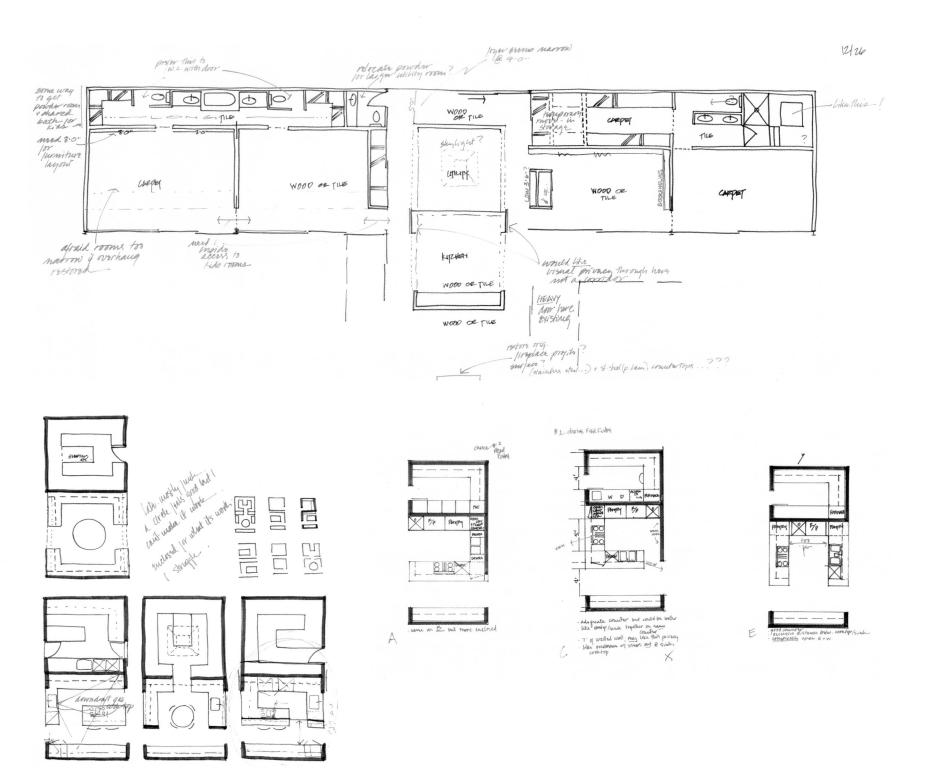

supported on two external columns. This is how they appear in the Johnsons' elevation drawing of 9 September 1961, but, as explained in chapter 6, they were never built like this. Instead, the columns were withdrawn within the glass envelope of the house and the protruding beam ends tapered. For Koenig to have shown the existing building other than how it appeared on the original drawings might have caused difficulties with the building department, so the earlier unbuilt design is perpetuated in the later drawings. Nevertheless, dotted lines on the beam ends suggest the taper, as if it were to be carried out as part of the new works (see pl. 60). This drawing also shows the floor of the carport raised two steps to accommodate the external ground level and the roofline run through contiguous with that of the house; in the end, the floor of the carport was cast one step lower than that of the house.

On 17 May, Koenig sent the Riebes copies of the finished working drawings for them to submit to the Building Department. "There will be one more round of changes when the plans come back from the building dept," he wrote. "Or there will be the *opportunity* for changes but that should be it."[29] He was now ready and, indeed, eager to start detailing the interior: "I think the new kitchen is great and I am very excited by it. I like the light gray color!" With the drawings, he included a bill totaling $3,000 for professional services.[30]

Cynthia also liked the light gray color. In a letter of 17 September, she wrote, "I would like to move away from white into a warm gray ie. wet concrete, no blues on the exterior decking with interior sheetrock walls a gray-tinted white—ceilings?, columns? and beams?—same as exterior? flat, satin or gloss? I'm enclosing some grays and would appreciate your sending them or others back (no FAX # yet) ASAP."[31] In a postscript, she told Koenig, who was a five-hour-drive away in Los Angeles, that the house was now "wired, sub-floored," with "insulation, sheet-rock" going in. The excavating for the carport was to start the next day and they were "awaiting glass, steel—the rest."[32]

Over the last few weeks, as his ideas developed, Koenig had been sending the Riebes sketch proposals for the kitchen and bathroom fittings. A drawing of 12 May shows the dimensions of the kitchen and laundry units, which follow version C. Some of the proposed fittings must have been imported from abroad, for a handwritten note warns about the "inches vs cm bug."[33] Another drawing for the master bathroom, dated 19 June, is annotated, "IDEA! BATH NEW PLAN. No doors! No Glass! No Mess! CINDY & FRED . . . Please chk out P.K."[34] A letter from Koenig of 15 June, addressing twelve separate points, indicates not only the extent of his attention to detail but also the depth of his ongoing dialogue with the Riebes. Regarding electrical outlets, he wrote, "I didn't show plugs at entry as they won't look so good right there. (You have them right around the corner) But I will put them back if you wish." And, regarding the closets, he comments, "Frameless doors look great in pictures and *terrible* in real life. Frames just the opposite. Reason: Frameless have a *huge* bevel around edge that looks like 1898. I'd buy them too if they were clean."[35]

Meanwhile, the Riebes, anxious not to forget the landscaping, had contacted the Los Angeles Conservancy, who had referred them to Garrett Eckbo, the landscape architect and Koenig's former teacher at the University of Southern California (USC), who was now based in Berkeley. "I hope Garrett Eckbo doesn't see the house in the shape it's in now!,"[36] Koenig commented in his letter of 19 June. By mid-September, however, the transformation of the house was already apparent. "We returned from Minnesota," Cynthia wrote to Koenig, "to what is now becoming the clear and lovely house you meant it to be. I was thrilled with the transformation."[37] It was then, amid the chaos of the building works, that Eckbo, who was in Carmel on another job, turned up. Cynthia recalled the visit in her letter: "In his words, he found it 'a structure of pure and classical modern elegance' which took him back to 'the brave new world of genuine modern architecture, while at the same time pointing to a future in which the confusions of postmodernism can be transcended.'"[38] This convinced Cynthia that Eckbo was the right man for the job.

On 1 November, Eckbo, working with his partner, William Yamamoto, sent the Riebes his first proposals for the garden.[39] These were only preliminary thoughts, but one that was taken up involved the closing off of the central road entrance that formed one end of a circular driveway to provide turning space for the carport and occasional guest parking.[40] However, ill health prevented Eckbo from pursuing the scheme, and, on his recommendation, Ken Wormhoudt from Santa Cruz, a USC contemporary and friend of Koenig, designed and executed the walkway to the west of the house. The hard landscape around the house was later finished off by Peter Walker from Berkeley. "It's amazing," he said of the house, "I see the ratios, I see the proportions, I see the discipline."[41]

The house, when completed, used the familiar Koenig materials and methods. But given it was a restoration, it had to be in keeping with the original. The specification for the roof was for either 18-gauge galvanized-steel T-decking manufactured by E. G. Smith and Co. or Robertson and Co., or for 18-gauge galvanized-steel Long Span E450 by EPIC Metals Corporation. The wall decking was similarly 18-gauge galvanized steel by H. H. Robertson Co.[42] Contemporaneous fascia details from the Seidel Associates House, dated 17 July 1959, were reemployed.[43] The great glass windows were replaced with double glazing, and the heating, lighting, wiring, and plumbing were all renewed.[44] The result was impressive. Even Koenig himself seemed surprised: "I am still thinking of that memorable day at your house. The house looked so beautiful, I don't know why the whole world would not want to live in one just like it. Maybe I'm prejudiced. You did a good job in finishing. I really liked the way the details came out.... I am grateful for your involvement. Thanks so much."[45] Koenig's gratitude was heartfelt. On 8 April 2001, he inscribed a copy of Steele and Jenkins's monograph:

Fred & Cindy
To my favorite clients
Pierre Koenig[46]

Another copy he signed, "For Fred and Cindy Riebe, good clients, now good friends."[47]

Koenig's last involvement with the Riebe House was to design the garden gate between the east wing of the house and the sloping ground beyond, for which two schemes exist in the archive. One is a computer-generated drawing for a pair of framed, ledged, and braced gates in perforated metal that were designed to align with the siding on the north elevation of the house (see pl. 61). The other is shown in a tracing paper overlay to a color photograph. Here, the steel frame of the house has been extended to form a framework or trellis into which a perforated sheet-metal doorway has been inserted (fig. 12.7). In the event, the gate was designed and installed after Koenig's death, by Jerrold "Jerry" Lomax, the Los Angeles architect and former associate of Craig Ellwood (with whom he designed Case Study House 18), who now lived nearby in Carmel Valley.

Koenig's second major restoration of one of his earlier houses was that of the Bailey House, Case Study House 21. It is perhaps ironic that when he first had the opportunity to revisit the building, Koenig proposed alterations that, although not extensive, would have changed the award-winning house considerably. The archive contains just one drawing, an undated site plan showing the extent of this work (see pl. 16). The client was the owner, Edson Newquist, who had approached Koenig in January 1986.[48]

The nature of the Bailey House was such that it could be easily extended by the regular repetition of the steel frame's transverse bays. This is what Koenig proposed for Newquist: the addition of two extra bays on the north end of the building to provide a new carport, and the enclosing of the existing carport to provide extra accommodation. The orientation of the vehicular access was to be turned through 90 degrees for a new driveway approaching the house from the east, with the cars entering the carport from the side, between the line of columns, rather than from the end. Since the new carport was to be open on three sides, the clarity of the previous arrangement, where the direction of traffic followed the linear form of the house, would be lost. Around the former carport, the existing cladding on the east wall would be retained, but the other three sides would now be enclosed with 10-foot sliding glass doors. This left the west wall exposed to the evening sun, so Koolshade sunscreens were specified for that elevation. The house had previously been surrounded on almost all sides by shallow lily ponds, and the idea now was that the pond between the former carport and the study should be extended outward and deepened to create a swimming pool. The thin red-brick terrace outside the study would be retained as a platform overhanging the new pool.

None of this work was attempted. However, by 1988, Newquist (or a previous owner) had rearranged the kitchen and introduced a roof light above the living room, where now stood a freestanding, circular, log-burning stove with a white enameled flue penetrating the galvanized-steel roof decking above.[49] So it remained when the house was bought by Dan Cracchiolo nine years later. "While the structural integrity was intact and the envelope in fair condition," Koenig later noted, "many of the interior finishes, including the floor, and appliances were damaged beyond repair."[50]

Dan Cracchiolo was a film producer and a vice president of Silver Pictures, whose most successful film, *The Matrix,* was to be released in 1999. He must have known of the significance of the house, for on 8 March 1997, even before the purchase was in escrow, he engaged Koenig.[51] On 12 March, Koenig signed an AIA agreement to "assist the owner during the Escrow period at 9038 Wonderland Park Avenue, also known as Case Study House No. 21."[52] At the end of escrow, a new contract was to be negotiated.[53]

Then, rather curiously, Cracchiolo approached another architect, Russell K. Johnson, who, on 24 March 1997, issued a Design Agreement to "Create a new kitchen with the same shape, form and

Fig. 12.7.
Riebe Addition to Johnson House, design for garden gate, view from south, ca. 2002. Photographer unknown.

finishes as the original, but with modern appliances and cabinets."[54] Johnson stated that his usual rate was $125 per hour, but he was giving Cracchiolo a special rate "because of the historic nature of this property."[55] Perhaps Johnson specialized in interiors, for Cracchiolo evidently wanted to re-create the kitchen as it had been. Johnson advised him of the impracticality of this: "Duplicate the original GE equipment. This would be very costly, and the functionality of the equipment would be questionable. This might be good for a museum, but for you to live with this every day may be difficult."[56] Instead, Johnson recommended Miele, "a European brand," for the appliances and the Subzero 700 series for the refrigerator. It is likely that this was the correspondence that Cracchiolo then forwarded to Koenig, saying, "Here is a copy of my Kitchen designer's memo regarding the restoration of the Case 21 kitchen. I am hoping to get your thoughts."[57] There is nothing in the archive to indicate what Koenig's thoughts might have been, but one can guess. The signing on 10 June of an AIA agreement issued by Koenig for the restoration of the house suggests that the negotiations with Johnson were to go no further and that Koenig was reclaiming the whole job.[58] For this, Cracchiolo was to make an initial payment of $5,000 and to pay 12 percent of all construction costs, which were estimated at $50,000.

The job fell into two main parts: the rebuilding of the kitchen and other interior fittings and the repair of the fabric. Joe Bavaro of Bavaro Design Studio was contracted to help with the design, sourcing, and drawing up of the interior parts, and Danny Moizel of Utopia Development Inc., building contractors in North Hollywood, was to take care of the external and internal restoration. The only structural work necessary was in the repair of the lily pond at the southwest corner, where subsidence had caused it to fracture. For this, Koenig engaged Richard Schwag of Aqua Concepts.

The kitchen, when rebuilt, was not an exact replica of the original but a close assimilation. The yellow Formica doors were now in stainless steel, and the Masonite panels that slid back to provide a window to the living room were replaced with etched glass. The dimensions varied slightly, probably to accommodate the new kitchen units, but they were nothing that a critical eye would notice, except perhaps that the structure was now 2 inches taller and, at 6 feet, 8 inches, that much closer to the 8-foot ceiling. The working drawings were prepared not by Koenig but by Bavaro (see pl. 17).

Koenig allowed Bavaro a certain amount of tolerance in sourcing components and obtaining quotations. The stereo cabinet—beside which, in one of Shulman's photographs, Koenig had stood while a model reclined on the sofa[59]—had been lost and needed to be replaced. This was entrusted to Bavaro, and numerous variations on the design are retained in the archive.[60] On 29 October, Koenig wrote to Bavaro with reference to scheme 4, "Do you think they can make this cabinet with a fine line across front where top meets panels? Let me know before I send to client."[61] And then on 19 November, he wrote again, asking, "Did you know that there was dead storage space under the turntable?" (see pl. 18).[62] Attached was the section drawing of scheme 5, with Koenig's handwritten note and an arrow indicating "Dead space."

In the archive, there are, in fact, no finished drawings in Koenig's own hand of the restoration of Case Study House 21. The working drawings, in as much as there are any, are by Bavaro. All the remaining drawings are computer generated and often no more than photocopies or fax printouts of originals. The only real evidence that they came from Koenig is that some bear a rubber stamp of his name and address. More often, however, his name is simply incorporated into the title. One such example shows the elegantly simple steel mailbox he designed for the restoration project. Supported on a 2-by-3-inch rectangular-section steel post, the black mailbox with white Helvetica numerals is almost a metaphor for the house itself (see pl. 19).

Perhaps because this building was his proudest achievement, Koenig kept a watchful eye on the job. When writing in April 1998 to Richard Schwag regarding the repair of the lily pond, he reminded him to focus on "reproducing the appearance of everything in this house as it was originally."[63] The same need for exactitude was impressed upon Danny Moizel. In July 1997, Koenig sent Moizel the paint specification for the exterior, noting that the "painting contractor shall furnish samples of finish work and colors for architects approval before starting work."[64] In the end, the paintwork did not turn out as intended, and in June 2000, following the completion of the restoration, he wrote, "When CSH #21 (Cracchiolo) was painted I know the painters didn't follow the specs. Now I need to know what they did use so we can touch up using the same paint otherwise there could be incompatibility."[65]

Koenig's site inspections were detailed and rigorous. His punch list (or snagging list) for the interior, drawn up on 12 May 1998, ran to over fifty points across three pages of notes, ranging from checking for overlaps of black-and-white paint on the walls, beams, and ceilings to touching up paint on the inside jamb of the bathroom pocket doors.[66] The punch list for the exterior, by comparison, contained only fourteen points, although some, like the following, should not have been overlooked by Moizel: "Coat all exposed G.S., flashing, Gravel stops, Flashing, etc., with Perma-Bar and after 2 weeks minimum paint black using a roller with Frazee Duratec."[67] Following an earlier visit, Koenig had had to send Moizel a firm order: "I was at the Job Site Thursday and noted that there was gravel at the Entrance Walk where brick is supposed to be installed. The gravel is not acceptable. See me if there is a problem with brick."[68] Through such attention to detail, Koenig ensured not only that the house was restored, as much as possible, to his original intent but also that, in doing so, a high standard of workmanship was maintained.

Although the work was less extensive, Cracchiolo was as involved with the redesign of his house as the Riebes had been with theirs. In response to one set of plans that Koenig sent him early on,[69] he replied, "As requested I have marked up the plans which you sent over. With regards to closets in the bedroom, I am only concerned with space for shoes. With regards to Bedroom #2, I wanted it to feel like a mini office desk that can be closed away by shutting the doors."[70] Cracchiolo had added, in red ink, a number of shelves to the elevation of the second bedroom wall and also a stool. On the floor plan, against the kitchen wall, he indicated "planter?" To further explain what he wanted for the second bedroom, Cracchiolo, like the Riebes before him, then sent Koenig a photocopy of a picture of a "study as a second living room" with a wall desk, a magazine shelf, and shelves above. The attached note says, "Here is a rough idea of the Desk-like design—this also shows the magazine shelf."[71] As well as attending to these details, Cracchiolo wanted to retain an overview. At the end of the initial letter, he added, "P.S. How are we doing with regards to the following: Tile for atrium, Lighting fixtures, Stainless Steel countertop, ovens, and designs for the cupboards that face North and South of the bathrooms?"[72] Koenig's response of 27 June 1997 was reassuring: "We are in good shape."[73]

The tiles for the atrium, to which Cracchiolo referred, provided a 5-by-8-foot backsplash to the fountain in the small court between the two bathrooms. When Cracchiolo bought the house, these tiles were uniformly gray, but now, in addition to restoring the fountain, Koenig intended to enliven the wall with a mosaic of eight red tiles. Although the tile work was completed by the time Koenig drew up his punch list in May 1998—a crooked tile was one of the items that had to be corrected—the fountain remained inoperative.[74] It fell to the house's next owner, Michael LaFetra, to complete that job.

While the house was still undergoing restoration, moves were afoot to secure its future as a historic-cultural monument. This began when Tony Merchell, vice president and founding board member of the Palm Springs Historic Site Preservation Foundation, wrote to Cracchiolo on 1 March 1999 saying that he had "observed with interest the restoration of your house and believe that it is most suitable for Designation."[75] On the same day, Merchell sent Koenig, with whom he had already been in discussion, the necessary application forms. "I expect Designation will be a shoe-in," he said.[76] It might have been a shoe-in, but, nevertheless, there were procedures to follow.

The first step was for the City of Los Angeles Cultural Heritage Commission to review the building and to decide whether it was significant enough to warrant further investigation. Jay Oren's staff report of 27 July briefly describes the house, putting it in its architectural context:

> Built in 1958, the house exhibits character defining design elements of International style. Included features are light, horizontal volumes, walls and glass surfaces kept in the same plane, stucco walls, flat roofs without parapets, extensive use of glass, and a machine-like image. There are five International style houses on the Commission's list of Monuments and no other buildings by the distinguished architect on record, Pierre Koenig FAIA.[77]

On Oren's recommendation, the house was accepted for consideration and a delegation, led by Catherine Schick, president of the Cultural Heritage Commission, and commissioners Kaye M. Beckham and Holly A. Wyman, visited the house on 18 August "in order to determine if the property qualifies for declaration as a Historic-Cultural Monument under the criteria set forth in Section 22.130 [of the Los Angeles Administrative Code]."[78] Koenig was there to show them the building. The visit must have gone well, for exactly a week later, Oren issued the commission's final determination on the house's monument status:

> Staff recommends that the Commission declare the house a Historic-Cultural Monument because it embodies the distinguishing characteristics of an architectural-type specimen, inherently invaluable for a study of a period style, and is a notable work of a prominent architect, Pierre Koenig FAIA. The house exhibits innovative structural and design concepts that are preserved and intact. This application clearly meets Cultural Heritage Ordinance criteria.[79]

This, however, was not the end of the matter. The commission's recommendation had to go to the city council's Arts, Health and Humanities Committee, which would then make a recommendation to the council, who would either confirm or deny the commission's action.[80] On 9 November 1999, the Los Angeles City Council confirmed the Cultural Heritage Commission's declaration and designated the house a historic-cultural monument, giving it the number 669.[81] A year later, in a move that appears almost to honor its own, the Cultural Heritage Commission selected Case Study House 21 as one of five buildings to be honored at the 2000 Cultural Heritage Commission Awards reception in January 2001.[82] The guest list for the awards reception did not include Dan Cracchiolo but rather the house's new owner, Michael LaFetra.[83]

Cracchiolo sold the house to LaFetra in the spring of 2000.[84] His last involvement with the building was to allow it to go forward that year for a Los Angeles Conservancy Preservation Award, which it duly won.[85] Eight awards were presented at the annual luncheon held at the Regal Biltmore Hotel on 3 May. Although Cracchiolo was still identified on the program as the house owner, Koenig was soon to be, if not already, communicating with LaFetra regarding the restoration of the fountain.[86] Cracchiolo had owned the house for barely three years, and it had been undergoing restoration for much of that time. As Koenig noted in his commentary on the house, "It took less than 9 months and cost 21,500 to build in 1958. It cost 100,000 and took 18 months to complete the restoration in 1998–1999."[87] Even then, the restoration was not fully complete. Four years later, on 14 June 2004, Dan Cracchiolo was killed in a motorcycle accident near Laurel Canyon in the Hollywood Hills. An obituary notice in *Hollywood Elsewhere* said that "part of Cracchiolo's creative energy went into interior decorating," and that "he was once profiled in *Architectural Digest* for restoring architect Pierre Koenig's 1960's 'Case Study House 21'—a 1950s-style thing—to its original condition."[88] That is true, but it rather underplays the story.

These two restorations, the Johnson House and Case Study House 21, show that, despite the dominance of postmodern architecture, a resurgence of interest in "1950s-style" things—what was to become known fashionably as "midcentury modern"—was beginning. Koenig himself remarked to the Riebes following the completion of their restoration that he couldn't "believe the sudden surge of interest in modern."[89] Yet compared with what Garrett Eckbo called "the confusions of postmodernism," these houses were remarkably calm and calming. It was the "pure and classical modern elegance" of the Riebes' house that struck Eckbo in the same way that the ratios, proportions, and discipline were not lost on Peter Walker. Koenig's stated determination to restore the Johnson House and to return the Case Study House to its original appearance show that he had never lost sight of Eckbo's "brave new world of genuine modern architecture." For Koenig, the future in which the confusions of postmodernism could be transcended lay in the past. As he told Joseph Giovannini, "Most architects were doing idealistic work: nobody thought about making money. All of my classmates and I thought design could change the way things were done.... Today," he added, "clients are into big trophy houses; they're business and legal people who aren't so interested in pioneering." Trophy houses were never Koenig's game, but the careful restoration of these houses, nevertheless, made them collector's items. In 2006, Case Study House 21 was sold by its then owner, Mark Haddawy,[90] at an auction in Chicago of "Important 20th Century Design" for $3,185,600.[91] Prototypical production houses, which is what Case Study House 21 was, do not usually sell for $2,400 a square foot.[92] The Riebes still live in their house but, as Giovannini remarked, "Once experimental, the house is now a classic."[93] □

## CHAPTER 13
# REVIVAL

When, in 1988, Pierre Koenig told Fred Riebe that most people thought he was dead,[1] he could not have foreseen what effect the exhibition *Blueprints for Modern Living: History and Legacy of the Case Study Houses* would have on his career. Held between 17 October 1989 and 18 February 1990 at the Museum of Contemporary Art's Temporary Contemporary in Los Angeles, as the museum's warehouse gallery in Little Tokyo was called, the exhibition featured two Case Study Houses built to full scale.[2] One was Ralph Rapson's Case Study House 4, the "Greenbelt House," designed in 1945 but never realized, and the other was Koenig's Case Study House 22. Buck and Carlotta Stahl were still living in the original house, and although they must have received a good income from renting it out for film, television, and advertising shoots, it had not yet gained the iconic status it has today. Nevertheless, Koenig now had two versions of Case Study House 22 on show in Los Angeles: the result was that he became famous for a second time.

The exhibition, first proposed in 1985, was tentatively called *Understanding the Case Study Concept* and was scheduled for spring or early summer 1986. Elizabeth A. T. Smith, then an assistant curator at the Museum of Contemporary Art (MOCA), Los Angeles, wrote to Koenig on 28 March 1985, floating the idea of the exhibition and asking if he still retained any drawings of his two Case Study Houses.[3] However, the plans for the exhibition stalled. In July, Richard Koshalek, the director of the museum, wrote to Koenig saying the exhibition had been rescheduled for the fall of 1988 and that the intention was to "focus on the history of the program through full-scale reconstructions of select Case Study designs." He continued,

> Your design for Case Study #22 is one of two that the curators have selected for full-scale reproduction. In our opinion, this method of presenting fully furnished and fitted houses as a major part of the exhibition will best convey to the Museum audience the innovations and vitality of the architecture that arose from the program. We ask your permission to utilize your design in this somewhat unusual, yet highly significant, way.[4]

Craig Hodgetts, the exhibition designer, wanted to re-create the design as closely as possible to the original specifications, complete with the correct furniture and fittings. Koenig was clearly willing to go along with the idea. In August 1988, Hodgetts and Smith interviewed him on videotape at home, and Smith, now an associate curator, wrote to thank him: "Your comments and insights were certainly enlightening . . . we look forward to continuing to work with you on the other aspects of the project over the course of the coming year."[5]

By now the date for the exhibition had slipped a further year, but in August 1989, Cynthia Campoy, the Temporary Contemporary's press officer, was able to issue a release declaring that "'Blueprints for Modern Living' includes two life-size, walk-through reconstructions of original Case

Study houses,"[6] and that "The reconstructed Koenig house, an icon of 1950s Los Angeles modernism, will simulate the dramatic, steel-and-glass pavilion-like quality of the original house which cantilevers over a cliff in the Hollywood Hills."[7] This was followed up in early October with a press conference at which Koenig spoke: "I am always happy to support your wonderful exhibit," Koenig told Campoy, "and I will always be willing to support your very worthwhile program."[8]

The exhibition, which opened on 17 October, was a huge success. On 27 October, Sherri Geldin, associate director at the museum, wrote to Koenig: "The public has responded overwhelmingly to the show, with a record number of visitors in the mere two weeks since it opened."[9] On 21 February 1990, three days after it closed, Smith wrote to Koenig once again, thanking him for his assistance and participation, and then adding, "Besides being one of the most well-attended shows ever presented by MOCA, *Blueprints for Modern Living* received extensive critical acclaim and an enthusiastic response from an extremely diverse group of visitors."[10] It is safe to say that the success of the exhibition, where Case Study House 22 was one of the prime exhibits, was due in no small part to Koenig's involvement. The University of Southern California had awarded him a sabbatical leave for the first semester of 1988 to work on the exhibition.[11] As Geldin wrote, "From the earliest stages of the planning process, you have played an instrumental role in the exhibition's success, and everyone at the museum is extremely grateful. . . . Thanks once again for your creative inspiration throughout this endeavor and the untold hours you've devoted to making the exhibition a breathtaking reality."[12]

On 21 October 1989, to coincide with the opening of the exhibition, the museum's Architecture and Design Council organized a symposium on the Case Study Houses at the Japan American Cultural Center. Like the exhibition, it turned out to be a great success. "The museum informs us," Katherine Rinne, the symposium chairperson, later wrote to Koenig, "that it was the best attended symposium/lecture series since their founding six years ago. This is due in large part to your participation."[13] The main part of the program was a ninety-minute dialogue between the *Los Angeles Times* columnist Art Seidenbaum[14] and a number of the Case Study House architects: Craig Ellwood, Don Hensman, Ed Killingsworth, Ralph Rapson, Whitney Smith, Calvin Straub, and, of course, Pierre Koenig.[15] As a practicing architect, Koenig was also to join Frank Gehry and Barton Myers later in the afternoon for the shorter roundtable discussion of the "Legacy of the Case Study Program." Two weeks later, Jim Tyler, a former associate of Craig Ellwood, wrote Koenig a disarmingly frank letter:

> I wanted to tell you how much I enjoyed your comments during the symposium on the Case Study House program on Saturday of last week. . . . Your remarks were well founded and struck to the heart of many of the problems that plague the architecture profession today. I appreciate very much your honesty in dealing with the challenges of building structures in a tough misunderstanding society that seems to always lean toward money making and fraud; unfortunately the people will not change much. Hopefully there will be enough clients around that will appreciate the quality of work that you continue to perpetuate.
>
> In addition, I should add that I have been happy for you during this new exposure of the Case Study Houses. I believe that it gives you some recognition that is long overdue; I always felt that you were short changed on publication of your work and maybe additional clients, because of your quiet demeanor and mannerly approach in dealing with people. Possibly this will bring you new projects and new opportunities for the future.[16]

The exposure to which Tyler referred included, in addition to the exhibition and the symposium, a lecture in November by Koenig as part of the Temporary Contemporary's *Art Talks* series[17] and, in Paul Goldberger's 10 December review of the exhibition for the *New York Times,* a large photograph of the mock-up of Case Study House 22.[18] "The full-size replicas of the houses are the real knock-'em-dead crowd-pleasers here," he wrote. "You can't build a whole house in most museums, but here are two of them with room to spare."[19] In what he referred to as "either a happy accident or devilishly clever irony," Goldberger noted how the twinkling lights of Los Angeles, when seen from the real Case Study House, had here been replaced with a bank of eighteen televisions for the video section of the exhibition. Allen Temko, writing on the same day in the *San Francisco Chronicle,* showed the same photograph, albeit smaller than the adjacent one of the Eames House and described how, "crossing a terrace beside a pool, the visitor walks backward in time, a third of a century and more, to enter these very different dwellings. Never mind that the steel columns and beams are simulated by painted wood and that some of the secondary spaces are omitted, or that there is a suggestion of stage scenery. Everything else has a convincing veracity."[20] Temko had more to say of the house, but the cutting retained in the archive, with a handwritten note in the margin and an arrow indicating "missing page," is incomplete.

Fred and Cynthia Riebe, Koenig's clients at that time, certainly visited the exhibition. "What are the dates of the L.A.M.O.C.A. show?"[21] Cynthia wrote to Koenig on 17 September. "If you are attending the opening on 14 October," came the reply, "I will send you tickets. (I know this guy . . .)."[22] The archive, however, does not indicate whether Martin and Mel Schwartz visited the exhibition, but in commissioning a new house from Koenig in 1990, they were not only the first to do so following the exhibition but also the first to do so since Michael Gantert had commissioned his house back in 1979. It had, for Koenig, been a long time since he had designed a new house for a new client, and it is perhaps not surprising that what emerged suggested a whole new approach to the steel house.

On 28 August 1990, Martin and Mel Schwartz went to visit Koenig at his home on Dorothy Street. This was their second meeting,[23] and Schwartz wanted to have a look at the house and to determine whether they had enough common ground for working together.[24] The meeting must have gone well, and the Schwartzes must have liked what they saw, for an American Institute of Architects (AIA) agreement was signed on 4 September,[25] and, the following day, Schwartz paid Koenig a retainer of $2,000.[26] The site was on Sycamore Road in Santa Monica. The preliminary specification, which Schwartz sent to Koenig, required, in addition to two bedrooms and bathrooms and the other necessary facilities, privacy and security from street level and good cross ventilation for passive cooling.[27] Schwartz suggested, with a sketch (not in the archive), a two-story structure with a subterranean two-car garage and an entry on the upper (first floor) level. The budget, excluding fees and interest, was to be $250,000.

Schwartz followed the design development closely and, like Cynthia Riebe, responded to Koenig's proposals with suggestions, questions, and sketches of alternative plan layouts. The preliminary studies that Koenig completed on 5 October comprised two overlapping squares, one rotated against the other. The upper-floor plans show each side to measure 30 feet and the angle of rotation to be 27 degrees. One square contained the accommodation, and the other was the steel frame that supported it. Common to both levels were a central bathroom/utility core and stairs that ran along the northeast side of the building (see pls. 112, 113). Martin Schwartz received the drawings on 20 October and wrote back two days later: "I am very pleased with the concept and appearance of your preliminary plans for my new home. In particular, I think that the exterior 'look' will be

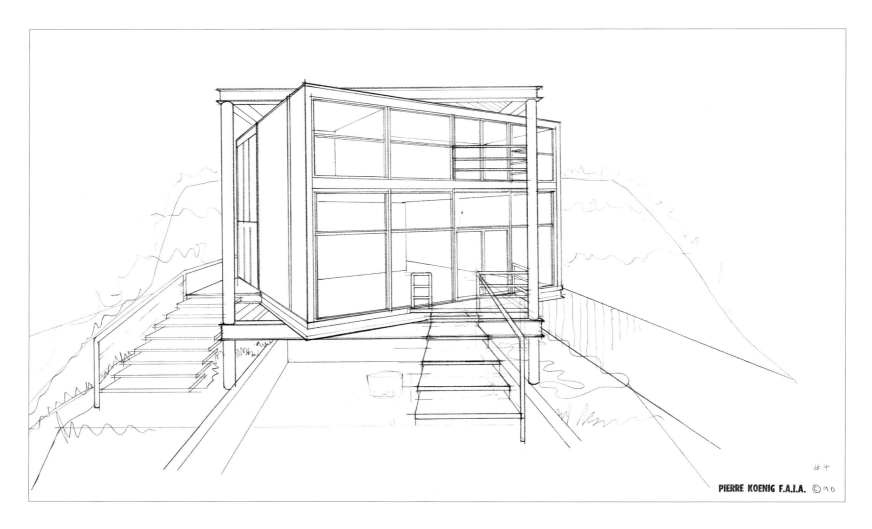

very exciting and dramatic."[28] There is, in the archive, a pencil perspective drawing of 1990 that must have provided the exterior "look" that so pleased Schwartz (fig. 13.1). Nevertheless, in his reply to Koenig, he made several attempts to improve the plans.

Schwartz's main concern was that the living room was too small, and so he suggested extending the structure back 5 feet, changing the plan to a 30-by-35-foot rectangle. As an alternative, he proposed reducing both the kitchen and the bathroom core while eliminating the utility room. He was also concerned that the bathrooms had no exterior window for ventilation and, with the same dissatisfaction that was felt by Cynthia Riebe when redesigning her kitchen, struggled to find an alternative arrangement for the rooms. "Drawings III(A) and III(B)," he wrote, "represent hours of frustration, in my feeble attempt to relocate the master bath to an outside wall. Please excuse the sloppiness. (. . . . I give up!)" (figs. 13.2, 13.3).[29] At the end of his letter, he apologized once again for his inarticulacy, saying, "Please excuse me, Pierre, if I come across as trying to tell the professional how to do his job. My crude sketches are only meant to help communicate my thoughts and concerns. I will follow up for your feedback within a few days."[30] Koenig's response, if not his feedback, was direct and to the point. In the margin of the letter he scribbled his reaction to Schwartz's various points: "ADD $15,000 . . . NO CHANGE . . . Not Feasable . . . POSSIBLE 2nd CHOICE . . . NO . . . ADD $25,000 . . . POSSIBLE . . . NIL."[31] The problem of the master bathroom, however, he carefully sidestepped, writing "ROOF MONITOR (SKY-LIGHTS)" in the margin.[32]

Fig. 13.1.
Schwartz House, view from west, 1990.

Fig. 13.2.
Martin Schwartz's sketch plan III(A), showing alternative master bathrooms for the Schwartz House, 22 October 1990.

Fig. 13.3.
Martin Schwartz's sketch plan III(B), showing alternative master bathrooms for the Schwartz House, 22 October 1990.

Fig. 13.4.
Martin Schwartz's sketch plan IV(1), showing alternative stair position for the Schwartz House, 23 October 1990.

Fig. 13.5.
Martin Schwartz's sketch plan IV(2), showing alternative stair position for the Schwartz House, 23 October 1990.

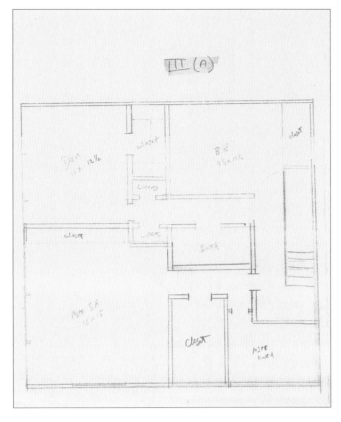

III (A)

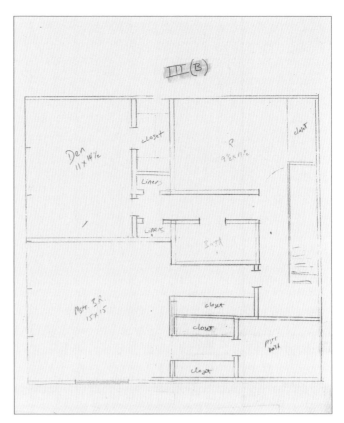

III (B)

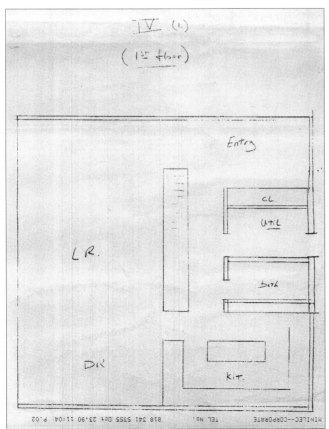

IV (1.)
(1st floor)

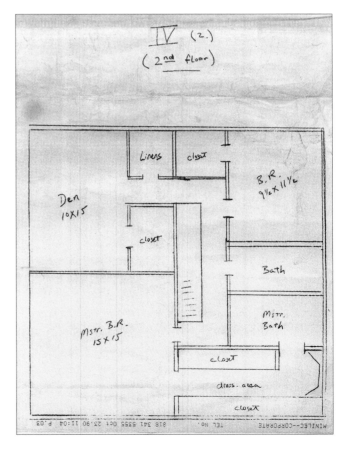

IV (2.)
(2nd floor)

The following day, Schwartz returned to the problem, sending Koenig, by fax, a third variation, III(C), on the master bathroom arrangement. At the bottom of the page he wrote, "P.S. Pierre—Just got back to the office. Also wanted to send you these sketches.... I promise, No more after this!!"[33] Koenig responded by fax the following day, apologizing for failing to point out the opening skylights to the bathrooms, adding: "I prefer this approach to the old windows as there is more light and privacy and better looks on the outside. If you need windows in the wall I will have to change the plan."[34] Schwartz's fax had included two more sketch plans, IV(1) and IV(2), suggesting how the stairs could be relocated in the center of the house in place of the bathroom core, which he now transferred to an outside wall (figs. 13.4, 13.5). Koenig responded to this idea with a fresh set of plans, undated but marked "ALTERNATE," which he dispatched six days later (see pl. 114).[35]

What happened in the next two weeks is not recorded in the archive, but there was something of a breakthrough. The alternate plan, showing the stairs in the center of the building, was clearly not satisfactory even though the living/dining room, which Schwartz had originally thought too small, was increased in size.[36] The clue to the breakthrough might be found in that letter of 22 October, when Schwartz wrote: "Another approach to possibly consider is far beyond my ability to draw. The idea would be to stay within your concept of a square structure rotating within a square frame, now introducing a third rotating square (or partial square) for the purpose of pushing out the rear of the building. This would allow for relocating the bath and utility rooms, leaving more space for the living area....?"[37]

Although Koenig had originally thought this unfeasible, it is, in fact, almost exactly what he did. By introducing a third square and thus pushing out the rear of the building, he managed to regroup the bathroom/utility room core within the body of the plan and provide a larger living/dining area. This he achieved by boxing in the external column on the northeast side of the building and wrapping a spiral stair around it.[38] A new preliminary drawing showing this arrangement was completed on 15 November and sent to Schwartz the next day (see pl. 116).[39] Five days later, Schwartz responded, "I have had a chance to review your 11/15 drawings, and will be calling to discuss shortly. The enclosed sketch is for discussion purposes."[40] There is, however, no such sketch in the archive.

Meanwhile, Koenig had undertaken a sun-study analysis to consider the problem of solar gain (see pl. 115). The living/dining room were on the southwest side of the house and would be subject to solar gain in the winter months but not, as he said, "any time during the day during the summer."[41] The problem he identified was with the September sun, when the "sun can be hot and must be kept out of the house."[42] This was the solution he recommended: "Tests show the vertical plane has more effect as a sun shade than an over-hang at this orientation (SW), therefore I am proposing some kind of 2 foot wide vertical fin along side some of the glass openings. This appears to be the most effective and feasible solution."[43] Schwartz replied that he understood the explanation and thought the solution appropriate.[44] Although photographs of a model of the house show fins projecting from the southwest facade, they were never implemented, and Koolshade screens were used instead.[45]

Koenig eventually completed the working drawings seven months later, on 10 June 1991. What had caused this hiatus is unclear, but as early as that January, Schwartz had written, in response to a fee claim, that he had "become somewhat concerned...over the status of our progress to date, given the extensive working drawings and specifications yet to be done."[46] He even suggested that Joe Bavaro, of Bavaro Design Studio, who had been waiting, as he said, "in the wings" and had been frequently copied on Schwartz's communications, should be brought in to help. After much insisting on Schwartz's part, this eventually happened.

Koenig completed a second round of revisions to the drawings at the beginning of September.[47] It might have been the receipt of these, together with a second cost estimate of $400,000, which was $150,000 over budget (excluding architectural fees, interest, and other soft costs),[48] that prompted Schwartz, on 11 September, to write to him once again. He had already sold his previous house in Tarzana and escrow was due to close on 1 November that year. The Internal Revenue Service allowed house owners two years from close of escrow to either buy or build a new house or tax would be charged on the house sale.[49] Even now, with twenty-six months to go, Schwartz anticipated problems:

> Should a redesign be necessitated by cost considerations, however, there simply may not be enough time to complete the project within the IRS deadline. We have been at it now for over a year, and we are still far from breaking ground. While it is possible that construction may be completed within 9 to 12 months, I have to leave some cushion for unforeseeable construction delays. Hence we *must* break ground within 6 months of my Nov. 1st escrow closing.
>
> Let me emphasize, Pierre, that if I do not have a Certificate of occupancy within 2 years of Nov. 1st, I risk bankruptcy. The IRS deadline is firm.[50]

Schwartz's concern, as it turned out, was well founded. The need to avoid delays was still uppermost in his mind when he wrote to Koenig following a meeting on 4 November: "Overriding concern: Time frame to complete design changes, obtain new bids and break ground? Our firm deadline is 6 months, at the latest."[51] The meeting had resulted in some further alterations to the design and a number of options from which Schwartz could choose. What Koenig now offered were three versions of the house: plans A, B, and C.[52] The current design was plan A, comprising three floors (one being inserted between the garage and the main living floor), which, at $125 per square foot, came in at $408,000. Plans B and C were reduced to two main stories, but with different-size garages. They measured 2,360 and 2,564 square feet, respectively. Plan B would cost $295,500 and plan C, $320,500. "These prices are estimates," Koenig sensibly added. "There is no guarantee we can attain or cannot attain our goal."[53] Schwartz's decision came the next day: "Thanks for the clarification. Based upon your rough cost estimates, I would like to forge ahead with 'Plan C' as discussed last week."[54]

Nevertheless, it was plan A that the building contractors priced, and, when the new bids came in two months later, they were between 6.5 and 10.75 percent over Koenig's September estimate:

| | |
|---|---|
| Ramfer | $434,390 |
| Grendel | $463,791 |
| Newhart | $451,687[55] |

Schwartz's analysis was that "Ramfer gave us a 'low ball' bid that can only go up.... We may be able to bring Grendel's quote down.... Both Ramfer and Grendel appear to have omitted kitchen appliances ($5,987) and 'koolshade' ($7,500) from their bids."[56] He then took things into his own hands and organized a meeting with Kemal Ramezani (whom he referred to incorrectly as Frank Kamel) at Ramfer Inc. and drew up a five-point agenda. But there was one overriding question he wanted answered: "Why is this 1900 sq. ft. home so costly, & what can be done?"[57] Whether or not it was this meeting that had the desired effect, Koenig's cost estimate, previously shown as $434,511, was soon revised down to $399,736.[58]

What negotiations there were over the following four months are not recorded in the archive, but on 3 June 1992, Ramezani wrote to Schwartz with the final price from Ramfer Inc., now called R. G. West Corporation: "Enclosed please find our final proposal for the above referenced project. During the past 11 months of investigation, our original bid of $434,390.00 has been modified to reflect changes in the specifications, the means in which these changes are to be handled, and negotiations with the sub-contractors to allow for the lowest possible price."[59] The price was accepted, and later that month, Schwartz signed the AIA owner/contractor agreement.[60]

At a meeting on 30 June between Koenig, Schwartz, Ramezani, and Joe Bavaro, the remaining questions were thrashed out. The minutes of the meeting start with an explanation of Koenig's intentions for the finished house:

> No extra or needless details. Presentable exposed structure and details, according to plan or approved by the architect. How the structure was the architecture and how this differs from other types of construction. Also, the need to exercise care after installation; the need to avoid spray paint, and holes cut into the exposed concrete and exposed steel frame or siding, etc. The structure is the finish detail.[61]

The next day, however, Schwartz wrote to Koenig with a further change:

> I have finally got around to reviewing your latest drawings in greater detail. . . . Please reinsert the (previously deleted) bridge from the garage rooftop deck to the front door landing at an added cost of $1,800. (I *swear* that this is the last time I will change my mind on this, but Melrose is distraught over the thought of window washers, gardeners, etc., trampling through the house with their equipment to get to the back deck.)[62]

This change was never effected, and even now the window washers and gardeners have to climb onto the rooftop deck using ladders.

A week after the 30 June meeting, and with the building contract now signed, Koenig wrote to Ramezani to say that he could "proceed, without delay, with the construction at 444 Sycamore Rd., Santa Monica,"[63] and, as if to reassure him, Schwartz sent a fax to Ramezani to say that he had received approval from the TransWorld Bank for his construction loan that morning.[64] It had been almost two years since Martin and Mel Schwartz had first gone to meet Pierre Koenig.

R. G. West subcontracted the steel work to F. B. Fabricators Inc. and proceeded with the site works. The first sign of trouble came when, on 17 December, F. B. Fabricators wrote to Schwartz saying that, for reasons beyond their control and that of R. G. West, the erection of the house would be delayed: they were awaiting products from Vulcraft (the truss-joist supplier) and approval notices from Koenig.[65] Schwartz forwarded the letter on to Ramezani at R. G. West saying, "Frankly, Kemal, I am entitled to a better explanation than this regarding any construction delays."[66] Ramezani, in his reply, admitted that Schwartz, as his client, should not have received that letter, but, to avoid saying the wrong thing, he first sent a draft of his intended response to Koenig for approval. The gist of the letter was that any delays due to the time it had taken to prepare the steel fabrication shop drawings, which admittedly had been omitted from the time schedule, had in fact been absorbed by the delay in the delivery of the truss joists, which was set by the manufacturers for mid-January. He went on to say, "Since without the truss joists, no other work can be started (even if all the steel structure is up),

We have to wait until the joists are installed in order to measure the height of the floors for the rough framing and roughing of the rest of the utilities."[67] In reworking Ramezani's draft, Koenig attempted to remove any possible causes of friction. "If you are still trying to look for a responsible party for the delay" was modified to "a reason for the delay"; and a paragraph in which Ramezani anticipated a four-week delay was reduced to "We will do our best to compensate for the lost time as much as we can."[68] "Keep the peace!" Koenig wrote in his cover note to Ramezani, adding, "It's a good idea to explain delays *after* they happen, *not before.*"[69]

On 5 January, Schwartz wrote to Koenig to say that he had been on-site that morning and saw the first shipment of structural steel being unloaded, adding, "Perhaps it would be a good time to give a call to your photographer friend, Julius Shulman."[70] Schwartz, in fact, had met Shulman the previous October at a Los Angeles Conservancy lecture he had attended with Joe Bavaro, and Shulman had expressed his interest in photographing the house. "I'm *thrilled!*" Schwartz told Koenig afterward.[71] When Shulman eventually came and took his photographs, they showed the bare skeleton of the house twisting above its concrete substructure (fig. 13.6).

The day after the first shipment of steel was delivered, it started to rain. On 21 January, Ramezani wrote to Schwartz: "Due to heavy rain in the last 15 days the job site was closed. Since the ground is very saturated, F. B. Fabricators will start their work from 01/22/93 at 7.00 am. We will push to compensate for the time lost due to rain as much as we can. Thank you for your understanding and patience."[72] Although the wet weather, not altogether unusual for Southern California, did not continue, site work started to fall behind. The threat of further rain on 27 March prevented the steel fabricators from coming to the site, so the work was rescheduled for 29 March.[73] The following day, Ramezani wrote to Mohamad Farrohki at F. B. Fabricators showing his frustration:

Despite our several telephone conversations and scheduling, the entry stairs was not delivered to the job site, nor did the welders show-up. I had to ask the deputy inspector to go back while I have to pay him the minimum service call. The painters are due for tomorrow and they do not cancell their schedule since it will be too costly to them. We are suffering all these confusions, while we have gone beyond our limits to help you-out.! So please send the stairs and your welders tomorrow to finish the job. It is forecasted that it may rain on Thursday and we are not able and cannot afford these losses any more![74]

These were not the only difficulties with F. B. Fabricators. The next month, an argument blew up over a delivery of steel joists with stud bolts attached. This was a surprise to everyone, including Schwartz. On 23 April, following a discussion with Koenig, he wrote to Ramezani saying that Koenig "still thinks that *you* should be responsible for letting Mohammad go forward with an unauthorized change."[75] Ramezani forwarded the fax to Koenig, declaring that he had opposed this decision and saying, "I have not been a party in the renegotiation of installing the bolts, and I have not authorized this change. In fact I was surprised to see them on joists when they were delivered." Then, quoting from Schwartz's letter, he added, "If you still feel that I 'should be responsible for letting Mohamad go forward with an unauthorized change' then let me know and I will take care of it."[76] Koenig's reply, sent the same afternoon, was firm:

You & I discussed FB installing bolts but I too had nothing to do with ordering the bolts. I send out specifications every day & nobody ever construes these to be work orders. I even put it in writing that authorization must come from *you,* as usual. And so I notified you by fax of this situation. You did not respond one way or the other. At that time you should have said NO!, I have other plans. FB went ahead and installed the bolts without authorization from you. (Under the fence, so to speak). So what now?[77]

Ramezani got the message and, in his reply to Koenig, accepted the responsibility for the stud bolts:

As is evidenced in this conflict, the only way to stop this confusion to happen is that no one should contact the sub-contractors except the G.C., otherwise the responsibility and the order of ranks will be lost. I am going to inform F. B. Fabricators to this fact that there has been no change order and do not bother you or Marty, and I will take care of it.[78]

As spring moved into summer, a revised construction schedule was drawn up. What had been a thirty-six-week construction period (as in article 7.8 of the building contract) was now projected to be sixty-eight weeks. Although twenty-three weeks of this were put down to extra work and rain delays, there were still eleven weeks unaccounted for.[79] In a fax to Ramezani dated 10 May, Schwartz wrote, "The truth is that . . . the steel fabricator/erector took substantially longer than anticipated."[80] He then continued with characteristic restraint:

It is *not* my desire to hold you responsible for these past delays. Rather, I only wish to look ahead to the timely completion of the job from this point forward. I *do* expect you to make every possible effort to make up for lost time, improving upon the original schedule wherever feasible from now on. To be honest, I have not seen this type of effort the past few weeks.[81]

The revised schedule had extended the time between the start of rough framing and the completion of the job from twenty-three weeks, as in the contract, to twenty-six weeks. Schwartz now asked that it be reduced to fewer than twenty-one weeks and that completion would be before 27 September that year.

Where Schwartz did show his irritation was with the issuing of change orders. At a site meeting that day, he had been asked to sign for almost $5,000 of extra work. As he told Ramezani:

> This is particularly upsetting in light of what has already transpired on the project. You know that I have already objected to change orders from Pierre or F. B. Fabricators that were issued after it was too late for me to question. Then you go ahead and do exactly the same thing! On the other hand, I know that these costs were legitimately incurred, and it is important that you and I remain on good terms.... Please don't force me to treat you in the same fashion as Mohammad with his belated extras.[82]

Schwartz then stated that no change order would be approved after the work was done and that, in such situations, R. G. West would have to absorb the cost.

The delays were, for Schwartz, not just an inconvenience. With the work still ongoing, he wrote to Ramezani on 1 July to say that his one-year construction loan with TransWorld Bank had expired that day, thus forcing him to request an extension for the loan and to pay an additional percentage of interest.[83] The problem of the spiral stair, which re-emerged on the same day, demonstrates well how the difficulties of the job often resulted in on-site delays and the subsequent expense of change orders. The design of the spiral stair was based on an idea first seen in the drawings for the Metcalf House in 1958 (see pl. 38) and repeated in the design of the Dzur House in 1959 (see fig. 6.4). The idea was to weld each tread, supported by a triangular gusset, directly to the shaft, which, at the Schwartz House, was one of the four circular columns of the outer structural frame (see pl. 117). On 1 July, a Thursday, Ramezani wrote to Koenig to say that he had had to employ a metal fabricator to remove all the treads and reinstall them in a way that would work. This would cost $10,000, for which he needed, immediately, change orders and final sketches so that the metal fabricator could start work two days later, on Saturday.[84] On Friday, he wrote again, sending a sketch of how he thought the treads should be positioned. "The steel man is working tomorrow," he said. "If you agree with my sketches, please advise me today, otherwise I have to close the work tomorrow."[85] Koenig's response, comprising two detail drawings, came after the weekend, on Monday. Meanwhile, the steel man, presumably, had been sent home. The problem clearly was that it was all done at the last minute; change orders and drawings were demanded with little time for their consideration or preparation. And, despite Schwartz's letter of 10 May to Ramezani regarding the protocol for change orders, there is, in the archive, no indication that he was consulted.

By mid-August, Schwartz's IRS watershed date of 1 November was just over ten weeks away. In a fax to Ramezani, in which he confirmed his acceptance of a quote of $29,671.16 for the sliding doors and windows, he tried once again to impress on his general contractor the urgency to complete the job: "I can't emphasize strongly enough, Kemal, that *time is of the essence.* As you know, I will suffer severe tax consequences if we cannot obtain the Certificate of Occupancy by December. I have also explained to you that the bank has extended my construction loan only through November.... I am relying on your assurance that construction will be completed around November 1st."[86]

The delays, to be fair to Ramezani, were not always of his making, and he was not assisted by the bad weather. At the start of October, Schwartz wrote to Jerry Peryman at Fleetwood Aluminum Products Inc. regarding the delay in the delivery of the sliding doors and windows for which a deposit of $11,800[87] had been paid on 20 August.[88] Due to a change order that affected a few upper-story windows, the whole shipment was delayed, with the result that the remainder of the building could not be made weather-tight and internal fitting-out could not proceed. "I won't bore you," he wrote to Peryman, "with the details of the time pressures we are facing on this house,"[89] but then he indicated that the financial risk caused by the delay was not his alone.

> Suffice it to say that I will incur substantial tax penalties should the project fail to meet deadline and, of course, I have structured Kemal's contract such as he would share in my pain. While we had experienced earlier delays on the job, Kemal felt comfortable in his ability to meet the deadline based on Fleetwood's original delivery quotation. This delay on your part has now left us in extreme jeopardy.[90]

It is here that all records in the archive of the building of the Schwartz House end. No response from Peryman can be found nor any indication of whether or not the house received its Certificate of Occupancy on time. This, however, seems unlikely, because the house was still lacking its front windows when a BBC Education film crew visited it on 13 October.[91] Their program, *Forging Ahead,* shows yellow tape across where the windows should be; and a 35 mm color slide retained in the archive and dated October 1993 shows the unfinished house with the BBC film crew outside.[92] The only document of a later date is the City of Los Angeles Department of Building and Safety Inspection Record, which shows that the final inspection for the grading was signed on 28 March 1994.[93] Martin and Mel Schwartz moved in on 9 March 1994, even though only a temporary Certificate of Occupancy had been issued.[94] It was now three and a half years since they had first visited Koenig at his home on Dorothy Street.

During this time, Martin Schwartz had steered and hustled the project toward completion with enormous patience and equal persistence. He might well be forgiven had he never commissioned any more building works. But there was the basement, that level between the garage and the main living floor, to be completed. On 28 July 1995, exactly sixteen months after the building passed its final inspection, the California Coastal Commission issued a letter of exemption for plans to "convert an unenclosed utility storage area into an enclosed basement/storage area at an existing 2-story single-family residence" (see pl. 118).[95] Approval from the Department of Building and Safety was received in early November, and Schwartz set Ramezani a prospective start date for the new building works of 2 January 1996.[96] It was not altogether wishful thinking, for Ramezani sent a fax to Koenig dated 4 January 1996 saying that he was "planning to pour conc. slab this week."[97] Compared with the building of the house itself, this small job went smoothly.[98]

The Schwartz House was the last house Koenig built but not quite his last completed work. The archive indicates that in the last ten years of his life, from the completion of the Schwartz House in March 1994 to his death in April 2004, Koenig received at least fifteen commissions, yet only what he called a "modular" extension for Jeffrey Ressner, a small pool house for William Koppany, and the restoration of Case Study House 21 were completed. Neither of the new works, however, shows the changes in his thinking regarding the use of structure anticipated by the Schwartz House. They were both almost retrogressive.

Jeffrey Ressner lived on Dorothy Street, next door to Koenig, in a small single-story timber cottage with a bay window. When it came to making an addition to his house, he turned to his neighbor. In January 2000, Koenig drew up an AIA agreement[99] for a single-story addition, and in April, Ressner paid him a $2,000 retainer.[100] This was, in fact, the second such retainer that Ressner had paid; an earlier payment of $1,000 was made in May 1988.[101] Although there is nothing in the archive to suggest what this might have been for, it could have been on the basis of this credit that Koenig began the preliminary designs in November 1999. These drawings, like those for the basement at the Schwartz House, were all computer generated and marked up by Koenig in red pencil. The intention, as in the extension he built for Della and Gary Rollé at the Seidel Associates House, was to straddle the rear part of the cottage with a steel frame. This comprised four 8-by-8-inch square-section columns, which supported, like a tabletop, a rectangle of 12-inch I-section steel beams (see pl. 123). On this was placed a single volume "modular" addition containing a recreation room (see pl. 121) or, as in another drawing, a large bedroom, off of which was a bathroom (see pl. 122). Whatever the function of the main space, it was to be split down the middle by a straight flight of stairs that rose from between the two existing bedrooms on the lower floor. The external cladding varied between stucco, when the space was to be a recreation room, and Texture 111, when it was to be a bedroom.[102] By the time the first set of working drawings was drawn up on 27 March 2000, the room was definitely a bedroom, although the external cladding varied between $1\frac{1}{2}$-inch galvanized-steel decking on half-inch ply (on the south elevation) and Texture 111 (on the north).[103] When the second set of working drawings was produced on 29 June, the Texture 111 had been replaced by 22-gauge galvanized-steel decking (see pl. 124).[104] Was it through a slow process of attrition that Koenig encouraged his client to move from stucco to Texture 111 to galvanized-steel decking? In the end, the result did not so much match as complement Koenig's own house next door.

Although Kemal Ramezani at R. G. West[105] quoted for the job, the contract was given to the Kausen Construction Company from San Fernando.[106] They had bid $96,936 against Ramezani's $115,800. Not only was Kausen's price about 17 percent less than Ramezani's, but it was also a much more considered quotation, itemizing the different trades and materials and charging a 20 percent contractor's fee. Ramezani's quotation contained no such detail. The AIA owner/contractor agreement was signed on 10 July and work proceeded.[107] Almost exactly a year later, on 20 July 2001, Koenig submitted his invoice for professional services comprising design, drawing, and supervision.[108] He had spent 42 hours on the job, at $100 per hour, and his assistant, Jan Ipach, had spent 402.5 hours, at $12 per hour: the total fee was $9,030.00. It is not difficult to guess who had done the computer-generated drawings and probably much of the supervision as well.

The other small project of this time was the swimming pool and pool house built for William and Cynthia Koppany adjacent to their house on Valley Oak Drive in the Hollywood Hills. Koenig had added William Koppany's name to a client index card in March 1999, and on 17 July of that year, they signed an AIA owner/architect agreement.[109] In August, Becker & Miyamoto were engaged as site surveyors on Koenig's recommendation, and Richard Garcia was contracted in November as the civil engineer for site works. But it was not until mid-December 2000, thirteen months later, that Koenig produced drawings of adequate detail to allow William H. Koh, the structural engineer, to provide a fee quote.[110] The slow start to the project did not improve in the New Year. On 20 June 2000, Garcia sent a fax to Koenig saying that a "grading permit is required for pool excavation and subdrain & backfill," and, in response, Koppany appears to have employed Randall Akers, a consulting inspector, to assist in obtaining the necessary permissions.[111] "Good luck in getting the City

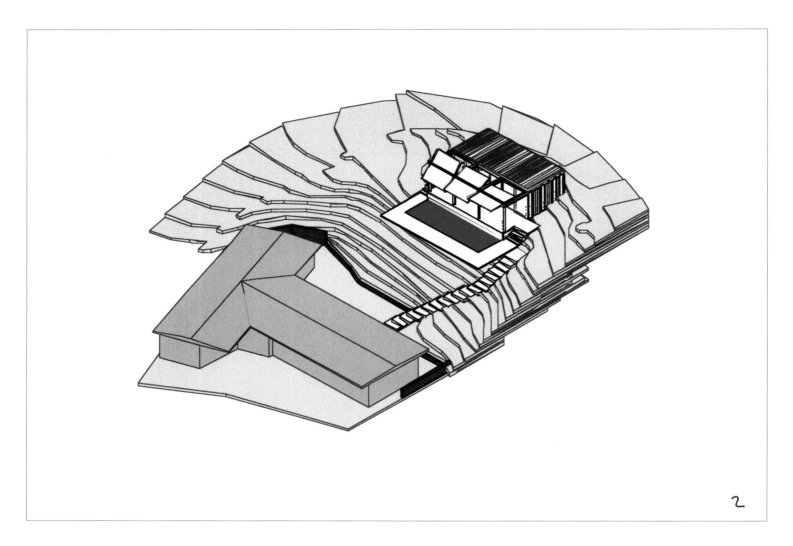

2

approval," he wrote on 14 August.[112] However, two months later, Garcia sent another fax to Koenig, asking, "Will you please bring me up to date on what is happening with this project?"[113] The problem, it would seem, was that Valley Oak Drive looped around the site, making it a "through lot." Therefore, the proposed pool, when seen from one point on the road, would be in the "rear yard," but when seen from another, it would be in the "front yard." This meant that the building of a swimming pool and pool house, together with the erection of a 6-foot chain-link fence around the site, would require a zoning adjustment, which, in turn, required a public hearing for the benefit of the neighbors and other affected parties. It was two years before the public hearing was eventually held on 6 August 2002.[114]

By then, it had been nearly a year since Koenig had written, almost triumphantly, to Wayne Schick, the geology and soils engineer, saying, "We Finally got Koppany into Plan Check."[115] Even so, the working drawings retained in the archive are dated 13 March 2002 or later,[116] although there is also an earlier, undated set.[117] The building they show is almost a reprise, in miniature, of his earlier pavilion houses. Comprising three 10-foot bays framed with 6-inch H-section columns and 12-inch I-section beams and clad in 18-gauge galvanized-steel decking, the 30-foot-long building defines the length of the lap pool that runs along its open west elevation (see pl. 120). Here, to provide shade to the interior, are three giant rectangular canvas sails colored red, yellow, and blue. Set between the steel frames, they tilt on central pivots to meet the angle of the setting sun. The printouts of the computer-generated model, although not showing the color of the tilted sails, indicate the steepness of the site and show the stepped pathway leading to the house below (fig. 13.7).

The length of time it took just to get the Koppany pool house on site was almost as long as it took, with all the delays, to build the Schwartz House. There is nothing in the archive to indicate any effort on Koenig's part to move the project along more quickly, although it would not be fair to judge his actions based solely on what little evidence the archive contains. However, it would be true to say that these last years of his life were characterized by a great number of incomplete or unrealized projects. Had some of these been built—specifically the houses for Randall Koenig and for Vida Tarassoly and Mohsen Mehran, as was that for Michael LaFetra, posthumously, by Jim Tyler—then the revival of his reputation following the *Blueprints for Modern Living* exhibition in 1989 might have had more substance. As it was, he received many awards and much public acclaim but, in the end, left little new work to show for it.

It was just six months after the closing of the exhibition that the Schwartzes had asked Koenig to build their house. In the decade since he had last built a house for a client—the Gantert House—both architectural fashion and practice had moved on. Postmodernism and its bastard progeny, deconstructivism, had swept through the fashionable architectural magazines and progressive offices, perhaps nowhere more so than in New York and Los Angeles. Yet for all the peculiarity of its twisted form, the Schwartz House cannot be seen as a response to these trends. The very fact that neither the Ressner modular addition nor the Koppany pool house betrayed any reflection of current architectural fashion would indicate that if the Schwartz House was cutting a new architectural path, then it was its own. Martin Schwartz's original requirement that the house should have privacy and security from the street and, at the same time, good cross ventilation for passive cooling explains the house's appearance. The constricted site did not allow for a pavilion-type house: the building had to extend upward. Consequently, the fortresslike garage at the lowest level addressed the street but kept it at bay. Above this, the street alignment was expressed through the exposed steel frame, but the house that sat within was turned to catch the cooling breeze coming up the canyon, Sycamore Road, from the ocean. As in Koenig's own house in Brentwood, a tall window slid open just a little would give all the cross ventilation and passive cooling the house needed. Far from following fashion, Koenig was, in the design of the Schwartz House, just doing what Jim Tyler had admired so much—dealing with the challenges of building structures in a tough, misunderstanding society. □

Fig. 13.7.
Koppany Pool House, computer-generated model, ca. 2002.

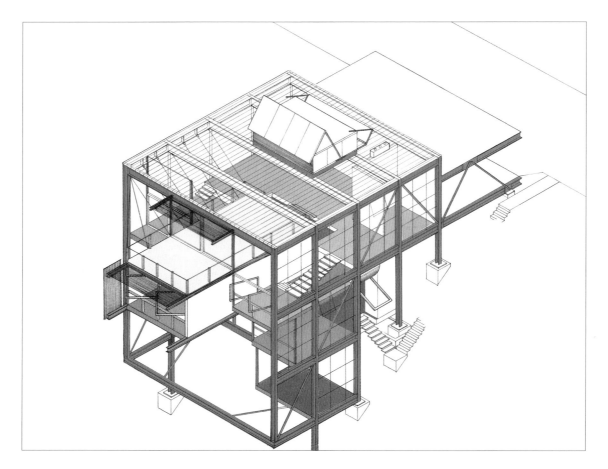

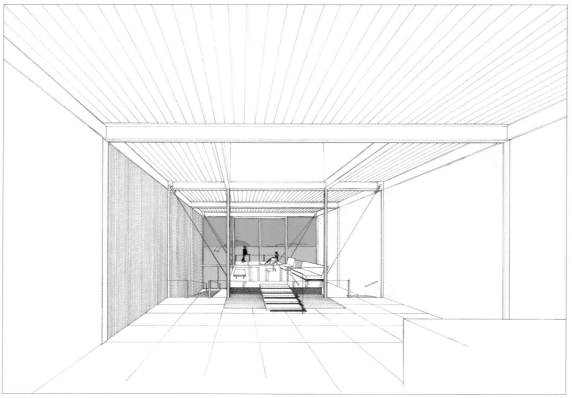

# PAYBACK TIME

In 1996, Pierre Koenig started on the design of a new house for his son Randall, a founding partner of the Orange County law firm Koenig Jacobsen, which specialized in, among other things, architecture, engineering, and construction law. The house was to be in the Orange County coastal community of Laguna Beach on a prominent, steeply sloping site overlooking the ocean. As at the Schwartz House, the design separated the structural frame from the living spaces that were positioned independently within it.

With an unintentional slip into legalese, Koenig described the design concept in a statement written for the Japanese journal *Global Architecture:*

> While determinate in plan, the section is indeterminate. Vertically, each space is arraigned autonomously without regard to other spaces above and below. In this manner an infinite variation is generated that gives each space a unique view. Many structural problems emerge using this system that cannot be solved by ordinary means. A combination of beams, columns and cable braces resolve the discontinuities. The end result is an unusual and dynamic interplay of space and supporting structure.[1]

The external steel frame, comprising 12-inch H-section columns and 18-inch I-section beams, stepped down the hillside in three 14-foot stages, resting, in a manner not unlike at the Beagles House, on three points of contact (fig. 14.1). "The ceilings," Koenig wrote, "are fourteen or more feet to increase the feeling of spaciousness and to convey the idea of many small and medium size boxes floating through a larger space."[2] Within this framework, the floors varied in position, facilitated by landings and half landings. "Individual spaces," Koenig noted, "are designed for restrained mobility during earthquakes, relieving some of the stress on the main frame."[3] To this end, the central part of the plan was a box suspended on cables projecting outward from the west elevation by 10 feet; it contained the master bedroom and bathroom, with the main entertainment area positioned above opening onto the roof (fig. 14.2). Although construction was scheduled for 1997–98 at a cost of $540,000, the design was never realized.

Far less innovative but more elaborate was the house designed for Vida Tarassoly and Mohsen Mehran on a steeply sloping site on Anacapa View Drive in Malibu. Although an American Institute of Architects (AIA) owner/architect agreement "to design and prepare contract documents for a single family dwelling" had been drawn up in July 2000, it was not until 19 August that Koenig added their names to a client index card,[4] a deposit of $2,000 being paid four days later.[5] Vida Tarassoly was a licensed civil and structural engineer, a registered contractor, and an attorney. Mohsen Mehran was a certified groundwater engineer. Like both Cynthia Riebe and Martin Schwartz before her, Tarassoly involved herself with the design of the building, challenging Koenig's ideas and suggesting her own solutions.

**Fig. 14.1.**
Randall Koenig House, axonometric drawing, 1996.

**Fig. 14.2.**
Randall Koenig House, interior view, entertainment area, 1996.

By early September, Koenig had hand drawn floor plans for the house and sent them to Taras-soly (see pls. 125, 126).[6] Arranged as two stories with a protruding central stair and parking at high level at the rear, Koenig's initial proposal was not unlike that for the Beagles House in section and the first version of the Beidleman House in plan—a two-story rectangle following the contours of the hillside, with the rooms facing the view and the circulation and services pushed to the rear. Some conversations must have ensued, for on 20 September, Tarassoly wrote, "Got your latest e-mail. Sorry I didn't get back to you earlier, I had a flu. The stepped down house seem to work towards taking care of the height problems. Mohsen was concerned about lower floor roof obstructing the view."[7] To make her point, she sent Koenig a cross section she had prepared using AutoCAD. What had been two stories, one on top of the other, was now a two-story stepped section.

After the stepped section was decided upon, the basic arrangement of the house altered little except for the addition of a third, lower level containing a swimming pool. The positioning of the garage, however, changed many times due to problems of access created by the curve of the road above the house and the slope of the hillside on which it sat. The earliest set of plans shows the garage at the rear of the house, but the adoption of the stepped section pushed the lower stories too far out from the hillside, thus contravening a local 28-foot height restriction.[8] Tarassoly's solu-tion was to put the garage at the lower level: "If the garage is at this lower elevation," she wrote, "driveway would have to start from the side to slope gradually down to this elevation."[9] Koenig's preference was to retain the garage at a higher level.

By adding an extra bay to the east end of the upper floor of the house, Koenig offered various permutations for the garage. One version, untitled but perhaps scheme 101, shows a two-car garage entered from the east; scheme 102 is for a two-car garage entered from the north; and scheme 103 shows a three-car garage entered from the east. Depending on the extent of the garage, the size and configuration of the adjacent living room, dining room, kitchen, and occasional family room varied. The next series of solutions, variations on scheme 103A, had the garage as a detached box to the northeast of the upper floor of the house. The advantage here was that the spatial arrange-ment for the living accommodation was not compromised by the size of the garage. What differed between these schemes was the connection from the house to the garage—sometimes steps, sometimes a terrace or even a bridge. Koenig's red pencil marked up Jan Ipach's computer print-outs with changes and revisions (see pl. 127).

Whatever the connection to the house, scheme 103A required a bridge to bring the cars in from Anacapa View Road, across a ravine, and to the garage. "I am trying to keep the bridge as level as possible for many reasons," Koenig wrote to his clients on 22 March 2001, "with the drive on grade sloped as much as possible. Also, I am tilting the bridge slightly so that the water is spread when it drains off bridge instead of pouring out in one place, creating erosion below."[10] The elevation of the bridge that accompanied the fax shows the bridge supported on slender legs 23 feet above the ravine (see pl. 130).

When a full set of drawings emerged six months later, they showed a building 70 feet long separated from the road above by a series of steps that led to a trellised entrance deck, off of which was set the three-car garage and entrance bridge (see pl. 128). The upper floor was 25 feet deep and comprised a living room, dining room (to seat twenty-two), kitchen, and family room overlooking the lower story. This, in turn, was 30 feet deep, with four bedrooms and three bathrooms (see pl. 129). A long flight of stairs, set within a glass walkway, cut through the center of the plan to connect to the swimming pool on the third and lowest level (see pl. 131). The whole structure was supported on nine

H columns (probably 12-inch square, but the size is unspecified) and I-section beams that spanned the width of the building in two 35-foot stages.

On 6 November, Koenig issued a fee statement for $4,660, of which $180 was for the "blueprints for submission to City."[11] Although this might indicate the completion of the design stage of the job, it would appear that Koenig was not satisfied with the solution. On a printout of the lower-floor plan for scheme 103B, there is the printed note "VIDA: I want to move this floor out as in the first scheme. I think we can get a variance for this. Nothing to lose."[12] The archive does not disclose whether or not the variance was granted, but Koenig did decide to raise the whole structure by 3 feet, which elevated the entrance deck, previously cut into the hillside, to a point higher than the natural grade, thereby obviating the need for a retaining wall.[13] One plan showing these alterations remains in the archive, with Koenig's instruction inscribed in red pencil: "7/13/02 Revise for final submission."[14]

The Tarassoly/Mehran House was never built, but it was never quite forgotten either. A new set of drawings was prepared in December 2003 and some sheets were further revised in March 2004.[15] Jan Ipach sent copies of structural and floor plans to Tarassoly on 9 March[16] and some additional drawings, including construction details, on 18 March. In his fax, he noted,

> I talked to Pierre about how to deal with the lateral loads on the downhill side of the house. Instead of adding a column (as you suggested on the phone), he would prefer to
> —increase size/weight of the existing columns
> —add X-bracing as shown in the attached floorplans
> I hope this works![17]

These were the last architectural instructions Pierre Koenig ever issued, for he died just over two weeks later.

In one last fax, dated 21 April 2004, Ipach told Tarassoly that "Gloria will call you tomorrow and give you information on Jim Tyler."[18] With Tyler, whose admiration for Koenig has already been noted, the building would be in safe hands. Two years later, with the house still unbuilt, Tarassoly wrote, "The house shall be true to Pierre's signature design and he wanted us to use Jim for the completion of the project. We have talked to Jim and are planning to use his services during construction."[19] Although Tyler did not get to build the Tarassoly/Mehran House, he did complete for Koenig one last building: the house for Michael LaFetra.

Michael LaFetra bought the Bailey House, Case Study House 21, in 2000 and saw the restoration work through to its completion. On 21 March 2002, he wrote to Koenig:

> Let me begin this letter with tremendous thanks for your brilliant architecture. I have had such a fantastic experience living in Case Study #21. I will fondly remember the calming sounds of water from the pond scuppers and the astonishing ability of this house to be indoors and outdoors at all times.

Then he continued with some regret:

> I have thought long and hard about how to maintain a life in this house with my two cats, Tarmac, and most importantly, Alison. Ultimately the house is just too small for two people to run

two different home businesses. I am deeply saddened that I will have to sell the house but regrettably, it has to be done.[20]

Case Study House 21 was only the first stage of LaFetra's involvement with Koenig's architecture, for, by this date, he had already commissioned another house from him. "I am thrilled at the potential of a new house in Malibu," he concluded, "and am excited for that process to really get rolling. I look forward to continuing our contact both as friends and as architect and client."[21]

LaFetra's intention was to replace the existing house at 6525 Point Lechuza Drive, Malibu, a building previously owned by the singer Pia Zadora. The site was a rocky promontory mostly taken up by a large house on the adjacent plot designed by John Lautner—the Beyer House of 1983. To facilitate the permit process, the designs for the new building were initially promoted as a remodel of the existing house, reflecting its scale and internal arrangement if not its appearance. It was the approach Koenig had taken when restoring and extending the Johnson House for Cynthia and Fred Riebe. Survey drawings dated 1 February 2001 show an awkwardly planned and rather featureless building with an undulating wall to the ocean view. A note on the drawings reads, "All interior and exterior wallls to be demolished."[22] Although this might suggest fairly extensive demolition work, the intention was to retain the footprint of the existing house, including a stepped walkway and retaining wall that ran around the northwest and northeast sides of the building, while straightening out and squaring off the undulating wall to the southeast. With the existing building now recorded, LaFetra and Koenig signed the AIA owner/architect agreement on 16 April 2001.[23]

By 1 October, when he sent LaFetra an invoice for $11,250, Koenig had completed the preliminary plans and preparations for submission to the City of Malibu.[24] Yet nothing can be found in the archive to suggest what these drawings might have been. If they showed a reworking of the existing house, then nothing of that remains. The earliest drawings in the archive are dated 17 December 2001, and although the building they show is clearly new, much of the disposition of the spaces reflects what had been there before (see pl. 132). The forecourt and garage are retained at basement level, with an entrance to the house in the same position. The office, bathroom, and utility room are still in the basement, in much the same configuration as before, but a screening room and gym have been added where previously there were storage and stairs. The main entrance on the floor above has been moved from the northeast side of the building to the northwest, but it still comes off the external passageway. The result is that the stairs, now top lit, are more central within the building's plan. On this level, the living room, dining room, and family room/den are still in the same location, but the kitchen and breakfast room have taken the position of the entrance hall and stairs; and an office, utility room, and bathroom have taken the place of the former kitchen toward the back of the building. To allow stairs to come up from the basement, much of the external deck on the side of the building facing the ocean has been removed and replaced with a rectangular deck and a hot tub. On the top floor, what was previously a rather chaotic plan is now rationalized in the manner of the Beidleman House and the later Tarassoly/Mehran House: the bedrooms face the view and the circulation and services are pushed to the rear. As an arrangement, the new plan of the lower floors differed little from the old, but it had better circulation and a more rational and regular use of space.

The conception of the new building was different in the three-dimensional use of space—an approach already explored in the house designed for Koenig's son Randall. Despite its siting, the existing house was a conventional layer cake of a building, and not a very tasty one at that. The new

Fig. 14.3.
LaFetra House, computer-generated model, ca. 2001.

design took advantage of the site, allowing the living and dining area along the oceanfront of the building to be a double-height, fully glazed space into which the bedrooms would look down from above. Here, the spatial sense of the building would be exploited by a bridge (as in Koenig's own house) that would pass through the volume from the master bedroom to a high-level external terrace that would cantilever out and beyond the hot tub on the level below. This was all made possible by a 10-by-20-foot grid of H-section steel columns and I-section steel beams through which views of the ocean were visible from almost any part of the building.

Very little about these plans changed between December 2001 and September 2003, which is the last date shown for revisions.[25] The house that Jim Tyler eventually completed in 2012 for LaFetra is very close to Koenig's original conception as shown in the computer-generated model (fig. 14.3). The interior volumes are essentially as Koenig conceived them, as are the finishes: exposed profiled roof decking to the ceilings and, externally, opaque glazed paneling to the walls. Only the adoption of an elevator for cars, in place of a sloped ramp, and the raising of the walkway around the exterior of the house would substantially change the approach to the building.

Koenig had added Michael LaFetra's name to a client index card on 12 June 2000,[26] and soon after, LaFetra took over the restoration of Case Study House 21. Two weeks later, Koenig received from Dallas, Texas, a small, white handwritten card embossed with an upturned golden horseshoe. It was dated 23 June and came from Hilre Hunt, who was married to Henry Frost IV:

Dear Mr Koenig,

A quick summer storm, resulting in a wet lingering twilight, I asked Henry to go with me to see the lot on Horseshoe. We walked the lot. He stopped, pointed at a spot with the toe of his shoe, and said, "I think the house should be a rectangle to about here." I replied, "I think we should put ourselves in the hands of the architect." Mutual silence. Will you be our architect? Hilre[27]

Hilre Hunt had begun her love affair with steel-and-glass houses on 1 April 1999, when she visited Case Study House 22 and met Carlotta Stahl and Pierre and Gloria Koenig.[28] In an email headed "Double Vision" sent to Koenig over a year later, she declared,

April first, I became a fool, for case study number 22. Always a sideline observer of my husband's passion, for the elegant steel and glass cloches, I attended the benefit, for the Friends of the Schindler House and my appreciation bloomed. "Ninety percent location, ninety percent architecture," I replied to all who enquired of my findings. The evening was a tonic, and I'm ready for a second draught.[29]

By 7 June 2000, Henry Frost and Hilre Hunt had been entered on one of Koenig's client index cards;[30] and, four days after Hunt penned her note, Koenig was on a morning flight from Los Angeles to Dallas.[31] The site was on Horseshoe Trail, in the wealthy Bluffview neighborhood, just behind where the Frosts then lived on Lilac Lane. Koenig stayed one night at the Guest Lodge at the Cooper Aerobics Center and then flew back to Los Angeles the next day.[32] It was a quick visit, but he saw all he needed to see. An AIA architect/owner agreement for one large residence and four small residences was soon drawn up,[33] and on 31 July, he acknowledged the receipt of the $2,000 retainer: "I'm off to a running start," he wrote.[34]

The site on Horseshoe Trail, a somewhat unlikely name for a suburban street, was a long rectangle measuring about 75 by 160 feet and oriented north-south. The scheme, as it emerged, was not for one large residence and four small residences, as the contract implied, but for four linked pavilions and a separate garage (see pl. 119). Accommodating, respectively, the living room, dining room/kitchen, and two separate bedrooms, these single-story pavilions were all the same size and shape—square with four corner columns supporting overhanging eaves. Only a variation in the paneled external envelope, a little reminiscent of the St. Jean housing in Quebec, suggests their different functions. A freehand sketch on the side of the site plan shows a pyramidal roof rising to a central lantern, but in the computer-generated perspective views, the roof is flat with a central clerestory (fig. 14.4). On one such view along the pathway running from the garage toward the living-room pavilion, Koenig has overdrawn the off-set rectangular paving slabs in red pencil and written, "Squares!"[35] There are no further drawings in the archive and satellite photographs of the site show the then existing building with additions. Hilre Hunt's love affair with steel-and-glass houses was never consummated.

Koenig's reputation, as it grew again in the 1990s, attracted other out-of-state clients. There is a survey drawing of a plot on Shelter Island in Gardiner's Bay, at the very eastern tip of Long Island, New York.[36] This came from Stuart Parr, a New York gallery owner who, in 2001, was looking for an architect to work with him on the design of a new house.[37] The resulting raised glass box, the eponymous Clearhouse, is credited to Michael P. Johnson of Cave Creek, Arizona, and Stuart

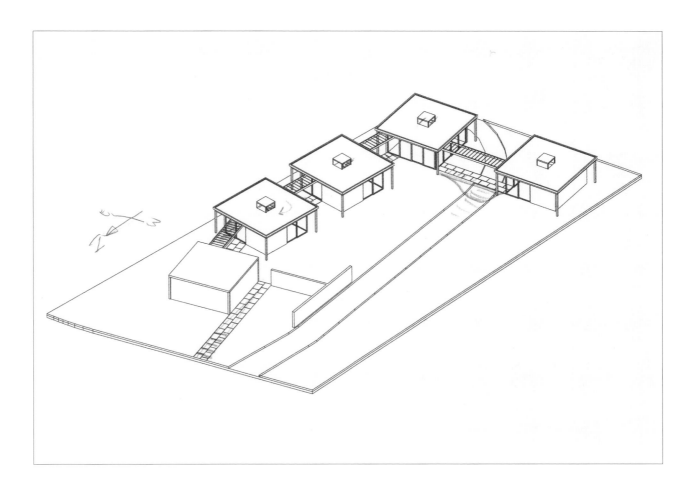

Fig. 14.4.
Frost/Hunt House, computer-generated model, 2000.

Parr Design, but, with different detailing, it could have been a design by Koenig. Also from New York came two opportunities to remodel apartments, the first for Nick Sands and the second for Kerri Scharlin.[38]

In December 1997, the New York art dealer Nick Sands flew out to Los Angeles to visit Koenig and also to see Case Study House 22, which was, as he later said in a handwritten thank-you note, "in many ways a dream come true!"[39] Enclosed with the note were some photographs of him and a female friend taken at the house at dusk. He wanted Koenig to remodel the New York apartment he was hoping to buy and offered to fly him out there to see it. A few months later, perhaps as a sweetener, Sands even offered to have Andy Warhol's chief collaborator and studio assistant, Gerard Malanga, do his portrait,[40] but Koenig had already declined, suggesting that they should wait until the sale had gone through.[41] It was not until the beginning of October 1998 that Sands obtained approval for the purchase from his bank, but by then he feared that he had lost his architect. "I ask for your understanding," he faxed on 9 October, "and hope that you will reconsider working for me."[42] Koenig must have replied immediately, and in the affirmative, for later the same day, Sands sent a second fax: "Many thanks for your message. I am breathing a sigh of relief as I was afraid I had lost you…whew!"[43] Koenig suggested waiting until the next summer, but Sands, anxious to get on with the job, offered once again to fly him to New York for a weekend to see the apartment. Failing that, he said he would film a walk-through on videotape so as to explain the space and then fly to Los Angeles himself to talk Koenig through it. Neither of these options, it seemed, appealed to Koenig, and the job went dead.

A little less than a year later, Sands wrote once more to say that, after living in the apartment for nine months, "the amount of square footage involved—a little over a thousand—does not justify the kind of project we had in mind."[44] His plan now was to buy the adjacent apartment and then have Koenig "do one large project and do it *right*...instead of some now and some later."[45] Sands clearly was a fan of Koenig: he kept James Steele and David Jenkins's recent book on Koenig on a night-stand next to his bed, and he did not want to lose his architect.[46] "I have followed the resurgence of your work in the popular press," he wrote, "reading articles in *House Beautiful, The New York Times, Echoes, Architectural Digest* and others. As you said to me the day we sat at your kitchen table, 'It's payback time!' I trust you are enjoying it."[47] Although he promised to keep Koenig informed as he moved forward with his plans, there is no further communication in the archive to suggest that he did.

Kerri Scharlin lived on Fifth Avenue, near Union Square, in Manhattan. On 21 November 1999, she wrote to Koenig, saying, "Your work has been an inspiration to me and has helped me imagine the possibilities of what our space could be."[48] Scharlin, her partner, Peter Klosowicz, and their daughter occupied three separate twelfth-floor apartments connected by a hallway and wished to bring them together as one cohesive home incorporating the external roof space. Scharlin sent Koenig a set of panoramic photographs of the apartments and the roof as well as an annotated floor plan. Koenig replied on 23 November: "It seems to be a challenge, which I like. It is also the kind of New York living space everyone dreams of."[49] Six days later, he wrote again with his ideas: "I would remove the existing walls, exposing the structure and determine, with my engineer, what has to be strengthened. Hopefully we can start with a clear space and really take advantage of the openness. I would also like to examine the possibility of opening the roof some place to accentuate the verti-cal—perhaps in conjunction with the roof development."[50] Koenig concluded by asking Scharlin for a "program," but no such document is to be found in the archive. Recent satellite photographs of the rooftop show that no improvements were made, and, in the absence of any further records in the archive, it must be assumed that this job did not go ahead either.

Closer to home, there were the possibilities of four new houses in California: one in Palm Springs, one near Santa Barbara, and two in Los Angeles. The first of these potential clients to contact Koenig was Nadir Safai, who, like Sands, had been reading Steele and Jenkins's book. On 14 August 1999, he wrote,

> I just finished your book cover to cover, so my mind may be racing a bit. About myself I was born in Hollywood and raised in Glendale. I then chose to go to USC and graduated in 91....Shortly thereafter I discovered architecture, primarily modern....My love of Palm Springs led me to consider buying a piece of land and building my first home there (this may be backward think-ing). This leads me to you. I don't really know where to begin. I love your ideas and designs. I would appreciate the opportunity to speak with you (this will allow me not to make this letter any longer as I feel I could go on forever).[51]

Koenig's response must have been positive, drawn, perhaps, by the Glendale and University of Southern California (USC) connections. A fortnight later, Safai sent him two site plans for plots in Palm Springs: one, his first choice, on Monte Vista Drive and the other on Cahuilla Road. Koenig then forwarded the plans to Tony Merchell in Palm Springs for an opinion. "Keep it under your hat until my client closes purchase," he wrote.[52] Safai, it would seem, never closed purchase, for the correspondence ends here. It was probably similar uncertainties about a site in the coastal community of Summerland, near Santa Barbara, that prevented the engineer and art collector Dr. J. W. Colin from building there. In January 2000, while pursuing site investigations, Colin sent Koenig a plan of plots around Evans Avenue. Then he wrote again to Koenig, in April, saying, "I finally got the info we needed. There is a 2nd fault line! . . . Please let me know if you feel you can put a home on the site whose cost would be in the $150/sqft area."[53] Although Koenig was never one to be put off by difficult sites, the price restriction might have been too hard to meet, for, once again, the correspondence retained in the archive ends.

While Nadir Safai was trying to purchase a plot of land in Palm Springs, Alan and Mary Anne Steinberger were pursuing a plot on the north side of Big Tujunga Canyon in the San Gabriel Mountains. Toward the end of September 1999, Alan sent Koenig a couple of maps to help identify the property and, on 30 September, directions for how to get there. "We're quite excited about the possibility of working with you!" he wrote, "(And I think you may find Mary Anne more knowledgeable about architecture than any layperson you've ever met!)."[54] The purchase, however, did not go well. By December, when he next wrote, Steinberger had spent $10,000 doing soil tests, and the seller was unwilling to split the costs or absorb them into the purchase price. During a site visit in October, Koenig had expressed his concerns about the impracticalities of the lower part of the site but seemed ambivalent about where to build. "The temperature and humidity is somewhat more pleasant down there," Alan observed.[55] "If you really think that spot would be lovely and merely a bit more expensive to build," he continued, "we'd consider going ahead with that test on our own. But if you see a laundry list of negatives, then we'll see if we can't find some other magical spot to build."[56] Koenig's response, which is not in the archive, must have equated to a laundry list, for here the correspondence ends.

Whereas neither Safai nor Colin nor the Steinbergers appear on Koenig's client index cards, Jefery and Pamela Levy do. They were added on 1 September 1999, and they paid a $5,000 retainer on 11 October, two days after signing an agreement for a new house, studio, and pool on a site on Woodrow Wilson Drive in the Hollywood Hills.[57] The next month, Koenig drew up a draft agreement to engage Joe Bavaro to provide interior design services as part of his team.[58] For this, Bavaro wanted a flat fee of $10,000 and $50 per hour for shopping tours with the clients.[59] Penciled notes from a morning telephone conversation give some idea of what the Levys had in mind: 18-foot ceilings, a stainless-steel kitchen, recessed and low-voltage lighting, a gym, and, because Jefery worked in the film industry, a mixing room and a preview room.[60] The Levys sent Koenig sketch plans showing how the house could be organized. It was to be a two-story, U-shaped pavilion approached centrally by a flight of steps. Although naive, these drawings, done on square-lined paper or on the back of discarded film scripts, give some clues to how the Levys saw their home (fig. 14.5). There were to be glass walls around the perimeter (except where the kitchen wall met the maid's room and bathroom), and floor-to-ceiling screens separating the interior spaces downstairs. Both the dining room and the den were to "soar" over the valley, and there was to be a centrally located fireplace in the living room. Water pools were to flank the entrance steps, and there was be an external patio to the rear. The Levys had clearly done their homework, for references to both of Koenig's Case Study Houses can be recognized in their proposals. However, this project, like so many others at this time, failed.

If what Nick Sands described as Koenig's "payback time" resulted in little more than a litany of incomplete or posthumous projects, the reasons might be found in the difficulties that had recently beset Koenig in the building of the Schwartz House. To the end of his life, he operated a small, almost one-man practice, and although he learned computer drafting techniques from his

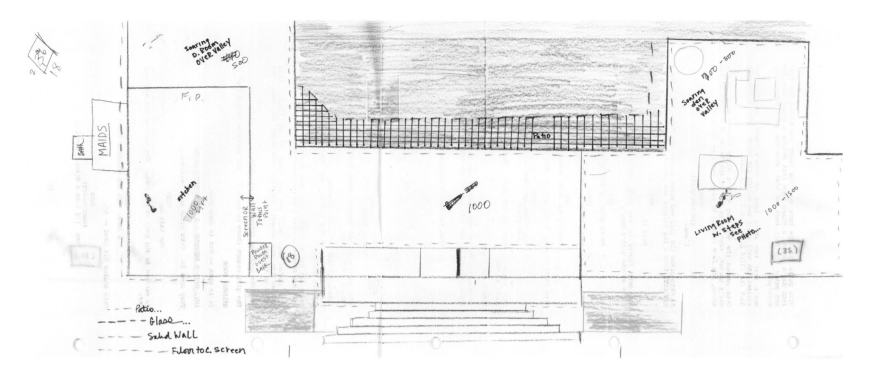

colleagues at USC,[61] the pressures and demands of the modern office seemed to have been too much for him. While building Case Study House 22 in 1960, his almost daily site visits had ensured that the demanding project had come to a satisfactory conclusion. But with the Schwartz House, no less complicated a building, the frequent if not incessant issuing of change orders and Koenig's slow response to urgent requests from the general contractor, Kemal Ramezani of R. G. West—as in the case of the spiral-stair treads—must have left him feeling greatly challenged. Nevertheless, his enthusiasm for architecture never waned, and every opportunity for designing a new house or an apartment was quickly seized upon. Whether or not it was the clients' decisions not to proceed cannot be said, but the very fact that almost none of these final commissions came to fruition during his lifetime would suggest that, as he approached seventy-five years of age, Koenig was recognizing the limits of his abilities. □

Fig. 14.5.
Jefery Levy's sketch plan for the Levy House, 1999.

# CHAPTER 15
# COOL TWICE

**NONDOMESTIC WORK**

This book's exploration of Pierre Koenig's archive demonstrates the great extent to which he was an architect of houses. There are, in fact, fewer than ten projects in the archive dating from after his move to the Dorothy Street office in 1959 that are not domestic or residential designs. Only one of them, the Electronic Enclosures Incorporated (EEI) Factory and Showroom in El Segundo, was built. Although the KYOR radio station building in Blythe, California, in 1958, provided little indication of the direction in which his architecture was soon to move (fig. 15.1), the EEI building, constructed nine years later, showed what could be achieved when his ideas were applied on a large scale.

Located on an awkward triangular plot of land between South Aviation Boulevard and the railway line, the EEI building, at 64,000 square feet, was Koenig's largest project. Of the original drawings, only the preliminary studies, dated September 1966 and marked "not for construction," remain in the archive. But they show very clearly how Koenig used the organization of space—perhaps a result of Kenneth Lind's influence—to address the problem. Apart from an early and undated scheme for a piano factory, in all probability a student project, there is nothing in the archive to suggest that Koenig had any experience with factory or production-line layout (see pl. 138).[1] Yet the solution he brought to the EEI building was very similar to that for the piano factory (see pl. 82). In both cases, the main production area was a rectangle of one-to-two proportions, through which the manufacturing and assembly process ran in a linear manner. At the piano factory, this was a five-stage process:[2]

1. humidity-controlled storage
2. preparation
3. action installation
4. assembly
5. finish

Whereas at EEI, it was more complicated but nevertheless as linear:[3]

1. raw material storage
2. shear
3. notch & punch
4. forming
5. welding
6. grind & finish
7. storage
8. preparation
9. painting

At the piano factory, the process moved around the outside of the space, while at EEI, in what was the preassembly area, it moved down the center, with storage and ancillary spaces to either side. Only the final assembly area, with its shipping office and loading bay, was located outside the linear plan. This part of the building stepped forward into the apex of the triangular site in four stages.

What made the EEI building work so well was Koenig's use of structure. The main factory floor was spanned by eight deep trusses set at 40-foot centers, which left the preassembly area free of

Fig. 15.1.
KYOR radio station, view from east, 1957.

columns while also providing habitable space within the depth of the truss. Whereas all manufacturing traffic was kept at ground level, staff and visitors approached the building from a ramped entrance at the north end that led to a mezzanine floor in the central core of the building between the preassembly and final-assembly areas. From there, stairs led up into the level of the trussed roof structure, where, above the final-assembly area, the display, sales, conference, accounting, design, and president's office were located (see pl. 83). Such an exploitation of structural space was quite innovative at the time and might be compared to the work of the Japanese Metabolists, specifically the Big Roof above the Festival Plaza at Expo '70 in Osaka or, later, European high-tech architecture as expressed at the Centre Georges Pompidou in Paris (1971–77). It is all the more regrettable, therefore, that Mike Jacobs, the president of EEI, chose to have the deep trusses replaced with lightweight, open-web joists.[4] Similarly, precast tilt-up concrete panels were substituted for the vertical steel decking that Koenig had specified for the exterior. However, none of the drawings describing this toned-down building remain in the archive.

Koenig had only recently begun to explore space and structure on a large scale with a medical building on Sunset Boulevard. Commissioned in April 1964 by Dr. Robert Franklyn—a celebrity "beauty surgeon" and the author of, among other books, *On Developing Bosom Beauty* and *The Art of Staying Young*[5]—the building was, in effect, an inverted pyramid held within a framework of fire-proofed steel. "As the structure gets larger as it goes up," Koenig wrote in his promotional statement, "each succeeding floor protects the floor under it from sun and rain.... As each level supports a floor load except the roof, the floor structural system ends at the top floor level and the roof support is a different but related system."[6] Since Franklyn wanted the greatest amount of natural light possible for the consulting rooms, Koenig located them on the top floor of the building, cantilevered out on long arms (fig. 15.2). It was an ambitious building, both spatially and structurally but, in the end, was never built. Instead, Franklyn commissioned a much smaller, circular building for the adjacent plot from the Brazilian architect Oscar Niemeyer.[7]

Franklyn was a good client for Koenig, even though only one of his commissions was realized. He seemed to encourage in Koenig more daring architectural solutions. A year before Koenig designed the Franklyn Medical Building, he had designed and built a poolside cabana for Franklyn and wife Wilma's 60-acre horse ranch on Potrero Road in Oxnard. This was to be an umbrella-like structure, 36 feet in diameter, with a steel frame, fly screens around the outside, and rough-hewn red-cedar shingles on the roof (see pl. 71).[8] In October 1969, Franklyn commissioned the survey of a leveled hilltop site in Thousand Oaks where he wanted to build a restaurant for his daughter Apryl.[9] For this exposed site, Koenig produced a number of steel-frame solutions, some circular, some octagonal, and some frankly awkward, before eventually deciding, in January 1977, upon an octagonal scheme to accommodate three-hundred diners and as many parking spaces.[10] The colored perspective drawing prepared to go with the plan shows an elegant but hardly discrete steel-and-glass structure with exposed roof trusses and a raised central clerestory. It was not in the locally preferred Spanish style, and it never, in the end, received a building permit (fig. 15.3).

Koenig was a modernist through and through, and to have compromised in such a situation is not what he would have done. Even his 1963 design for a mosque, perhaps as traditional a building type as can be imagined, was rational and regular, with a reinforced-concrete frame and brick infill panels. The plan, first conceived, quite literally, on the back of an envelope, comprised a grid of six 30-foot-square bays, with the rounded mihrab on the east wall. The building was surrounded by a

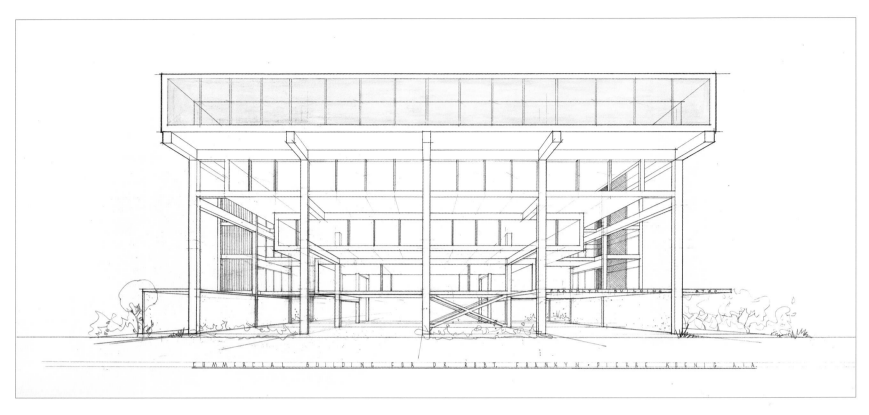

COMMERCIAL BUILDING FOR DR. ROBT. FRANKLYN · PIERRE KOENIG A.I.A.

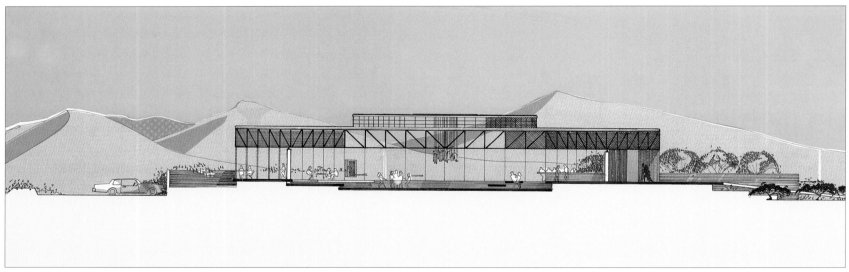

Fig. 15.2.
Franklyn Medical Building, view from northwest, 1965.

Fig. 15.3.
Franklyn Dinner Club, view from west, 1976.

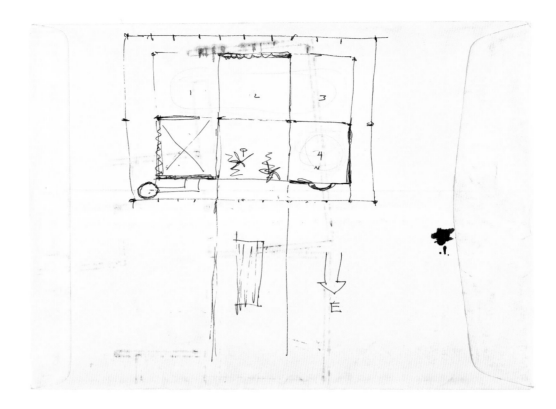

Fig. 15.4.
Mosque, sketch plan on envelope, 1963.

colonnade, set 10 feet out, supporting an overreaching roof, through the southeast corner of which rose the freestanding minaret (fig. 15.4). Although commissioned by the Muslim Association of America and funded by the newly independent state of Kuwait, it was never built.[11] In 1963, the same year that Koenig drew plans for the building, Kuwait held its first parliamentary elections, became a member of the United Nations, and was finally recognized by Iraq, which had until then maintained territorial claims on the country, its sea access, and its oil—as it was to do once again twenty-seven years later. Perhaps, amid these political upheavals, the funding for the mosque got overlooked.

## PHILOSOPHY

Koenig's choice of reinforced concrete makes the mosque unique in his oeuvre. Although he is largely associated with steel-frame buildings, he maintained an open mind as to the choice of material. As he said, "I don't want to give you the idea that I believe there is only one valid material. I say only that one should work within the limitations of the particular material. I object to wooden buildings that look like they should be steel buildings and *visa versa.* By knowing the limitations of a material, we are able to use the material to its maximum capabilities."[12]

This brief statement comes from a three-page set of handwritten notes on yellow legal-size paper that were prepared, most probably, for a lecture. There is, however, no indication of the intended audience or when the notes were written. These pages represent one of about ten similar sets of lecture notes or position statements contained in the archive. Some have titles or give the name of the intended audience, or indicate by their content to whom they were addressed, but few have dates. Apart from those lectures, which were purely reminiscences—such as "The Way We Were USC Architecture in the 40's,"[13] delivered on 10 April 1995—most of the lecture notes or position statements deal with industrialization or prefabrication, the responsibility of the architect, the role of the building industry, and the attitude of the public. A number of ideas are rehearsed more than once, which, while this suggests a consistency in Koenig's thinking, makes it more difficult in the absence of dates to identify a development of thought. So where does one start?

In the archive, there is one small, torn, and tatty piece of paper typed in upper case (as were most of Koenig's typescripts) that gives a brief and succinct, if incomplete, position statement:

1. WHAT I AM DOING:
    NOT WITH STEEL CO.'S
    NOT A STYLE BUT WITH A MEAN
    ANY MATERIAL O.K. IF USED PROPERLY
    PLAN IS STILL MOST IMPORTANT
    PRE-FAB CURTAIN WALLS
2. PHILOSOPHY:
    NOT HAVE TO BE PERSONAL EXPRE
    KEEP EMOTIONS UNDER CONTROL
    AS RELATED TO OTHERS PUBLICLY
    TO RAISE TOTAL ENVIRONMENT NOT
    ISOLATED EXAMPLES.

    WE HAVEN'T TRIED IT YET
    ONE MAN DOESN'T DO IT–TIMES
    REJECT BECAUSE CAN"T DO.

3. HOW I DESIGN
    HISTORY (EXPOSED, DECK, ETC.
    PRELIMINARYS
    SIMPLICITY FOR 2 REASONS
        ECONOMY & DESIGN[14]

The idea this contains—a meaningful, plan-generated, prefabricated architecture that is controlled in appearance and responsive to context and climate—weaves through the various lecture notes and position statements, three of which stand out. One, already quoted above, is the hand-written lecture on yellow legal paper;[15] the second is a single sheet with the simple title "PIERRE KOENIG," which, by its indirect reference to the "sun-control devices" at the Iwata House, dates probably from 1965 or 1966;[16] and the third, probably of a similar or slightly earlier date due to its references to the psychologist Walter Bailey and the limited extent of Koenig's own practice, is a five-page marked-up typescript of a lecture.[17] None of these indicate their intended audience or their actual date of delivery, but their arguments are similar, if not sometimes identical. Inasmuch as a few passing remarks help date these papers to the early to mid-1960s, they could be seen as a position statement following the success of two Case Study Houses.

In the early 1960s, few architects were involved in mass production, and, as Koenig then complained, it had become the business of the large building companies, who failed to understand the value of the architect and for whom production planning was usually done by their own engineers.[18] "It is the error of the Detroit type of thinking," he wrote on the yellow legal paper, "that produces machine made items without aforethought or design considerations." "More intelligent manufacturers," he added, "employ architects to assist in producing manufactured items."[19]

He did not blame the public for being uncritical about their architecture; rather, he blamed the housing developers for providing them with a lack of choice: "The public cannot choose insofar as they (the public) can only make decisions from amongst items shown to them and always this selection is quite limited. The developer decides to build three types of 'Cinderella' houses and comes to the conclusion later that people like 'Cinderella' houses because that's all he's sold."[20] Koenig saw housing as the most direct and most challenging need in the country, but he argued that it would not be resolved until it was "proven over and over again that a really good contemporary factory produced house can be a pleasure to live in and will be a lot less expensive than the handi-crafted houses of old."[21] Recognizing that, for many, mass production meant repetition, he wrote, "You don't have to have mass production to have repitition. We have look alike things now whether they are mass produced or not. The basic problem," he argued, "is once again whether or not the product is well designed in the first place. There are too many advantages to mass production to ignore it. We must accept mass production but we must insist on well designed products."[22] Rather than inducing monotony (as opposed to repetition) in the built environment, Koenig argued that mass production would lead instead to diversity: "I do *not* believe that standardization of building activity will necessarily induce monotony. We have lots of monotony now, at least in the U.S., with everyone using the same techniques and the same forms. Production can lead to multi parts that lead to multi forms. With a wide variety of parts, an infinite variation of form can take place."[23]

In addition to criticizing the large building companies for failing to make adequate use of architects, he criticized the architecture profession for its inability to adapt to new conditions, resulting in a loss of position within the building industry: "As I see it the problem is not mass production but the inability to be able to cope with change in regard to mass production or any other means to architecture. Students and young architects must be trained to be able to deal with change in an organized manner or eventually there will be no architecture."[24]

In 1963, Koenig took the argument to a meeting of the American Institute of Architects (AIA),[25] explaining how he saw each commission as "a duality—solving the immediate problems of the client and at the same time to create the prototype for mass production." "Each job," he explained, "in its own way has the ability to encompass the needs of many people. Each job is a statement of what can or cannot be done within the limitations of mass production and standard components."[26] This he demonstrated, both in kind and in content, with the exhibition pavilion he had recently designed for the Bethlehem Steel Company, in which a display of his steel houses was shown. Made from bolted steel sections and intended to be easily transported and quickly assembled, it had had its first exposure at the 31st Annual Garden and Home Show in Oakland, California, on 19–21 April and was now on display at the Construction Industries Exposition and Home Show in Los Angeles.[27] In a statement headed "Commercial Exhibit for Bethlehem Steel Company," he wrote, "This travelling exhibit is a successful creation of an atmosphere of the interior of a steel-framed house. It is also a solution to the problem of maximum space utilization."[28] The intention of the pavilion, as the client's brief said, was to "show maximum possibilities in the use of steel for residences and to develop a demountable display unit that could be easily assembled with a minimum of skilled labor."[29] In the archive, there is, in pencil, a rough assembly drawing together with an eight-stage Field Erection Order (fig. 15.5).[30]

In the third and longest of these lecture notes and position statements, Koenig summarized his position: "To me, a building is significant if it fulfills the function of use and beauty (and this is the

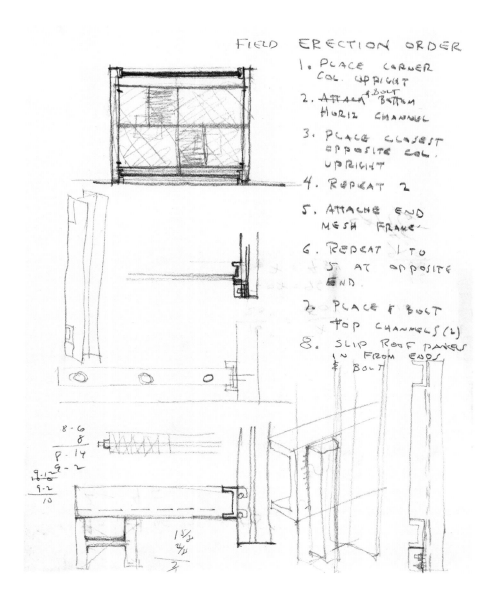

big and) makes use of or contributes to modern technology & well being. This then is the framework of my work and my endeavor: to create through the advantages of modern industrialism, a high level of physical environment for all through example and education."[31]

Koenig remained consistent to this philosophy, and almost thirty years later, in 1991, when addressing students at the Harvard University Graduate School of Design, he told them, "I view industrialization as a freedom giving tool. I use the industrialization process help to produce architecture, to take advantage of its capabilities, to do things that cannot be done by hand-crafted methods. To quote Barbara Goldstein: 'Science in the service of Architecture.'"[32]

When in 1988 Koenig told Fred Riebe, "Most people think I am dead," it was not without feeling.[33] His client index cards show how slow business was. Since 1983, when Frank Stuermer of the Los Angeles Department of City Planning had come to him asking for a house in Hawaii, his only new clients had been either the owners of his older houses, such as Della and Gary Rollé, Frank South, and Edson Newquist, or his neighbor on Dorothy Street, Arlette Mosher, who had asked him to do a few small domestic jobs. In 1984, the Irish actor Pierce Brosnan, then starring in the televi-

Fig. 15.5.
Bethlehem Steel Company Pavilion, Field Erection Order, 1963.

sion series *Remington Steele,* and his wife, Cassandra Harris, met with Koenig, and he added their names to a client index card. But no retainer was paid, and there is no evidence in the archive of any work.[34] The truth is that architectural fashion, now in the guise of postmodernism, had left Koenig and his philosophy behind. The closest he ever came to playing the postmodernist's game, for it was a game, was when, in 1986, Jeffrey Klawans (his one other new client) commissioned him to design sliding steel gates at the rear of his shop on Melrose Place.[35] Although the gates themselves were clean and straightforward, Koenig added ornamental lanterns to the top of the masonry piers.[36] But such is the nature of West Hollywood.

## RICHARD NEUTRA

By the end of 1961, Case Study House 21 had been published twenty-three times, by Koenig's own count.[37] As well as featuring five times in *Arts & Architecture,* it had appeared in a number of professional and popular magazines, including the *LA Examiner, Sunset, House & Home, L'architecture d'aujourd'hui, Zodiac,* and *Bauen+Wohnen.* Case Study House 22, although more recent, was also already widely published. Koenig, therefore, should not have been altogether surprised when on 19 April 1962, Richard Neutra, his former design-studio critic from the University of Southern California (USC), wrote to him, saying, "I wanted you to know how much I enjoyed seeing your work. Would you like to visit with me some time?"[38] There is no record in the archive to indicate where Neutra saw Koenig's work or to suggest the immediate outcome of this invitation, which might have been no more than a friendly chat, although it is more likely that Neutra had his eye on Koenig for a potential role in his office.

The situation was brought to a head a year later when, on 27 March 1963, Neutra's home and small office on Silver Lake Boulevard was destroyed by fire. Although business could continue from the main office on nearby Glendale Boulevard, Neutra must have been in touch with Koenig once again with the aim of engaging assistance to cope with the undiminishing workload if not the rebuilding of the practice following the disaster of the fire. Less than three weeks after the fire, on Easter Monday, Neutra wrote to Koenig from Grand Rapids, Michigan:

> Just before leaving, I had, as so often, all sorts of offers reaching at least part of California and the middle West.
>
> The easter weekend was not a good time to talk with my associates of many years or yourself, although I enjoyed conversing with your nine year old Randy who told me of your two year old whom you train to be an architect! Like tightrope dancing, architecture, balancing with clients, bankers and building inspectors, should be trained early.
>
> Perhaps you are good enough to let me know what, besides domestic design, has held your interest and what range of working drawings you may feel comfortable to tackle. Probably smaller projects might be a good start, but how small and what kinds.
>
> Perhaps you are so good to send me a list to show it to our officers.[39]

It was an offer with which Koenig was not wholly comfortable, and, three days later, he wrote to John Entenza asking for a little free advice:

> Richard Neutra has asked me to associate with him. He is not too clear in explaining how but it sounds like it would be on a particular job basis. He has other architects on jobs with him from

time to time but they are usually relatively unknown and on their first job. He wants me to move into his "Foundation" which is fine as I need an office badly except it's on the other side of town and away from my clients. Neutra also wants me to teach nights at his "Foundation" but I have a contract with USC which I value highly.

I suppose I'm really concerned about losing my identity under the hand of this overwhelming personality but this may be irrational, I don't know.

I would appreciate a word from you on this. Mr. Neutra is away now but he will be back in a week so I have until then. He is very anxious.[40]

A week later, Entenza, now director of the Graham Foundation in Chicago, wrote a candid reply advocating caution:

Naturally he is terribly affected by the consequences of the fire, but deeply concerned about his future work and the image he will leave behind him. He needs new blood; new muscles, and if that is to be you, I must say that you must be careful to retain your own identity, and to work in terms of realities. Otherwise, before you realize it, you will be a creature, and be lost in the legend. I am sure that there is are practical and useful consideration from your point of view, and if you can limit your participation to that, the association might work out. . . .

I know this is very tempting, and it might very well be very good for you. If you feel you can maintain your own identity—and I mean *really* retain it—it could be a productive association. However, do remember that these are the last few years of a great career of a man who is determined to fill out his own image, and I think that is the first and only consideration involved. This is understandable and courageous on his part, but be sure that you can handle any consequences to you as an individual, and to you as a professional.[41]

Although he had little work at the time—only the Beagles House was on the drawing board[42]— Koenig listened to Entenza's advice and did not take up the offer. He valued not only his independence and identity but also, as he said, his new role at USC.

## USC

As a single practitioner, Koenig had, since the early 1960s, been employed at USC, first as an instructor and then as an assistant professor of architecture.[43] The decision to join USC must have been not only to supplement his income but also to give him independence and a freedom of approach, something his growing architectural reputation needed.

During a teaching career that lasted about forty years, Koenig contributed widely to the USC School of Architecture. In undated lecture notes held in the archive, he recalls his early intentions: "When I came to the Dept. of Arch. in 1962, I came with a commitment to teach fundamentals. Having practiced architecture at the fundamental level and working within strict limits I looked forward to extending my comprehension in these areas of interest."[44] The programs he subsequently taught reflected this pragmatic structure-and-construction-driven approach. In his Building Science (205) class, he asked his students "to identify and analyze an example of an outstanding historic building that is known for its' structural clarity and resultant excellent design."[45] A list of twelve buildings was offered, ranging from the Gothic cathedrals of the Île de France to the Crystal Palace in London, the AEG Turbine Factory in Berlin, and the John Hancock Building in Chicago. All were buildings that were structurally expressive. "Find out why your building was built," he told his students, "and how it was built and how it solved the problem."[46] For the studio reviews of student work, he invited architects and engineers, including Jim Tyler and Dimitry Vergun, to join him.[47] In Materials and Methods of Building Construction (211), he lectured on wood, masonry, metal, and concrete, as well as roofing, glass, cladding, and interiors,[48] and in Graphic Communication (490), he taught students shadow projection and trained them "to think in three dimensional graphic terms."[49]

Koenig's greatest contribution to the School of Architecture came through his interest in natural forces design. This had begun with the arrival in 1963 of Ralph Knowles, who introduced him to phenomenology and the use of natural forces as organizing determinates. As a design teacher, Koenig realized that if the parameters were tightly set, then a student who could work successfully within those confines could do so in any situation. As he put it, "The more stringent the limits the wider the range of possibilities."[50] By altering the number of determinates, he could set design programs to suit students of any level. "By adding a minimum of only two determinates every year for the 6 years a student is in school," he argued, "he will have dealt with more variables than the average architect does in a lifetime."[51] This is how one third-year program was set out:

SITE WITH DETERMINATE LIGHT
SITE WITH DETERMINATE SLOPE
A MATERIAL WITH THE DETERMINATE GRAVITY
PEOPLE WITH THE DETERMINATE GROUP

WE WILL COPE WITH THESE SETS ONE AT A TIME AT THE RESEARCH AND ANALYTICAL LEVELS AND THEN TOGETHER AT THE ANALYTICAL AND SYNTHETIC LEVELS.

SUN IN RELATION TO SIMPLE ELEMENT PRODUCES SPACE
SITE AT VARIABLE SLOPE & ORIENTATION PRODUCES CHANGE[52]

It can be seen, then, that the Chemehuevi project, with its variable housing units and extreme climatic conditions, was the perfect vehicle for this approach to design teaching.

Following his work with Konrad Wachsmann as assistant director of the Institute of Building Research, Koenig set up the Natural Forces Laboratory, complete with a heliodon, a 30-foot-long wind tunnel, and a shake table for earthquake simulation. Here, he taught Natural Forces Design (307, 418, 199, and 599), heading the 1992 reading list with Robert Mark's *Light, Wind, and Structure: The Mystery of the Master Builders* (1990).[53] In 1980, he applied for sabbatical leave to document the data collected using the wind tunnel for various research projects.[54] The leave was approved for the first semester of 1981.[55] He applied for another sabbatical leave in the second semester of 1996 to further investigate, with new measuring devices, the data collected from the wind tunnel.[56] The archive does not indicate if this leave was granted nor does it contain any of the research findings.

In the late 1990s, Koenig, now well into his seventies, developed a course that should have already been a permanent feature in the architecture curriculum at USC: History of Modern Architecture in Southern California (499). On 4 August 1998, he sent Julius Shulman a fax:

Although my new course, "History of Modern Architecture in Southern California" is not to start until January, it's not too early to start planning. . . . I am counting on you for support in this most important project. As we both know this course is long over-due and will help to put Los Angeles modern architecture back in the hearts and minds of young people for long time to come.

I hope you are as excited about this project as I am.[57]

In addition to asking Shulman for a large number of 35 mm color slides, he invited him, along with Eames Demetrios, Don Hensman, Ed Killingsworth, and Jim Tyler to lecture.[58] Not long after the course started in January 1999, Elaine Sewell, A. Quincy Jones's widow, wrote to him: "I was delighted to hear of the progress you are making in the shaping of your new course at USC. It must be stimulating for you to add new dimensions to your work."[59] To accompany the course, Koenig published two CDs comprising two hundred photographs of modern architecture in Southern California.[60] Of his own houses, he included Koenig 1, Lamel, Squire, Koenig 2, and Schwartz, but excluded both of the Case Study Houses. These were included in the program as house tours.

As his annual records show, Koenig played a full role in the School of Architecture at USC.[61] Rising from assistant professor, he gained tenure and was eventually made a full professor of architecture on 1 September 1997.[62] On this occasion, Dean Robert Timme wrote to, among others, Neil Jackson asking for "a candid statement that specifically addresses itself to . . . the quality and potential of his scholarship and its impact on the field."[63] It seemed a somewhat redundant question. Although, at the age of almost seventy-two, this promotion was late in coming, the following year he was named a distinguished professor of architecture. As the provost, Lloyd Armstrong, said in his congratulatory letter, this was an award made to the very few professors who have brought special renown to the university, and it was in recognition of both "the impact your work has had on the field of architecture in the United States and the high esteem in which you are held internationally" and "your reputation as an important guiding influence on your students for thirty years, the personal vitality you have brought to the university community, and your role as a catalyst for social change through the designs you created for a new modern lifestyle in the 1950's and 1960's."[64] In the same year, the USC School of Architecture gave Koenig a Distinguished Alumni Award and, posthumously, named a lecture hall after him.

**RECOGNITION**

An invitation to speak at Harvard University in 1991 was one of many similar invitations in the years following the *Blueprints for Modern Living: History and Legacy of the Case Study Houses* exhibition at the Museum of Contemporary Art's Temporary Contemporary in Los Angeles. Earliest among these, and coincident with the exhibition, was the invitation to speak at California State Polytechnic University (Cal Poly), Pomona.[65] In June 1990, the San Francisco Museum of Modern Art invited him to participate in their fall lecture series, *The Aesthetics of Technology,* alongside Charles Correa, Jean Nouvel, Richard Rogers, and Sir Jack Zunz.[66] It was a heady cast. In October 1991, Koenig's work was shown in the *Los Angeles—City on the Move* exhibition at the fourth Salon international de l'architecture in Milan, a show that was presented in Los Angeles a year later.[67] In March 1994, he was included in the exhibition *100 Projects/100 Years* at the National Convention of the AIA to celebrate the centenary of the Los Angeles chapter.[68] Eighteen months later, in September 1995, he contributed drawings to Neil Jackson's exhibition *Steel Houses,* held at the RIBA Heinz Gallery in London.[69] That October, the Los Angeles Conservancy included his house on Dorothy Street in their *Architects' Own Homes Tour* series, and Koenig joined the subsequent panel discussion at the Pacific Design Center.[70] He was always generous with his time and willing to contribute: "Received your FAX regarding the renderings," he wrote to Jackson, "Your wish is my command."[71] More lecture invitations from schools of architecture followed: the University of Texas and a second from Cal Poly Pomona, in 1997; Arizona State University and yet another from Cal Poly Pomona, in 1999; and, in 2000, the AIA Student Forum 2000.[72]

The success of the restoration of Case Study House 21 seems to have attracted a different audience. In March 2000, Koenig received an invitation from Thomas Jester of the United States Department of the Interior inviting him to participate in a keynote panel discussion at the international conference *Preserving the Recent Past II* to be held that October in Philadelphia. In that same month, he participated in the series *Architecture L.A. at the Hammer* held at the University of California, Los Angeles's Hammer Museum.[73] "It was great!" the museum director Ann Philbin wrote on the bottom of her thank-you letter.[74] Then, at the beginning of November, the National Trust for Historic Preservation held its National Preservation Conference 2000 in Los Angeles. Delegates visited Case Study House 22, and Koenig signed copies of James Steele and David Jenkins's book, although perhaps not as many as hoped due to other distractions.[75] "In future," Renée Harrison, the conference coordinator wrote, "we will schedule fewer activities during the book-signings."[76] In April 2001, Koenig went up the coast to the AIA Monterey Design Conference at Pacific Grove. In a program that included Michael Graves, Craig Hodgetts, and Rem Koolhaas,[77] Koenig delivered a lecture, "Modernism in CA: Our Legacy and Our Future." Following the event, Amy Eliot, the conference chair, wrote to thank him, commenting, "Your presentation received great reviews!"[78] But for Koenig, it was business as well as pleasure: he came away with 13.5 learning units of continuing education credit.[79]

With the newfound exposure came the awards, not just those for buildings but also those for achievement.[80] In the fifteen years after 1967, Koenig received no awards at all. Then, in 1983, he was named as one of the best two hundred architects at the AIA 200/2000 Awards, and, in the following year, when Los Angeles played host to the Olympics, the city's chapter of the AIA selected him as an "Olympic architect whose work has been deemed outstanding."[81]

It was not until the 1990s, however, that the awards really flooded in. In 1996, the California Council of the AIA gave him the Maybeck Award "in recognition of outstanding lifelong achievement in architectural design."[82] The Pacific Design Center presented him with the Star of Design for Lifetime Achievement in Architecture Award in 1998, and, the following year, he received the AIA Los Angeles Gold Medal Citation, "the highest honor that the Chapter may bestow."[83] In 2000, he accepted the Gold Medal Lifetime Achievement Award from the Tau Sigma Delta Society of Architects and Landscape Architects and, perhaps claiming recognition where it was due, a Distinguished Alumni Award from Pasadena City College. These were all Los Angeles or California awards, but that is not to diminish them: after all, the population of California in 2000 was almost 34 million. That same year, he was elevated onto the world stage, with an honorary fellowship of the Royal Institute of British Architects (RIBA), and then, in 2001, was recognized on the national stage, as a finalist for the National Design Awards.

The attempt to secure Koenig a RIBA honorary fellowship began in 1996, the year in which he won the Maybeck Award, when Neil Jackson, himself a member of the RIBA, nominated Koenig for the honor.[84] That nomination was unsuccessful.[85] A second attempt was made by Jackson in 1998, this time supported by a letter from Sir Norman Foster. "I agree whole heartedly," Foster wrote, "with everything that you state in support of Pierre Koenig. Like many of my generation I was influenced by his seminal works—particularly the case study houses. More recently I had the opportunity to see his own house to which you also refer. It is refreshing to see the same continuity of approach which in the context of the LA environment is still as fresh and valid as ever."[86]

The selection committee did not meet until early 1999. In anticipation of this, Koenig forwarded a copy of Steele and Jenkins's book for the committee's consideration and eventual deposit in the RIBA Library.[87] However, when the meeting convened, it was found that, due to a recent widening of membership of the RIBA to include, among others, members of the AIA, Koenig was no longer eligible for an honorary fellowship. Julie Grover from the president's office wrote to explain the situation: "I can report however that the matter was discussed in some detail by the Committee and consequently a paper will be submitted to the next Council meeting on 17 March to address the problem. The Committee therefore hope that by next year, Pierre Koenig's name can once again automatically come forward for consideration by the Committee."[88] The committee was true to its word: on 6 April 2000, Alex Reid, the director general, wrote to Koenig to say that the president proposed to nominate him to the RIBA Council for election as an honorary fellow of the Institute.[89] On 18 May, Reid wrote to Koenig again to say that, at a meeting held on the previous day, the council had elected him an honorary fellow.[90]

Koenig was delighted. A draft copy of his acceptance letter remains in the archive: "It is with great pleasure that I accept the Royal Institute of British Architects honorary fellowship and the international recognition that the award brings to my work. I want to thank Neil Jackson and Sir Norman Foster for their steadfast advocacy on my behalf. resolute."[91] On 3 June 2000, he sent a fax to Jackson:

> I checked my records and found you first submitted my name to the RIBA in 1996! It's hard to believe it's been that long. A big thank you doesn't seem enough but here goes: THANK YOU. I guess Sir Norman Foster had to give them a nudge at the end, which I appreciate very much but you did all of the work on this long road.[92]

The awards ceremony, which Koenig did not attend due as much as anything to the distance involved, was held at the Banqueting House in Whitehall, London, on 18 October 2000. Honorary fellowships were awarded to four other international architects—Ricardo Legoretta, Kjell Lund, Jo Noero, and Peter Zumthor—but the main event was the award of the Royal Gold Medal to Frank Gehry.[93] It had been a long road to this particular evening not only for Koenig but also for his sponsors. In his absence, Koenig asked Jackson to receive the award for him.

The last award documented in the archive is the Cooper-Hewitt, National Design Museum's Architecture Design Award for 2001, which is part of their annual National Design Awards program.[94] This was the second year of the awards, and Koenig was short-listed with the New York design practice Asymptote and the architect and theorist Peter Eisenman. No three finalists could have been more different. Koenig did not win—the prize went to Eisenman—but he did attend the awards reception at the White House in July 2002, where Laura Bush, the awards' honorary patron, made an address. "Design," she said, "in all its disciplines, is the world's greatest facilitator—it allows us to enjoy life and all of its pursuits."[95] Koenig would have concurred.

The arrival of awards, invitations, and celebrity clients that characterized the last fifteen years of Koenig's life show a remarkable revival of fortune. Throughout a fifty-year career, he had, as Foster observed, maintained "the same continuity of approach . . . as fresh and valid as ever."[96] The trajectory of Koenig's architectural career was very much a straight line largely independent of the undulating wave of architectural fashion, although the two overlapped for a few years at the end of the 1950s and once again over thirty years later. On the second occasion, *Time* magazine could write without hyperbole, "The current renaissance in midcentury modernism is particularly sweet for Koenig, 73, who has lived long enough to become cool twice."[97]

## INDETERMINACY

There are perhaps two ways of looking at Pierre Koenig's career: The first is as a struggle against the changing whims of architectural fashion, during which there were two peaks, his Case Study Houses and his latter-day recognition, separated by troughs of lean years during which his teaching at USC and the opportunities to revisit his earlier buildings sustained him. It is an experience not unfamiliar to practitioners who work alone. The second way is more characteristic of the man and suggests a strength of mind and resoluteness born of his wartime experience. As he said, "You take chances. You do things you wouldn't ordinarily."[98] This was apparent from the beginning in his single-minded obsession with production houses. "I have always tried to do real buildings," he told an AIA audience in 1963, "buildings that are what they purport to be, without fantasy or romance."[99] Whether this was the Burwash House, published in *Arts & Architecture* as a "low-cost production house," or Case Study House 21, the intention was the same.[100] "Each steel house that I produced was a prototype for a mass-production program," he wrote. "Some examples are identical frames with varying interiors and there is one tract. Most are thought of as 'custom' houses. Most of my work is now concerned with the extension of the pre-fabrication method in terms of producing the most variation with the minimum of parts and the maximum economy."[101] Case Study House 21, as he later said, was "the perfect example of what you can do. Perfect. It's non-site-specific whereas Case Study House 22 is site specific. I had no intention of producing that again. But 21, it can go anywhere and it can make any kind of a house."[102]

Case Study House 22 is famous, ultimately, not because of its architecture but because of its photograph. This concerned Koenig considerably—not that the house was famous but that the continual revenue that it generated went not to him but to Julius Shulman and to Buck and Carlotta Stahl. There were no "royalties" in the building for him. Even before the house was finished, Koenig had drawn up a contract to be signed by the Stahls and Bethlehem Steel that stated, "Pierre Koenig, AIA, shall receive full credit as the architect each and every time the photographs are used in advertising or are offered for public showing in periodicals or exhibits."[103] In the same way, the quick sale and resale of Case Study House 21, once the house had been restored at the end of the 1990s, generated a tidy profit for its sequential owners. But when interviewed in 2003, Koenig could only be phlegmatic: "Everybody has gained something from it," he laughed. "The architect never gets very much out of these things, you know. . . . The architects get nothing but the notoriety, and I can't complain about that because with the two Case Study Houses, 22 and 21, they've been all over the world."[104]

Even if his late-flowering success brought him little financial reward and, as has been shown, little new work, it did bring him new admirers. The fan letters that followed the publication of Steele and Jenkins's book in 1998 must have been rewarding, for they are carefully filed in the archive. "I must confess I shed a few tears over your book," wrote Edward Allen, an architect from South Natick, Massachusetts. "There were so many reasons to do so. In looking at its pages, I realized how much more completely your work had influenced me during my student days than I had remembered. . . . Your name was magic to me then. . . . As a student, I would have given anything to have a career exactly like yours."[105] But it was not just the book that brought plaudits. A few months later, on 26 December 1999, Hassan Cham sent Koenig a fax with the subject line "Impressed":

> Happy holidays to you. I am from a country called he Gambia with very little marvellous architectural pieces of work. Your work came to me after watching a program on American homes that aired on cable TV in the Takoma Park, MD.
>
> I knew about Frank Lloyd Wright but never heard about you till today. Well, I am very thankful to have discovered your art..Steel homes. The most appealing to me being your Stahl house Design or Case Study House 22. Very impressive.[106]

Koenig was now in good company.

The archive reveals much about Koenig, yet, in many ways, little of his private life. Koenig's first marriage, to Merry Sue Thompson, ended in 1959, and the following year, he married Gaile Elodie Carson, with whom he had a son, Jean Pierre, in 1961. It was during the fifteen years of this marriage that he became politically active, joining the American Civil Liberties Union (1966, 1967), the Planning and Conservation League for Legislative Action (1966, 1967), the American Association for the United Nations (1966), and the United Nations Association of the USA (1967, 1968, and 1969).[107] His thinking was clearly liberal, but there is no evidence of him being a registered Democrat or, less likely, a Republican. It is doubtful that it was the political events in Paris in May 1968 that drew him to France that year, probably his first visit since the war, but his passport, issued just a few months earlier, bears entry stamps for London and Paris that July and August, and, for the same trip, he obtained an international driving permit. His next passport, issued in 2000, bears no foreign-entry stamps at all.[108] Perhaps he, like many Californians, felt no great need to travel abroad. As a young man at home in Santa Monica, he enjoyed watersports, was a member of the California Council of Diving Clubs, and became a keen sport fisherman.[109] By 1961, he was an active member of the Santa Monica Sea Lancers, promoting lectures—such as those by Billy Anderson on "Diving in Hawaii" and by Don Turner on "Porpoises"—and diving adventures, including a trophy dive from the ship the *Tom Boy,* a beach meet and clam dive at Zuma Beach, and a weekend dive at Refugio State Beach.[110] In March 2003, with his diving days long behind him, he received a letter and a selection of old diving photographs from one of the Sea Lancers, Dick Schreiber, a retired orthopedic surgeon who was still living in his beach house at Point Dume, Malibu. "For a long time," Schreiber wrote, "we have watched your professional success with pleasure, via the occasional story in the newspaper."[111] Another of Koenig's interests, ever since his childhood in San Francisco, was railroads, and in 1976, he attended the UCLA Extension evening lecture series *Railroads: The Romance and the Reality.* On the feedback form, he rated it "Very Informative."[112] In his sixties and feeling perhaps too old for scuba diving, Koenig turned his attention again to railroads, becoming a supporter of the National Railroad Museum[113] and a keen collector of model trains.[114]

Koenig's other great passion, which was reflected in his architecture, was music. In the new house he built on Dorothy Street with his third wife, Gloria Kaufman, whom he had married in 1984, he kept an extensive collection of vinyl records. Usually hidden behind sliding etched-glass doors, the music room would open onto the living room, where, on large loudspeakers flanking the fireplace, he would listen to John Cage: "I love that kind of music because it wipes the head out. That's great. That's why I have the big speakers. When I get through playing it's like I've been away on another planet for six months."[115] For his students, who often came to the house, he would analyze

Johann Sebastian Bach's Brandenburg Concertos or read Igor Stravinsky's book *Poetics of Music in the Form of Six Lessons* (1970). "Igor Stravinsky was a very strong influence on my life," he said. "Everything he talked about, almost everything, can be applied to architecture."[116] For Koenig, the music and the architecture of the modern movement were one and the same: "The nothingness, the spaces, the spaces between, repeating things, not repeating things, how things work when they go together, how they work when they don't go together . . . the indeterminacy."[117] In the white-and-gray interior of that steel house where indeterminacy infused the music as much as it did the architecture, Pierre Koenig died on 4 April 2004.[118] His work as an architect had spanned over half a century and his legacy, in Los Angeles, was assured. □

PLATES

**Pl. 1.** *A Branch Library,* plan analysis, plan, ca. 1948–49.

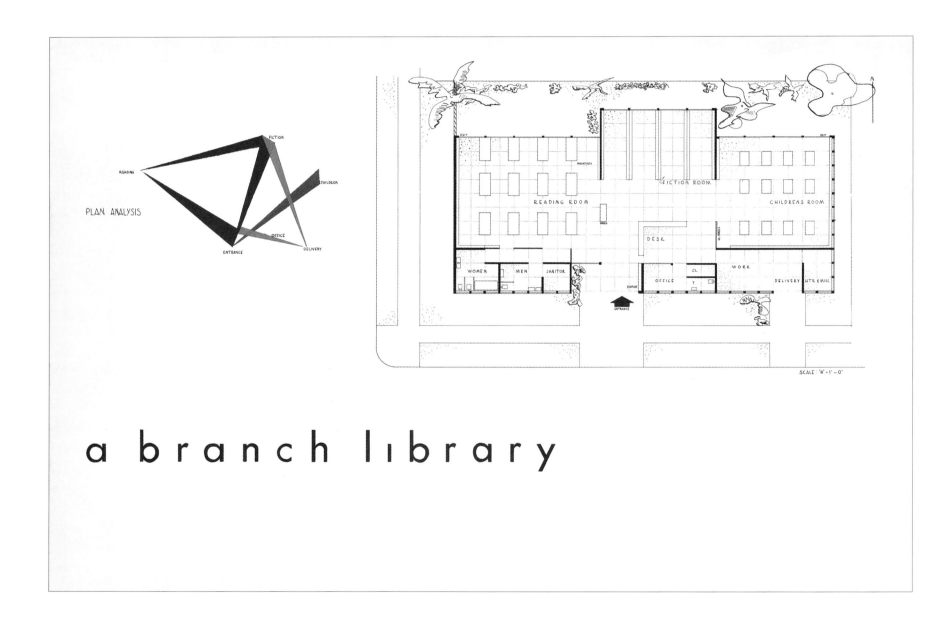

KOENIG HOUSE 1

**Pl. 2.** Koenig House 1, Glendale, plan, details, plot plan, 23 August 1950.

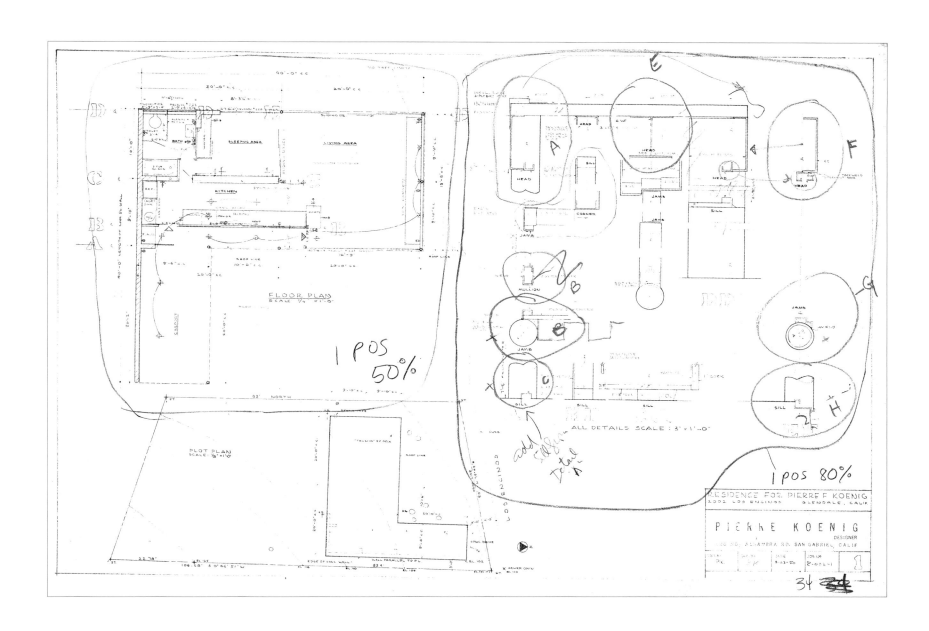

**Pl. 3.** Lamel House, plan, elevations, 4 April 1953.

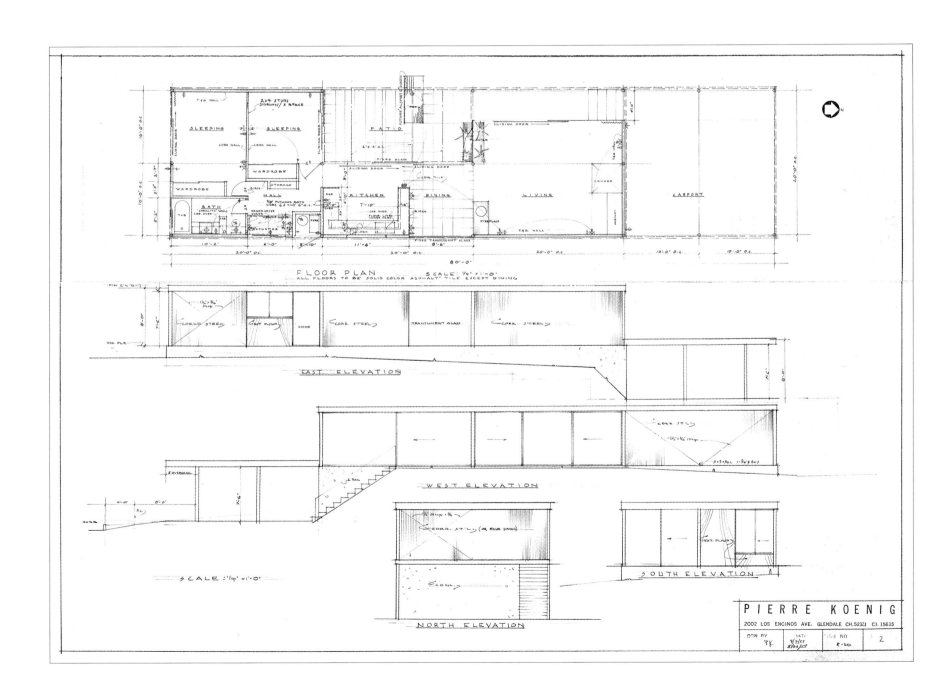

**Pl. 4.** Scott House, plan, ca. 1953.
**Pl. 5.** Scott House, details, 21 September 1953.
**Pl. 6.** Scott House, fireplace details, 21 September 1953.

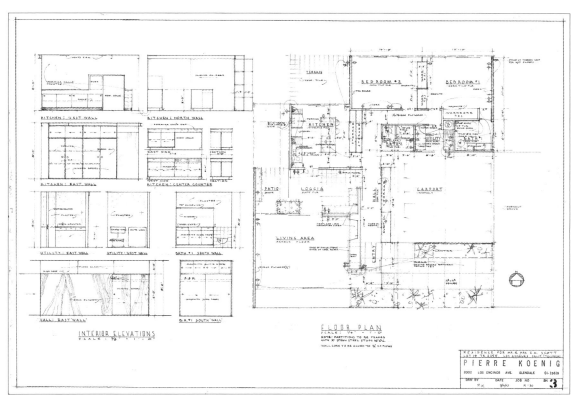

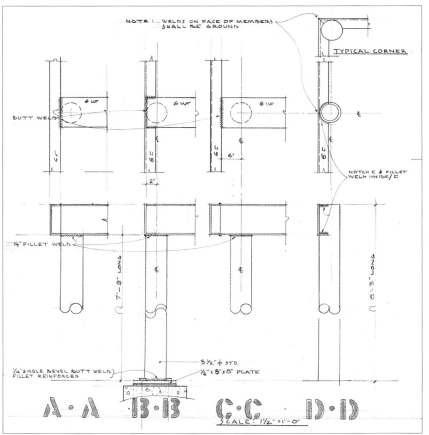

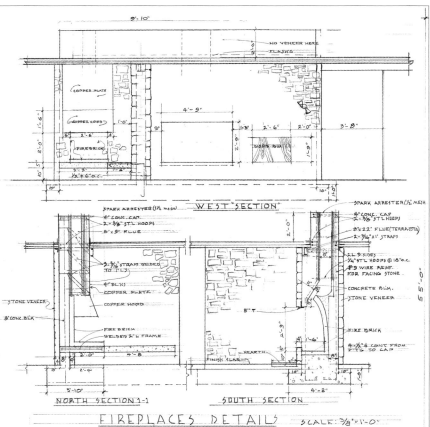

**Pl. 7.** Squire House, plan, 1 October 1953.

**Pl. 8.** Squire House, fireplace details, 7 October 1953.

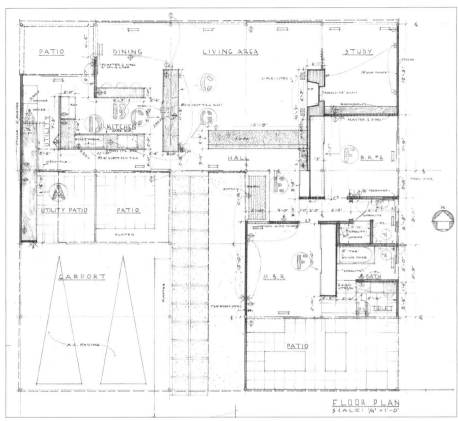

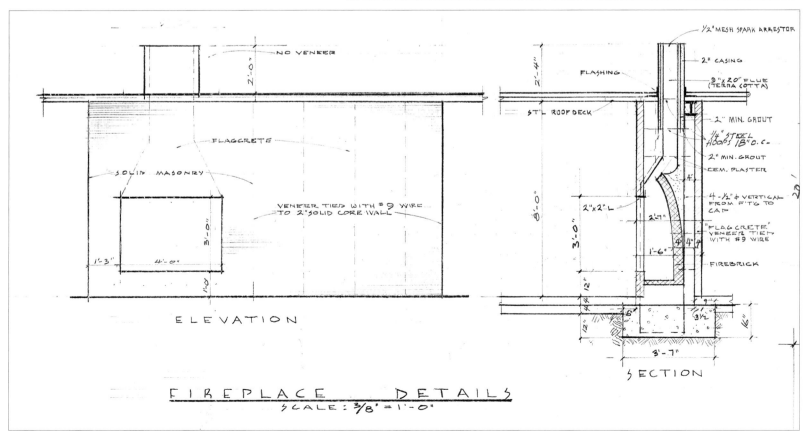

**SQUIRE HOUSE** I SOUTH ADDITION

**Pl. 9.** South Addition to Squire House, plan, details, 11 November 1987.

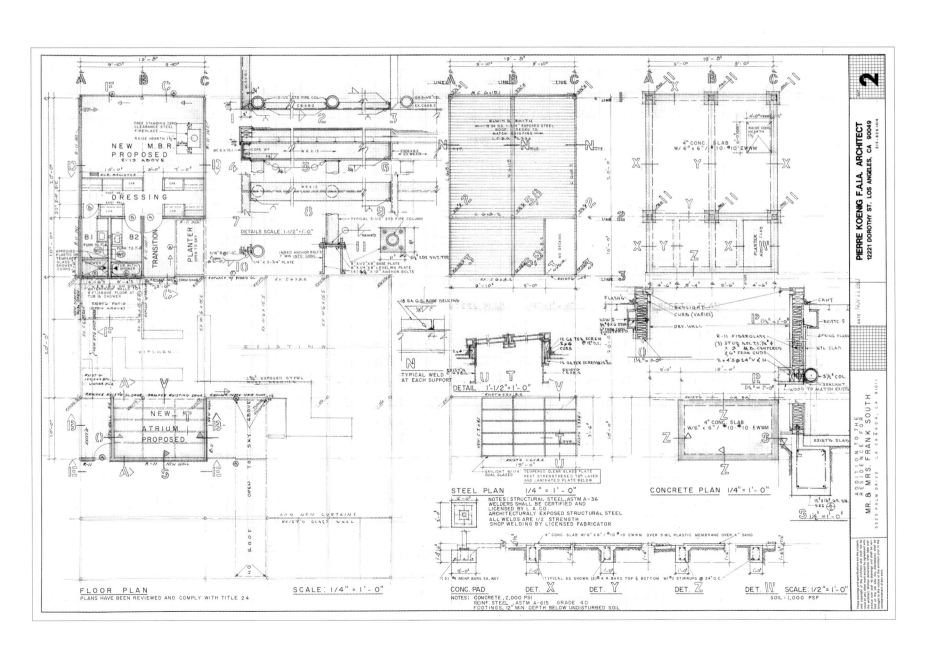

**Pl. 10.** Bailey House, version 1, steel frame, details, 16 April 1956.

**Pl. 11.** Bailey House, version 1, plan details, 16 April 1956.

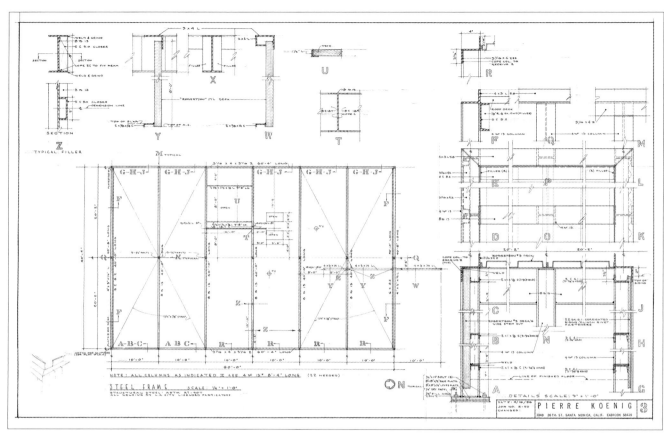

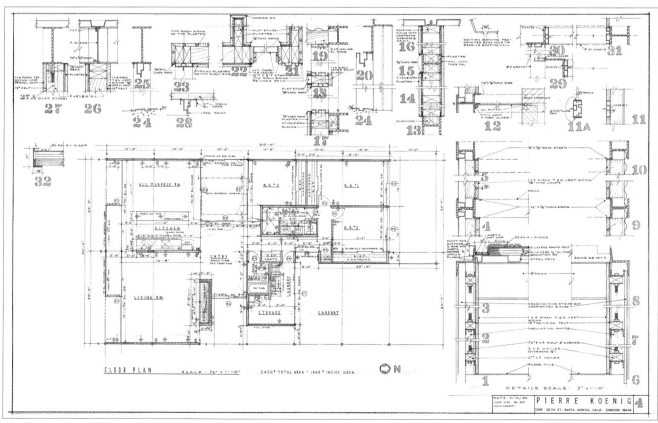

**BAILEY HOUSE** | VERSION 1

**Pl. 12.** Bailey House, version 1, foundation details, 16 April 1956.

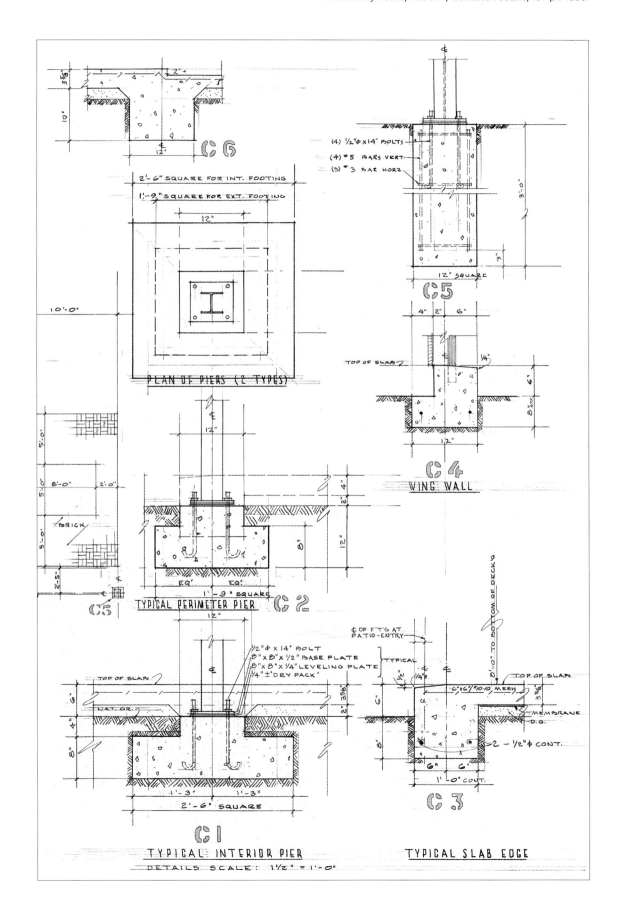

**Pl. 13.** Bailey House, version 2, foundation details, 22 April 1958.

**Pl. 14.** Bailey House, version 2, plan, ca. 1958.

**Pl. 15.** Bailey House, version 2, foundation detail, 22 April 1958.

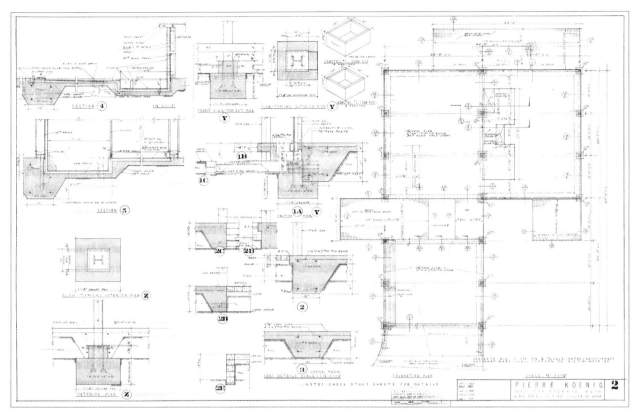

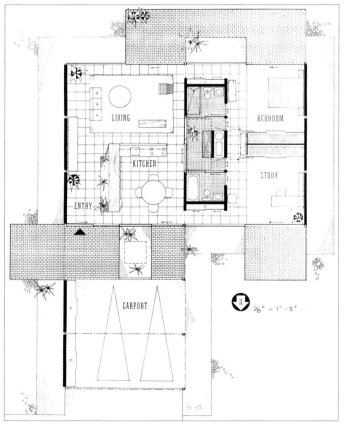

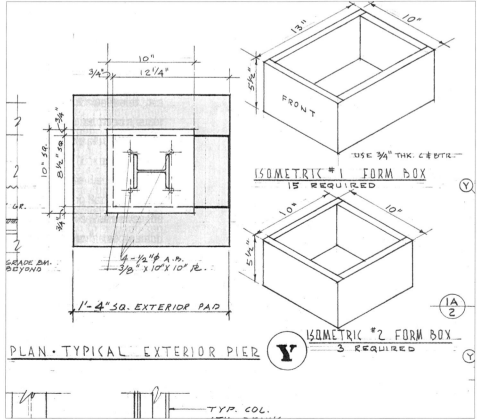

**BAILEY HOUSE** | NEWQUIST ADDITION

**Pl. 16.** Newquist Addition to Bailey House, plan, ca. 1986.

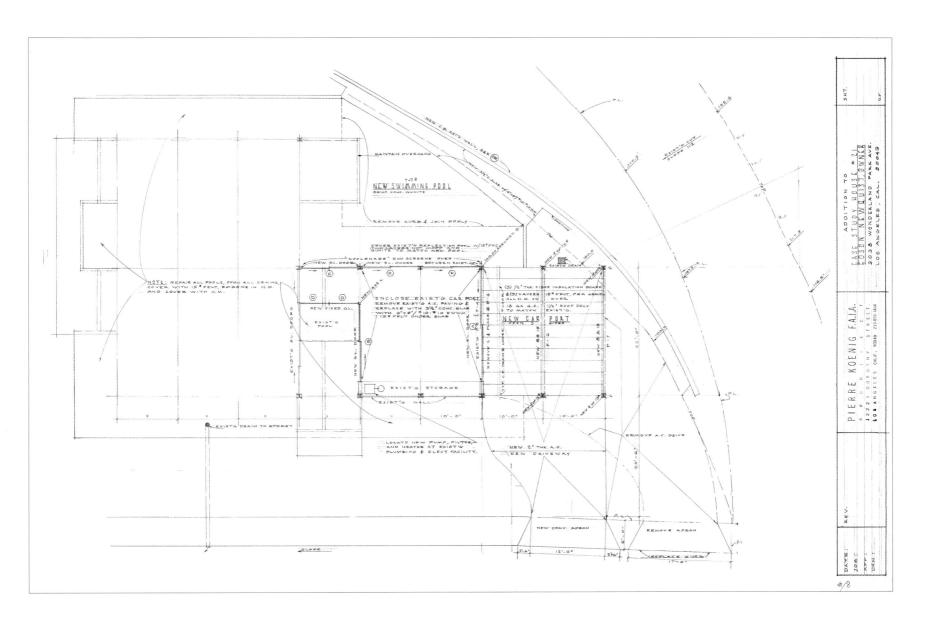

**Pl. 17.** Bavaro Design Studio, Cracchiolo Restoration of Bailey House, kitchen, elevations, sections, ca. 1997.

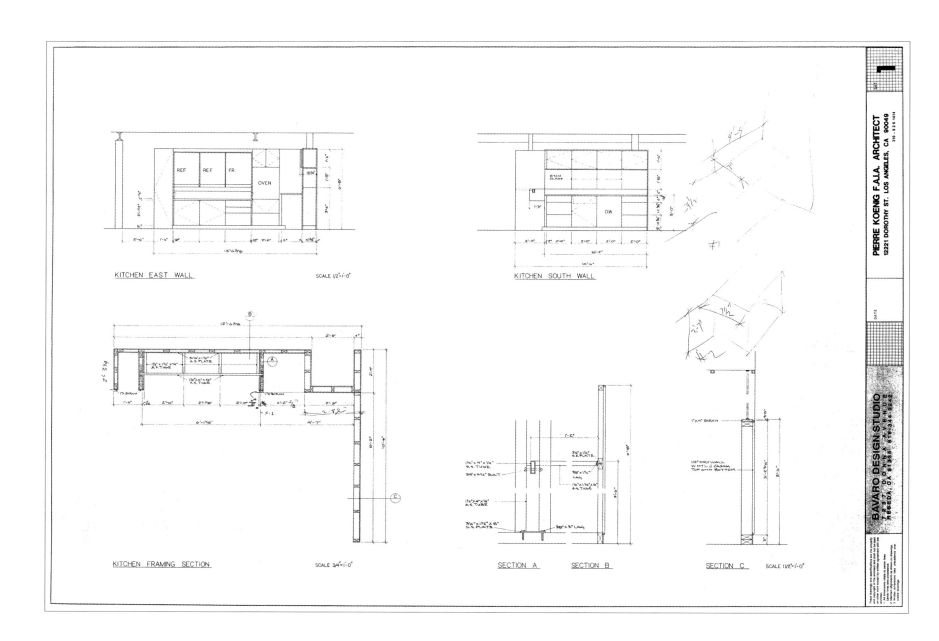

**Pl. 18.** Stereo cabinet for Cracchiolo Restoration of Bailey House, section, plan, scheme 5, ca. 1997.

**Pl. 19.** Mailbox for Cracchiolo Restoration of Bailey House, elevations, ca. 1997.

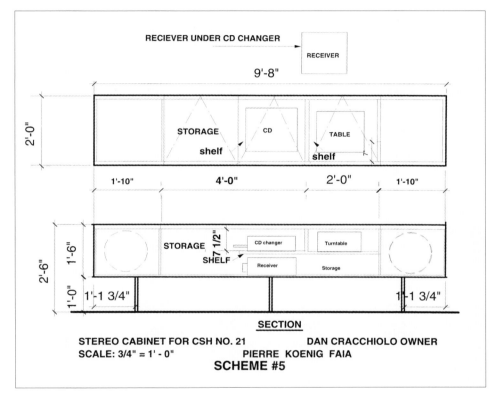

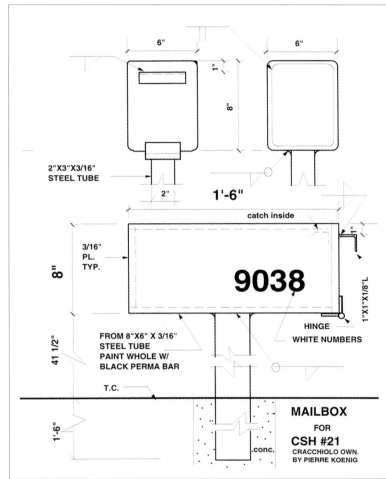

**Pl. 20.** Burwash House, steel structure, plan, details, 15 February 1957.

**Pl. 21.** Burwash House, plan, 15 February 1957.

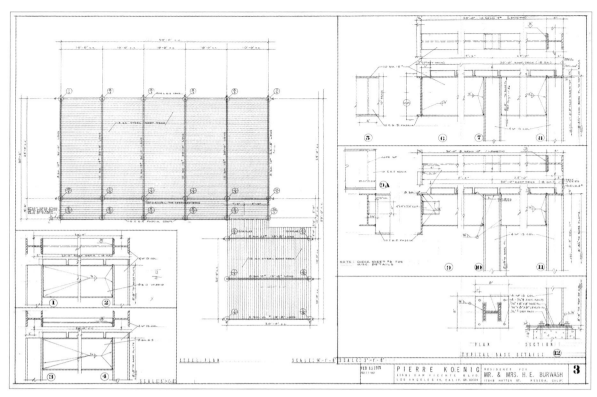

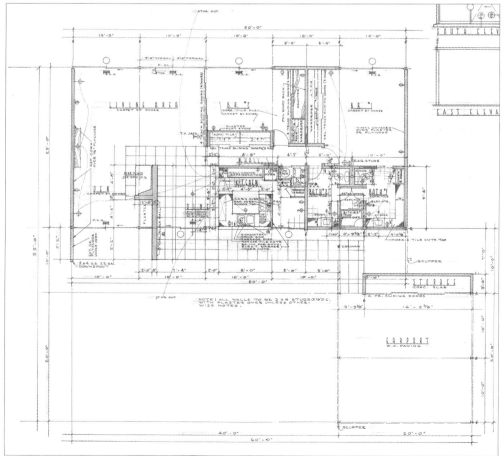

**Pl. 22.** Burwash House, fireplace, plan, elevations, section, 15 February 1957.

**Pl. 23.** Burwash House, kitchen and bathroom cabinet details, 15 February 1957.

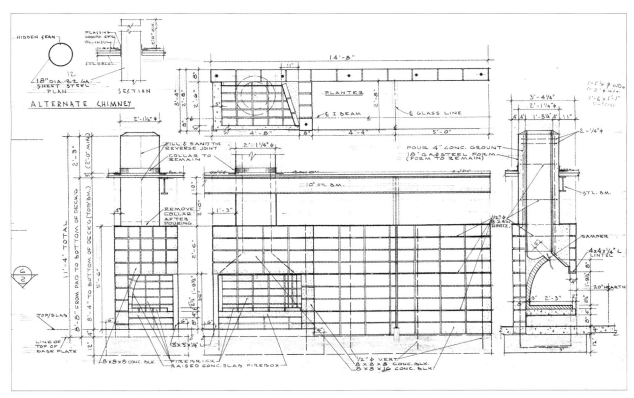

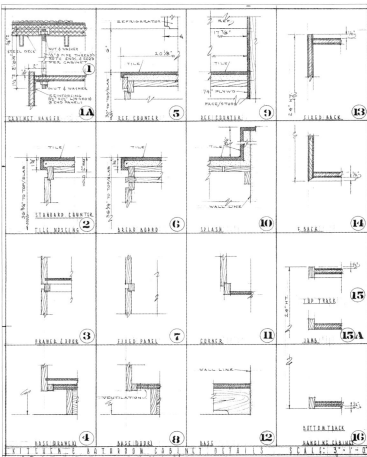

**Pl. 24.** Whitehead Addition to Burwash House, plan, elevations, sections, 10 February 1965.

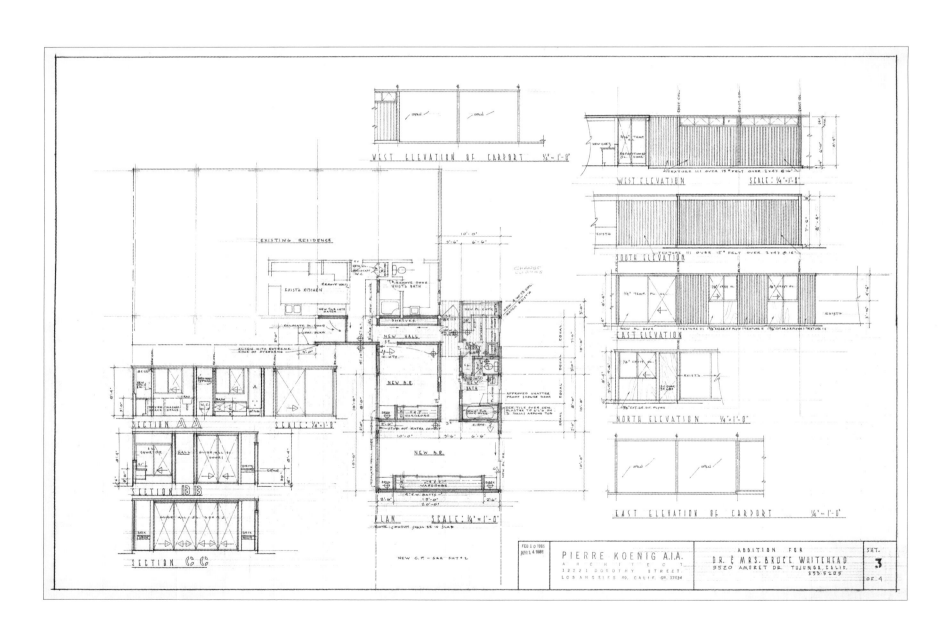

**Pl. 25.** Beidleman House, version 1, plan, ca. 1956.

**Pl. 26.** Beidleman House, version 1, steel-frame plans, section, elevations, details, 12 August 1957.

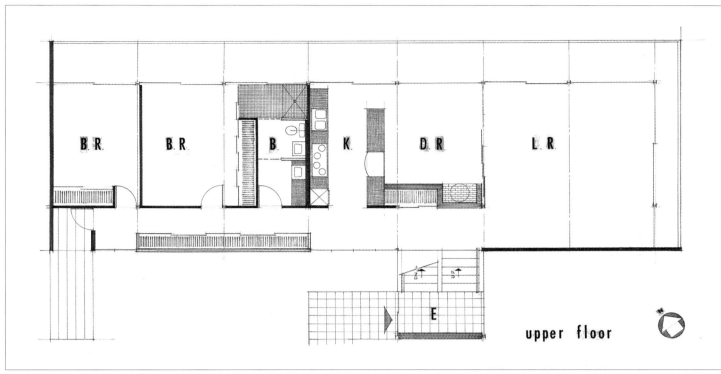

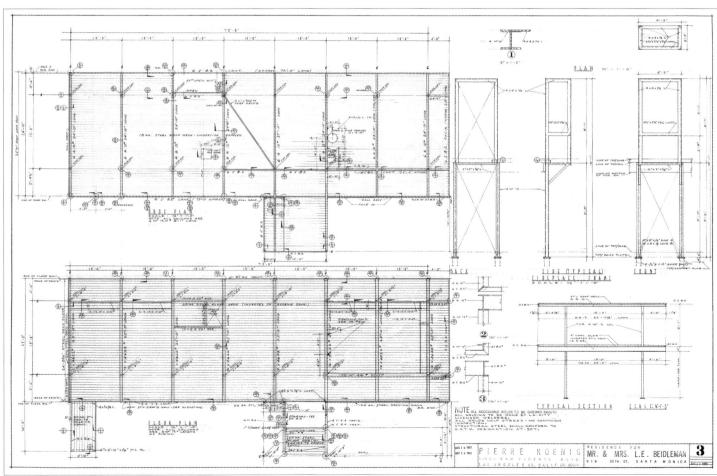

**BEIDLEMAN HOUSE** | VERSION 1

**Pl. 27.** Beidleman House, version 1, elevations, section, 12 August 1957.

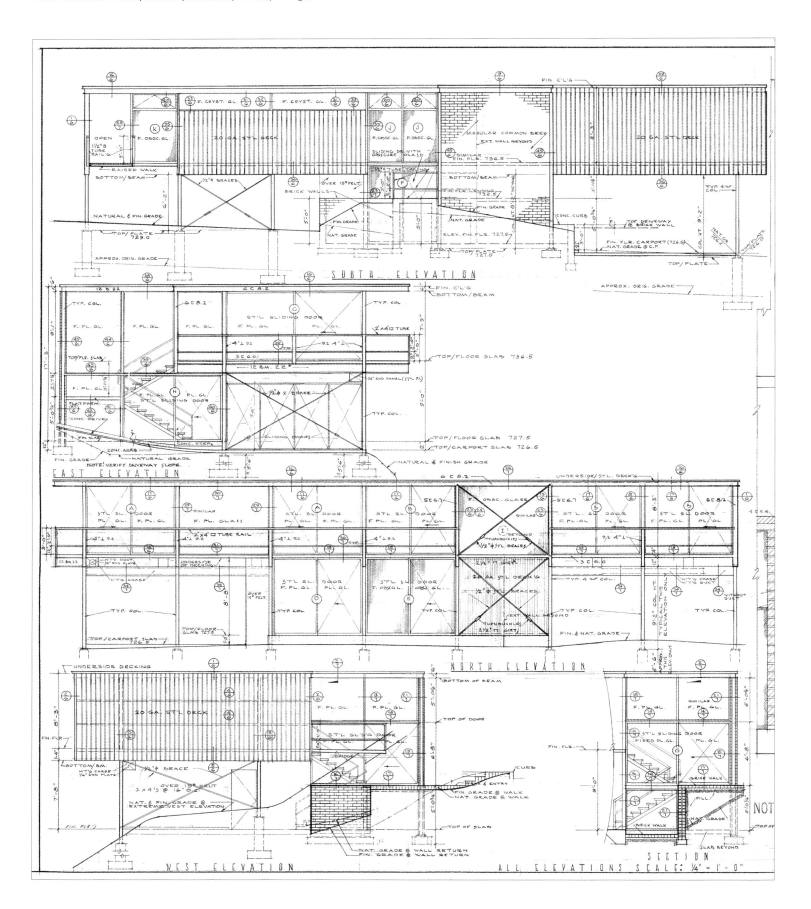

**Pl. 28.** Beidleman House, version 2, "first floor" preliminary plan, 7 January 1960.

**Pl. 29.** Beidleman House, version 2, rear elevation, ca. 1960.

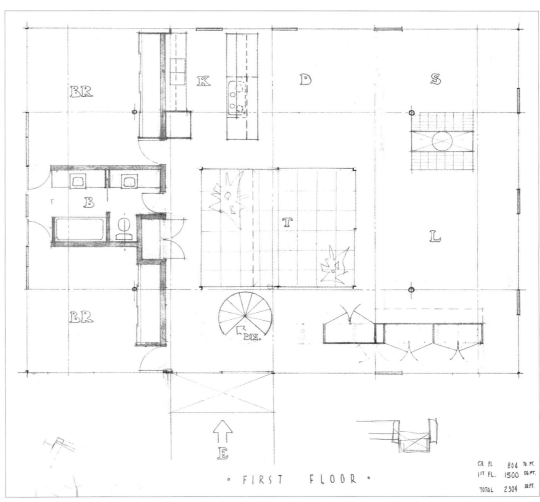

· FIRST FLOOR ·

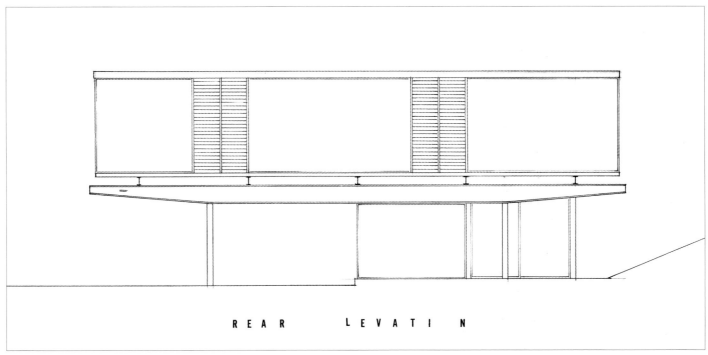

REAR    ELEVATION

**Pl. 30.** Beidleman House, version 2, lower-floor plan, 19 February 1962.

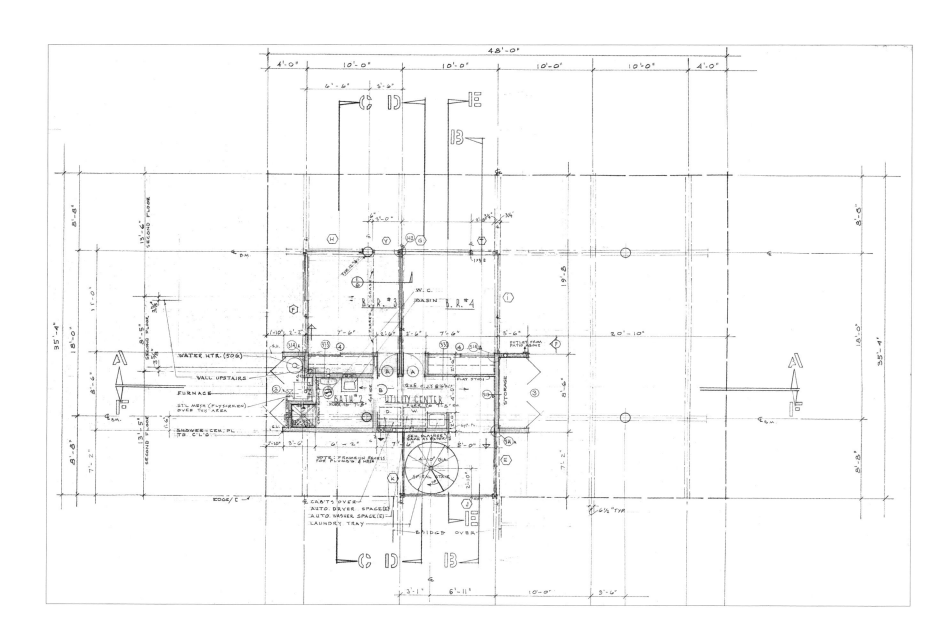

**Pl. 31.** Stahl House, site sections, ca. 1959.

**Pl. 32.** Stahl House, plan, ca. 1959.

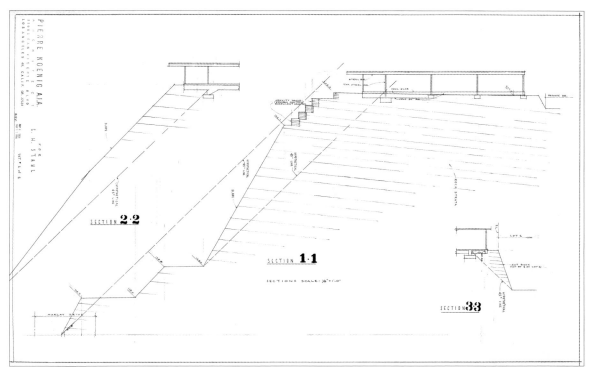

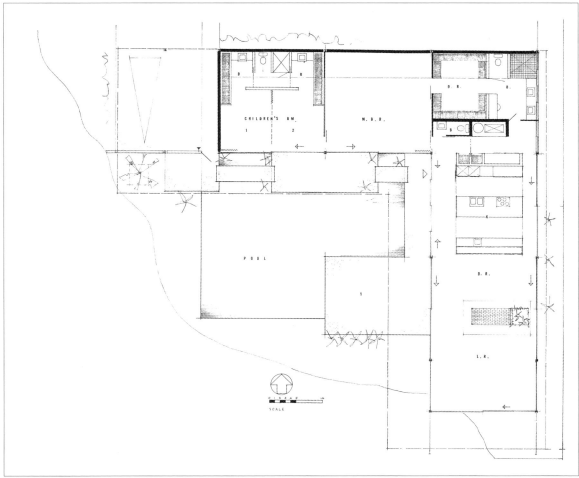

**Pl. 33.** Stahl House, sketch plan. From "Logs 1958," book 1, n.p.

**Pl. 34.** Stahl House, fireplace, elevations, sections, 3 July 1958.

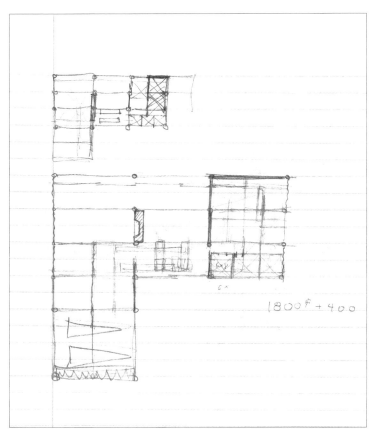

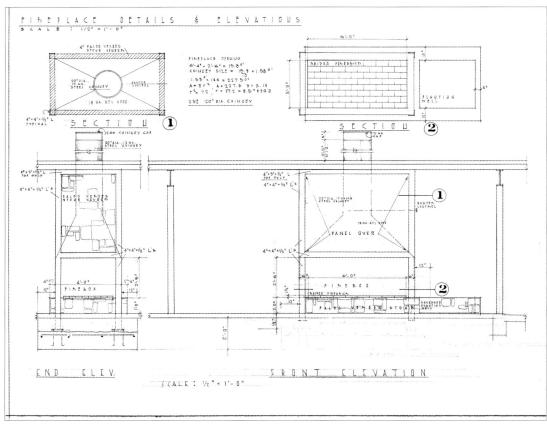

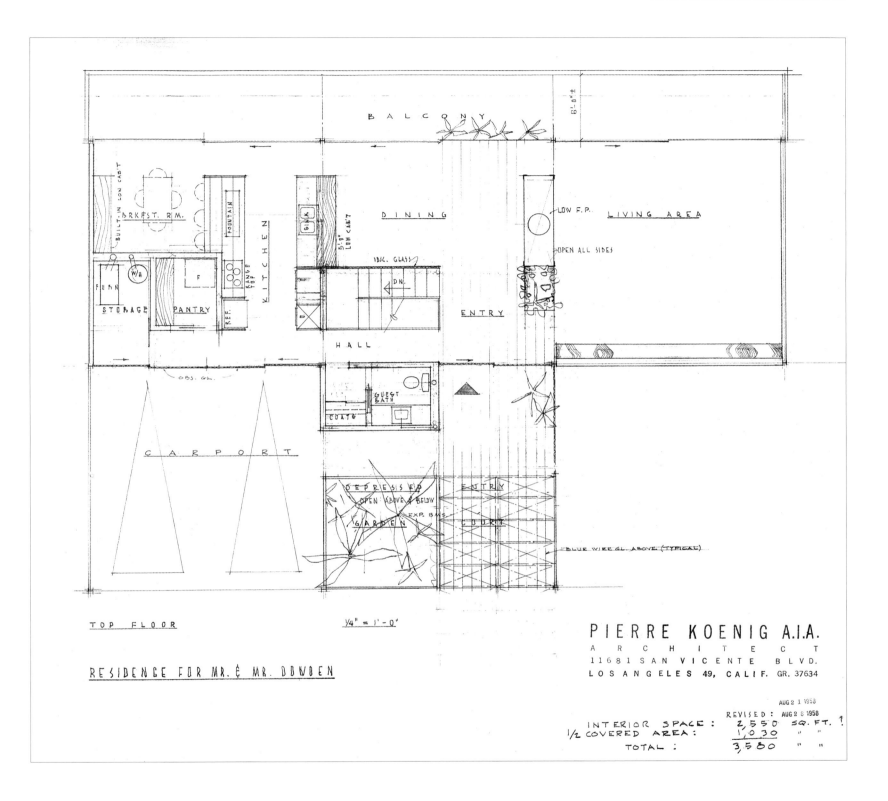

TOP FLOOR

1/4" = 1'-0"

RESIDENCE FOR MR. & MR. DOWDEN

PIERRE KOENIG A.I.A.
A R C H I T E C T
11681 SAN VICENTE BLVD.
LOS ANGELES 49, CALIF. GR. 37634

AUG 2 1 1958
REVISED : AUG 2 8 1958
INTERIOR SPACE : 2,550 SQ. FT.
1/2 COVERED AREA : 1,030 " "
TOTAL : 3,580 " "

**Pl. 36.** Metcalf House, upper-floor plan, 20 August 1958.

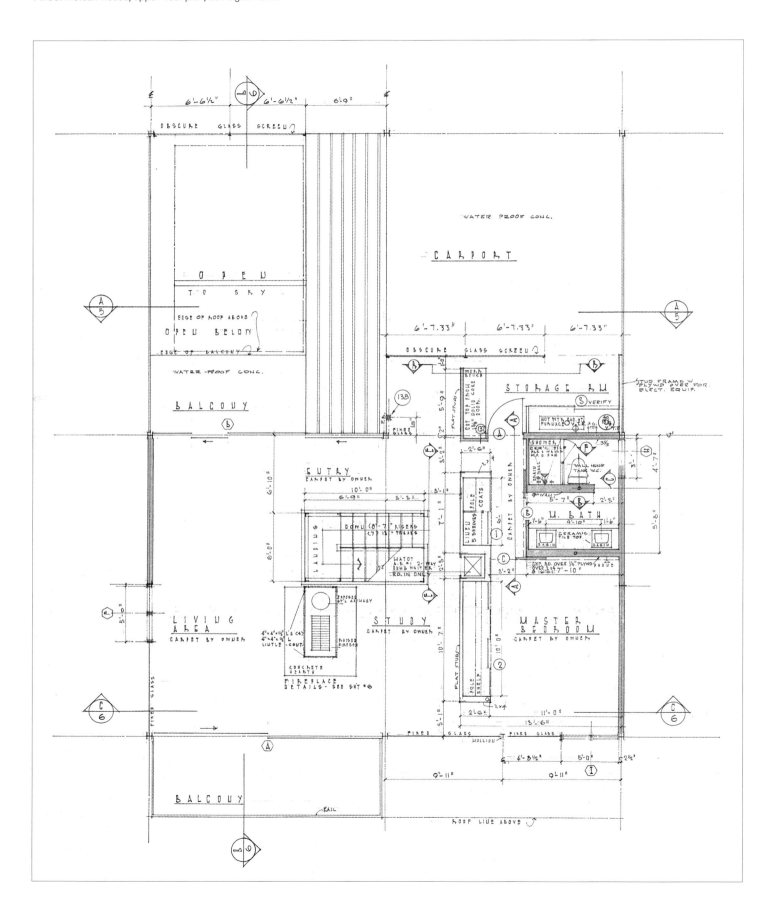

**Pl. 37.** Metcalf House, middle-floor plan, 20 August 1958.
**Pl. 38.** Metcalf House, elevations, sections, 20 August 1958.

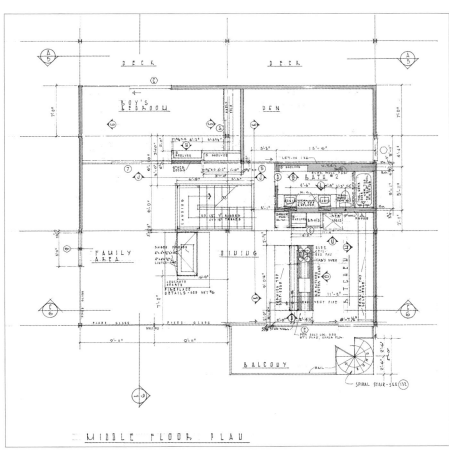

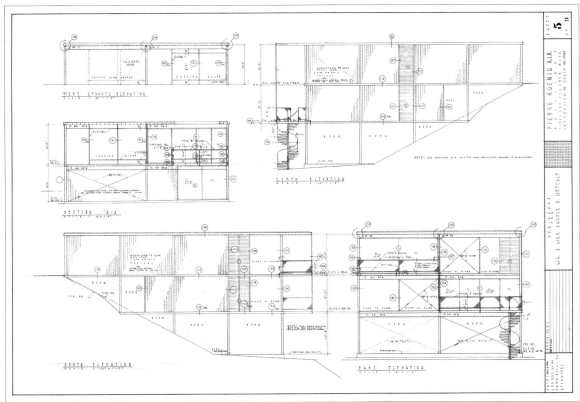

**Pl. 39.** Seidel Associates House, plan, ca. 1959.

**Pl. 40.** Seidel Associates House, elevations, sections, 8 June 1959.

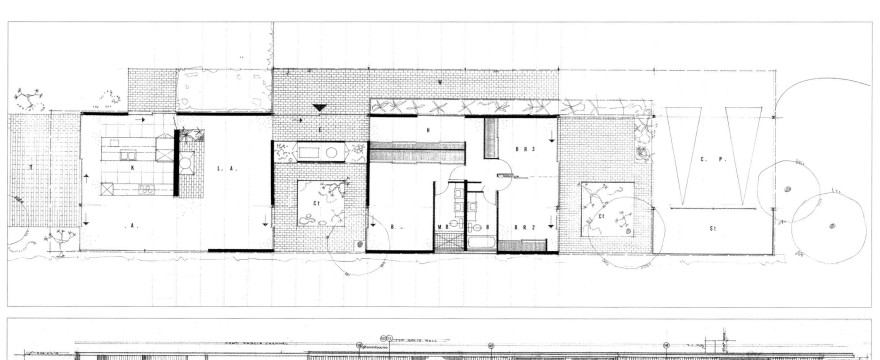

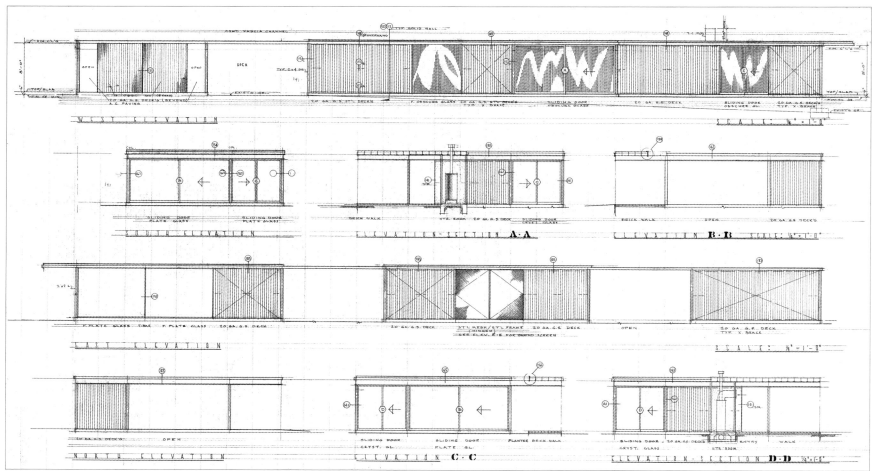

**Pl. 41.** Second Valensi Addition to Seidel Associates House, plan, elevations, details, 1 September 1965.

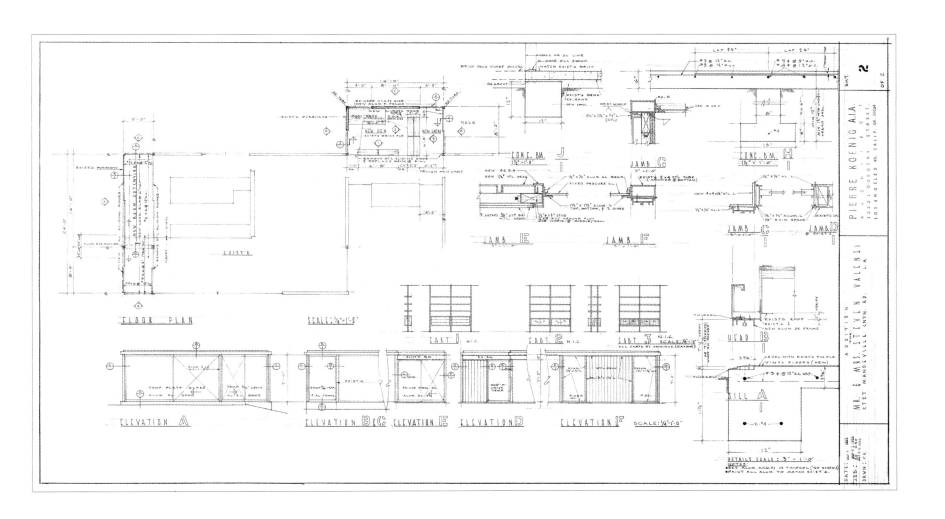

**Pl. 42.** First Rollé Addition to Seidel Associates House, plans, elevation, 3 December 1982.

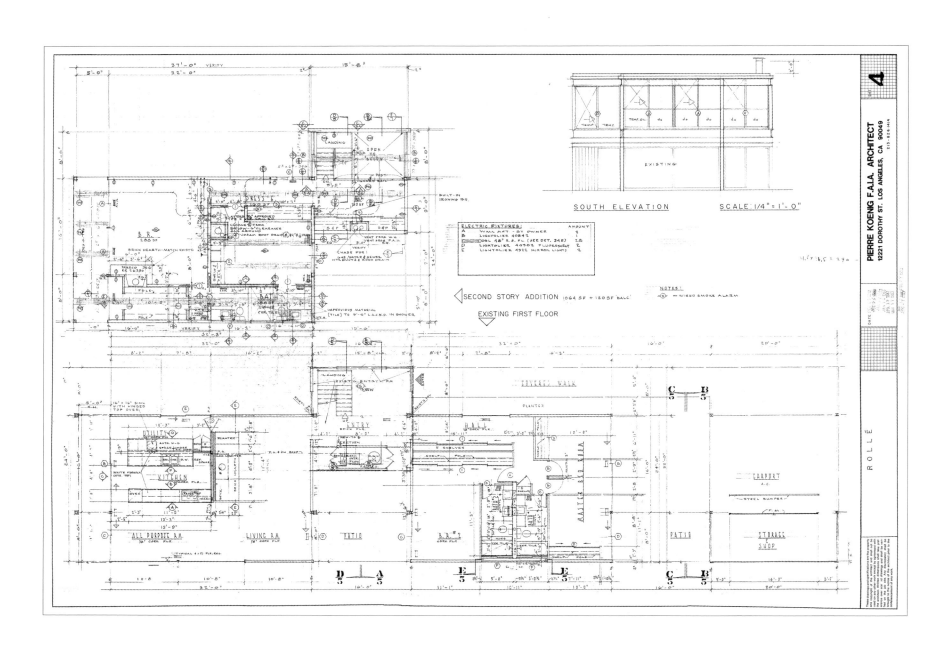

**SEIDEL ASSOCIATES HOUSE** | SECOND ROLLÉ ADDITION

**Pl. 43.** Second Rollé Addition to Seidel Associates House, sections, elevations, 20 August 1993.

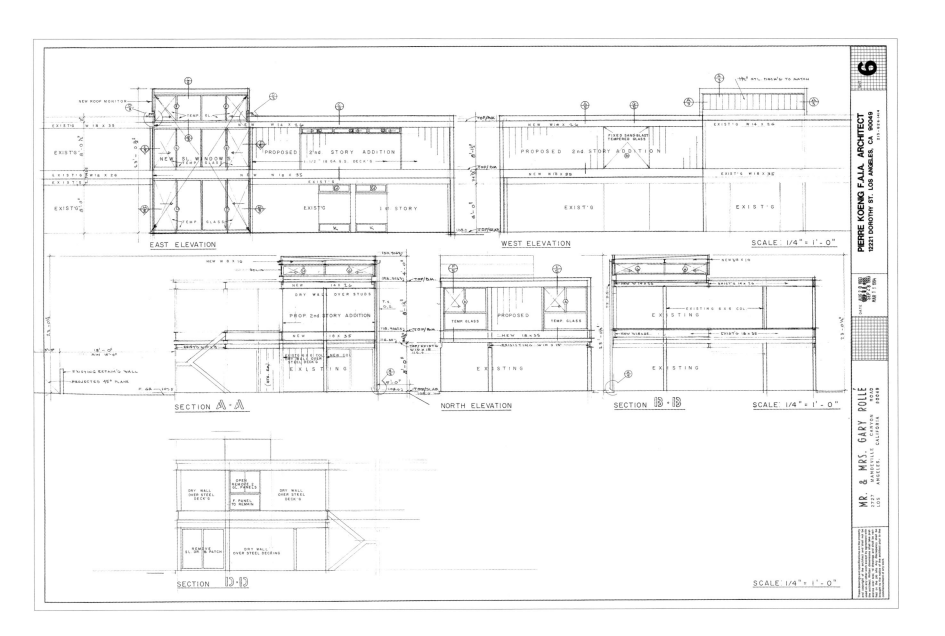

**Pl. 44.** Dzur House and guest house, final lower-floor plan, section, signed by Dzur and dated 21 June 1959.

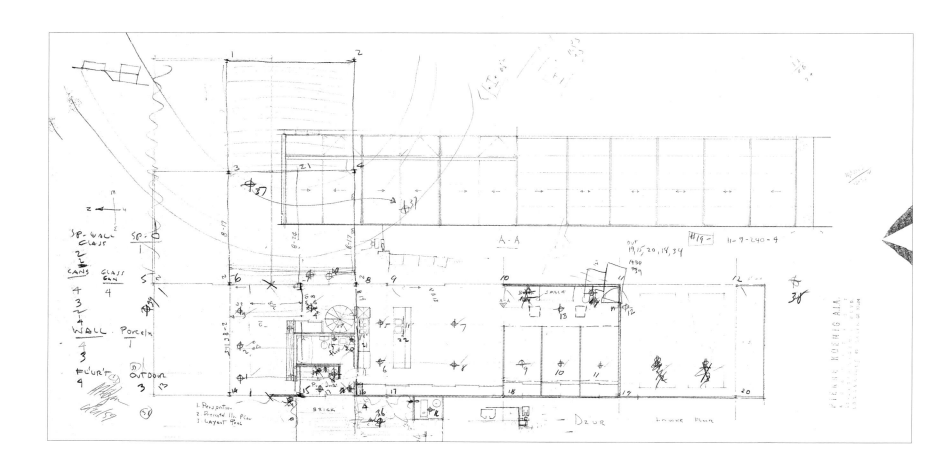

**Pl. 45.** Dzur House and guest house, sketch plan, 1959.
**Pl. 46.** Dzur House and guest house, axonometric and perspective sketches, ca. 1959.

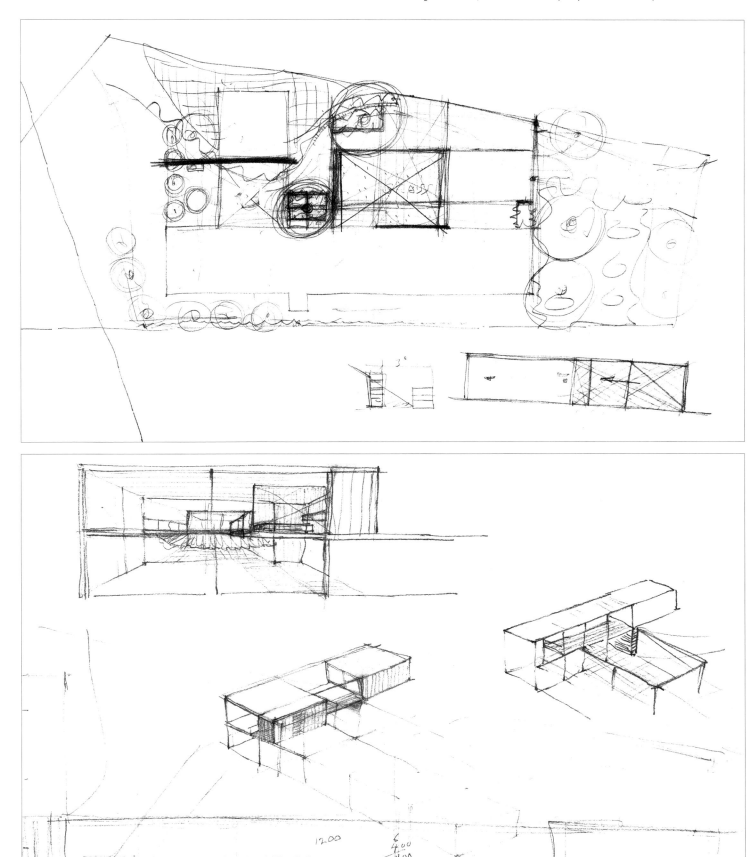

**Pl. 47.** Dzur House and guest house, proposed lower-floor plan, ca. 1959.

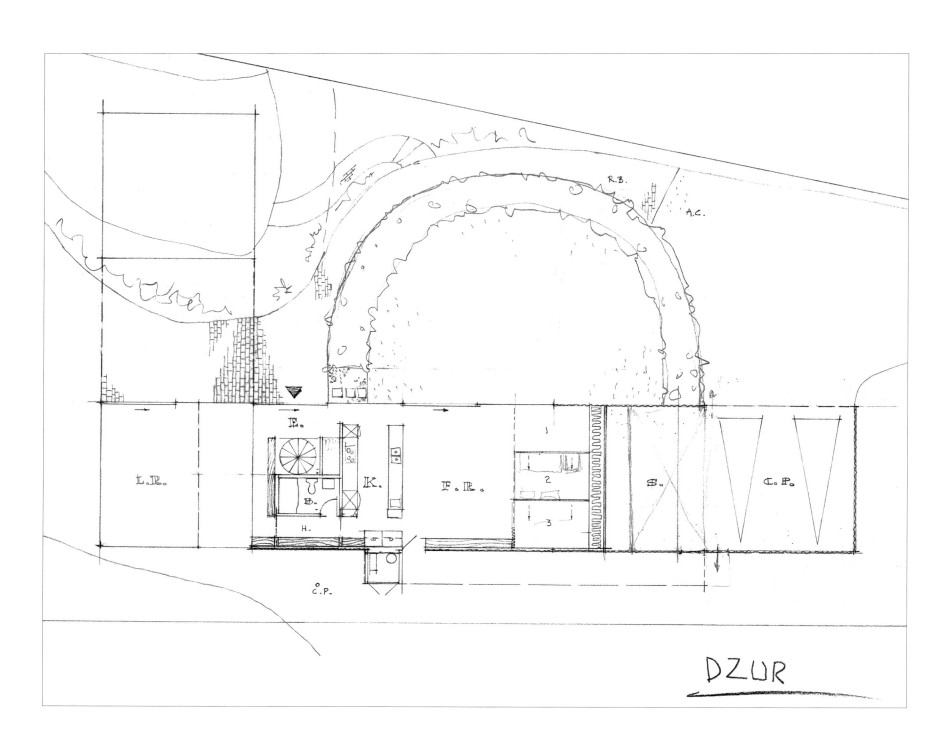

**Pl. 48.** Dzur House and guest house, proposed upper-floor plan with dogleg stair, ca. 1959.

**Pl. 49.** Dzur House and guest house, proposed upper-floor plan with spiral stair, ca. 1959.

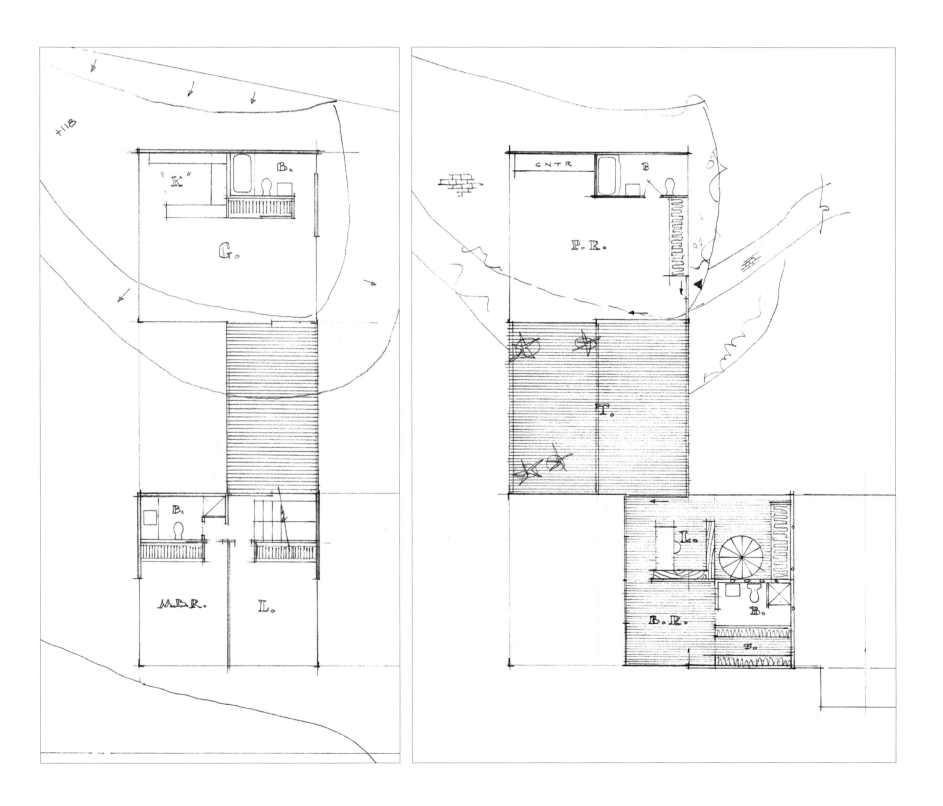

**Pl. 50.** Seidel Beach House, plan, elevations, 14 January 1960.

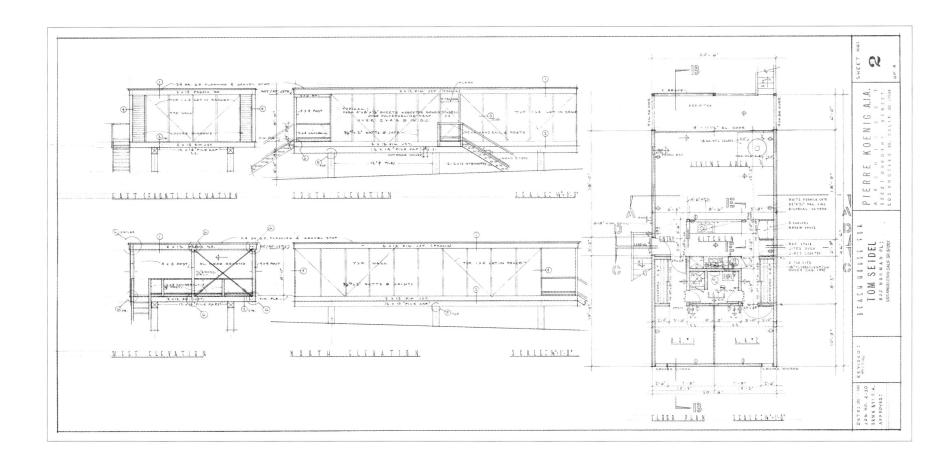

**Pl. 51.** Oberman House, plan, ca. 1960.

**Pl. 52.** Oberman House, standardized construction detail no. 187, 13 June 1960.

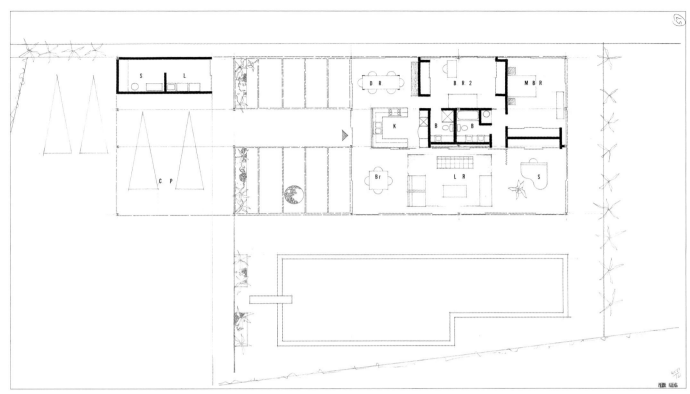

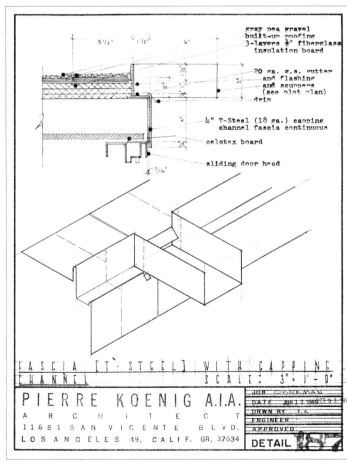

**Pl. 53.** Production Houses, St. Jean, Quebec, elevations, 8 August 1960.

**Pl. 54.** Production Houses, St. Jean, Quebec, lower-floor plan, details, 8 August 1960.

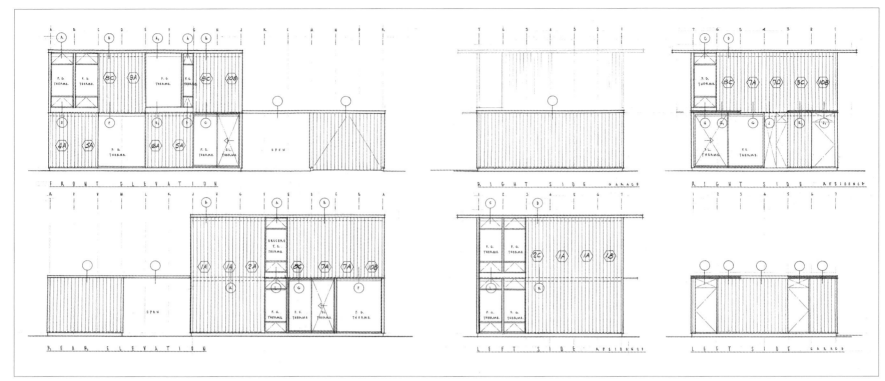

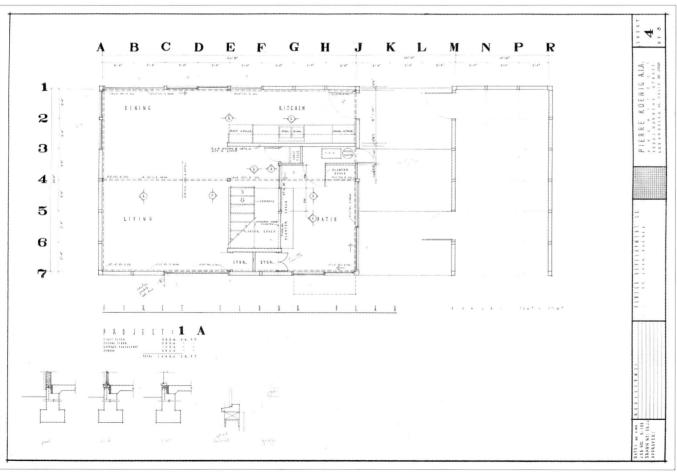

**Pl. 55.** Whittlesey House, elevations, 3 December 1960.
**Pl. 56.** Whittlesey House, upper-floor plan, 3 December 1960.
**Pl. 57.** Whittlesey House, lower-floor plan, 3 December 1960.

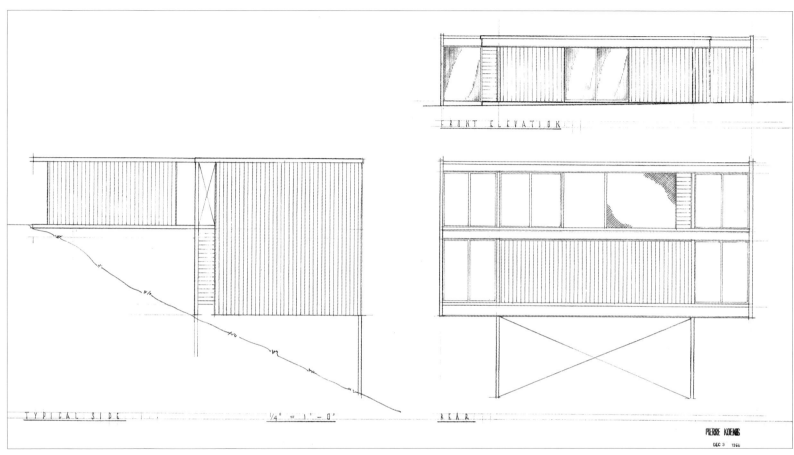

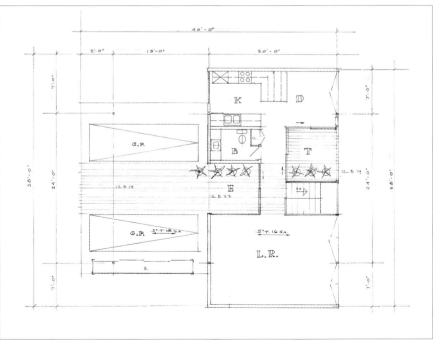

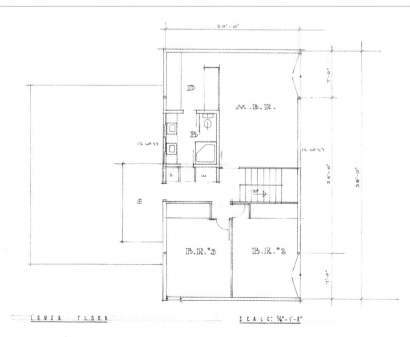

**Pl. 58.** Plaut Vacation House, plan, 16 February 1961.

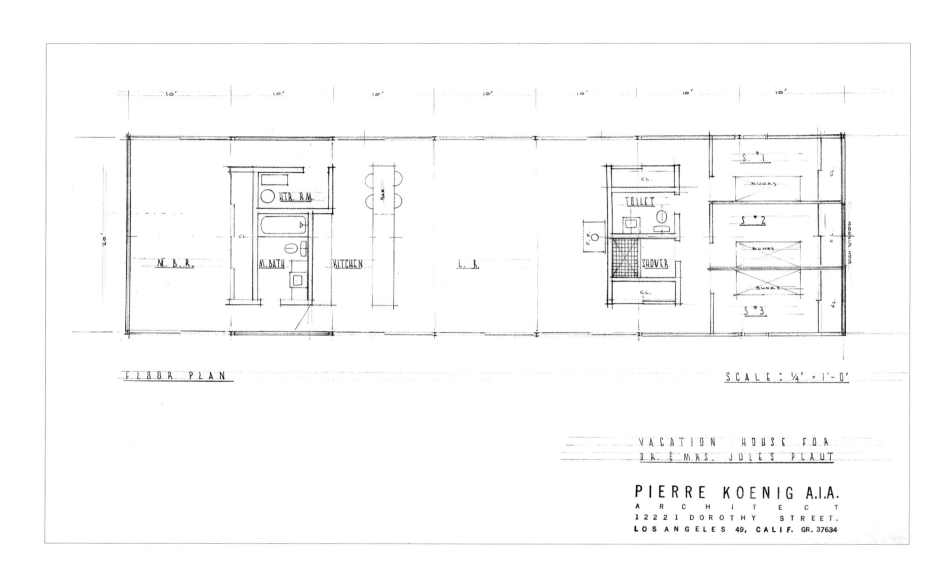

FLOOR PLAN

SCALE: ¼" = 1'-0"

VACATION HOUSE FOR
DR. & MRS. JULES PLAUT

**PIERRE KOENIG A.I.A.**
ARCHITECT
12221 DOROTHY STREET.
LOS ANGELES 49, CALIF. GR. 37634

**Pl. 59.** Johnson House, plan, detail, 9 September 1961.

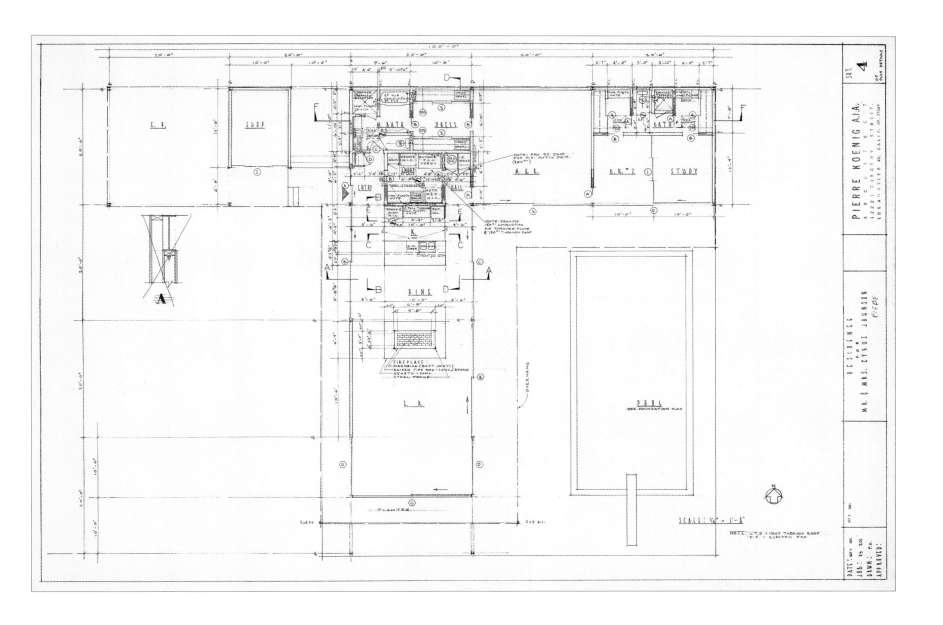

**Pl. 60.** Riebe Addition to Johnson House, elevations, 17 May 1989.

**Pl. 61.** Riebe Addition to Johnson House, garden gate, elevations, ca. 2002.

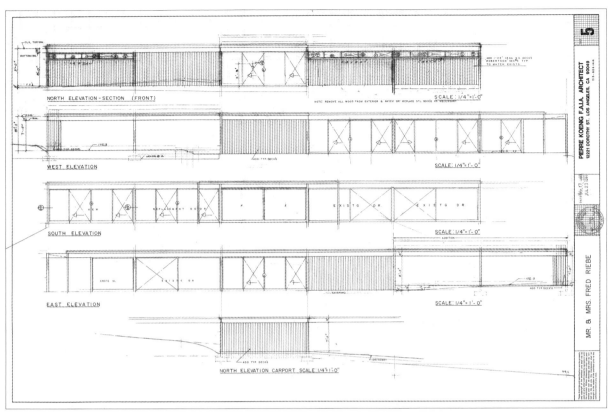

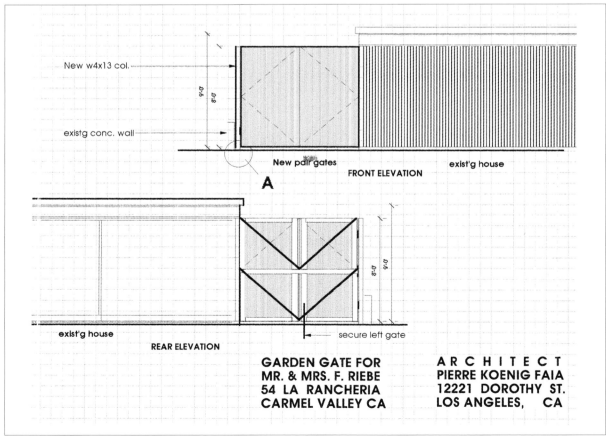

**Pl. 62.** De Winter House, plans, 9 January 1962.
**Pl. 63.** De Winter House, elevations, sections, details, 9 January 1962.

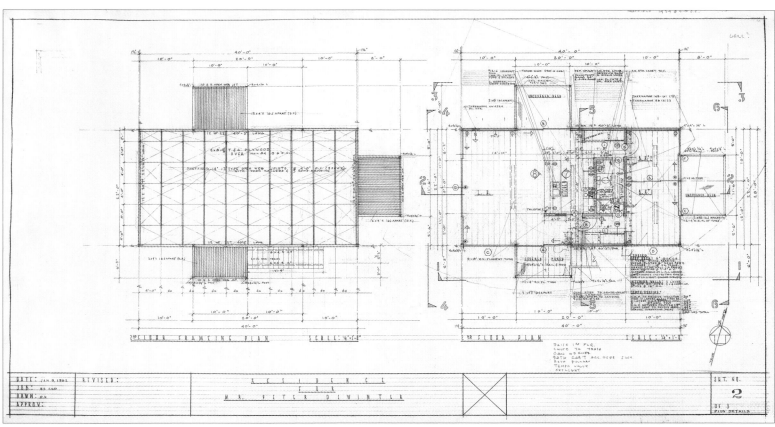

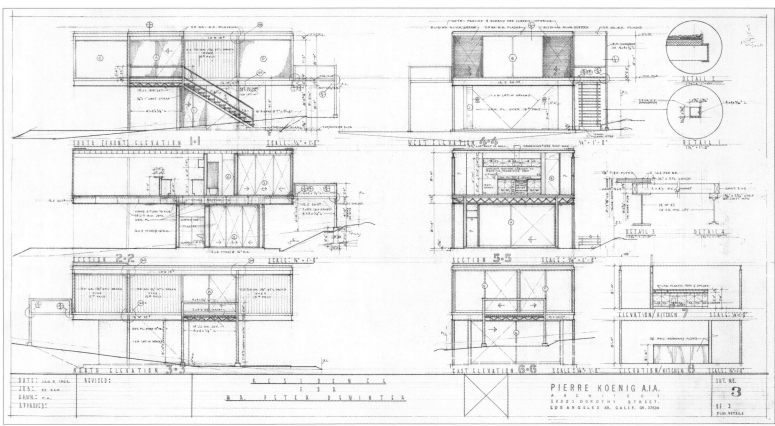

**Pl. 64.** Herrington House 1, lower-floor plan, 20 February 1961.

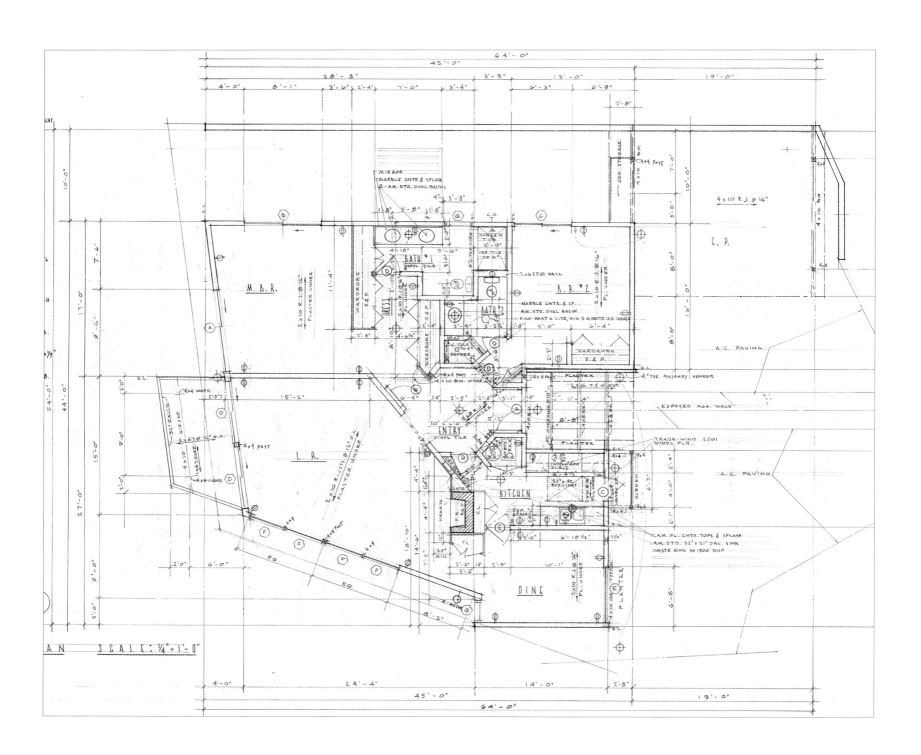

**WILLHEIM HOUSE**

**Pl. 65.** Willheim House, sketch plan, lower floor, ca. 1962.

**Pl. 66.** Willheim House, preliminary design, lower-floor plan, ca. 1962.

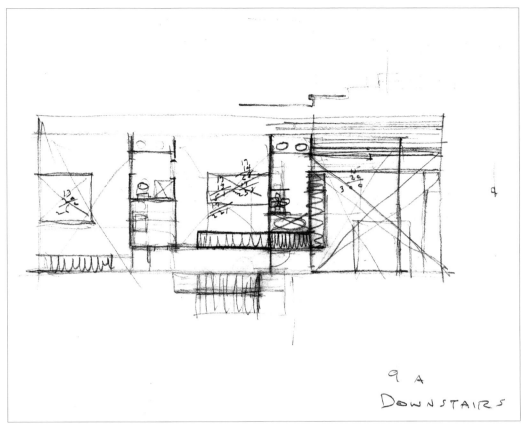

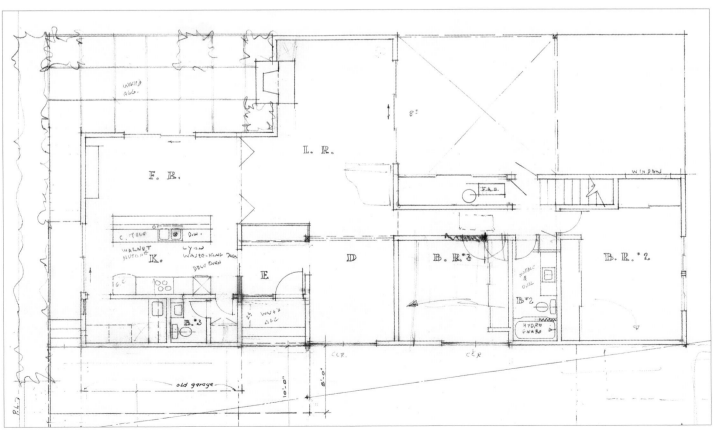

**Pl. 67.** Willheim House, east (front) elevation, 10 May 1962.

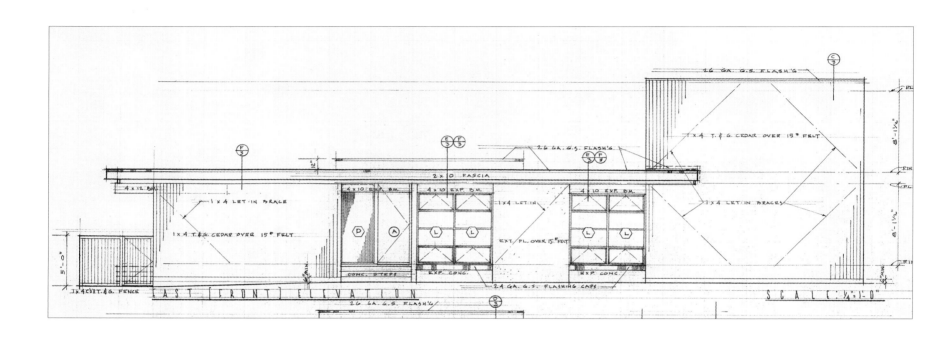

**Pl. 68.** Beagles House, foundation, plan, section, detail, 2 November 1962.

**Pl. 69.** Beagles House, elevations, 2 November 1962.

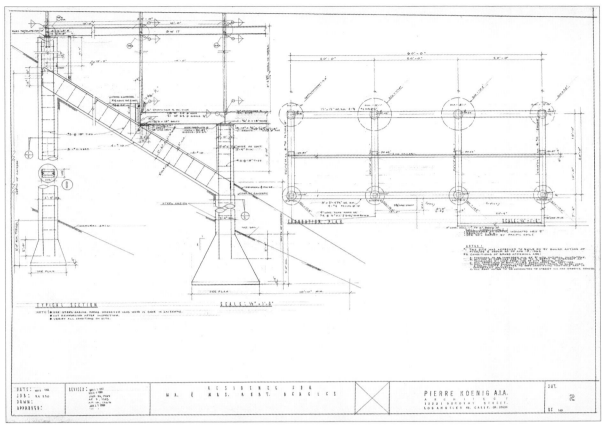

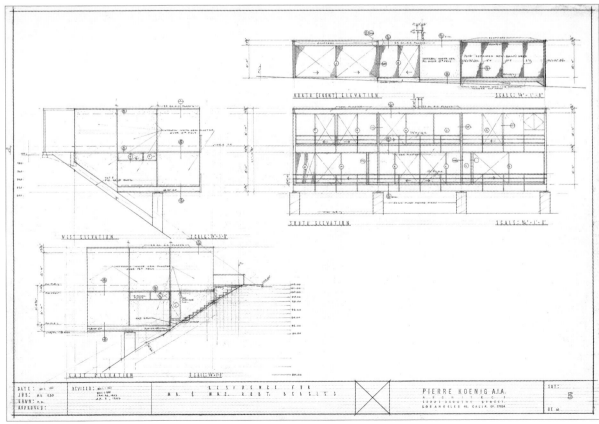

**Pl. 70.** Herrington House 2, lower-floor plan, 4 November 1963.

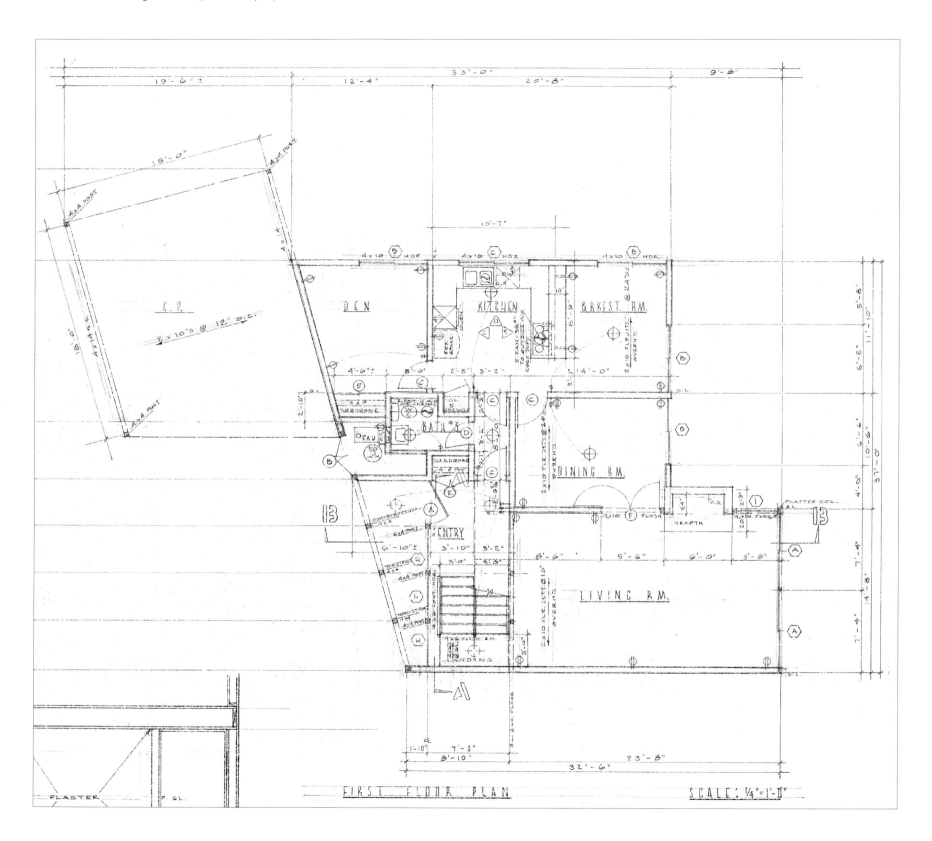

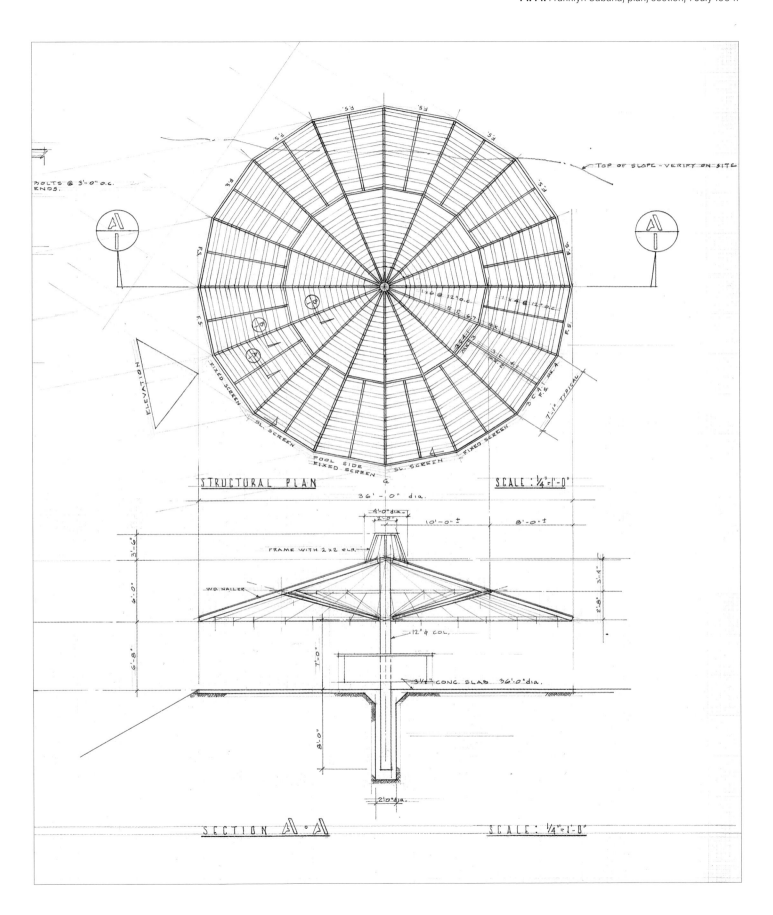

STRUCTURAL PLAN                                    SCALE : ¼"=1'-0"

SECTION A·A                                        SCALE: ¼"=1'-0"

**Pl. 72.** Iwata House, stair sections, details, 4 May 1965.

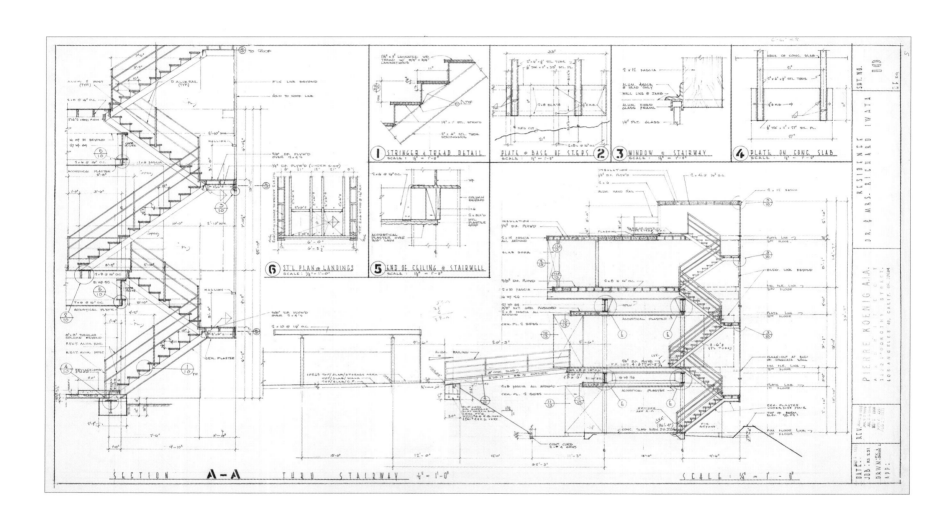

**Pl. 73.** Henbest House on Crest Road, elevations, sections, details, 11 August 1965.

**Pl. 74.** Henbest House on Crest Road, plan, 11 August 1965.

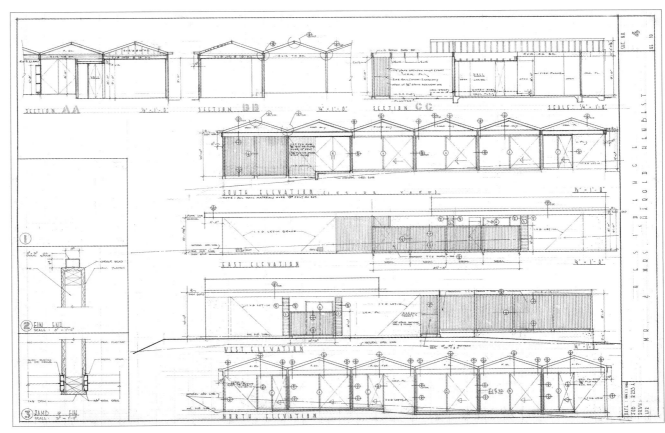

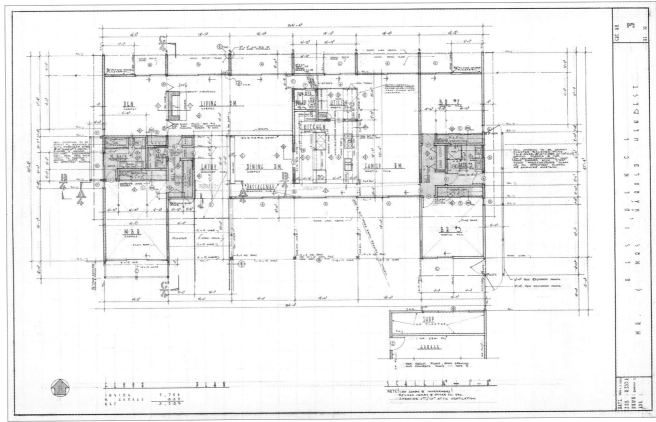

**Pl. 75.** Koenig House 2, carport, plan, elevations, details, 18 July 1966.

**Pl. 76.** Koenig House 2, carport and recreation room, plan, section, after 1985.

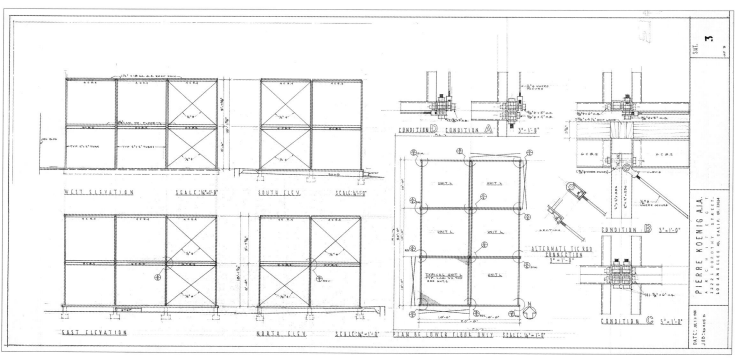

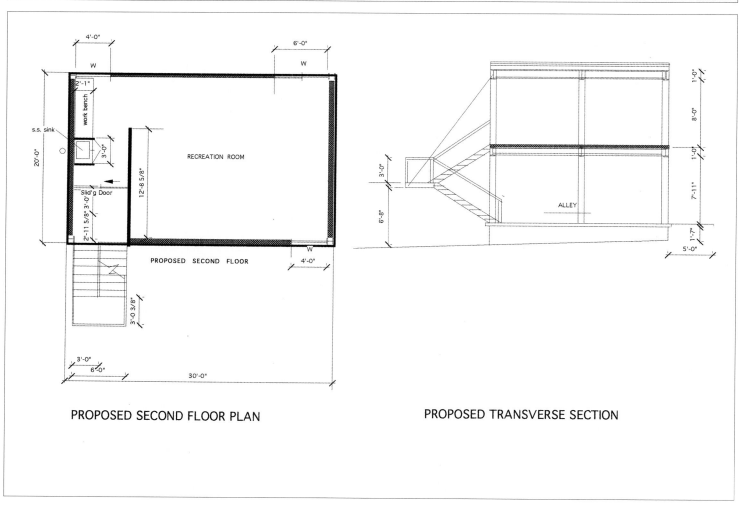

PROPOSED SECOND FLOOR PLAN

PROPOSED TRANSVERSE SECTION

KOENIG HOUSE 2

**Pl. 77.** Koenig House 2, steel structure, plans, details, 5 January 1983.

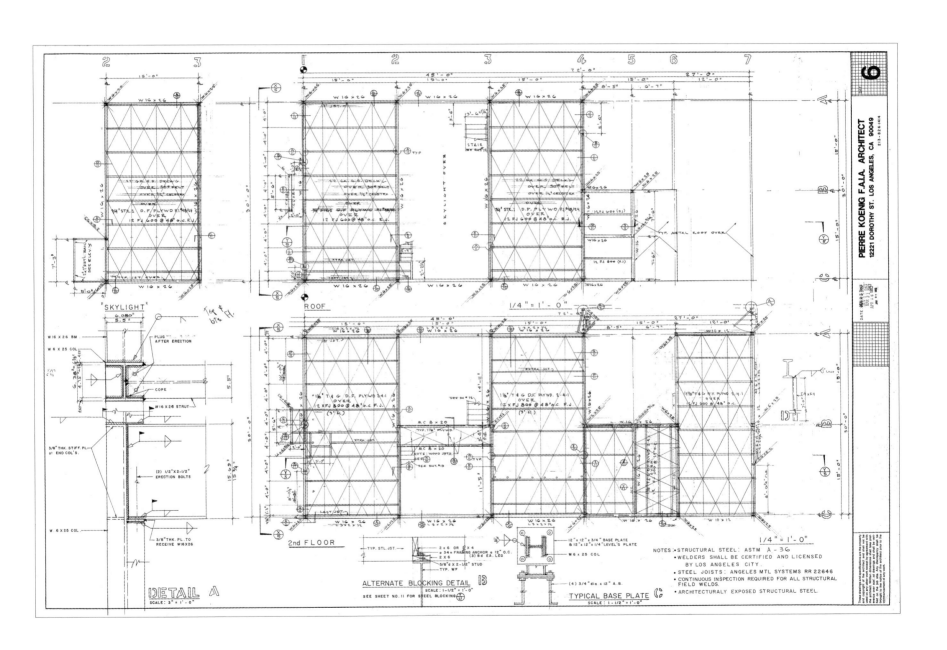

**Pl. 78.** Koenig House 2, elevations, section, 5 January 1983.

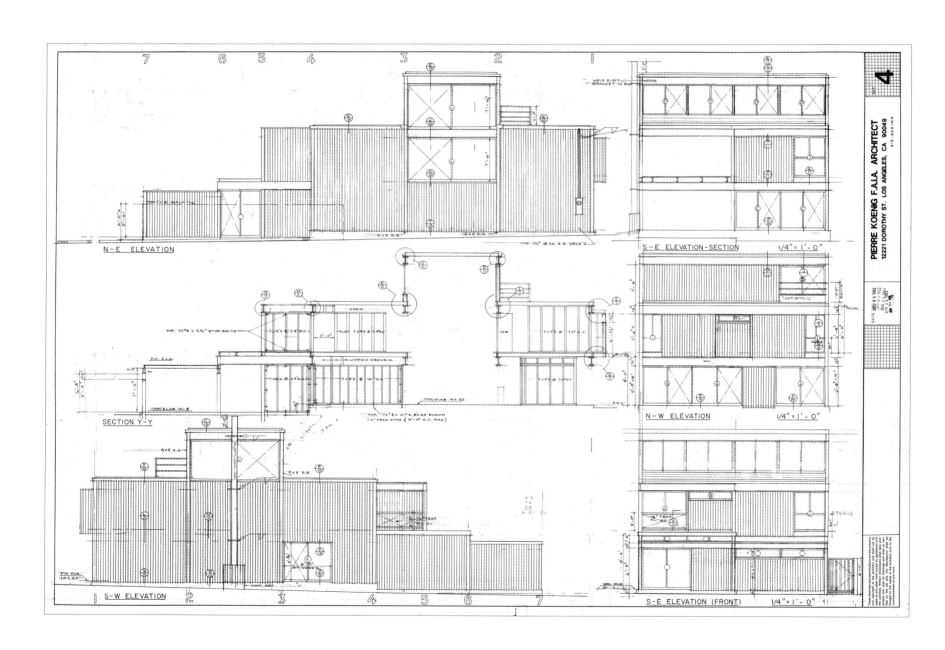

KOENIG HOUSE 2

**Pl. 79.** Koenig House 2, twelve-stage axonometric steel-assembly drawing, 5 January 1983.

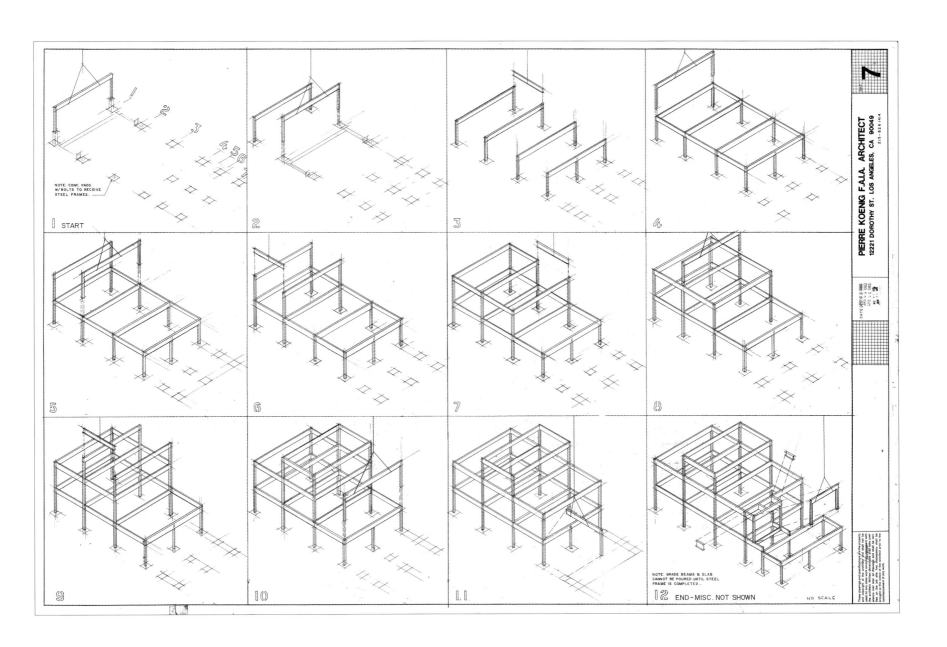

**Pl. 80.** Bosley House, preliminary study, plan, 5 August 1966.

**Pl. 81.** Bosley House, elevations, 9 March 1967.

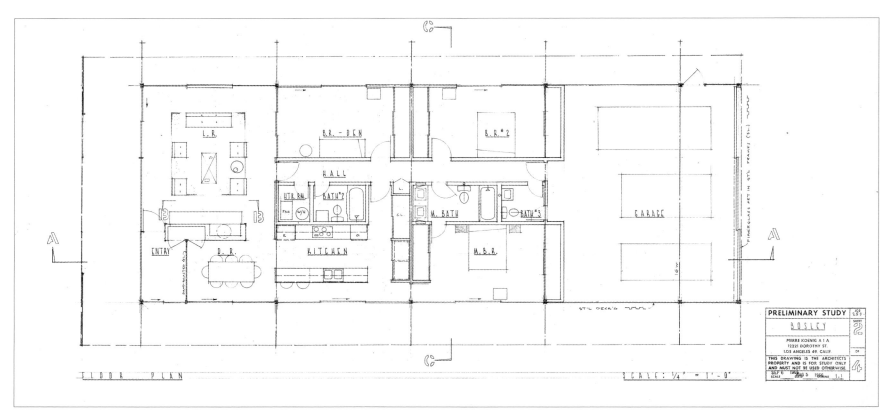

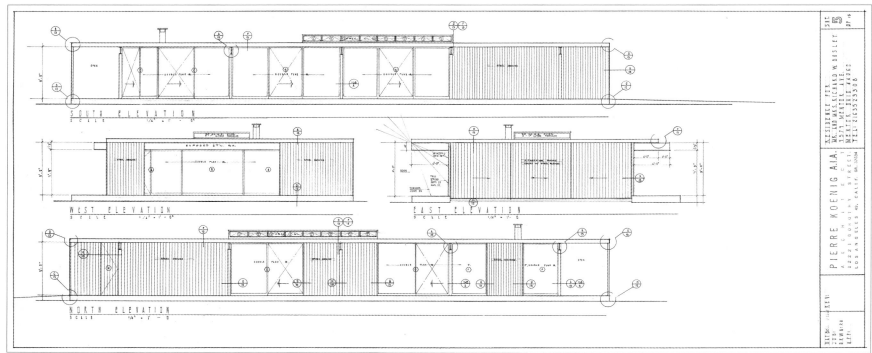

**Pl. 82.** EEI Factory and Showroom, preliminary study, lower-level plan, 13 September 1966.

**Pl. 83.** EEI Factory and Showroom, axonometric drawing of roof structure, ca. 1966.

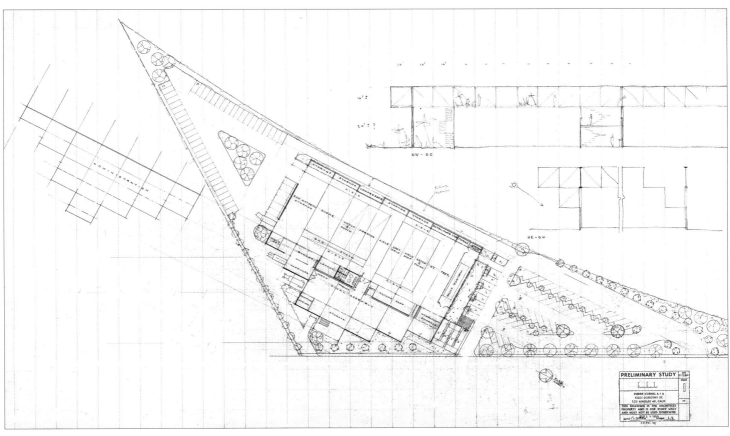

**Pl. 84.** Colwes House, elevations, ca. 1968.

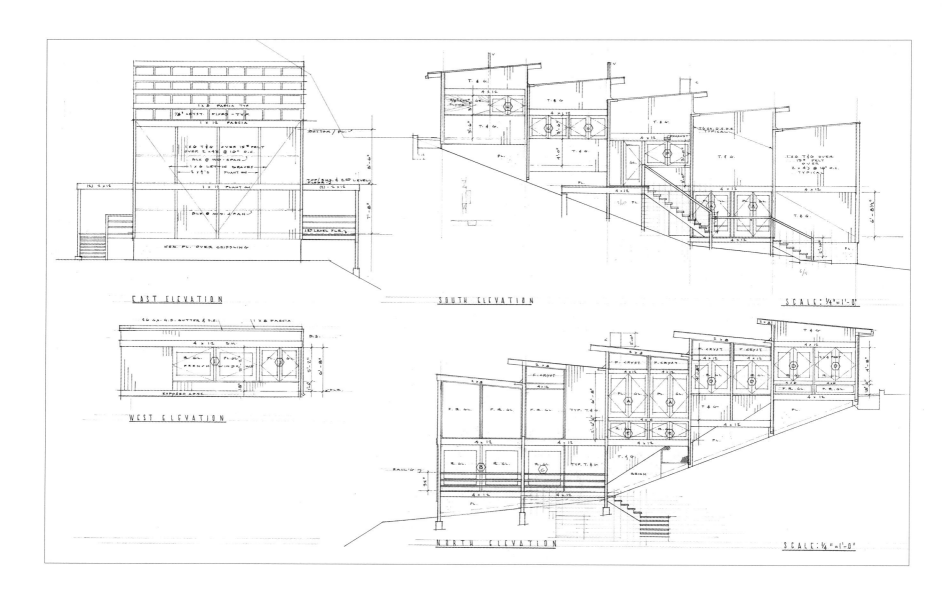

EAST ELEVATION

SOUTH ELEVATION

SCALE: 1/4"=1'-0"

WEST ELEVATION

NORTH ELEVATION

SCALE: 1/4"=1'-0"

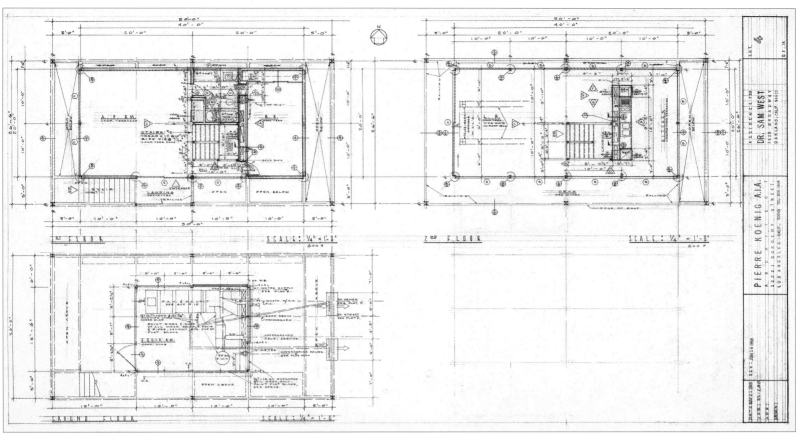

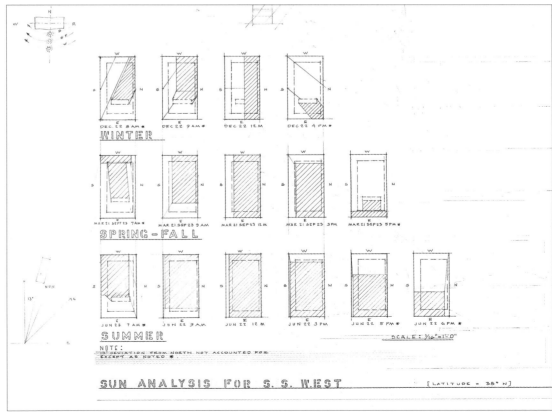

**Pl. 87.** Chemehuevi Housing Project, Community Facility, preliminary plan, 16 August 1972.

**Pl. 88.** Chemehuevi Housing Project, Tribal Council House, plan, ca. 1972.

**Pl. 89.** Chemehuevi Housing Project, Tribal Neighborhood Center, plan, section, ca. 1972.

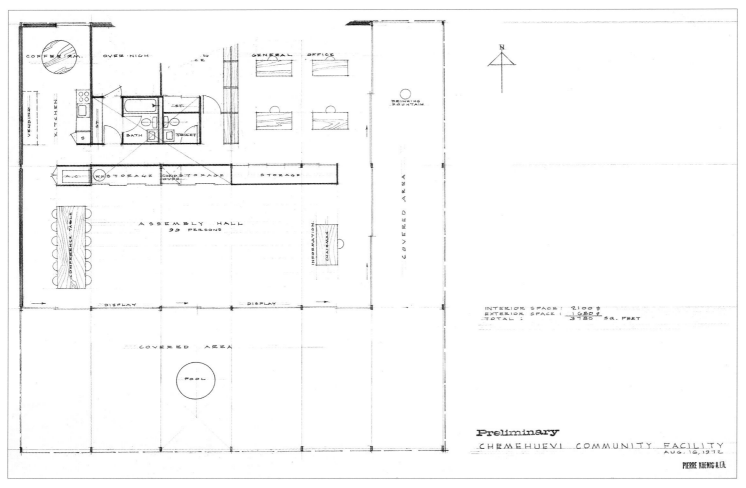

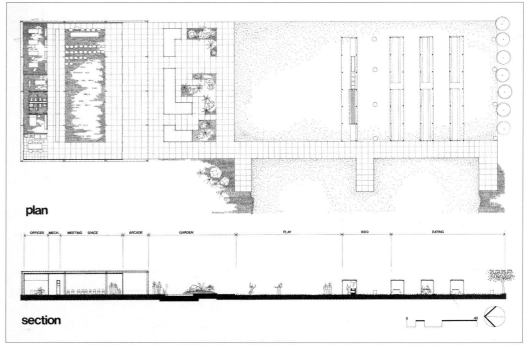

**Pl. 90.** Chemehuevi Housing Project, sun-path analysis, July 1973.

**Pl. 91.** Chemehuevi Housing Project, shower and toilet building, plan, elevations, sections, details, July 1973.

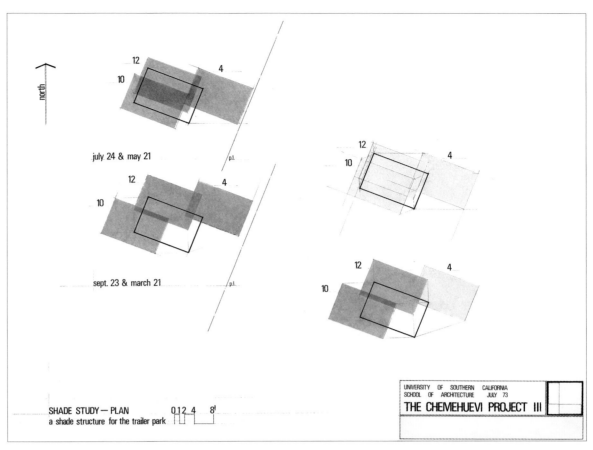

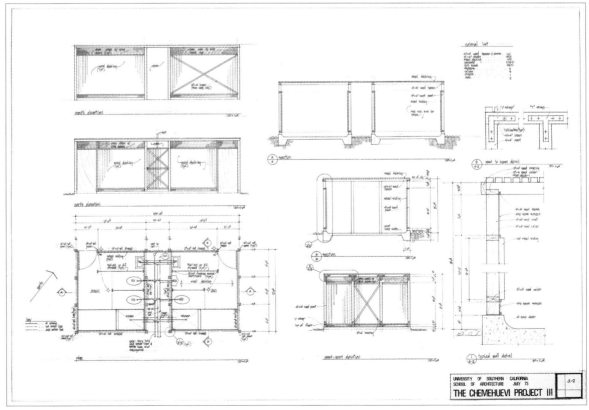

**Pl. 92.** Chemehuevi Housing Project, 400-square-foot house, type A5, plan, June 1971.

**Pl. 93.** Chemehuevi Housing Project, 1,200-square-foot house, type H1, plan, June 1971.

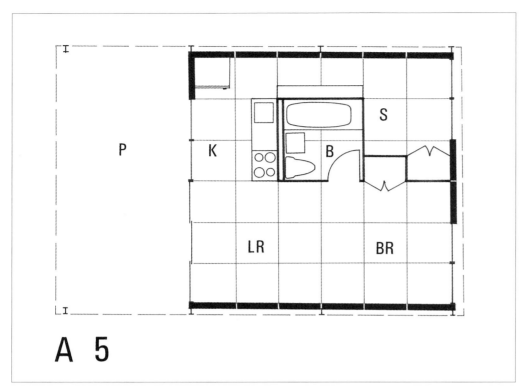

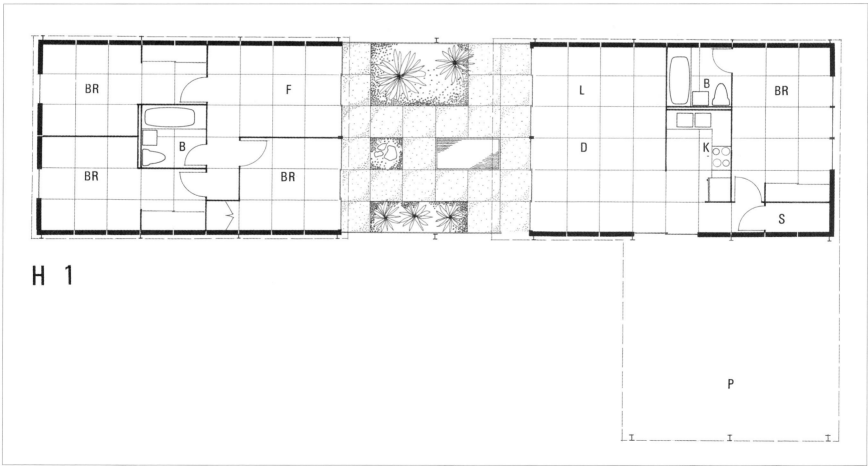

CHEMEHUEVI HOUSING PROJECT

**Pl. 94.** Chemehuevi Housing Project, interior panel details, June 1971.

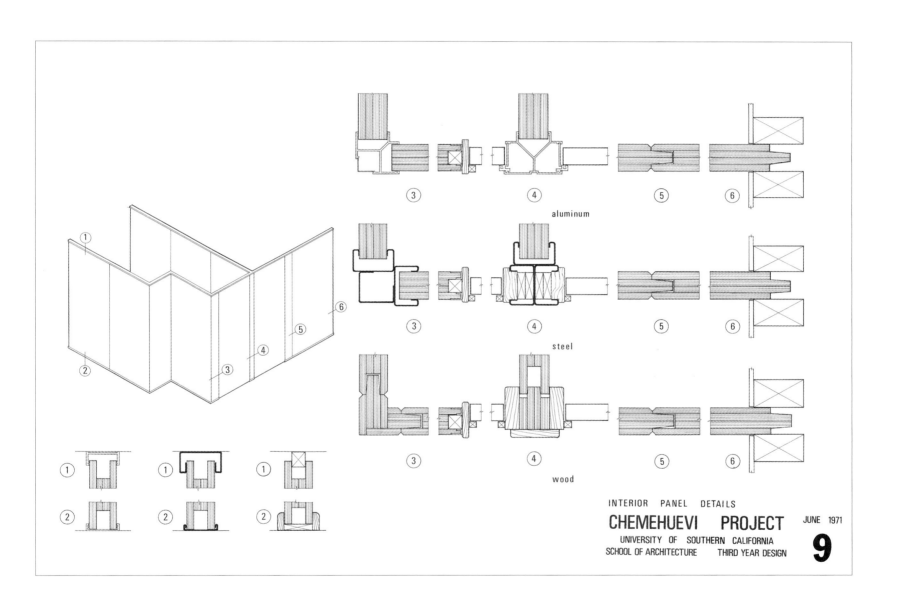

aluminum

steel

wood

INTERIOR PANEL DETAILS
CHEMEHUEVI PROJECT    JUNE 1971
UNIVERSITY OF SOUTHERN CALIFORNIA
SCHOOL OF ARCHITECTURE    THIRD YEAR DESIGN    9

**Pl. 95.** David Brindle, Evaluation of Dwelling Plans . . . , A-400:B-600 housing unit, plan, 1 June 1974.

**Pl. 96.** Chemehuevi Housing Project, A-400:B-600 housing unit, July 1974.

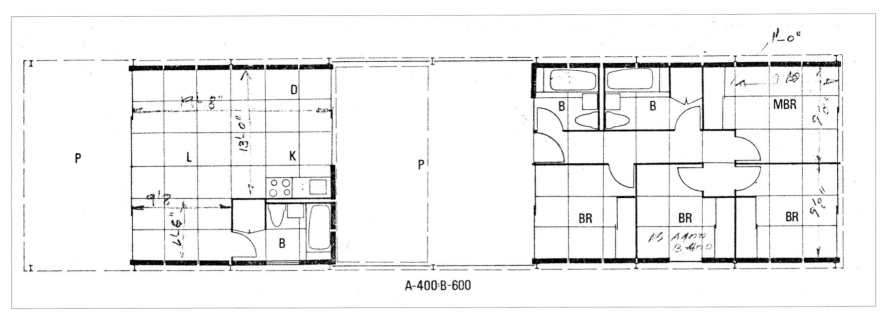

A-400:B-600

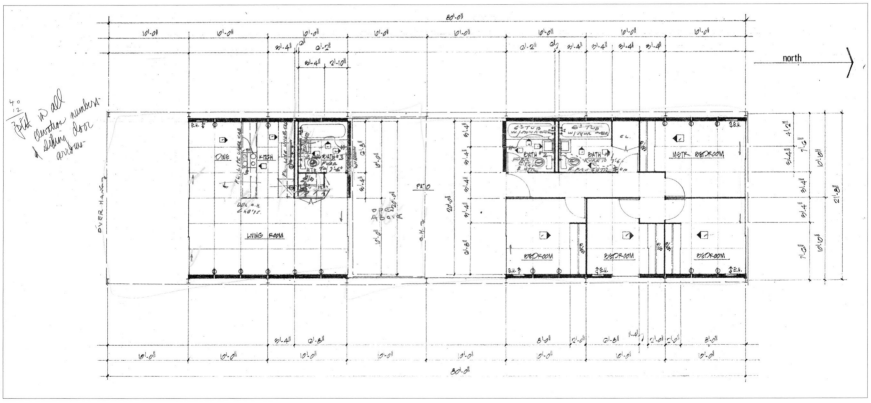

north

**Pl. 97.** Chemehuevi Housing Project, axonometric drawing of sixteen house types, 18 July 1976.

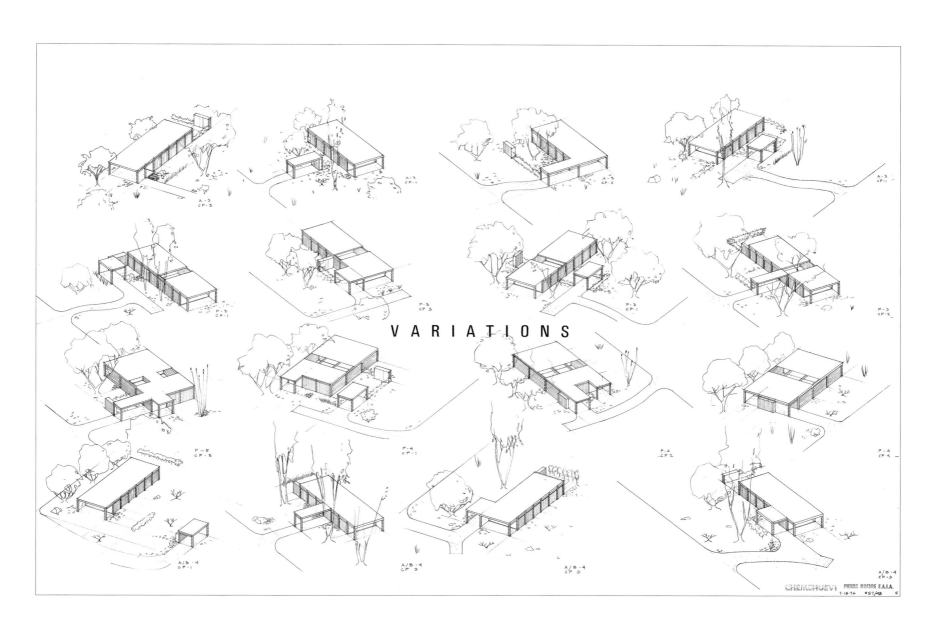

VARIATIONS

**Pl. 98.** Korzeniowski House and Apartment, details, 13 October 1971.

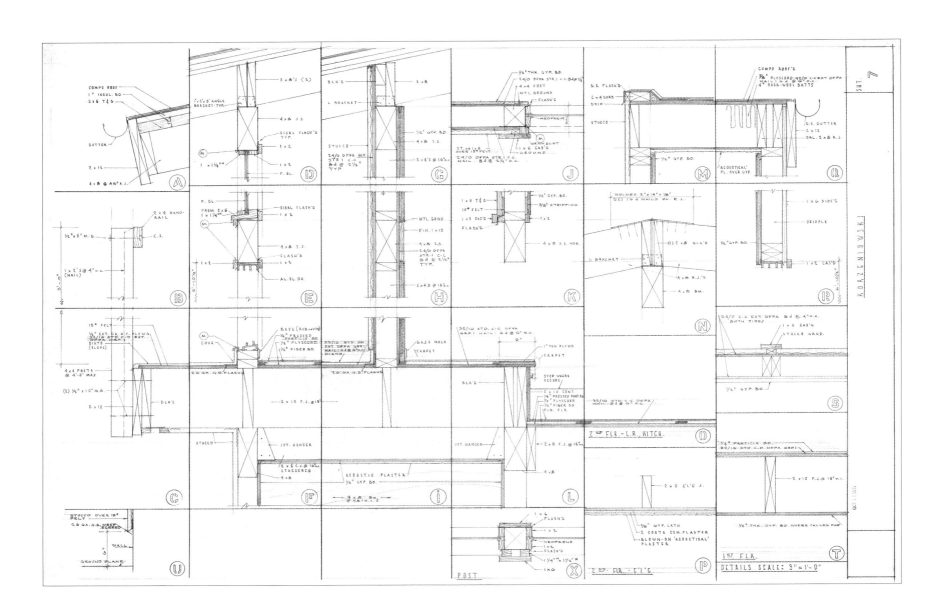

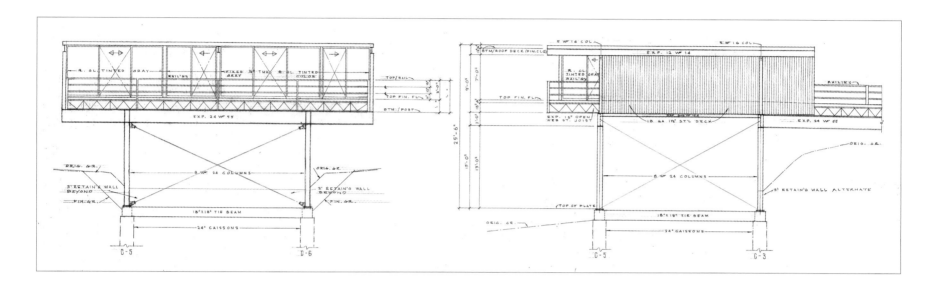

**Pl. 100.** Whittemore House, site sections, ca. 1973.

**Pl. 101.** Whittemore House, plan, ca. 1973.

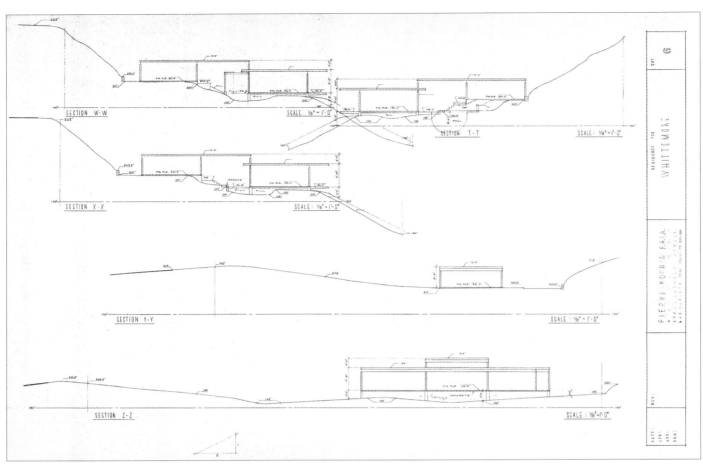

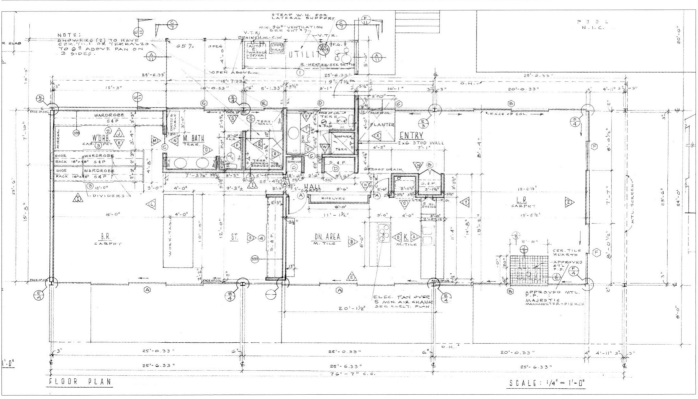

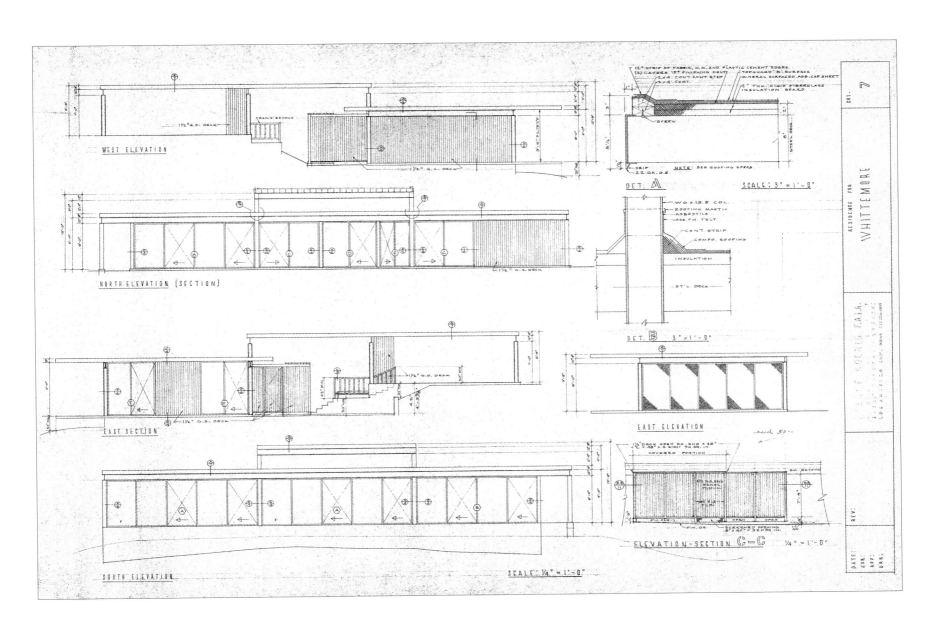

**Pl. 103.** Burton House, elevations, ca. 1978.

**Pl. 104.** Burton House, plan, ca. 1978.

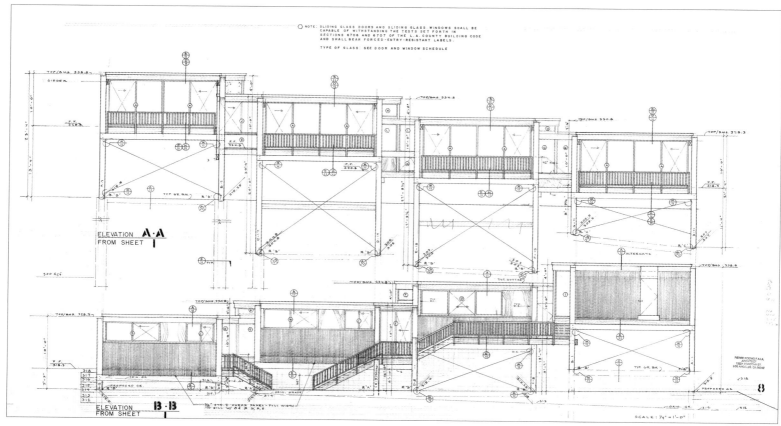

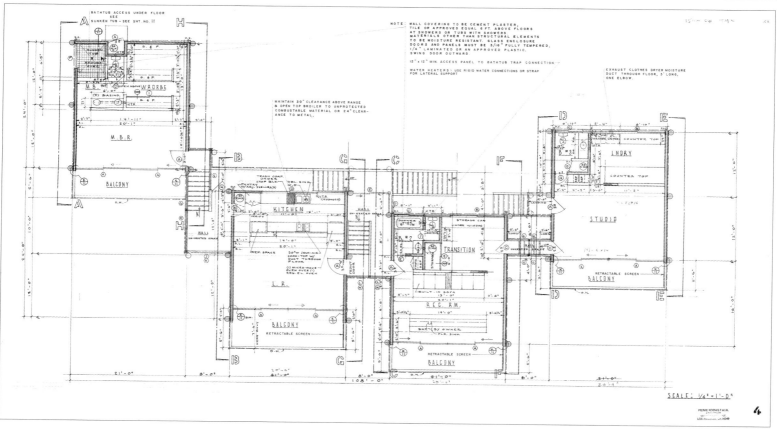

**Pl. 105.** Burton House, sections, ca. 1978.
**Pl. 106.** Burton House, sun-path analysis, ca. 1978.

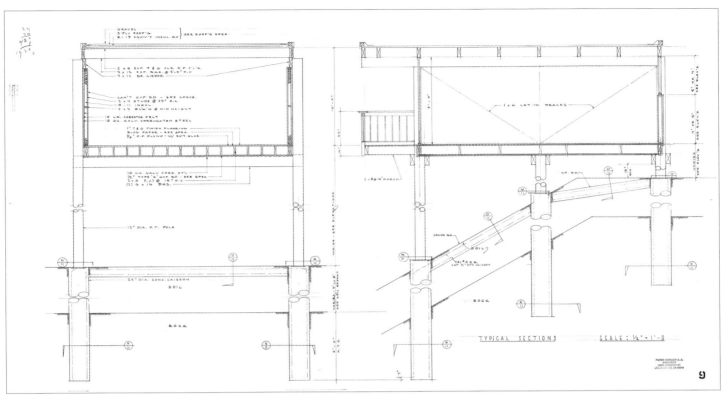

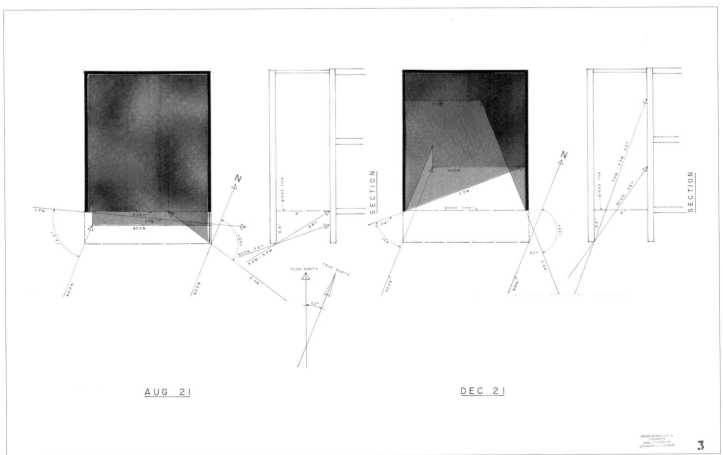

AUG 21

DEC 21

**Pl. 107.** Holland House, plan, elevation, section, details, 11 May 1979.

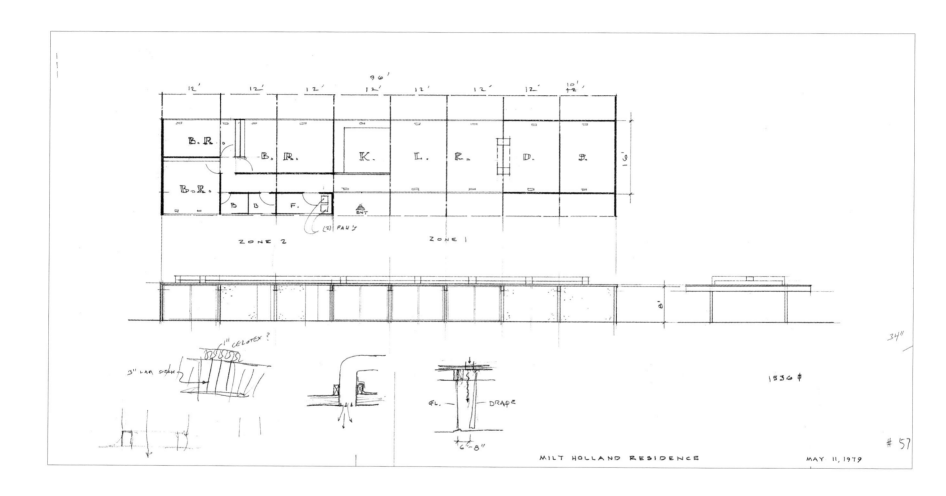

**Pl. 108.** Bayer House, plan, section, perspective drawing, 19 February 1982.

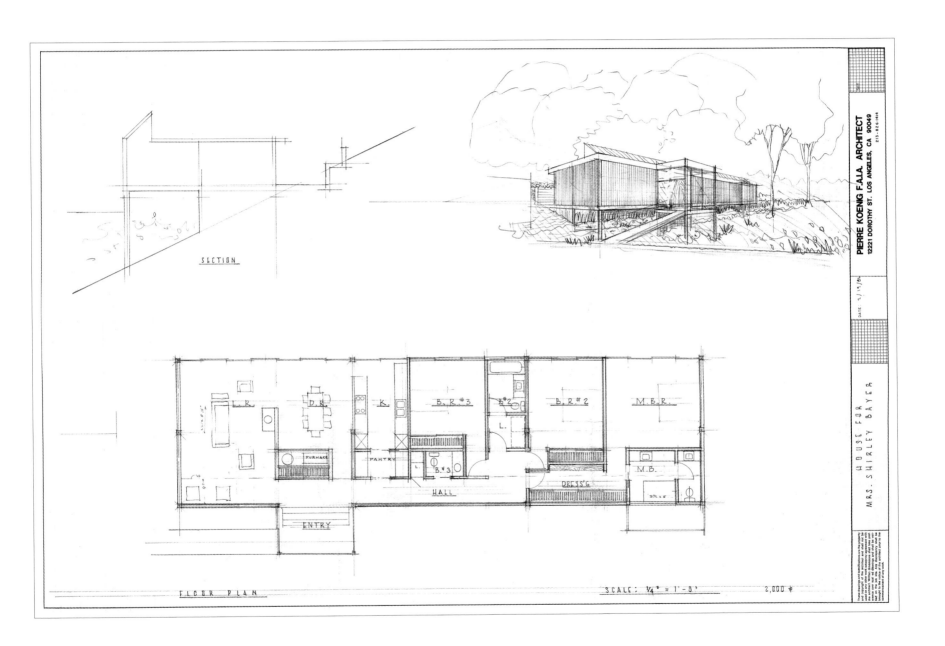

SECTION

PIERRE KOENIG F.A.I.A. ARCHITECT
12221 DOROTHY ST. LOS ANGELES, CA 90049
213-826-1444

HOUSE FOR
MRS. SHIRLEY BAYER

L.R.

D.R.

K.

PANTRY

FURNACE

B.R.#3

B.#3

B.#2

L.

B.R.#2

M.B.R.

M.B.

DRESS'G

HALL

ENTRY

FLOOR PLAN

SCALE: 1/4" = 1'-0"

2,000 #

**Pl. 109.** Gantert House, plans, 11 August 1980.

**Pl. 110.** Gantert House, elevations, details, 11 August 1980.

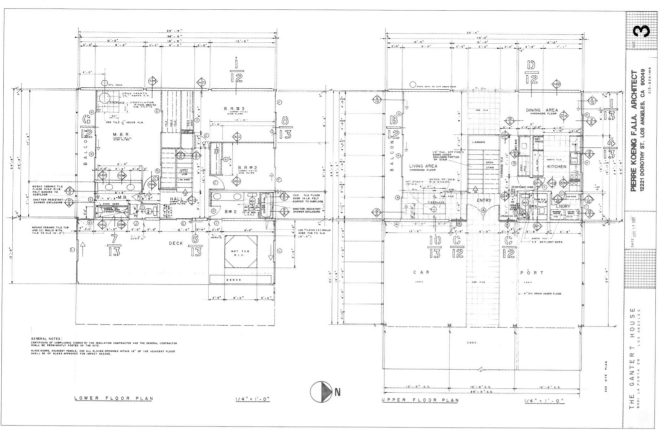

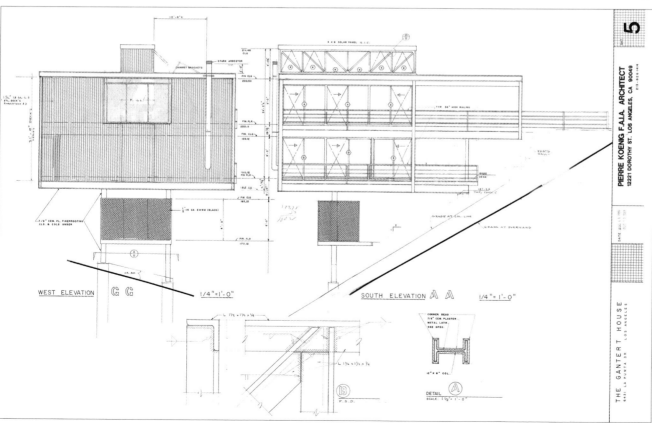

STUERMER HOUSE

**Pl. 111.** Stuermer House, version 4, elevations, details, 5 February 1985.

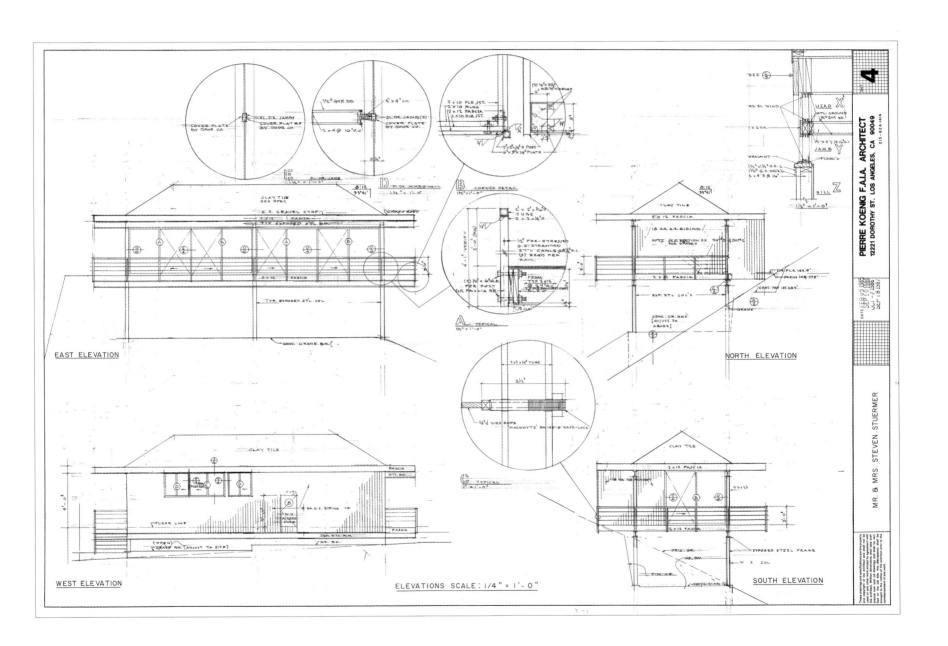

**Pl. 112.** Schwartz House, preliminary study, lower-floor plan, 5 October 1990.

**Pl. 113.** Schwartz House, preliminary study, upper-floor plan, 5 October 1990.

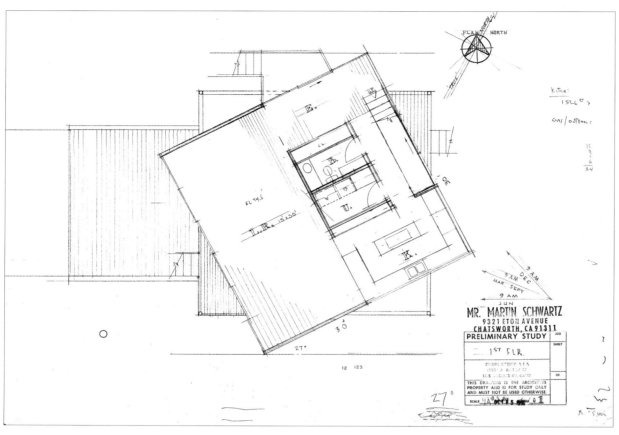

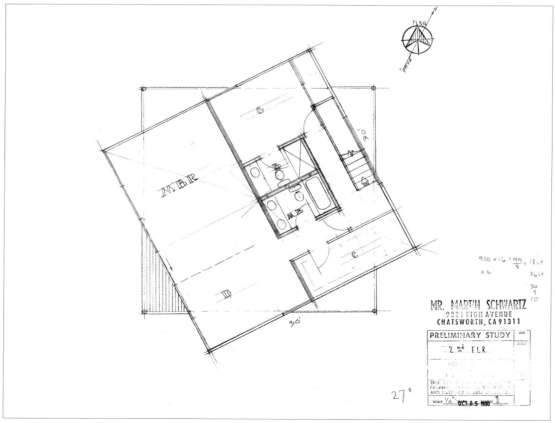

**Pl. 114.** Schwartz House, alternate plans, ca. 30 October 1990.

**Pl. 115.** Schwartz House, sun, ventilation, and view diagrams, ca. 16 November 1990.

**Pl. 116.** Schwartz House, preliminary study, lower-floor plan, 15 November 1990.

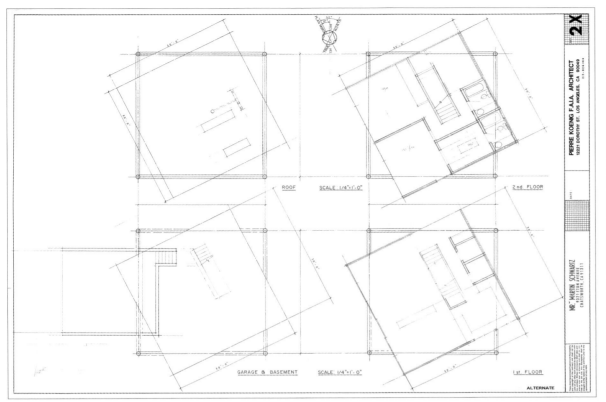

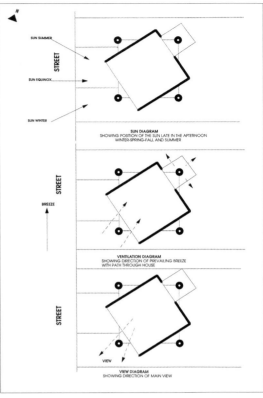

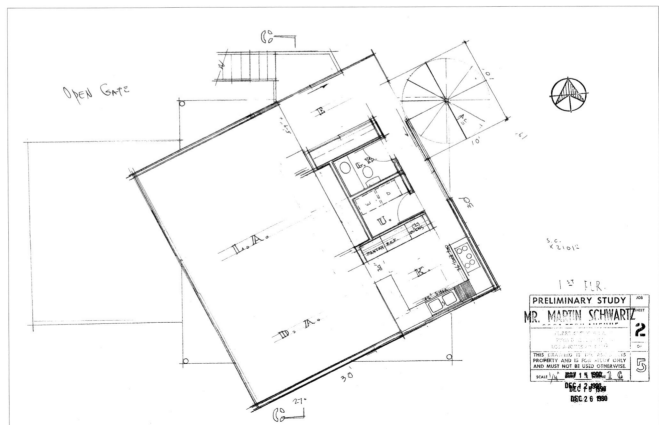

**Pl. 117.** Schwartz House, spiral stair, plan, elevation, details, 10 June 1992.

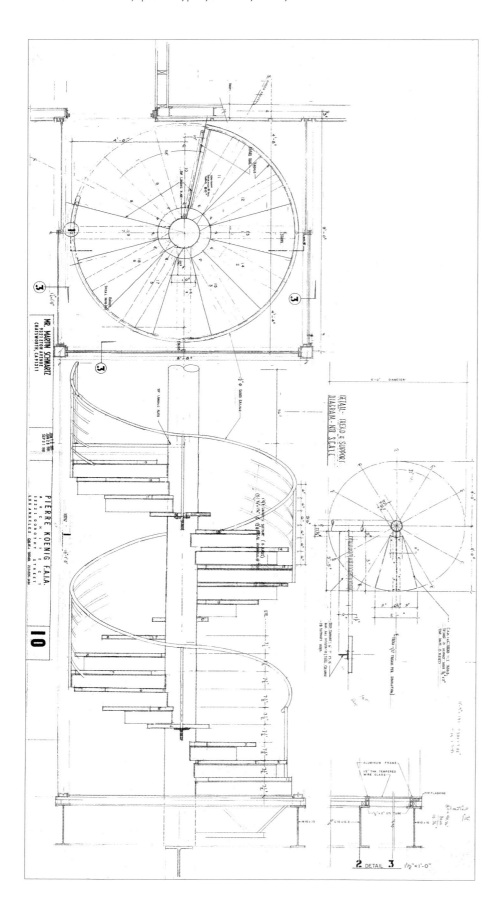

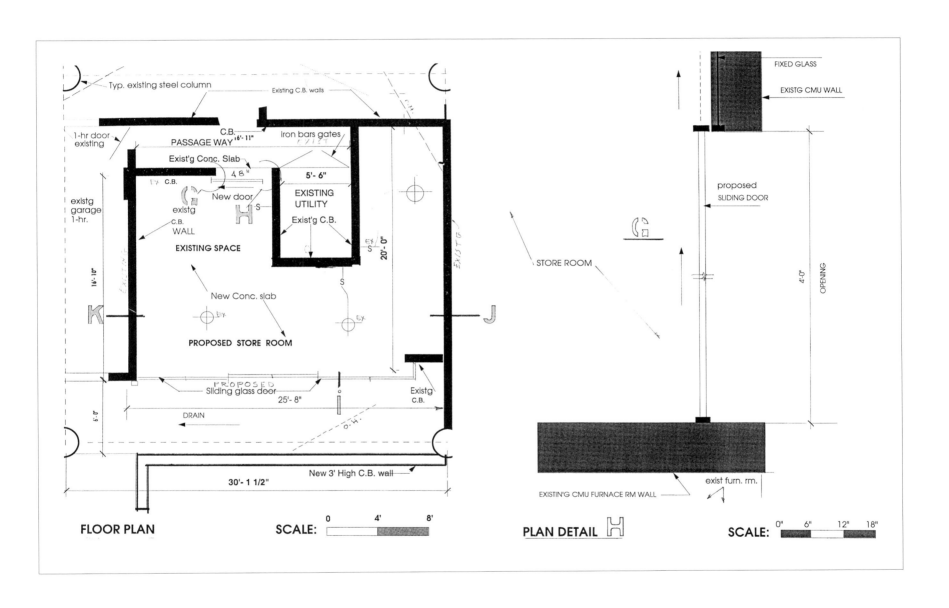

Typ. existing steel column

Existing C.B. walls

1-hr door existing

C.B.
PASSAGE WAY '6'- 11"

Iron bars gates

Exist'g Conc. Slab

4 8"

C.B.

New door

5'- 6"

EXISTING UTILITY

existg

existg garage 1-hr.

C.B. WALL

Exist'g C.B.

EXISTING SPACE

16'-10"

New Conc. slab

20'- 0"

K

J

PROPOSED  STORE  ROOM

PROPOSED
Sliding glass door

Existg C.B.

25'- 8"

DRAIN

New 3' High C.B. wall

30'- 1 1/2"

FLOOR PLAN

SCALE:

0      4'      8'

FIXED GLASS

EXISTG CMU WALL

proposed
SLIDING DOOR

STORE ROOM

4'-0"

OPENING

exist furn. rm.

EXISTIN'G CMU FURNACE RM WALL

PLAN DETAIL

SCALE:      0"      6"      12"      18"

**Pl. 119.** Frost/Hunt House, plan, details, axonometric drawing, ca. 2000.

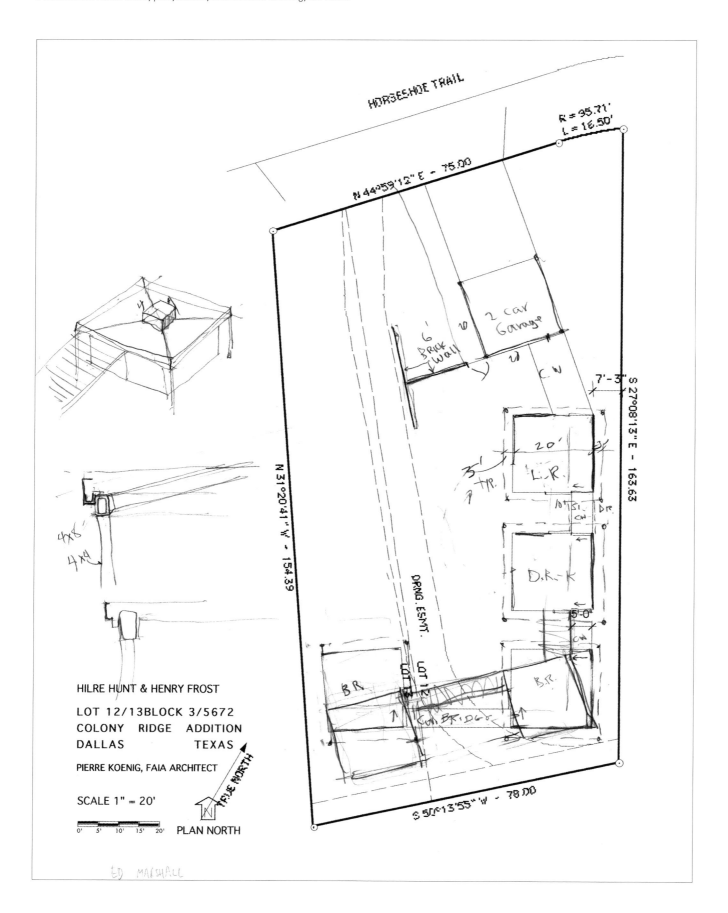

HORSESHOE TRAIL

R = 35.71'
L = 16.50'

N 44°59'12" E – 75.00

S 27°08'13" E – 163.63

N 31°20'41" W – 154.39

2 car Garage

6 BRICK WALL

C.W

7'-3

20'

L.R.

3'
TYP.

LOT 13    D.R
C.W

D.R-K

5'-0

CW

DRNG. ESMT.

BR

LOT 13
LOT 12

Con BRIDGE

B.R.

S 50°13'55" W – 78.00

4X8
4X4

HILRE HUNT & HENRY FROST

LOT 12/13 BLOCK 3/5672
COLONY   RIDGE   ADDITION
DALLAS            TEXAS

PIERRE KOENIG, FAIA ARCHITECT

SCALE 1" = 20'

0'   5'   10'   15'   20'

TRUE NORTH

N

PLAN NORTH

ED MARSHALL

KOPPANY POOL HOUSE

**Pl. 120.** Koppany Pool House, steel structure, plans, sections, details, axonometric drawing, 13 March 2002.

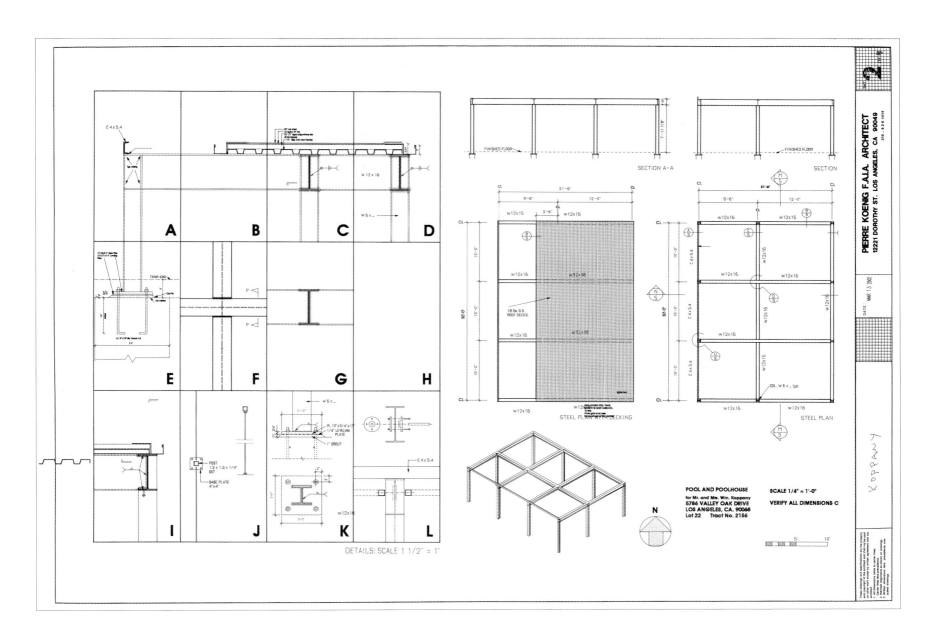

SECTION A-A

SECTION

STEEL PLAN WITH DECKING

STEEL PLAN

DETAILS: SCALE 1 1/2" = 1'

POOL AND POOLHOUSE
for Mr. and Mrs. Wm. Koppany
5786 VALLEY OAK DRIVE
LOS ANGELES, CA. 90068
Lot 22    Tract No. 2156

SCALE 1/4" = 1'-0"

VERIFY ALL DIMENSIONS C

PIERRE KOENG F.A.I.A. ARCHITECT
12221 DOROTHY ST. LOS ANGELES, CA 90049
310-826-1616

DATE  MAR 13 2002

**Pl. 121.** Ressner Modular Addition, recreation room, plans, ca. 1999.

**Pl. 122.** Ressner Modular Addition, bedroom and bathroom, plans, 29 November 1999.

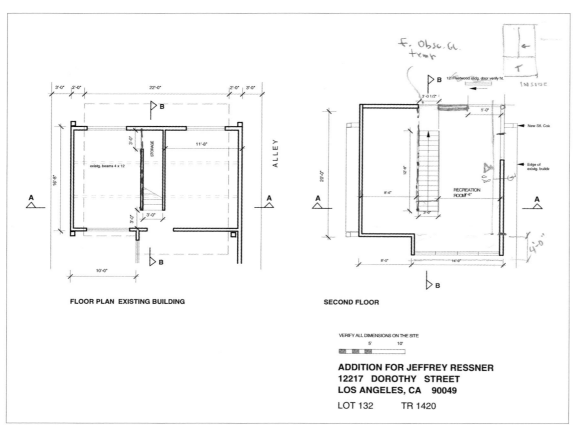

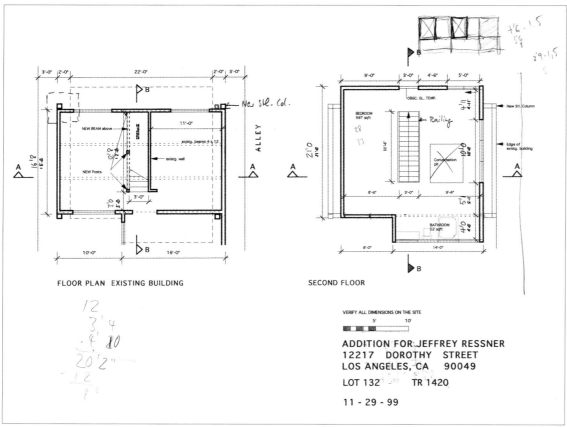

**Pl. 123.** Ressner Modular Addition, steel structure, plan, elevations, details, axonometric drawing, 29 June 2000.

**Pl. 124.** Ressner Modular Addition, elevations, sections, 29 June 2000.

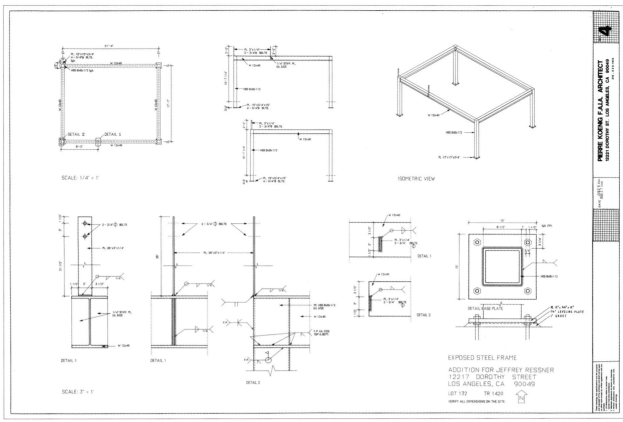

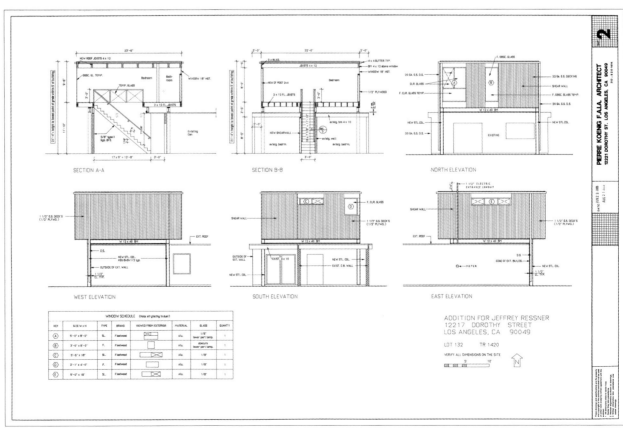

**Pl. 125.** Tarassoly and Mehran House, upper-floor plan, 6 September 2000.

**Pl. 126.** Tarassoly and Mehran House, lower-floor plan, 6 September 2000.

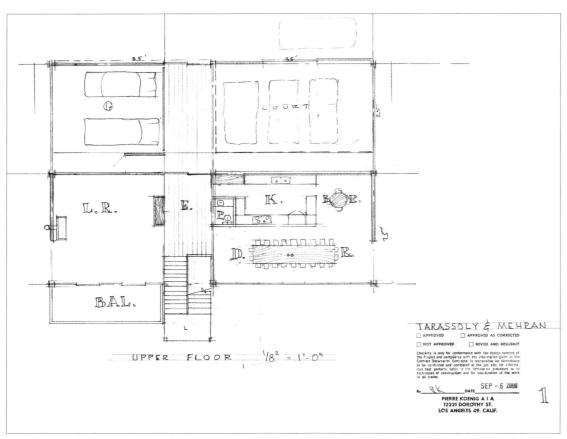

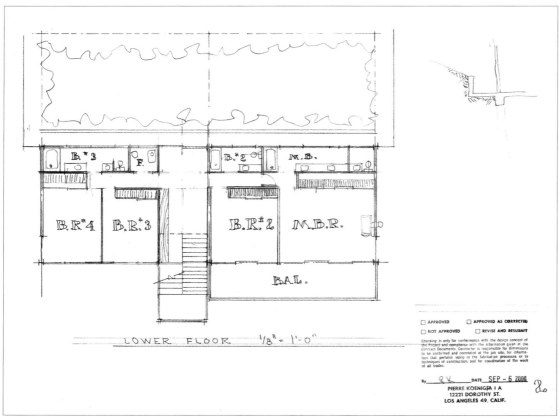

TARASSOLY AND MEHRAN HOUSE

Pl. 127. Tarassoly and Mehran House, scheme 103A, upper-floor and garage plan, ca. 2000.

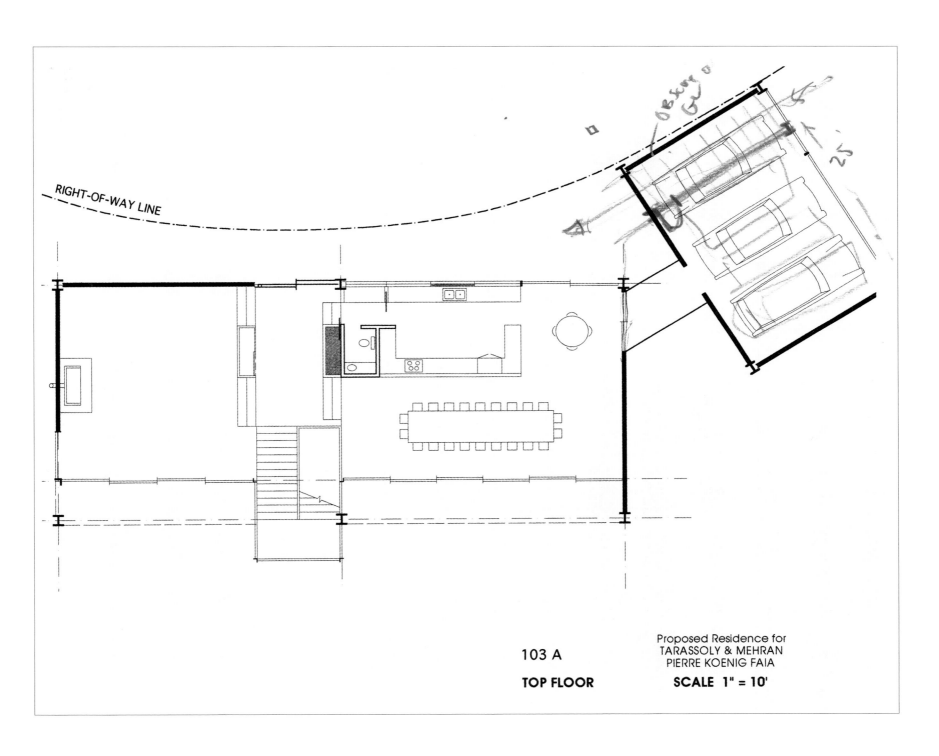

RIGHT-OF-WAY LINE

103 A

TOP FLOOR

Proposed Residence for
TARASSOLY & MEHRAN
PIERRE KOENIG FAIA

SCALE 1" = 10'

**Pl. 128.** Tarassoly and Mehran House, scheme 103A, upper-floor and garage plan, 1 September 2001.

**Pl. 129.** Tarassoly and Mehran House, lower-floor plan, 1 September 2001.

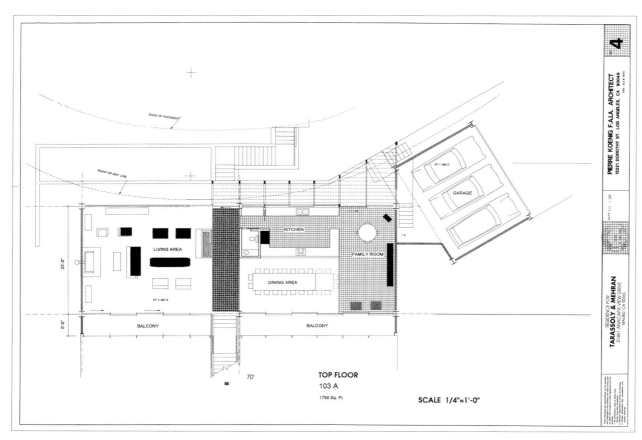

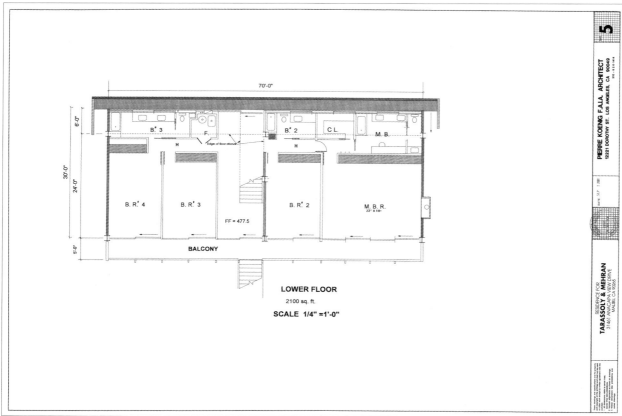

**Pl. 130.** Tarassoly and Mehran House, garage and bridge section, 21 March 2001.

**Pl. 131.** Tarassoly and Mehran House, view from northeast, 17 September 2001.

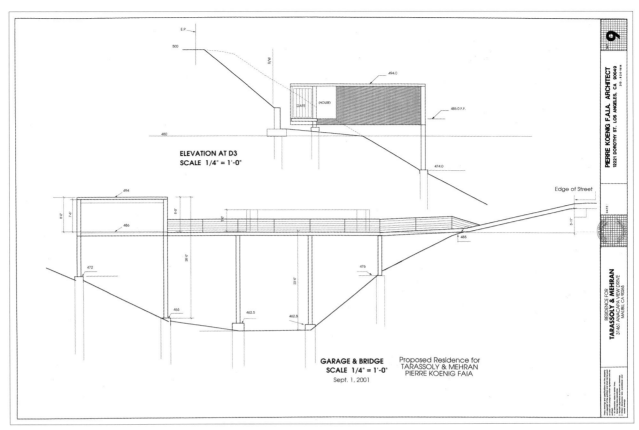

ELEVATION AT D3
SCALE 1/4" = 1'-0"

GARAGE & BRIDGE
SCALE 1/4" = 1'-0"
Sept. 1, 2001

Proposed Residence for
TARASSOLY & MEHRAN
PIERRE KOENIG FAIA

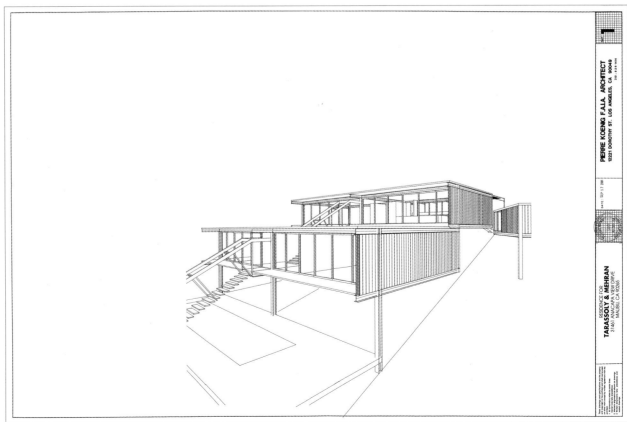

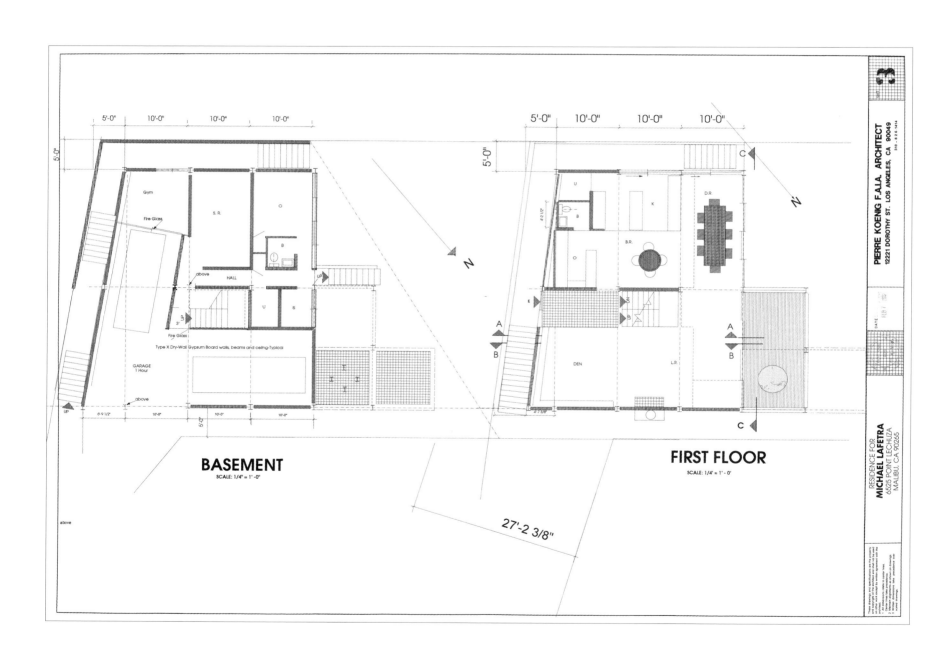

PIERRE KOENIG F.A.I.A. ARCHITECT
12221 DOROTHY ST. LOS ANGELES, CA 90049
310.826.1414

RESIDENCE FOR
**MICHAEL LAFETRA**
6525 POINT LECHUZA
MALIBU, CA 90265

**BASEMENT**
SCALE: 1/4" = 1'-0"

**FIRST FLOOR**
SCALE: 1/4" = 1' - 0'

27'-2 3/8"

**Pl. 133.** Fujioka Rental Units, alternative steel and timber designs, plans, elevations, n.d.

**Pl. 134.** Markel's Auto Upholstery Shop, plans, section, elevations, detail, n.d.

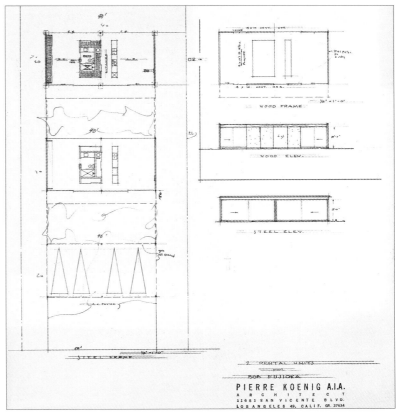

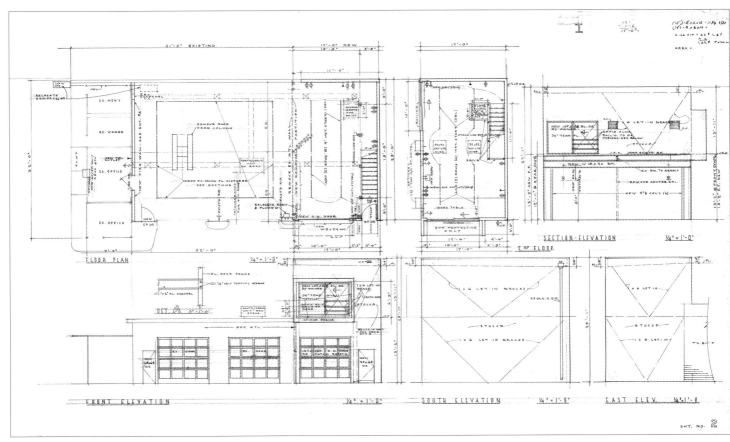

**Pl. 135.** Stern Addition, plans, section, elevations, plot plan, details, n.d.

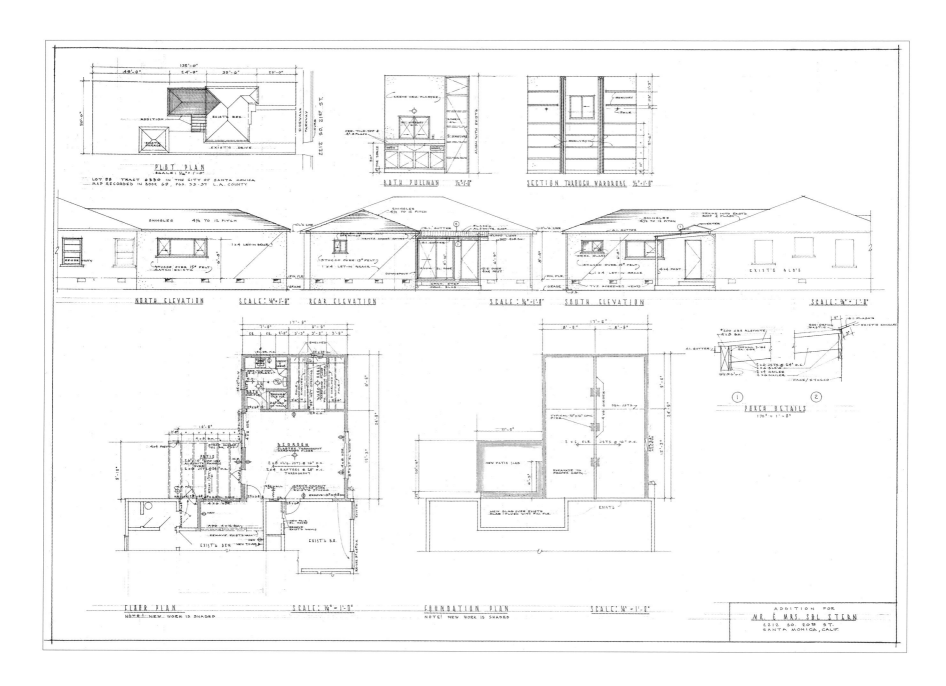

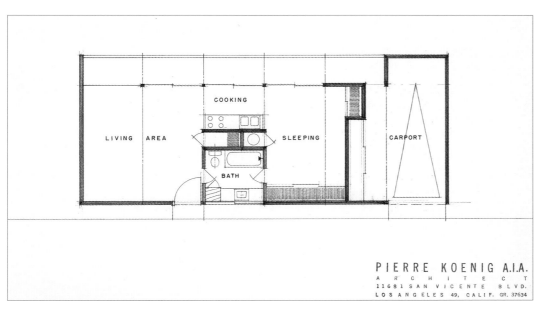

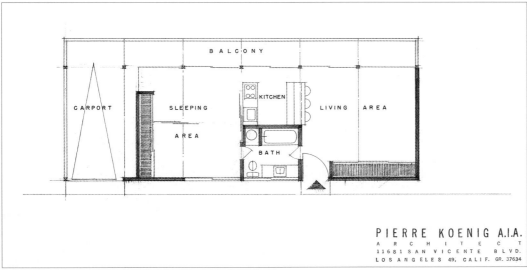

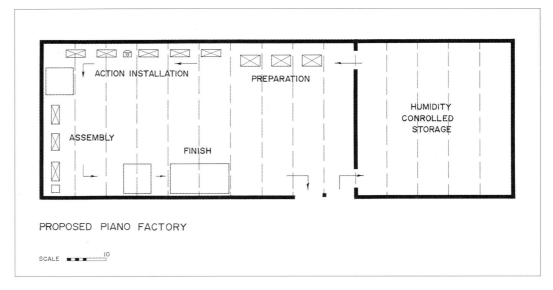

# ACKNOWLEDGMENTS

This book, which is based on an exploration of the Pierre Koenig archive held at the Getty Research Institute, would not have been possible without the enormous help of Sally McKay, head of Special Collections Services, and her team. To those guardians of Koenig's legacy, I am immensely grateful. I would also like to thank Gail Feigenbaum, Michele Ciaccio, and Janelle Gatchalian of Getty Research Institute Publications, who encouraged this project into the light, and Lauren Edson, Catherine Lorenz, and Victoria Gallina, who helped bring it to completion.

The book relies heavily on material held in the archive, but inevitably questions arose. I would like to thank Kenneth Breisch, David Buhler, Albert Dzur, Debi Howell-Ardila, Jan Ipach, Alissa McBeth, Billy Rose, and Janie Stewart, who patiently answered my correspondence, as well as Mohamed Sharif, who kindly gave me copies of his taped interviews with Koenig. In England, Graham Mancha shared with me his special knowledge of midcentury modern furniture, and June Lawrence and Simon Pepper commented on the text.

I have been visiting Pierre Koenig's houses for almost thirty years. This book has brought me back to many of them and to some of them for the first time. I would like to thank those other guardians of Koenig's legacy who have welcomed me into their houses: Alice Beagles, Ferrell and Christine Burton, Beth Cristales, Mark Haddawy, Jacob Koo, Bill Koppany, Michael LaFetra, Cynthia and Fred Riebe, Della and Gary Rollé, Martin and Mel Schwartz, Steven Slomkowski, Buck and Carlotta Stahl, and Geoff and Eda Wainwright.

Finally, I must thank Randall Koenig for those memories of his father; Gloria Koenig, for those of her husband; and Pierre Koenig himself, for the support and interest he showed me during the sixteen years I knew him. I hope that I have adequately reciprocated.

This book is dedicated to two Angelenos, Elizabeth and Grace.

*Neil Jackson*
*London, April 2018*

# CHRONOLOGICAL LIST OF WORKS

| Client | Work | Location | (E) Extant (D) Demolished (P) Project (U) Unknown status | Earliest Dated Drawing or Document | Drawing or Document Type Showing the Given Date | Date on Client Index Card | Archive Location for Dating (FF) Flat File (B) Box (F) Folder |
|---|---|---|---|---|---|---|---|
| Pierre Koenig | house 1 | 2002 Los Encinos Avenue, Glendale | D | 23 August 1950 | plan, elevation, section, construction detail | | FF1 |
| Jacqueline and Edward Lamel | house | 1884 Los Encinos Avenue, Glendale | E | 4 April 1953 | plan, elevation | 1953 | FF2 |
| Aurora and Edwin Scott | house | 10300 Haines Canyon, Tujunga | D | 21 September 1953 | plan, elevation | 1953 | FF5 |
| William Squire | house | 5323 Palm Drive, La Cañada | E | 1 October 1953 | plan | 1953 | FF3 |
| Mary and Walter Bailey | house 1 | 9038 Wonderland Park Avenue, Los Angeles | P | 16 April 1956 | plot plan, plan, construction detail | 1958 | FF17 |
| Mr. and Mrs. Henry E. Burwash | house | 9520 Amoret Drive, Tujunga | E | 15 February 1957 | plot plan, plan elevation, construction detail | 1957 | FF7 |
| Francis and Larry Beidleman | house 1 | Hanley Avenue, Los Angeles | P | 12 April 1957 | plan, elevation, construction detail | 1954 | FF26 |
| Mary and Walter Bailey | house 2 | 9038 Wonderland Park Avenue, Los Angeles | E | 22 April 1957 | plan, elevation, construction detail | 1958 | FF18 |
| Mr. and Mrs. Frank K. Danzig | house remodel | 1156 San Ysidro Drive, Beverly Hills | E | 2 May 1957 | plan, elevation | 1 May 1957 | FF9 |
| Seidel Associates | house | 2727 Mandeville Canyon Road, Los Angeles | E | 20 May 1957 | approval of variation request | | B1A.F6 |
| Frank Danzig, J. E. Mason, KYOR radio station | commercial building | 127 North Broadway, Blythe | E | 1 August 1957 | section, elevation, preliminary design | 1 May 1957 (Danzig), 1958 (Mason) | FF10 |
| Carlotta and Clarence "Buck" Stahl | house | 1635 Woods Drive, Los Angeles | E | 3 July 1958 | elevation | 1959–60 | FF20, FF21 |
| Seidel Investment Co. | commercial building remodel | Waldorf Hotel, 5 Westminster Avenue, Venice | U | 1 August 1958 | plan, elevation, section, detail | | FF24A |

| Client | Work | Location | (E) Extant (D) Demolished (P) Project (U) Unknown status | Earliest Dated Drawing or Document | Drawing or Document Type Showing the Given Date | Date on Client Index Card | Archive Location for Dating (FF) Flat File (B) Box (F) Folder |
|---|---|---|---|---|---|---|---|
| Mr. and Mrs. B. Dowden | house | | P | 15 August 1958 | perspective | | FF14 |
| Mr. and Mrs. Arnold D. Metcalf | house | 2342 Moreno Drive, Los Angeles | P | 20 August 1958 | plan, section, construction detail | August 1958 | FF13 |
| Seidel Investment Co. | commercial building remodel | Casa Loma Apartments, 101 Dudley Avenue, Venice | U | 5 November 1958 | plan, elevation, section | | FF24A |
| Seidel Investment Co. | commercial building remodel | 30 Dudley Avenue, Venice | U | 13 November 1958 | plan, elevations | | FF24A |
| Seidel Investment Co. | commercial building remodel | Sidewalker Café, Saint Mark's Hotel, Windward Avenue and Ocean Front Walk, Venice | U | 22 January 1959 | plan, elevation, details | | FF24A |
| Seidel Investment Co. | commercial building remodel (front) | 40 Brooks Avenue, Venice | P | 9 March 1959 | plot plan, elevation, construction detail | | FF24A |
| Seidel Investment Co. | commercial building remodel | Knickerbocker Building, 431 Ocean Front Walk, Venice | D | 21 April 1959 | plan, elevation | | FF24A |
| Seidel Associates | house | 2727 Mandeville Canyon Road, Los Angeles | E | 8 June 1959 | plan, elevation | | FF23 |
| Albert A. Dzur | house | San Pedro | P | 21 June 1959 | plan (signed and dated by Dzur) | | FF15 |
| Albert A. Dzur | guest house | San Pedro | P | 29 September 1959 | plan | | FF16 |
| Larry Beidleman | house 2 | Hanley Avenue, Los Angeles | P | 7 January 1960 | preliminary plan (signed by Beidleman) | 1954 | FF26 |
| Tom Seidel | beach house | 42560 Pacific Coast Highway, Malibu | E | 15 January 1960 | plan, elevation | undated | FF29 |
| Janet and Mayer Oberman | house | 24 Crestwind Drive, Palos Verdes (given as 5200 Crestwind Drive on the client index card) | E | 13 June 1960 | elevation, section | 1962 | FF38 |
| Venice Development Co. | prefabricated tract houses | St. Jean, Quebec | P | 17 August 1960 | plan, construction detail | | FF34 |
| Mr. and Mrs. P. E. Philbrick | new porch | 530 Georgina Avenue, Santa Monica | U | 29 August 1960 | working drawings | | FF25 |
| Andrew Whittlesey | house | | P | 3 December 1960 | plan, elevation | undated | FF25 |

| Client | Work | Location | (E) Extant (D) Demolished (P) Project (U) Unknown status | Earliest Dated Drawing or Document | Drawing or Document Type Showing the Given Date | Date on Client Index Card | Archive Location for Dating (FF) Flat File (B) Box (F) Folder |
|---|---|---|---|---|---|---|---|
| Dr. and Mrs. Jules Alan Plaut | house | | P | 14 February 1961 | plan | undated | FF25 |
| Tom Seidel | carport addition | 42560 Pacific Coast Highway, Malibu | P | 2 June 1961 | plan, elevation, section | undated | FF29 |
| Elizabeth Donahue | | | | | | 24 June 1961 | B36 |
| Elizabeth and Cyrus Johnson | house | 54 La Rancheria, Carmel Valley | E | 7 August 1961 | elevation, plan | 1962 | FF148 |
| Felicia and Leon Papernow | house addition | 989 Corsica Drive, Pacific Palisades | E | 4 December 1961 | plot plan, plan, elevation, section | undated | FF41 |
| Tom Seidel | The Stover apartments | Stoner Avenue, Los Angeles | U | 4 December 1961 | working drawings | | FF31 |
| Peter de Winter | house | 6331 Deep Dell Place, Los Angeles | P | 9 January 1962 | plot plan, plan, elevation, section, construction detail | undated | FF40 |
| David Herrington | house 1 | 1907 North Beverly Drive, Beverly Hills | E | 20 February 1962 | plot plan, plan, elevation, construction detail | undated | FF49 |
| Jerry and Robert Willheim | Seidel House rebuild | 1355 North Bundy Drive, Los Angeles | E | 15 March 1962 | plan, construction detail | 1961 | FF36 |
| Seidel Investment Co. | commercial building remodel (rear) | 40 Brooks Avenue, Venice | E | 6 August 1962 | plan | | FF24A |
| Alice and Robert Beagles | house | 17446 Revello Drive, Pacific Palisades | E | 2 November 1962 | plan, elevation, section, construction detail | 1962 | FF48 |
| Lorain and Steven Valensi | first addition to Seidel Associates House | 2727 Mandeville Canyon Road, Los Angeles | P | 27 December 1962 | plan, perspective | undated | FF24, FF23 |
| Mohammed Alsabery, Muslim Association of America | mosque | Hollywood | P | | | 1963 | B36 |
| Bethlehem Steel Co. | exhibition stand | | D | 27 February 1963 | plan, elevation | | FF39 |
| Mr. and Mrs. David Herrington | house 2 | 1911 North Beverly Drive, Beverly Hills | E | 4 November 1963 | plot plan, plan, elevation | undated | FF49 |

| Client | Work | Location | (E) Extant (D) Demolished (P) Project (U) Unknown status | Earliest Dated Drawing or Document | Drawing or Document Type Showing the Given Date | Date on Client Index Card | Archive Location for Dating (FF) Flat File (B) Box (F) Folder |
|---|---|---|---|---|---|---|---|
| Mr. and Mrs. Ira Lawrence | house | 3440 Meier Street (later 3442), Mar Vista | E | 24 February 1964 | elevation, section, axonometric | | FF140 |
| Jacob Rosenberg | | | | | | 10 April 1964 | B36 |
| Wilma and Robert Alan Franklyn | cabana | 782 West Portrero Road, Thousand Oaks (given as 52 Potrero Road in drawing title) | P | 1 July 1964 | plan, elevation section, construction detail | 23 April 1964 | FF50 |
| Neal Levine | | | | | | 5 February 1965 | B36 |
| A. Bruce Whitehead | Burwash House addition | 9520 Amoret Drive, Tujunga | E | 10 February 1965 | plan, elevation, section | 29 November 1965 | FF51 |
| Vickie Kabuko and Richard Iwata | house | 912 Summit Place, Monterey Park | E | 4 May 1965 | section, construction detail | 9 October 1963 | FF42, FF43 |
| Dr. Robert Alan Franklyn | office building | 8778/8782 Sunset Boulevard, Los Angeles | P | 1 July 1965 | plan | 23 April 1964 | FF72 |
| Martha and Harold Henbest | house | 7127 Crest Road, Rancho Palos Verdes | E | 11 August 1965 | elevation, section, construction detail | 19 February 1963 | FF65 |
| Lorain and Steven Valensi | second addition to Seidel Associates House | 2727 Mandeville Canyon Road, Los Angeles | E | 1 September 1965 | plan, elevation | undated | FF23 |
| Pierre Koenig | house addition 1 | 12221 Dorothy Street, Brentwood | E | 19 January 1966 | plot plan, plan, elevation, section, construction detail | | FF56 |
| Pierre Koenig | house addition 2 | 12221 Dorothy Street, Brentwood | P | 18 July 1966 | plot plan, plan, section, construction detail | | FF56 |
| Carol E. and Richard W. Bosley | house | 9579 Mentor Avenue, Mentor, OH | P | 5 August 1966 | preliminary studies | 29 June 1966 | FF57 |
| Mike Jacobs, Electronic Enclosures Inc. | factory | 225 South Aviation Boulevard, Los Angeles | E | 13 September 1966 | preliminary study, plan, section | 1 August 1966 | FF53 |
| Alban Katz | | 1301 Summit Ridge, Beverly Hills | | | | 11 August 1967 | B36 |
| Alice and Carmine Pagano | | Navesink Park, Monmouth County, NJ | | | | 31 August 1967 | B36 |
| Marianne and Jacob Marschak | house | | P | | | 4 January 1968 | B36 |

| Client | Work | Location | (E) Extant (D) Demolished (P) Project (U) Unknown status | Earliest Dated Drawing or Document | Drawing or Document Type Showing the Given Date | Date on Client Index Card | Archive Location for Dating (FF) Flat File (B) Box (F) Folder |
|---|---|---|---|---|---|---|---|
| Howard E. Johnson | | | | | | 30 March 1968 | B36 |
| Louie Cruz, Manuel's Carnitas | 18 vacation units, El Campo Turistico "Manuel's" | Rio Hardy, near Mexicali, Baja California, Mexico | P | | | 8 September 1968 | B36 |
| Matthew J. Colwes | | Vanetta Drive, Los Angeles | P | | | 13 December 1968 | B36 |
| Dr. Samuel A. West | house | Carquinez Heights, Vallejo | D | 21 May 1969 | plan, elevation | 1 October 1967 | FF61 |
| Laurie and Bruce Rozet | house remodel | 681 Brooktree Road, Pacific Palisades | U | 7 July 1969 | plan | 1 February 1969 | FF60 |
| Joe Koevner | | 9119 St. Ives Drive, Los Angeles | | | | 10 January 1970 | B36 |
| Mort Freeman, Marion Cantor | | | | | | 7 July 1970 | B36 |
| Evelyn Heller | pavilion, house | 1773 Olinda Road, Makawao, Maui, HI | | | | 1 August 1970 | B36 |
| John Calveti, Leon Papernow | | Cypress Communications television station building | | | payment recorded on client index card | 11 May 1971 | B36 |
| Chemehuevi: USC Third-Year Design Project | housing | Chemehuevi Reservation, Lake Havasu | P | June 1971 | plan | | B65 |
| Harold Henbest | house | 30159 Avenida de Calma, Palos Verdes | E | 7 July 1971 | elevation, section | 19 February 1963 | FF67 |
| Bev and Al Lawson | | 1216 North Sepulveda, Los Angeles | | | | 10 August 1971 | B36 |
| Roxanne and Josef Korzeniowski | house and apartment | 6520 Vista del Mar, Playa del Rey | D | 13 October 1971 | plan, elevation, construction detail | 27 April 1971 | FF68 |
| Patricia and John Dye | house remodel | 1201 Kings Road, Newport Beach | P | | | 22 June 1972 | B36 |
| Therona and Alex Whittemore | house | 3504 Coast View Drive, Malibu | P | 1 June 1973 | specification | undated | B2.F20 |
| Michael Nemo | house remodel | 2665 Hollyridge Drive, Los Angeles | E | 14 August 1975 | plan, section, construction detail | June 1975 | FF76 |
| Pierre Koenig | house addition 3 | 12221 Dorothy Street, Brentwood | P | 7 October 1975 | William Porush steel calculations | | B2.F21 |
| Rose Peterson | house remodel | 610 Mildred Avenue, Venice | U | 19 April 1976 | plan, elevation, section | | FF76 |

| Client | Work | Location | (E) Extant (D) Demolished (P) Project (U) Unknown status | Earliest Dated Drawing or Document | Drawing or Document Type Showing the Given Date | Date on Client Index Card | Archive Location for Dating (FF) Flat File (B) Box (F) Folder |
|---|---|---|---|---|---|---|---|
| Dr. Robert A. Franklyn | Restaurant for Apryl Franklyn | McCloud Avenue, Thousand Oaks | P | 8 June 1976 | preliminary study, axonometric | 23 April 1964 | FF101 |
| Mr. and Mrs. Hubert H. Grebe | house addition | 12567 Everglade Street, Los Angeles | E | 5 December 1976 | plot plan | November 1976 | FF76 |
| Christine and Ferrell Burton III | house | Looshen Road, at 31371 Pacific Coast Highway, Malibu | E | 26 September 1978 | Robert L. Covell and Associates topographical map | 4 July 1978 | FF99 |
| Mildred and Milt Holland | house | | P | 11 May 1979 | plan, elevation | 1 May 1979 | FF100 |
| Michael G. Gantert | house | 6431 La Punta Drive, Los Angeles | E | 11 August 1980 | plan, elevation, section | 4 June 1979 | FF110 |
| Carol May and Robert van der Linde | addition to Lawrence House | 3442 Meier Street (formerly 3440), Mar Vista | P | 12 August 1980 | plan | | FF142 |
| Pierre Koenig | house 2 | 12221 Dorothy Street, Brentwood | E | 12 June 1981 | quotation from Weld-Rite | | B8.F1 |
| Shirley Bayer | house | 3500 Mandeville Canyon Road, Los Angeles | P | 19 February 1982 | plan, section, perspective | 21 March 1980 | FF106 |
| Della and Gary Rollé | first addition to Seidel Associates House | 2727 Mandeville Canyon Road, Los Angeles | E | 3 December 1982 | plan, elevation, construction detail | 10 January 1981 | FF120 |
| Pierre Koenig | house 2 | 12221 Dorothy Street, Brentwood | E | 5 January 1983 | plan, elevation, section, construction detail | | FF131 |
| Eiko and Steven Stuermer | house | Alina Place, Kaneohe, Oahu, HI | P | 24 June 1984 | preliminary plan, elevation | 12 August 1983 | FF125 |
| Cassandra and Pierce Brosnan | | | | | | 15 September 1984 | B36 |
| Pam Wayne | house addition | 425 32nd Street, Manhattan Beach | E | 2 December 1985 | site plan, plan, elevation, section, construction detail | | FF138 |
| Edson Newquist | Bailey House addition | 9038 Wonderland Park Avenue, Los Angeles | P | | | 15 January 1986 | B36 |
| Jeffrey Klawans, Connoisseur Antiques | shop addition | 8468 Melrose Place, Los Angeles | E | January 1986 | plot plan, plan, section | 24 January 1986 | FF139 |

| Client | Work | Location | (E) Extant (D) Demolished (P) Project (U) Unknown status | Earliest Dated Drawing or Document | Drawing or Document Type Showing the Given Date | Date on Client Index Card | Archive Location for Dating (FF) Flat File (B) Box (F) Folder |
|---|---|---|---|---|---|---|---|
| Margaret and Frank South | Squire House addition | 5323 Palm Drive, La Cañada | P | 11 November 1987 | site plan, plan, elevation, section | 1986 | FF144 |
| Cynthia and Fred Riebe | remodel of Johnson house | 54 La Rancheria, Carmel Valley | E | 21 September 1988 | letter from Fred Riebe to Pierre Koenig | 14 October 1988 | B10.F6 |
| Arlette Mosher | carport remodel | 12229 Dorothy Street, Brentwood | P | 15 March 1988 | plan | 19 December 1986 | FF147 |
| Jeffrey Ressner | house addition | 12217 Dorothy Street, Brentwood | P | | | 1 May 1988 | B36 |
| Martin Schwartz and Mel Cunanan | house | 444 Sycamore Road, Santa Monica | E | 5 October 1990 | plan | 9 August 1990 | FF159 |
| Della and Gary Rollé | second addition to Seidel Associates House | 2727 Mandeville Canyon Road, Los Angeles | E | 21 July 1991 | plan | 10 January 1981 | FF153 |
| Ted H. Weitzel, Indian River Investment Management Company, Inc. | housing | Dade County, FL | P | 24 October 1991 | letter from Ted Weitzel to Pierre Koenig | | B10.F13 |
| Martin Schwartz and Mel Cunanan | basement addition to Schwartz House | 444 Sycamore Road, Santa Monica | E | 28 July 1995 | exemption letter from California Coastal Commission to Martin Schwartz | 9 August 1990 | B15.F11 |
| John Hunke | | | | | | 8 March 1996 | B36 |
| Randall Koenig | house | Laguna Beach | P | 19 December 1996 | fax from Pierre Koenig to GA House Project '97 | | B16.F1 |
| Daniel Cracchiolo | Bailey House restoration | 9038 Wonderland Park Avenue, Los Angeles | E | 12 March 1997 | AIA agreement | 8 March 1997 | B16.F3 |
| Nick Sands | apartment remodel | New York, NY | P | 29 December 1997 | letter from Nick Sands to Pierre Koenig (dated postmark on envelope) | | B16.F7A |
| Hilre Hunt and Henry Frost | house | 5141 Horseshoe Trail, Bluff View, Dallas, TX | P | 21 April 1999 | letter from Hilre Frost to Pierre Koenig | 7 June 2000 | B17.F1 |
| Cynthia and William Koppany | pool house | 5786 Valley Oak Drive, Los Angeles | E | 17 July 1999 | AIA agreement | 19 March 1999 | B18.F3 |

| Client | Work | Location | (E) Extant (D) Demolished (P) Project (U) Unknown status | Earliest Dated Drawing or Document | Drawing or Document Type Showing the Given Date | Date on Client Index Card | Archive Location for Dating (FF) Flat File (B) Box (F) Folder |
|---|---|---|---|---|---|---|---|
| Nadir Safai | house | 433 South Cahuilla Road, Palm Springs | P | 14 August 1999 | letter from Nadir Safai to Pierre Koenig | | B16.F9A |
| Mary Anne and Alan Steinberger | house | 2446 Big Tujunga Canyon, Tujunga | P | 28 September 1999 | location plan sent from Alan Steinberger to Pierre Koenig | | B16.F10 |
| Pamela and Jefery Levy | house | 7315 Woodrow Wilson Drive, Los Angeles | P | 9 October 1999 | AIA agreement | 1 September 1999 | B16.F8 |
| Kerri Scharlin and Peter Klosowicz | apartment remodel | 74 5th Avenue, Apt. 12, New York, NY | P | 21 November 1999 | letter from Kerri Scharlin to Pierre Koenig | | B16.F11 |
| Jeffrey Ressner | house addition | 12217 Dorothy Street, Brentwood | E | 22 November 1999 | plan | 2 April 1999 | B17.F7 |
| J. W. Colin | house | 173 Evans Avenue, Summerland, Santa Barbara | P | 21 January 2000 | plot plan sent by J. W. Colin to Pierre Koenig | | B16.F12 |
| Denise and Alan Schier | Squire House restoration and addition | 5323 Palm Drive, La Cañada | P | May 2000 | AIA agreement | | B16.F13 |
| Vida Tarassoly and Mohsen Mehran | house | 31461 Anacapa View Drive, Malibu | P | July 2000 | AIA agreement | 19 August 2000 | B19.F1 |
| Mr. and Mrs. Anthony Christian | house | 906 Lathrop Avenue, River Forest, IL | P | 2001 | AIA agreement | | B18.F11 |
| Stuart Parr | house | Shore Road, Shelter Island, NY | P | | | 25 January 2001 | B36 |
| Michael LaFetra | house | 6525 Point Lechuza Drive, Malibu | E | 3 July 2001 | plan | 12 June 2000 | FF207 |
| Michael LaFetra | Bailey House restoration | 9038 Wonderland Park Avenue, Los Angeles | E | 21 March 2002 | letter from Michael LaFetra to Pierre Koenig | 12 June 2000 | B18.F11A |
| Mark Haddawy | Bailey House restoration | 9038 Wonderland Park Avenue, Los Angeles | E | | | 24 July 2002 | B36 |
| Billy Rose | Gantert House remodel | 6431 La Punta Drive, Los Angeles | E | 20 September 2003 | letter from Billy Rose to Pierre Koenig; contractual agreement between Joseph J. Bavaro and Pierre Koenig | 12 September 2003 | B20.F1 |

| Client | Work | Location | (E) Extant (D) Demolished (P) Project (U) Unknown status | Earliest Dated Drawing or Document | Drawing or Document Type Showing the Given Date | Date on Client Index Card | Archive Location for Dating (FF) Flat File (B) Box (F) Folder |
|---|---|---|---|---|---|---|---|
| **UNDATED WORKS** | | | | | | | |
| Bob Fujioka | 2 rental units | | U | ca. 1957–59 | | | |
| Pierre Koenig | house addition 4 | 12221 Dorothy Street, Brentwood | P | after 1985 | | | |
| Lincoln "Link" Paola, Paola Oldsmobile | car showroom | 2865 Foothill Boulevard, La Crescenta | E | ca. 1954–55 | | | |
| | addition to Markel's Auto Upholstery Shop | 8498 Melrose Avenue, Los Angeles | D | ca. 1957–59 | | | |
| Benjamin Pass | hotel remodel | Charles Hotel, 25 Windward Avenue, Venice | U | ca. 1957–59 | | | |
| Tom Seidel | house | 1355 North Bundy Drive, Los Angeles | E | ca. 1955–60 | | | |
| | alterations to Sarkisian Building | | U | | | | |
| Mr. and Mrs. Sol Stern | house addition | 2212 South 21st Street, Santa Monica (given as 2212 South 20th Street in drawing title) | E | | | | |

# NOTES

All quotations are printed with typographical, grammatical, and spelling errors intact. All references to the Pierre Koenig archive correspond to the Preliminary Inventory of 2013.

## CHAPTER 1

1.  Pierre Koenig, untitled lecture at the San Francisco Museum of Modern Art, 20 June 1990, 1, Pierre Koenig papers and drawings, 1925–2007 (hereafter PKPD), 2006.M.30, box 147, folder 12, Getty Research Institute, Los Angeles.

2.  See State of California, Department of Public Health, Standard Certificate of Birth, City and County of San Francisco (District No. 3801; Local Registered No. 7189), PKPD, box 57, folder 8. Blanche was born on 1 May 1900, and Harold was on born 15 March 1898. See index card marked "Family," PKPD, box 36.

3.  James Steele and David Jenkins, *Pierre Koenig* (London: Phaidon, 1998), 8.

4.  Koenig, untitled lecture at the San Francisco Museum of Modern Art, 1.

5.  *The Alhambran,* 1943. PKPD, box 51, folder 1.

6.  "Civic Body Accepts Youth as Member," *Spokesman-Review,* 20 November 1936, 25.

7.  Pierre Koenig, interview by Mohamed Sharif, Los Angeles, January–November 2003, QuickTime movie, © 2016 by in-D media. See also PKPD, flat file 256.

8.  Koenig's attendance at the School of Engineering at the University of Utah in 1943 is listed in his curriculum vitae dated 10 July 1996, in the possession of the author. It is also recorded in Steele and Jenkins, *Pierre Koenig,* 9, 152. However, inquiries made to the University of Utah have found no records of Koenig's time there. See David Buhler (University of Utah Archives), email to the author, 26 July 2016; and Alissa McBeth (Office of the Registrar, Transcripts and Verifications Division, University of Utah), email to the author, 8 August 2016.

9.  Enlisted Record and Report of Separation: Honorable Discharge, 1946, PKPD, box 54, folder 2.

10. For the ASTP, see V. R. Cardozier, *Colleges and Universities in World War II* (Santa Barbara: ABC-CLIO, 1993), esp. 24. See also Robert R. Palmer, Bell I. Wiley, and William R. Keast, *The Army Ground Forces: The Procurement and Training of Ground Combat Troops* (Washington, D.C.: United States, Office of Military History, 1948), 28–39.

11. In January 1944, Colonel Herman Beukema, a professor of economics, government, and history at the US Military Academy at West Point and director of the program, reported this to a US congressional investigating committee. See US House of Representatives Committee on Military Affairs, "Inquiry into Army and Navy Educational Program," 19–21 January 1944, 51, https://babel.hathitrust.org/cgi/pt?id=mdp.39015024639471;view=1up;seq=5.

12. Pierre Koenig, *A Computer Generated Presentation about the 292 Field Artillery Observation Battalion in Combat during World War II 1944–1945,* 1997, typescript, 6, PKPD, box 54, folder 3.

13. The Union-Castle Line commissioned the passenger liner in 1926. The Royal Navy requisitioned it on 8 September 1939 and converted it to a merchant cruiser armed with eight six-inch guns. A five-hour running battle in the South Atlantic with the German auxiliary cruiser *Thor* in December 1940 had left her badly damaged, and Koenig remembered the ship as being patched with steel plates covering the many holes. Koenig, *A Computer Generated Presentation,* 1.

14. Pierre Koenig, "Combat Diary," 22 November 1944 to 2 August 1945, 1, PKPD, box 54, folder 1.

15. For reasons of both security and psychological comfort, the staging posts across the Pays de Caux had been named after brands of American cigarettes—Camp Lucky Strike, Camp Pall Mall, and so on.

16. Koenig, *A Computer Generated Presentation,* 4.

17. *Travelogue of the 292 F.A. OSBN. BN.*, n.d., PKPD, box 78, folder 3.

18. For observation post number 3, see Koenig, *A Computer Generated Presentation,* 6.

19. Koenig, "Combat Diary," 8.

20. Koenig, "Combat Diary," 9.

21. Koenig, "Combat Diary," 2.

22. Koenig, "Combat Diary," 2.

23. Koenig, "Combat Diary," 3.

24. Koenig, "Combat Diary," 3.

25. The diary is ambiguous about the date; it can be read both ways. See Koenig, "Combat Diary," 3.

26. Koenig, "Combat Diary," 3.

27. Koenig, "Combat Diary," 4.

28. Koenig, "Combat Diary," 4.

29. "The Cigarette Camps: The US Army in the Le Havre Area," www.skylighters.org/special/cigcamps/cigintro.html.

30. An undated index card marked "Guns" shows the following: "9mm Lugar #1625 Erfurt '25 1920 1917 with bayonet; 9mm Mauser 1943 dot #6777 rear site; 30c M-1 carbine Inland #523169." See PKPD, box 36.

31. Koenig, "Combat Diary," 5.

32. Koenig, "Combat Diary," 5.

33. Koenig, "Combat Diary," 5.

34. Enlisted Record and Report of Separation.

35. Koenig frequently misspells the names of the town and cities through which his battalion moved. Those mentioned in this chapter are "Bidding" (Betting),

"Forback" (Forbach), "Morsback" (Morsbach), "Spichern" (Spicheren), "Benren" (Behren-lès-Forbach) "Lampersheim" (Lampertheim), "Grossunderfield" (Grossrinderfeld), "Guttigen" (Gützingen), "Rotting" (Rottingen; the *Travelogue* map calls it "Hottingen"), "Neckersulm" (Neckarsulm), "Hiedleburg" (Heidelberg), "Manhiem" (Mannheim), "Zuzamaltheim" (Zusamaltheim), and "Marktl" (Markt). See Koenig, "Combat Diary," 1–4; and the *Travelogue* map.

36.  Joe Knipps to Pierre Koenig, 6 July 1997, PKPD, box 54, folder 6.

37.  Joe Knipps to Pierre Koenig, 2 September 1997, PKPD, box 54, folder 6.

38.  Koenig, *A Computer Generated Presentation,* 6. The videotape was produced with the assistance of Steve Diskin at Art Center College of Design, Pasadena, and Douglas Noble and Karen Kesnek at the University of Southern California.

39.  Koenig, *A Computer Generated Presentation,* 1.

40.  Enlisted Record and Report of Separation.

41.  Koenig, *A Computer Generated Presentation,* 6.

42.  Koenig, *A Computer Generated Presentation,* 4.

43.  Koenig, *A Computer Generated Presentation,* 8.

44.  Koenig, *A Computer Generated Presentation,* 6.

45.  Koenig, *A Computer Generated Presentation,* 8.

46.  Operation Spring Awakening was launched in Hungary with the intention of securing the oil reserves there, but, after some initial success, it was defeated by the much larger Soviet forces. The Germans were pushed back toward Vienna, which fell on 13 April. On 8 May, while still in Austria, the 12th SS Panzer Division surrendered near Enns, and the 1st near Linz. Neither Division, it seems, was anywhere near Höchstädt an der Donau where A Battery crossed the river Danube. Information on Operation Spring Awakening, the 6th SS Panzer Army, the 1st SS Panzer Division, and the 12th SS Panzer Division was taken from the corresponding Wikipedia entries.

47.  William C. Hudelson to Pierre Koenig, 2 September 1997, 1, PKPD, box 54, folder 7. Colonel Arthur Raster Hercz was the battalion colonel to whom Hudelson was assigned.

48.  Hudelson to Koenig, 2 September 1997, 2.

49.  Hudelson to Koenig, 2 September 1997, 2. Emphasis Hudelson (underlined in the original).

50.  Hudelson to Koenig, 2 September 1997, 2.

51.  Recent research at the Universiteit Leiden and elsewhere has investigated what the architectural and military historian Simon Pepper has referred to as *"the circumstances and processes by which memories of violence are maintained or suppressed, sometimes to be resurrected many years after the original events."* Simon Pepper, "War Stories," *Social History* 41, no. 2 (May 2016): 32.

52.  Koenig, "Combat Diary," 2.

CHAPTER 2

1.  Pierre Koenig, *A Computer Generated Presentation about the 292 Field Artillery Observation Battalion in Combat during World War II 1944–1945,* 5, Pierre Koenig papers and drawings, 1925–2007 (hereafter PKPD), 2006.M.30, box 54, folder 3, Getty Research Institute, Los Angeles. This particular quotation is crossed out in the script.

2.  Pierre Koenig, interview by Mohamed Sharif, Los Angeles, January–November 2003, QuickTime Movie, © 2016 by in-D media.

3.  Pierre Koenig, interview by Mohamed Sharif.

4.  Pierre Koenig, untitled lecture at the San Francisco Museum of Modern Art, 20 June 1990, 1, PKPD, box 147, folder 12.

5.  Koenig, untitled lecture at the San Francisco Museum of Modern Art, 1.

6.  See Ralph Rapson, "Proposal for Case Study House #4," *Arts & Architecture* (August 1945): 30–34; and Ralph Rapson, "Proposal for Case Study House 4, Part 2," *Arts & Architecture* (September 1945): 33–37.

7.  For the Miller Boat House, see "Boat House: Rudolph and Twitchell Architects," *Arts & Architecture* (August 1948): 34–35. For the Shute House, see "House in Florida," *Arts & Architecture* (November 1948): 32–34. For the Leavengood House, see "House in Florida by Twitchell and Rudolph, Architects," *Arts & Architecture* (January 1951): 24–25.

8.  Pierre Koenig, untitled lecture given at Harvard University, 30 October 1991, 2, PKPD, box 147, folder 14.

9.  Drawing, 29 September 1947, PKPD, box 51, folder 2.

10.  Drawing, 11 December 1947, PKPD, box 51, folder 2.

11.  Interior decoration, 27 January 1948, PKPD, box 51, folder 3.

12.  James Steele and David Jenkins, *Pierre Koenig* (London: Phaidon, 1998), 9.

13.  The Department of Architecture was established within the School of Fine Arts at USC in 1919.

14.  Deborah Howell-Ardila, "'Writing Our Own Program': The USC Experiment in Modern Architectural Pedagogy, 1930 to 1960" (master's thesis, USC School of Architecture, 2012), 131.

15.  For example, the Crane/Sedlachek House in Bel Air (1949). See Pierluigi Serraino and Julius Shulman, *Modernism Rediscovered* (Cologne: Taschen, 2000), 66.

16.  Frank Gehry, preface to *Architecture and Its Photography,* by Julius Shulman (Cologne: Taschen, 1998), 10.

17.  Ken Breisch, "Professional and Educational Discourse: Training the Next Generation of Architects in Los Angeles," in *Overdrive: L.A. Constructs the Future, 1940–1990,* edited by Wim de Wit and Christopher James Alexander (Los Angeles: Getty Research Institute, 2013), 83.

18.  Esther McCoy, *The Second Generation* (Salt Lake City: Peregrine Smith, 1984), 28.

19.  See *University of Southern California Bulletin* 42, no. 8 (September 1947), and vol. 44, no. 12 (1 October 1949), PKPD, box 28, folder 7. Harwell Hamilton Harris left in 1951 to be head of architecture at the University of Texas at Austin. See Lisa Germany, *Harwell Hamilton Harris* (Austin: University of Texas Press, 1991), 140.

20.  Gordon Drake moved to San Francisco in the autumn of 1949. See Neil Jackson, "Californian Promise," *Architectural Review* (March 1996): 84.

21.  A. Quincy Jones was a visiting professor from 1951 to 1967 and the dean of the School of Architecture and Fine Arts from 1975 to 1978. "A. Quincy Jones: The Oneness of Architecture," *Process: Architecture,* no. 41 (1983): 162.

22.  Pierre Koenig, "Acceptance Speech Gold Medal Award Ceremony, Oct. 28, 1999," PKPD, box 33, folder 17.

23.  Pierre Koenig, "Housing, Wood, and the Community: An Analysis" (course project, USC, January 1950), PKPD, box 51, folder 6.

24.  Pierre Koenig, "Does a Housing Problem Exist?," in idem, "Housing, Wood, and the Community," n.p.

25. Pierre Koenig, "What Is the Best Dwelling Type?," in idem, "Housing, Wood, and the Community," n.p.

26. Pierre Koenig, "Areas in Relation to Structure," in idem, "Housing, Wood, and the Community," n.p.

27. Pierre Koenig, "Wood in Relation to Housing," in idem, "Housing, Wood, and the Community," n.p. Koenig's use of the word "new" here is intended to be ironic, which explains his use of "(sic)" beside it.

28. Pierre Koenig, "Pierre Koenig, Candidate for Promotion to the Rank of Full Professor, School of Architecture, University of Southern California," 1996, n.p., collection of the author.

29. Koenig, "Acceptance Speech."

30. Pierre Koenig, interview by Mohamed Sharif.

31. See Steele and Jenkins, *Pierre Koenig,* 10.

32. Koenig, "Candidate for Promotion," n.p.

33. Both the site and the house were lost with the construction of the Glendale Freeway (State Route 2). Pierre Koenig drew sheets 1 and 2, and George Foy drew sheet 3. All are dated 23 August 1950. See PKPD, flat file 1.

34. Pierre Koenig, interview by Neil Jackson, Los Angeles, 13 July 1988.

35. The drawings for the Curtis House, held at California State Polytechnic University (CSPU), Pomona, are dated 12 May 1949 and 8 and 28 June 1949, but those for the Shulman House and the Olds (Case Study) House are undated. Esther McCoy states that the Case Study House was designed while the Curtis House was being finished. See Neil Jackson, *The Modern Steel House* (London: E. & F. N. Spon, 1996), 118n24.

36. See drawing 37/PS/004 in the Soriano Collection held at CSPU Pomona. Drawing 37/PS/001 says, "Experimental unit development. Alexander Curtis residence, Los Angeles." See Jackson, *The Modern Steel House,* 119n27.

37. Raphael Soriano, interview by Neil Jackson, Los Angeles, 11 July 1988.

38. "Preview of the Future," *Architectural Forum* (November 1951): 214–15.

39. "Preview of the Future," 218.

40. "Case Study House 1950," *Arts & Architecture* (August 1950): 20, 22.

41. See "Hillside House by Raphael Soriano, Architect," *Arts & Architecture* (April 1948): 39.

42. "Case Study House 1950," *Arts & Architecture* (December 1949): 22; and "Diagrammatic Analysis of Site Plan, Case Study House 1950 by Raphael Soriano, Architect," *Arts & Architecture* (February 1950): 24.

43. "Diagrammatic Analysis of Site Plan, Case Study House 1950 by Raphael Soriano, Architect," *Arts & Architecture* (February 1950): 24.

44. Many years later, he credited J & F Ironworks of Hawthorne for teaching him how to design in steel. Koenig, "Acceptance Speech."

45. Earlier drawings for Koenig's house show the columns to be set on a grid measuring 9 feet, 10 inches by 20 feet. See Residence for Pierre Koenig, sheet 1, 23 August 1950, PKPD, flat file 1. Later drawings prepared for publication show a 10-by-10-foot grid. See PKPD, box 1, folder 2.

46. For Soriano, see Jackson, *The Modern Steel House,* 64. For Koenig, see PKPD, flat file 1.

47. There were seven photographs taken. See the Julius Shulman Photography Archive, 1936–97, 2004.R.10, Series II, Job 1247, Getty Research Institute, Los Angeles. Koenig, when interviewed by Mohamed Sharif, suggested that *Arts & Architecture* had commissioned these photographs, but Shulman's archive shows that they were for *Living for Young Homemakers,* who first published them.

48. Edith Brazwell Evans, "The Pioneering Urge in Action," *Living for Young Homemakers,* February 1953, 68–69.

49. "Steel Frame House," *Arts & Architecture* (October 1953): 25.

50. In the photograph, Koenig is not, as might be thought, doing an architectural drawing; rather, he is editing a film.

51. Koenig, *A Computer Generated Presentation,* 4.

52. Pierre Koenig, interview by Mohamed Sharif.

## CHAPTER 3

1. Edith Brazwell Evans, "The Pioneering Urge in Action," *Living for Young Homemakers,* February 1953, 68–69.

2. The Lamel House was located at 1884 Los Encinos Avenue. Koenig's own house was at 2002 Los Encinos Avenue.

3. "Steel Frame House," *Arts & Architecture* (October 1953): 25.

4. The Scott House was located at 10300 Haines Canyon Avenue, Tujunga. The Squire House was located at 5323 Palm Drive, La Cañada.

5. Residence for Pierre Koenig, sheet 1, 23 August 1950, Pierre Koenig papers and drawings, 1925–2007 (hereafter PKPD), 2006.M.30, flat file 1, Getty Research Institute, Los Angeles.

6. Residence for Mr. Edward M. Lamel, sheet 3, 6 April 1953, PKPD, flat file 2.

7. Residence for Mr. Edward M. Lamel, sheet 4, half full-size steel plan, 6 April 1953, PKPD, flat file 2.

8. Roof framing plan, n.d.; and Typical section, n.d., PKPD, box 61, folder 2.

9. "Case Study House for 1949," *Arts & Architecture* (December 1949): 26–39.

10. Michael Brawne, "The Wit of Technology," *Architectural Design* (September 1966): 440–51.

11. See *The Herman Miller Collection* (Zeeland, MI: The Herman Miller Furniture Company, 1952), 52–53, 94, 111.

12. For example, the work Koenig did for Della and Gary Rollé. See Joe Bavaro to Pierre Koenig, fax dated 14 October 1994, PKPD, box 11, folder 1.

13. See a photo taken in ca. 1956, after Koenig sold the house to Mr. and Mrs. Lynn Sawyer, reproduced in *Time,* 9 April 1956, 75.

14. Hairpin legs were designed by Henry P. Glass in 1941 but never patented. They have been used, therefore, by many table manufacturers.

15. "Small House by Pierre Koenig, Designer," *Arts & Architecture* (January 1954): 25.

16. "Steel Frame House," *Arts & Architecture* (June 1955): 23.

17. Barbara East, "There May Be a Steel House . . . In Your Very Near Future," Modern Living, *San Francisco Examiner,* 18 September 1955, 2.

18. Pierre Koenig, quoted in Esther McCoy, "Steel around the Pacific," Pictorial Living, *Los Angeles Examiner,* 25 February 1956, 8.

19. Pierre Koenig, quoted in Esther McCoy, "What I Believe . . . A Statement of Architectural Principles by Pierre Koenig," *Los Angeles Times Home Magazine,* 21 July 1957, 25.

20. McCoy, "What I Believe," 25, 38.

21. Margaret Stovall, "Home of the Week," *Independent Star News,* 31 August 1958, B5.

22. "An Economical House Results from an Adventurous Spirit," *Living for Young Homemakers,* February 1956, 102. "Framed and Roofed…in 2 days," *Sunset, The Magazine of Western Living,* April 1959, 112.

23. "Jeunes architectes dans le monde," *L'architecture d'aujourd'hui,* September 1957, 73.

24. Randall "Randy" Koenig was born on 18 January 1954.

25. On a card in box 36, which contains Koenig's client index cards, is a list of thirteen cars that he owned. Many were foreign sports cars, including the following: 1952 MG T Mk2, 1962 Austin Healey 3000, 1964 Triumph Spitfire, 1973 Fiat 124 Spider, and the 1965 Porsche 356 C Coupe that he still had when he died.

26. See Robert Newcombe and Mike Lawler, *The Crescenta Valley* (Charleston, SC: Arcadia, 2010), 35.

27. Pierre Koenig, interview by Mohamed Sharif.

## CHAPTER 4

1. The drawings for the Lamel, Scott, and Squire Houses were all prepared at 2402 Los Encinos Ave., Glendale, CA. The rented apartment was at 1349 26th Street, Santa Monica, CA.

2. On 2 January 1957, Koenig made an application to Walter C. Peterson, the city clerk at City Hall, for a license to run a limited business from 11681 San Vicente Boulevard. The fee of twelve dollars was paid in cash on 7 January, and the license was granted two days later. See Pierre Koenig papers and drawings, 1925–2007 (hereafter PKPD), 2006.M.30, box 32, folder 8, Getty Research Institute, Los Angeles.

3. James Steele and David Jenkins, *Pierre Koenig* (London: Phaidon, 1998), 12.

4. The Eichler Homes X-100 opened in October 1956.

5. For Jones's steel houses, see Neil Jackson, *The Modern Steel House* (London: E. & F. N. Spon, 1996), 76–84.

6. Pierre Koenig, interview by Mohamed Sharif, Los Angeles, January–November 2003, QuickTime movie, © 2016 by in-D media.

7. Peter J. Candreva to Douglas Lathrop, jury commissioner, Los Angeles Municipal Court, n.d. (but after 29 April 1957), PKPD, box 34, folder 10. The dispensation was served on 20 May 1957. Virginia Nielsen, assistant jury commissioner, Los Angeles Municipal Court Judicial District, to Pierre Koenig, 20 May 1957, PKPD, box 34, folder 10.

8. In his letter of 2 January 1957 to Walter C. Peterson, the city clerk at City Hall, he states, "I am an Architectural Draftsman." See PKPD, box 32, folder 8.

9. "An Economical House Results from an Adventurous Spirit," *Living for Young Homemakers,* February 1956, 102.

10. Western Union telegram from Pierre Koenig to Edith Evans, 23 January 1956. Author's collection.

11. Pierre Koenig, "The Way We Were USC Students in the 40's," 10 April 1995, PKPD, box 48, folder 2.

12. Toni Edgerton, "Redesigning Venice Is Koenig Mission," *Roberts News,* 21 November 1957, 1, 13.

13. Edgerton, "Redesigning Venice," 1.

14. Edgerton, "Redesigning Venice," 1. *Sputnik* 1 had gone into orbit on 4 October 1957, two days after Koenig had qualified as an architect.

15. Pierre Koenig, quoted in Edgerton, "Redesigning Venice," 1.

16. Arthur Drexler, *The Architecture of Japan* (New York: Museum of Modern Art, 1955).

17. City of Los Angeles Department of Building and Safety, Notice to Comply issued to the Venice Development Company, showing the job address of 1500 Pacific, Venice, Job Order B 5408, 9 April 1959, PKPD, uncatalogued. Receipt issued by the City of Los Angeles Department of Building and Safety, 13 April 1959, PKPD, uncatalogued.

18. Pierre Koenig to Venice Development Company, 17 July 1959, PKPD, uncatalogued.

19. See drawing for remodel for 40 Brooks Avenue, sheet 1, 6 August 1962, PKPD, flat file 24A.

20. See designs for house at 9038 Wonderland Park Avenue, sheets 1–5, 16 April 1956, and two undated perspective drawings, PKPD, flat file 17.

21. See Residence for Mr. & Mrs. H. E. Burwash, sheets 1–5, 15–20 February 1957, PKPD, flat file 7; promotional statement, n.d., PKPD, box 1, folder 7; and *Logs 1958,* book 1, 5 March–6 June 1958, PKPD, box 38, folder 1.

22. The Burwash House was built at 9520 Amoret Drive, Tujunga. The Scott House was located at 10300 Haines Canyon Avenue, Tujunga. For the Bailey House, see designs for 9038 Wonderland Park Avenue and two undated perspective drawings. For the Beidleman House, see "Steel House by Pierre Koenig," *Arts & Architecture* (April 1956): 18–19.

23. Bailey House, sheet 3, 16 April 1956, PKPD, flat file 17.

24. Residence for Mr. and Mrs. H. E. Burwash, sheet 3, 15 February 1957, PKPD, flat file 7.

25. Working drawings for the Beidleman House are dated 12 April 1957; those for the Burwash House, 15 February 1957. See, respectively, PKPD, flat files 26 and 7.

26. Burwash residence statement, n.d., PKPD, box, 1, folder 7.

27. Residence for Mr. and Mrs. H. E. Burwash, sheet 4, 15 February 1957, PKPD, flat file 7.

28. "Low-Cost Production House," *Arts & Architecture* (March 1957): 24–25.

29. "Low-Cost Production House," 25.

30. "Low-Cost Production House," 25.

31. These houses are all discussed later in this volume. For the Seidel Beach House, see ch. 8; for the Dzur House, see ch. 6; for the Dowden House, see ch. 7; for the Metcalf House, see ch. 7.

32. "Two Commercial Projects by Pierre Koenig, Architect," *Arts & Architecture* (July 1958): 24–25. For the Playa del Rey shopping center, see also Esther McCoy, "Pierre Koenig," *Zodiac* 5 (1959): 162–63.

33. See Markel's Auto Upholstery Shop, n.d., PKPD, flat file 225.

34. See Addition for Mr. and Mrs. Sol Stern, n.d., PKPD, flat file 226.

35. See Remodel for Mr. & Mrs. Frank K. Danzig, 2 May 1957, PKPD, flat file 9.

36. See Koenig client index card, PKPD, box 36. For KYOR, see PKPD, flat file 10.

## CHAPTER 5

1. "Announcement—Case Study House Program," *Arts & Architecture* (January 1945): 37, 39.

2. "Project for Case Study House XXI," *Arts & Architecture* (May 1958): 14–15, 30. This house should not be confused with Richard Neutra's unbuilt Case Study

House 21 (1947) or with Neutra's Case Study House 20 (1947–48), also called the Bailey House.

3. "Case Study House 18," *Arts & Architecture* (April 1957): 18.

4. Pierre Koenig, interview by the author, Los Angeles, 13 July 1988.

5. "Project for Case Study House XXI," 14–15, 30.

6. Pierre Koenig, interview by the author.

7. Bailey House, perspective drawings, n.d., Pierre Koenig papers and drawings, 1925–2007 (hereafter PKPD), 2006.M.30, flat file 17, Getty Research Institute, Los Angeles; and Bailey House floor plan, sheet 4, 16 April 1956, PKPD, flat file 17.

8. Publicity statement prepared by Pierre Koenig, n.d., PKPD, box 1A, folder 10.

9. Bailey House, foundation plan, sheet 2, 2 April 1958, PKPD, flat file 18.

10. This was the material used on the 1986 space shuttle *Challenger,* which broke apart shortly after launching.

11. For construction details, see Detail W (typical interior section) and Detail 162, both dated 26 June 1958, PKPD, box 1, folder 14.

12. Pierre Koenig, interview by Mohamed Sharif, Los Angeles, January-November 2003, QuickTime movie, © 2016 by in-D media.

13. Pierre Koenig, interview by Mohamed Sharif.

14. Pierre Koenig, interview by Mohamed Sharif.

15. "Progress Report," *Arts & Architecture* (August 1958): 14–15; "Case Study House 21," *Arts & Architecture* (November 1958): 29. "Arts & Architecture Case Study House #21," *Arts & Architecture* (January 1959): 8.

16. Visitors' book, Case Study House 21, January 1959, 7, 8, 15, 25, 26, 28, 31, PKPD, uncatalogued.

17. See Residence for Mr. and Mrs. Arnold D. Metcalf, working drawings, flat file 13. A "written agreement" with the Stahls had been made in November 1957. See Jeffrey Head, "Creating the Iconic Stahl House: Two Dreamers, an Architect, a Photographer, and the Making of America's Most Famous House," *Curbed,* 24 August 2017, https://www.curbed.com/2017/8/24/16156818/stahl-house-julius-shulman-case-study-22-pierre-koenig.

18. "Case Study House No. 21," *Arts & Architecture* (February 1959): 19.

19. Pierre Koenig, interview by Mohamed Sharif.

20. See Head, "Creating the Iconic Stahl House."

21. Pierre Koenig, interview by Mohamed Sharif.

22. See Residence for Mr. and Mrs. C. H. Stahl, 3 July 1958, PKPD, flat files 20, 21.

23. "Project for a Case Study House," *Arts & Architecture* (May 1959): 15.

24. This date is quoted by Barbara Thornburg in "Koenig's Case Study House 22 as Home," *Los Angeles Times,* 27 June 2009, http://www.latimes.com/home/la-hm-stahl27-2009jun27-story.html.

25. Pierre Koenig, typescript, "Case Study House 22 Pierre Koenig," n.d., PKPD, box 1A, folder 1.

26. Pierre Koenig, interview by author.

27. Untitled typescript, n.d., PKPD, box 1A, folder 1. Much of the wording of this statement is used in "Case Study House No. 22," *Arts & Architecture* (May 1960): 14–21.

28. See Thornburg, "Koenig's Case Study House 22."

29. See Head, "Creating the Iconic Stahl House."

30. The two Stahl children were Bruce and Sharon. Bruce was two years old when the family moved into the house. Sharon, aged 49 when Thornburg's article in the *Los Angeles Times* was published in 2009, would have been a baby when the house was finished in May 1960. This suggests that the client index card was written at that time (and certainly before the third child, Mark, aged 42 in 2009, was born). See Koenig client index card, PKPD, box 36.

31. See Head, "Creating the Iconic Stahl House."

32. Pierre Koenig, interview by author.

33. Pierre Koenig, "Logs 1958," 33, PKPD, box 38, folder 1.

34. The revised concrete plan shows, in blue, the foundations for the fireplace overwritten with the word "omit." See Residence for Mr. & Mrs. C. H. Stahl, concrete plan, sheet 2 of 8, 3 July 1958, revised 2 November 1958 and 5 January 1959, PKPD, flat file 20.

35. See Residence for Mr. & Mrs. C. H. Stahl, concrete plan.

36. See Section 1.1 and 1.2, "For C. H. Stahl," sheet 2 of 2, 6 September 1958, revised 1 November 1958, PKPD, flat file 21.

37. See Residence for Mr. & Mrs. C. H. Stahl, concrete plan. The site plan (sheet 1, revised 14 July 1958 and 5 January 1959), the steel plan (sheet 3, revised 14 July 1958 and 5 January 1959), and the electrical floor plan (sheet 4, revised 14 July 1958) all show the reduced end bay and evidence of lines being scratched out and subsequently overdrawn. PKPD, flat file 20.

38. Residence for Mr. & Mrs. C. H. Stahl, elevations, sheet 5 of 8, 3 July 1958, revised 14 July, 16 July 1958, and 5 January 1959, PKPD, flat file 21.

39. See Head, "Creating the Iconic Stahl House." Emphasis Head.

40. "Case Study House 22 Pierre Koenig," 1, n.d., PKPD, box 1A, folder 1.

41. Pierre Koenig, interview by Mohamed Sharif.

42. Pierre Koenig, interview by Mohamed Sharif.

43. Pierre Koenig to Bob Brady, 19 April 1960, PKPD, box 1A, folder 1.

44. Julius Shulman's ledger indicates that the shoot took place on 9 May 1960. There are no additional dates listed. His client index cards confirm this date. See Job 2980: Case Study House No. 22 (Los Angeles, Calif.), 1960, Julius Shulman photography archive, 1935–2009, 2004.R.10, boxes 190, 195, 198, 199, 200, 1053–1054, and 1110.

45. "Sunday Pictorial," *Los Angeles Times,* 17 July 1960, front cover.

46. "Case Study House No. 22 by Pierre Koenig, Architect," *Arts & Architecture* (June 1960): 14–21.

47. Reyner Banham, *Los Angeles: The Architecture of Four Ecologies* (Harmondsworth, UK: Penguin, 1971), 229.

48. Koenig, interview by Mohamed Sharif; and Gloria Koenig in conversation with the author, 9 February 2013.

49. Koenig, interview by Mohamed Sharif.

CHAPTER 6

1. Notes prepared by Tom Seidel, 20 May 1957, Pierre Koenig papers and drawings, 1925–2007 (hereafter PKPD), 2006.M.30, box 1A, folder 6, Getty Research Institute, Los Angeles.

2. W. E. Milburn to Tom Seidel, 29 January 1959, PKPD, box 1A, folder 6.

3. House for Tom Seidel Associates, plan, interior elevations, sheet 4, 8 June 1959, PKPD, flat file 23.

4. Tom Seidel and Pierre Koenig, Appeal for Modification of Building Ordinance, submitted to the Board of Building and Safety Commissioners, City of Los Angeles, 16 June 1959, PKPD, box 1A, folder 6.

5. Notice of Hearing in City Hall, Los Angeles, on 2 July 1959, sent to Tom Seidel on 18 June 1959, PKPD, box 1A, folder 6.

6. Notes prepared by Tom Seidel.

7. T-Steel Corporation packing sheet, 6 August 1959, PKPD, box 1A, folder 6.

8. On 11 March 1960, Pierre Koenig wrote to Gerald B. Carter regarding incomplete tiling work in the bathrooms and threatened to give the contract to another tiler to finish. PKPD, box 1A, folder 6.

9. Recapitulation, drawn up by Koenig and checked by Seidel, 16 May 1960, PKPD, box 1A, folder 6. A second, undated estimate of $38,007.05 is retained in the archive. Recapitulation, n.d., PKPD, box 1A, folder 7.

10. Pierre Koenig, "The Use of Steel in the Work of Pierre Koenig," 1993, PKPD, box 48, folder 2.

11. Pierre Koenig, "Builders Steel House," typescript, n.d., 1, PKPD, box 1A, folder 7.

12. Pierre Koenig, untitled typescript, n.d., 2, PKPD, box 1A, folder 7. "Steel House by Pierre Koenig, Architect," *Arts & Architecture* (April 1961): 30.

13. "Steel House," 22–23, 30.

14. "Steel House," 22–23, 30. American Institute of Architects and Sunset Magazine Honor Award for the Walter C. Bailey House presented to Pierre Koenig, October 1959; see certificate and letter to Pierre Koenig from Proctor Mellquist, 7 July 1959, PKPD, box 33, folder 11.

15. Advertisement, *Arts & Architecture* (October 1961): 31. See also "Copy for Ken Kremith ad to appear in next issue of *Arts & Architecture* magazine: 1/16 page," box 1A, folder 6.

16. For background details of the Dzur House, I am grateful to Albert W. Dzur. Albert Dzur, email to the author, 28 January 2017.

17. "Guest House Dzur Residence," 29 September 1959, PKPD, flat file 15.

18. Mayer Oberman was a violinist for the Chicago Symphony Orchestra from 1939 to 1942.

19. See Pierre Koenig, "General Notes & Specifications," n.d., PKPD, box 2, folder 3.

20. See "Steel House," 27.

21. Publicity statement for the Oberman House, draft, n.d., 2, PKPD, box 2, folder 3.

22. Invoice from Knoll Associates to Pierre Koenig for $990, 4 January 1962, PKPD, box 42, folder 4.

23. "Steel House," 30.

24. Publicity statement for the Oberman House.

25. *Log 4,* 9 June 1962, PKPD, box 38, folder 5.

26. *Log 4,* 13 June 1962, PKPD, box 38, folder 5.

27. Kurt Meyer to Pierre Koenig, 26 July 1967, 1, PKPD, box 2, folder 3.

28. See "30. Eames House, Pacific Palisades" and "25. Rosen House, Pacific Palisades," *Architectural Grand Prix of the Greater Los Angeles Area on the 186th Birthday of the City of Los Angeles,* sponsored by the City of Los Angeles and the American Institute of Architects, 1967, PKPD, box 2, folder 3.

29. "26. Palos Verdes Residence," *Architectural Grand Prix.*

30. Grand Prix Award certificate, 1 September 1967, PKPD, box 33, folder 13.

31. See Neil Jackson, *Pierre Koenig* (Cologne: Taschen, 2007), 60–61.

32. Advertisement, Coldwell Banker & Company, dated 1968 by Pierre Koenig, PKPD, box 2, folder 3.

33. Pierre Koenig, publicity statement for the Reibe addition, n.d., PKPD, box 10, folder 11.

34. For confirmation of Bosley's professional career, see *International Plant Propagators' Society 1965–66 Membership and Guests List,* http://ipps-admin .datahost.co.za/uploads/15_E.PDF.

35. Koenig had previously owned a 1962 Austin Healy 3000 and a 1964 Triumph. See PKPD, box 36.

36. In Palm Springs, William Cody built the Cannon House (1963) and the Shamel House (1964), both at the El Dorado Country Club. Albert Frey built the second Frey House (1964) on Palisades Drive.

37. Raphael Soriano built the Grossman House (1965) in the Studio City neighborhood of Los Angeles.

38. "Mies van der Rohe," *Arts & Architecture* (March 1952): 22–25.

## CHAPTER 7

1. Calvin Straub built the Sedlachek House at 3385 North Beverly Glen Boulevard in 1949. Arthur Gallion signed the drawings.

2. Gordon Drake built the Rucker House (1947) in Los Angeles; Gregory Ain built the Miller House (1949) in Beverly Hills; and Whitney Smith and Wayne Williams built the Levanant House (1953) in Pasadena.

3. "Steel House," *Arts & Architecture* (April 1956): 18–19.

4. The house was designed for a family of three adults. See the publicity statement for the first Beidleman residence, untitled typescript stamped "5 294," n.d., 1, Pierre Koenig papers and drawings, 1925–2007 (hereafter PKPD), box 1A, folder 10.

5. See Residence for Mr. and Mrs. L. E. Beidleman, set of drawings dated 12 April and 12 August 1957, PKPD, flat files 26 and 27.

6. "Steel House," 19.

7. "Steel and Concrete Hillside House," *Arts & Architecture* (January 1959): 20–21, 28.

8. Residence for Mr. and Mrs. L. E. Beidleman, 12 August 1957, sheet 3, PKPD, flat file 26. See also the publicity statement prepared by Pierre Koenig, n.d., PKPD, box 1A, folder 10.

9. Visitors' book for Case Study House 21, January 1959, 7, PKPD, not catalogued.

10. James Steele and David Jenkins, *Pierre Koenig* (London: Phaidon, 1998), 37.

11. Residence for Mr. and Mrs. Arnold B. Metcalf, steel and concrete plan, middle floor, sheet 5, 20 August 1958, PKPD, flat file 13.

12. Elevations and sections, Residence for Mr. and Mrs. Arnold B. Metcalf.

13. Application to Construct New Building, submitted to the Department of Building and Safety, City of Los Angeles, September 1958, PKPD, box 1, folder 11.

14. Steele and Jenkins, *Pierre Koenig,* 37.

15. See Beidleman House, preliminary drawings, "Upper Level," January 1960, "Upper Floor" and "First Floor," n.d., PKPD, flat file 26.

16. Steele and Jenkins, *Pierre Koenig,* 73.

17. See the Beidleman House drawings, PKPD, box 1A, folder 11.

18. "Survey & Contour Map of Lot 5, Blk. 18, TR. 8923 M.B. 118-35. Los Angeles, Calif. For Beagles. Date May 1962," PKPD, flat file 48.

19. Pierre Koenig, interview by Mohamed Sharif, Los Angeles, January–November 2003, QuickTime movie, © 2016 by in-D media. See also, Tom Freeman, *Environmental Geology Laboratory* (New York: John Wiley & Sons, 2003), 130.

20. Pierre Koenig, publicity statement for the Iwata House, n.d., PKPD, box 2, folder 9.

21. Koenig, publicity statement for the Iwata House.

22. Pierre Koenig, structural notes and publicity statement for the Iwata House, n.d., PKPD, box 2, folder 9.

23. Pierre Koenig, publicity statement for the Iwata House.

24. Pierre Koenig, publicity statement for the Iwata House.

25. Elizabeth Morinaka to Pierre Koenig, email, 20 June 2002, PKPD box 2, folder 9.

CHAPTER 8

1. See Addition for Mr. and Mrs. P. E. Philbrick, sheet 1, 29 August 1960, Pierre Koenig papers and drawings, 1925–2007 (hereafter PKPD), 2006.M.30, flat file 25; box 1A, folder 9.

2. In 1953, Jean Hagen was nominated for the Best Supporting Actress Oscar for her role as Lina Lamont in *Singin' in the Rain* (1952).

3. See working drawings for Tom Seidel, sheet 2 of 2, 2 June 1961, PKPD, flat file 29.

4. Application to Alter–Repair–Demolish for 1355 North Bundy Drive, Brentwood, n.d., PKPD, box 1A, folder 13.

5. See Residence for Mr. and Mrs. David Herrington, plot plan, sheet 1, 4 November 1963, PKPD, flat file 49.

6. See the entry dated 31 May 1965 in Koenig's spiral sketchbook for 10 March 1965 to 12 May 1966, PKPD, box 38, folder 6.

7. The DuPont House was published in *Architecture/West* (April 1964): n.p. See Pierluigi Serraino and Julius Shulman, *Modernism Rediscovered* (Cologne: Taschen, 2000), 344.

8. See Residence for Mr. and Mrs. Harold Henbest, sheets 3 and 4, 11 August 1965, PKPD, flat file 65.

9. The drawings are undated, but Evelyn Heller's name was added to the Koenig client index cards on 1 August 1970. See PKPD, box 36.

10. See Koenig client index cards, PKPD, box 36.

11. House for Mr. Harold Henbest, floor plan, sheet 4, n.d., PKPD, flat file 67; and Residence for Mr. & Mrs. Harold Henbest, floor plan, sheet 3, 11 August 1965, PKPD, flat file 65. Sheet 4 is clearly a reworked copy negative of sheet 3.

12. Matthew J. Colwes paid Koenig a $400 retainer on 14 December 1968. See Koenig client index cards. Although the drawings are undated, there is a reference on sheet 1 to a soil report by Converse, Davis and Associates dated 25 February 1968. See Colwes House drawings, sheet 1, n.d., PKPD, flat file 59.

13. See Koenig client index cards.

14. See Burton House drawings, n.d., PKPD, flat files 97 and 98.

15. In the end, the side walls were boarded in timber.

16. See Bayer House drawings, PKPD, flat file 108.

17. See Koenig client index cards.

18. See Remodel for Mr. and Mrs. Leon Papernow, 4 December 1961, PKPD, flat file 41. Leon Papernow and John Calveti represented Cypress Communications and were the clients in 1971 for the proposed Cypress Television Building.

19. See Wayne Addition drawings, PKPD, flat file 138.

20. For the Lawrence House and the Van der Linde addition, see Lawrence House drawings, PKPD, flat files 140 and 143, respectively. Although the Lawrence House drawings give the street address as 3440 Meier Street, the Van der

Lindes' Public Record Application for Inspection—to Add–Alter–Repair–Demolish—give it as 3442. (See Van der Linde Addition, PKPD, box 9, folder 9.) The current street number is 3442.

21. See Rozet House drawings, PKPD, flat file 60.

22. See Nemo Remodel drawing, PKPD, flat file 76.

23. See Peterson Remodel drawings, PKPD, flat file 76.

24. See Grebe Addition drawings, PKPD, flat file 76.

25. See Mosher Remodel drawings, PKPD, flat file 147.

26. See Koenig client index cards.

CHAPTER 9

1. American Institute of Architects Certificate of Fellowship, 21 June 1971, Pierre Koenig papers and drawings, 1925–2007 (hereafter PKPD), 2006.M.30, box 36, folder 7, Getty Research Institute, Los Angeles.

2. Reyner Banham, "Klarheit, Ehrlichkeit, Einfachkeit...and Wit Too! The Case Study Houses in the World's Eyes," in *Blueprints for Modern Living: History and Legacy of the Case Study Houses,* ed. Elizabeth A. T. Smith (Cambridge, MA: MIT Press, 1989), 188.

3. Morphosis was led by Thom Mayne and Michael Rotondi.

4. See Addition for Mr. and Mrs. Pierre Koenig, sheet 1, 19 January 1966, PKPD, flat file 56.

5. See Porush's calculations for carport and den, 7 October 1975, PKPD, box 2, folder 21.

6. At the time of writing, these drawings were misfiled under the West House, PKPD, flat file 63.

7. See undated drawings for a proposed recreation room at 12221 Dorothy Street, PKPD, box 2, folder 21.

8. See Koenig client index cards, PKPD, box 36.

9. Inspection docket, County of Los Angeles, Department of County Engineer, Building and Safety Division, 12 July 1972, PKPD, flat file 75. See also General Notes and Specification, dated 1 June 1973, box 2, folder 20. The first page says, "Job Whittemore."

10. Pierre Koenig, publicity notes for 6431 La Punta Drive, n.d., PKPD, box 1A, folder 10.

11. Koenig, publicity notes for 6431 La Punta Drive.

12. Plan check references BB4601 (30 December 1981) and BB5739 (22 June 1982). See Residence for Pierre Koenig, site plan, sheet 1, 28 December 1981, PKPD, flat file 131.

13. Zoning Application for Slight Modification of Area Requirements, receipt no. 120214, 20 December 1982, PKPD, box 8, folder 7.

14. Letter on Pierre Koenig's stationery, signed by Mr. and Mrs. Robert Irmas of 12217 Dorothy Street, and by Ms. Bonnie Bates of 12225 Dorothy Street, 23 January 1983, PKPD, box 8, folder 2.

15. Zoning Application for Slight Modification of Area Requirements, draft copy, n.d., 2, PKPD, box 8, folder 6.

16. Zoning Application for Slight Modification of Area Requirements, draft copy.

17. Zoning Application for Slight Modification of Area Requirements, receipt no. 120214.

18. The outline of the L-shaped office plan is sketched on one undated print of the twelve-stage assembly drawing mentioned below. See "Box 12 End Misc. not

19. "shown" panel on print of twelve-stage assembly drawing for Koenig House 2, sheet 7, n.d., PKPD, flat file 133. The master drawing (flat file 131), started on 5 January 1983, was revised on various dates through to 5 January 1985. One of these dates would indicate when the L-shaped office plan was added in hard line.

19. James Moreland of Weld-Rite Welding Services to Pierre Koenig, quotation, 12 June 1981, PKPD, box 8, folder 1.

20. See Dimitry Vergun, steelwork calculation for Pierre Koenig Residence, 24 February 1982, revised 17 June 1982, PKPD, box 8, folder 1.

21. In a series that runs up to sheet 13 (and maybe further), sheets 2, 5, 8, 9 10, and 12 are missing. PKPD, flat file 131.

22. John Mansfield of Brace Engineering to Pierre Koenig, quotation, 6 April 1983, PKPD, box 8, folder 4.

23. Robert D. Anderson to Pierre Koenig, 17 January 1983, PKPD, box 8, folder 4. The house project to which Anderson refers is likely to have been the Gantert House.

24. Standard Form of Agreement between Owner and Contractor, made between Pierre Koenig and Robert D. Anderson, 22 November 1983, PKPD, box 8, folder 4. This reduction was due to a separate agreement for materials, for which Koenig agreed to pay Viking Steel Corporation $8,714 directly. See Robert D. Anderson to Pierre Koenig, 14 December 1983, PKPD, box 8, folder 4.

25. Pierre Koenig, interview by Mohamed Sharif, Los Angeles, January–November 2003, QuickTime movie, © 2016 by in-D media. See also Neil Jackson, *The Modern Steel House* (London: E. & F. N. Spon, 1996), 6.

26. Pierre Koenig, untitled lecture at the San Francisco Museum of Modern Art, 20 June 1990, 1, PKPD, box 147, folder 12.

27. Payment requests made by Pierre Koenig to California Federal Savings and Loan Association, no. 4709 for $17,128, 12 December 1983; no. 4710 for $1,562, 12 December 1983, PKPD, box 8, folder 4.

28. Robert D. Anderson to Pierre Koenig, invoice, 14 December 1983, PKPD, box 8, folder 4.

29. Robert D. Anderson to Pierre Koenig, invoice, 30 December 1983, PKPD, box 8, folder 4.

30. Dave Carey of Besteel to Pierre Koenig, quotation, 17 February 1928, PKPD, box 8, folder 4; invoice, Robert D. Anderson to Pierre Koenig, 14 December 1983.

31. Besteel to Pierre Koenig, invoice, 28 February 1984, PKPD, box 8, folder 4.

32. Robert D. Anderson to Pierre Koenig, invoice, 11 May 1984, PKPD, box 8, folder 4.

33. Robert D. Anderson to Pierre Koenig, invoice, 11 May 1984.

34. Pierre Koenig to Larry Wolf of St. Charles of Southern California, 3 May 1984, PKPD, box 8, folder 5.

35. Dana Clarrissimeaux of St. Charles of Los Angeles to Pierre Koenig, 3 June 1984, PKPD, box 8, folder 5.

36. Contract made between Pierre Koenig and Dana Clarrissimeaux of St. Charles of Los Angeles, no. LA–0355, 3 and 9 August 1984, PKPD, box 8, folder 5.

37. Contract made between Pierre Koenig and Dana Clarrissimeaux of St. Charles of Los Angeles, not numbered, 14 and 17 August 1984, PKPD, box 8, folder 5.

38. St. Charles of Los Angeles to Pierre Koenig, statement no. 8483, 1 November 1984; Dana Clarrissimeaux of St. Charles of Los Angeles to Pierre Koenig, 19 December 1984 (with reference to invoice 8484 dated 1 November 1984), PKPD, box 8, folder 5.

39. Dana Clarrissimeaux of St. Charles of Los Angeles to Pierre Koenig, 19 December 1984.

40. Elkan Custom Made Furniture to Pierre Koenig, invoice, 30 November 1984, PKPD, box 8, folder 5.

41. See Koenig client index cards.

42. Stuermer Preliminary, plans and elevations, sheet 1, 24 June 1984, PKPD, flat file 125.

43. Stuermer Preliminary, plans and elevations, sheet 2, 8 July 1984, PKPD, flat file 125.

44. Stuermer Preliminary, plans and elevations, sheet 1, 24 June 1984, PKPD, flat file 127.

45. Stuermer House, elevations, sheet 3, 9 November 1984, PKPD, flat file 125.

46. See Stuermer House, structural steel drawing, sheet 3, 5 February 1985, PKPD, flat file 126.

47. See Stuermer House, structural steel drawing, sheet 5, 5 February 1985, PKPD, flat file 126.

48. See Koenig client index cards.

49. The final amendments to the Stuermer drawings of 5 February 1985 were made on 18 September 1987. See Residence for Mr. & Mrs. Steven Stuermer, sheets 1, 2, 3, PKPD, flat file 126; and Mr. & Mrs. Steven Stuermer, sheet 4, PKPD, flat file 126.

## CHAPTER 10

1. The exact location of the site remains obscure. The plot plan is titled "Paroisse de St.-Luc, Division d'Enrégistrément de St.-Jean." Saint-Luc is on the northwest corner of Saint-Jean-sur-Richelieu, Quebec. Although it is more correct to use the spelling Saint-Jean, related documents in the archive have been catalogued under St. Jean, so that is the form used here.

2. See Plan montrant une partie du lot no: 15, paroisse de St.-Luc, Division d'enrégistration de St.-Jean, 24 September 1959, Pierre Koenig papers and drawings, 1925–2007 (hereafter PKPD), 2006.M.30, flat file 35, Getty Research Institute, Los Angeles.

3. "Modern Production House," *Arts & Architecture* (January 1961): 22.

4. Sheets 1–4 and 6–13, and one numbered E1, are retained in the archive. PKPD, flat file 34.

5. See internal wall elevations, Venice Development Co., Saint-Jean, Quebec, sheet 4, 8 August 1960, PKPD, flat file 33.

6. "Modern Production House," 22.

7. Pierre Koenig, interview by Mohamed Sharif, Los Angeles, January–November 2003, QuickTime movie, © 2016 by in-D media.

8. See El Campo Turistico "Manuel's," Baja California, n.d., PKPD, flat file 224.

9. Wim de Wit, "Modernism Thwarted: Pierre Koenig's Work for the Chemehuevi Indians," *Getty Research Journal*, no. 3 (2011): 87.

10. De Wit, "Modernism Thwarted," 97n5.

11. Konrad Wachsmann, who was famous for his promotion of the factory-made house, worked at USC from 1964 to 1974.

12. Pierre Koenig, interview by Mohamed Sharif.

13. This led to the use of the suffix on the drawings, as in the Chemehuevi Project I, Chemehuevi Project II, and Chemehuevi Project III.

14. Pierre Koenig, quoted in De Wit, "Modernism Thwarted," 97n6, which cites his speech at a general tribal meeting as recorded in appendices, vol. 1,

general Tribal Meeting, tape 2, in *Chemehuevi Today: Annual Report, University of Southern California, School of Architecture, Chemehuevi Program,* 1 July 1975–30 June 1976, 17.

15.   De Wit, "Modernism Thwarted," 98n15.

16.   Chemehuevi Indian Tribe, Resolution, signed by Herbert W. Pencille, chairman, and Georgia Laird Culp, secretary-treasurer, 28 October 1971, PKPD, box 4, folder 2.

17.   Chemehuevi Indian Tribe, Resolution.

18.   Site plan, n.d., PKPD, flat file 79.

19.   There is also a colored and annotated sketch on yellow tracing paper in the archive that does not appear to be in Koenig's hand showing shade structures and their relationship, in section, to the main building. See PKPD, flat file 94.

20.   See Regional Climatic Data Temperature, n.d., PKPD, box 66.

21.   The Chemehuevi Project III, public toilet location map, July 1973, PKPD, flat file 89.

22.   Keith H. Grey, Pierre Koenig, and Peter Rodemeier, eds., *The Chemehuevi Project: An Exploratory Land Use, Planning, and Housing Study* (Los Angeles: Department of Architecture, University of Southern California, July 1971), PKPD, box 3, folder 1.

23.   Part I: "An Exploratory Land Use Study of the Chemehuevi Reservation," by Keith H. Grey, for the Department of Architecture, USC, with Jaime Gesundheight, Jack Groswith, Robert Holder, Millard Lee, Robert Mosteller, Michael Robinson, and Robert Simonian; Part II: "Study of Planning Alternatives for Section 19 of the Chemehuevi Reservation," by Peter Rodemeier, for the Department of Architecture, USC, with James Van Dalfsen, John Davis, William Nighswonger, Byron Pinckert, Leonard Roberts, Ralph Spargo, and Timothy Twomey; Part III: "Low Cost Tribal Housing Study for the Chemehuevi Reservation," by Pierre Koenig, for the Department of Architecture, USC, with Michael Chan, Minoru Chen, Robert Freeman, Steven Parmelee, Donald Puddy, Geoffry Reeslund, and Lowell Warren.

24.   Grey, Koenig, and Rodemeier, eds., *The Chemehuevi Project,* 221.

25.   40 inches (1 meter) was also the width of the Mahon panels specified for the Saint-Jean production houses.

26.   Grey, Koenig, and Rodemeier, eds., *The Chemehuevi Project,* 225.

27.   Grey, Koenig, and Rodemeier, eds., *The Chemehuevi Project,* 225.

28.   David Brindle, "Part One of a Study to Determine the Roof and Wall Components for the Chemehuevi Project" (Department of Architecture, University of Southern California, Los Angeles, CA, 21 February 1973), PKPD, box 3, folder 2.

29.   Brindle, "Part One," 1–2. The lettered requirements are an indirect quotation.

30.   Brindle, "Part One," 23–24, 68.

31.   Brindle, "Part One," 67.

32.   Brindle, "Part One," 21.

33.   David Brindle and Anne Vernez, "Part Two of a Study to Determine the Roof and Wall Components for the Chemehuevi Project" (Department of Architecture, University of Southern California, Los Angeles, CA, 21 June 1973), 8, PKPD, box 3, folder 3.

34.   David Brindle, "Evaluation of Dwelling Plans to Meet the FHA Minimum Property Standards for the Chemehuevi Project" (Department of Architecture, University of Southern California, Los Angeles, CA, 1 June 1974), PKPD, box 3, folder 4.

35.   Brindle, "Evaluation of Dwelling Plans," 1.

36.   Joseph W. Janick to Jack Turner, chairman, 15 July 1976, PKPD, box 3, folder 5.

37.   See Pierre Koenig to Jayne Hulbert, 7 March 1977, PKPD, box 3, folder 7.

38.   The Outline Specification is stamped by HUD with the date 3 January 1977, PKPD, box 3, folder 5.

39.   Pierre Koenig, Outline Specification for the US Department of Housing and Urban Development, Chemehuevi Indian Housing, 22 November 1976 and 3 January 1977, PKPD, box 3, folder 5.

40.   Statement presented to the All Mission Indian Housing Authority, 21 December 1976, PKPD, box 3, folder 7. See also De Wit, "Modernism Thwarted," 96, 90n20.

41.   See Pierre Koenig to Jayne Hulbert.

42.   Pierre Koenig to Jayne Hulbert.

43.   See De Wit, "Modernism Thwarted," 96.

44.   Henry Knox to George Washington, 7 July 1789, PKPD, box 36.

45.   Ted Weitzel to Pierre Koenig, 4 October 1991, PKPD, box 10, folder 13.

46.   Ted Weitzel to Pierre Koenig, 24 October 1991, PKPD, box 10, folder 13.

47.   Pierre Koenig to Ted Weitzel, 26 September 1992, PKPD, box 10, folder 13.

48.   Ted Weitzel to Pierre Koenig, 1 October 1992, PKPD, box 10, folder 13.

49.   See Don Finefrock, "Owners to Get Variances on a Case-by-Case Basis," *Miami Herald,* 21 November 1992, 4B; and Don Finefrock, "Lax Rules on Flood Standards Could Cost," *Miami Herald,* n.d., 1B, 4B. PKPD, box 10, folder 13.

50.   Ted Weitzel to Pierre Koenig, 11 October 1992, PKPD, box 10, folder 13.

51.   See "House in Industry: A System for the Manufacture of Industrialized Building Components by Konrad Wachsmann and Walter Gropius," *Arts & Architecture* (November 1947): 28–37.

52.   See "House in a Factory by Henry Dreyfuss, Designer, and Edward L. Barnes, Architect," *Arts & Architecture* (September 1947): 31–35, 49–50.

53.   Pierre Koenig in conversation with the author, 23 February 1990, Los Angeles.

54.   Pierre Koenig, interview by Kimberly Kirkpatrick, 16 October 1992, in James Steele, *Los Angeles Architecture: The Contemporary Condition* (London: Phaidon, 1993), 150.

**CHAPTER 11**

1.   Author interview with Della and Gary Rollé, 6 April 2016, Los Angeles. Confirmed in an email from Della Rollé to the author, 8 April 2018.

2.   Author interview with Della and Gary Rollé, 6 April 2016, Los Angeles.

3.   Description of Burwash House, n.d., 1, Pierre Koenig papers and drawings, 1925–2007 (hereafter PKPD), 2006.M.30, box 1, folder 7, Getty Research Institute, Los Angeles.

4.   See Addition for Dr. and Mrs. Bruce Whitehead, plan, sections, and elevations, sheet 3, 10 February 1965, PKPD, flat file 51.

5.   See Addition to the Residence of Mr. and Mrs. Frank South, elevations and sections, sheet 3, 11 November 1987, PKPD, flat file 144.

6.   See AIA Abbreviated Standard Form of Agreement between Owner and Architect, between Mr. and Mrs. Alan Schier and Pierre Koenig, unsigned, May 2000, PKPD, box 16, folder 13.

7.   See also "Copy for Ken Kremith ad to appear in next issue of *Arts & Architecture* magazine: 1/16 page," 5 September 1961, PKPD, box 1A, folder 6.

8.   See Valensi House, preliminary study, 7 August 1965, PKPD, flat file 24.

9. On 4 March 1981, Koenig invoiced the Rollés $2,514.37 for "design develop-ment stage 35% of fee." An advance of $1,000 had already been paid. Another invoice for $2,000 for "completion of working drawing stage" followed on 1 May 1981. PKPD, box 7, folder 1.

10. From the videotape recording of the San Francisco Museum of Modern Art (SFMOMA) lecture on 20 June 1990, PKPD, box 111, v4.

11. Pierre Koenig, "Addition by Pierre Koenig," n.d., PKPD, box 7, folder 1. A typescript version of this statement dated 10 April 1985 is held in PKPD, box 7, folder 3.

12. Vergun's calculations are dated 15 June 1981 and the plan check receipt is dated 9 December 1982. PKPD, box 7, folder 1.

13. Pierre Koenig to Mr. and Mrs. Gary Rollé, statement, 1 September 1982, PKPD, box 7, folder 2.

14. Pierre Koenig to Mr. and Mrs. Gary Rollé, statements dated 1 August 1982 and 1 September–1 December 1982, PKPD, box 7, folder 2.

15. Gary Rollé to Pierre Koenig, 20 December 1982, PKPD, box 7, folder 2.

16. Pierre Koenig to Mr. and Mrs. Gary Rollé, statement, 21 December 1982, PKPD, box 7, folder 2.

17. Pierre Koenig to Mr. and Mrs. Gary Rollé, statements dated 1 June to 1 Septem-ber 1983, PKPD, box 7, folder 2.

18. Rollé House, column detail, 30 March 1984, PKPD, box 7, folder 3.

19. John Mutlow to Pierre Koenig, 28 June 1985, PKPD, box 7, folder 3.

20. AIA Standard Form of Agreement between Owner and Architect, between Pierre Koenig and Mr. and Mrs. Gary Rollé, signed, 1 July 1991, PKPD, box 11, folder 1.

21. Pierre Koenig to Kemal Ramezani of R. G. West Corporation, 31 July 1993, PKPD, box 11, folder 4.

22. Kemal Ramezani of R. G. West Corporation to Mr. and Mrs. Gary Rollé, 22 February 1994, PKPD, box 11, folder 11.

23. Estimated Cost Breakdown, Mr. and Mrs. Gary Rollé, 9 July 1993, PKPD, box 11, folder 1.

24. R. G. West Corporation Payment Request, Final, 23 January 1995, PKPD, box 11, folder 1.

25. R. G. West Letter of Transmittal, Rollé Residence, 21 February 1994, PKPD, box 11, folder 11.

26. Pierre Koenig to Joe Bavaro, 12 October 1992, PKPD, box 11, folder 1.

27. Pierre Koenig to Joe Bavaro, 12 October 1992, PKPD, box 11, folder 1.

28. Joe Bavaro to Pierre Koenig, fax, 14 October 1994, PKPD, box 11, folder 12.

29. Jules Seltzer Associates to Pierre Koenig (client), invoices dated 18 May, 20 June, and 12 September 1995, PKPD, box 11, folder 11.

30. Knoll Group to Pierre Koenig, order confirmation, 30 June 1995, PKPD, box 11, folder 11. The order confirmation does not identify the furniture other than say-ing "glass top table," "chair," "left module," "end module." However, Bavaro's fax of 14 October 1994 listed the two Wassily chairs as coming from Knoll.

31. Billy Rose to Barry Sloane of Sotheby's International Realty, 25 August 2003, PKPD, box 20, folder 2.

32. Rose to Sloane, 25 August 2003.

33. See Sotheby's sales literature, which lists the house at $950,000. PKPD, box 6, folder 7.

34. AIA Abbreviated Standard Form of Agreement between Owner and Architect, between Billy Rose and Pierre Koenig, 12 September 2003, PKPD, box 20, folder 1.

35. Billy Rose to Pierre Koenig, 20 September 2003, PKPD, box 20, folder 1.

36. Rose to Koenig, 20 September 2003.

37. Billy Rose, "Magazines Contacted or in the Process of Being Contacted for Pierre Koenig Remodel of Gantert House," n.d., PKPD, box 20, folder 1.

38. Joseph J. Bavaro to Pierre Koenig, 20 September 2003, PKPD, box 20, folder 1.

39. Joe Bavaro to Pierre Koenig, "Gantert House," n.d., PKPD, box 20, folder 1. A copy of this list, dated 17 December 2003, is held in PKPD, box 20, folder 2.

40. See Pierre Koenig to Billy Rose, fax, 26 September 2003, and attached perspective drawing of kitchen island stamped "Preliminary Study," 26 Sep-tember 2003, PKPD, box 20, folder 1.

41. See Pierre Koenig to Billy Rose, fax, 26 September 2003, and attached plans of master bedroom and new bedroom, both stamped "Preliminary Study," 29 September 2003, PKPD, box 20, folder 1. The Preliminary Study plans, which were sent on 20 September, were date-stamped by Koenig on 29 September, nine days after they were sent. Presumably the date-stamp should have said 19 September.

42. See Pierre Koenig to Billy Rose, fax, 10 October 2003, and attached plan of bathroom 3 and laundry stamped "Preliminary Study," n.d., PKPD, box 20, folder 1.

43. Billy Rose to Pierre Koenig, fax, 22 December 2003, PKPD, box 20, folder 1.

44. Billy Rose to Pierre Koenig, 12 January 2004, PKPD, box 20, folder 1.

45. Koenig's assistant Jan Ipach sent Joe Bavaro a fax on 3 March 2004 saying, "Dear Joe—These are the window details for the new fixed glazing in the Gantert/Rose House. (2 sheets) Greetings from Pierre's office —Jan." PKPD, box 20, folder 1.

## CHAPTER 12

1. Information on the remodeling of 54 La Rancheria supplied by Cynthia Riebe, dated January 2008, revised 2016.

2. See "Interview Questions, Andrea Truppin, Ed. *Modernism* 01/09/07," 1, Pierre Koenig papers and drawings, 1925–2007 (hereafter PKPD), 2006.M.30, box 10, folder 4.

3. Joseph Giovannini, "A Modernist Jewel Rescued from Disgrace," *New York Times,* 1 January 1998, F8, PKPD, box 10, folder 4.

4. Andrea Truppin, "Pierre Koenig Round Two," *Modernism* (Spring 2007): 44.

5. "Interview Questions, Andrea Truppin," 2.

6. "Interview Questions, Andrea Truppin," 2.

7. Fred Riebe to Pierre Koenig, 21 September 1988, PKPD, box 10, folder 6.

8. "Interview Questions, Andrea Truppin," 1, PKPD, box 10, folder 4.

9. The sale closed on 29 November 1988. Cynthia Riebe, email to the author, 24 November 2016.

10. "Interview Questions, Andrea Truppin," 2, PKPD.

11. "Interview Questions, Andrea Truppin," 3.

12. Koenig client index cards, PKPD, box 36. AIA Standard Form of Agreement between Owner and Architect, between Mr. and Mrs. Frederick C. Riebe and Pierre Koenig, 14 October 1988, PKPD, box 10, folder 7.

13. Handwritten, undated note from Fred Riebe to Pierre Koenig attached to the AIA Standard Form of Agreement between Owner and Architect, between Mr. and Mrs. Frederick C. Riebe and Pierre Koenig.

14. See Koenig client index cards.

15. See plan, 54 La Rancheria, Carmel Valley, 18 November 1988, PKPD, flat file 149.

16. "It required a complete gutting of the house right down to its steel skeleton." "Interview Questions, Andrea Truppin," 5.

17. See Cynthia Riebe's handwritten list of seven actions, n.d., PKPD, box 10, folder 11. These include:

    1. enclose carport to 4th bedroom
    2. design new garage/storage/entry wing
    3. re-consider approach to house i.e., location of present driveway
    5. re-locate kitchen/laundry to central core, consider bathroom/bath configuration and access

18. Cynthia Riebe to Pierre Koenig, 28 November 1988, PKPD, box 10, folder 6.

19. Cynthia Riebe, untitled plan, 28 November 1988, PKPD, flat file 149.

20. Floor Plan Preliminary ID, Mr. and Mrs. Fred Riebe, 54 La Rancheria, Carmel, CA, 8 December 1988, PKPD, flat file 150. Only one sheet of this set remains in the archive. See also "Interview Questions, Andrea Truppin," 3, PKPD.

21. Cynthia Riebe, untitled plan, 26 December 1988, PKPD, flat file 149.

22. Cynthia Riebe, untitled plan, 26 December 1988. Water legislation at the time permitted only one additional shower or bathtub, but two handwashing basins and two water closets were allowed. For that reason, the bathtub appears to be shared between the two children's bathrooms.

23. Cynthia Riebe, Outline plan of house showing interior partitions, n.d., PKPD, flat file 149.

24. Cynthia Riebe, Alternative kitchen/laundry room layouts (four large, six small), n.d., PKPD, flat file 149. Emphasis Riebe.

25. Cynthia Riebe to Pierre Koenig, 28 December 1988, PKPD, box 10, folder 6.

26. Handwritten note (n.d.) from Cynthia Riebe to Pierre Koenig attached to photocopy of *Designers' Kitchens & Baths,* n.d., 33, PKPD, box 10, folder 9.

27. "Interview Questions, Andrea Truppin," 3.

28. Pierre Koenig to Mr. and Mrs. Fred Riebe, 23 March 1989, PKPD, box 10, folder 7.

29. Pierre Koenig to Mr. and Mrs. Fred Riebe, 17 May 1989, PKPD, box 10, folder 7. Emphasis Koenig.

30. Pierre Koenig to Mr. and Mrs. Fred Riebe, statement, 17 May 1989, PKPD, box 10, folder 7. Koenig client index cards show that, by 12 September 1991, the Riebes had paid $18,000. PKPD, box 36.

31. Cynthia Riebe to Pierre Koenig, 17 September 1989, PKPD, box 10, folder 6.

32. Cynthia Riebe to Pierre Koenig, 17 September 1989.

33. Kitchen plan, Riebe House, 12 May 1989, PKPD, box 10, folder 2.

34. Master bathroom plan, Riebe House, 19 June 1989, PKPD, box 10, folder 2.

35. Pierre Koenig to Cindy and Fred Riebe, 15 June 1989, PKPD, box 10, folder 3. Emphasis Koenig.

36. Pierre Koenig to Cindy and Fred Riebe, 15 June 1989.

37. Cynthia Riebe to Pierre Koenig, 17 September 1989, PKPD, box 10, folder 6.

38. Cynthia Riebe to Pierre Koenig, 17 September 1989, quoting a letter from Garrett Eckbo dated 9 September 1989, PKPD, box 10, folder 6.

39. Garrett Eckbo and William K. Yamamoto to Cynthia and Fred Riebe, 1 November 1989, PKPD, box 10, folder 3.

40. Garrett Eckbo and William K. Yamamoto to Cynthia and Fred Riebe, 1 November 1989, 2.

41. "Interview Questions, Andrea Truppin," 7. Walker also designed a landscape plan for the entire site.

42. Robertson and Co. and H. H. Robertson Co. are the same company of sheet metal suppliers. It is written both ways here to match how Koenig wrote the names on the specification: Specification for Mr. and Mrs. Riebe, n.d., 5, PKPD, box 10, folder 8.

43. Typical fascia, Seidel House, detail 165, 17 July 1959, PKPD, box 10, folder 8.

44. "Interview Questions, Andrea Truppin," 5.

45. "Interview Questions, Andrea Truppin," 3.

46. Copy shown to the author by Cynthia Riebe, 18 October 2016.

47. "Interview Questions, Andrea Truppin," 4.

48. See Koenig client index cards. There was no retainer paid.

49. This was the interior as seen by this author in 1988. For a photograph of the space and a longer discussion of the restoration of the house, see Neil Jackson, "Case Study House 21: The (Re)making of a Collector's Item," *Getty Research Journal,* no. 7 (2015): 53–66.

50. Pierre Koenig, Statement starting "Case Study House #21 was designed for Dr. & Mrs. Walter C. Bailey . . . ," n.d., PKPD, box 1, folder 13.

51. See Koenig client index cards.

52. AIA Standard Form of Agreement between Owner and Architect, between Daniel Cracchiolo and Pierre Koenig, 12 March 1997, PKPD, box 16, folder 3. Cracchiolo made his first payment to Koenig on 27 March 1997. See Koenig client index cards.

53. For more on the restoration of the Bailey House, see Jackson, "Case Study House 21: The (Re)making of a Collector's Item," 53–66.

54. Russell K. Johnson to Dan Cracchiolo, memo, 24 March 1997, 1, PKPD, box 16, folder 3.

55. Russell K. Johnson to Dan Cracchiolo, memo, 1.

56. Russell K. Johnson to Dan Cracchiolo, memo, 1.

57. Dan Cracchiolo to Pierre Koenig, note, n.d., PKPD, box 16, folder 5.

58. AIA Standard Form of Agreement between Owner and Architect, between Daniel Cracchiolo and Pierre Koenig, for Restoration of 9038 Wonderland Park Ave., Los Angeles, CA (Case Study House No. 21), 10 June 1997, PKPD, box 16, folder 3.

59. See Julius Shulman, Job 26222: Case Study House No. 21, Julius Shulman photography archive, 1935–2009, 2004.R.10, Getty Research Institute, Los Angeles, http://hdl.handle.net/10020/2004r10_job2622 (Links/display item: color photograph no. 2622.53K).

60. For the various designs for the credenza, see PKPD, box 16, folders 4 and 7. There were at least five versions of the stereo cabinet, although it is schemes 3, 4, and 5 that mostly feature in the archive. One unnumbered version has two integral speakers and a fixed top above each of them. The opening top panels are divided two-thirds to the left, with turntable, storage, and CD changer below, and one-third to the right, with storage below. There is no overhanging lip. The design for scheme 4 incorporates walnut plywood, with the grain running horizontally, and a white solid-core, laminated, plastic, hinged top with

an overhanging lip. Dimensions are 9 feet, 8 inches long, 2 feet, 6 inches tall (on 12-inch legs), and 2 feet deep, with a 12-inch-diameter coaxial speaker, and Electric Voice and Kroll fabric W321-9 covering the speakers. There is a note on the drawing of a plywood panel with a speaker cutout: "Turn fabric around corner so that no wood shows from front." This refers specifically to the mitered corner where the fabric-covered plywood meets the walnut side panel. There is very little to distinguish scheme 3 from scheme 5, apart from the greater amount of accessible storage provided in the latter, where the central three (of five) panels of the top open separately. On scheme 3, there is a single opening panel for the central three-fifths of the top. An earlier version, not numbered, shows a separate speaker box, 18 inches square, in place of the left-hand speaker and a 12-inch-long, quarter-inch-thick smoked acrylic panel set into the upper edge of the left-hand end of the cabinet. This version has four opening panels on the top, the panel over the right-hand speaker being fixed. There is even another version of this design with the separate speaker panel. Here, there is a single hinged panel over the smoked acrylic panel and a long panel covering the position of the other three in the previous design.

61. Pierre Koenig to Joe Bavaro, fax, 29 October 1997, PKPD, box 14, folder 4.
62. Pierre Koenig to Joe Bavaro, fax, 19 November 1997, PKPD, box 14, folder 4.
63. Pierre Koenig to Richard Schwag, fax, 9 April 1998, PKPD, box 16, folder 4.
64. Pierre Koenig to Danny Moizel, fax, 14 July 1997, PKPD, box 1, folder 12.
65. Pierre Koenig to Danny Moizel, fax, 12 June 2000, PKPD, box 16, folder 6A
66. Punch list, 12 May 1998, PKPD, box 16, folder 4.
67. Punch list faxed by Pierre Koenig to Danny Moizel, 13 May 1998, PKPD, box 16, folder 4.
68. Pierre Koenig to Danny Moizel, fax, 16 May 1998, PKPD, box 16, folder 4.
69. A preliminary plan for the kitchen, pending owner approval, was faxed by Koenig to Danny Moizel on 17 June 1997. It is therefore likely that he sent Cracchiolo plans at the same time. Preliminary kitchen plan faxed by Pierre Koenig to Danny Moizel, PKPD, box 16, folder 3.
70. Letter on Silver Pictures [Warner Brothers] letterhead from Dan Cracchiolo to Pierre Koenig, n.d., PKPD, box 16, folder 3.
71. Note on Decade Pictures letterhead with attached photocopy from Dan Cracchiolo to Pierre Koenig, n.d., PKPD, box 16, folder 5.
72. Letter on Silver Pictures [Warner Brothers] letterhead from Dan Cracchiolo to Pierre Koenig.
73. Pierre Koenig to Dan Cracchiolo, fax, 27 June 1997, PKPD, box 16, folder 3.
74. Punch list faxed by Pierre Koenig to Danny Moizel.
75. Tony Merchell to Dan Cracchiolo, 1 March 1999, PKPD, box 1, folder 13A.
76. Tony Merchell to Pierre Koenig, 1 March 1999, PKPD, box 1, folder 13A.
77. Jay Oren to Los Angeles Cultural Heritage Commission, staff report, 27 July 1999, PKPD, box 16, folder 6A.
78. Susan H. Ioka, executive assistant II for the Los Angeles Cultural Heritage Commission, to Daniel Cracchiolo, 4 August 1999, PKPD, box 16, folder 6A.
79. Jay Oren to Los Angeles Cultural Heritage Commission, 25 August 1999, PKPD, box 16, folder 6A.
80. See Susan H. Ioka to Daniel Cracchiolo.
81. See Marjorie Thayne, executive assistant II for the Los Angeles Cultural Heritage Commission, to Daniel Cracchiolo via certified mail, 19 November 1999,

PKPD, box 16, folder 6A. With the announcement came the offer for a bronze plaque for the building.

82. Holly A. Wyman, president, Los Angeles Cultural Heritage Commission, to Pierre Koenig, 1 November 2000, PKPD, box 16, folder 6A.
83. Los Angeles Cultural Heritage Commission guest list, 12 December 2000, PKPD, box 1, folder 13A.
84. This can be judged by the dates on letters, first to Cracchiolo and then to LaFetra, which are retained in the archive.
85. See Linda Dishman, executive director of the Los Angeles Conservancy, to Pierre Koenig, 6 March 2000, PKPD, box 1, folder 13A.
86. See Pierre Koenig to Michael LaFetra, fax, showing drawing for the fountain, 2 June 2000, PKPD, box 16, folder 6A.
87. Pierre Koenig, Statement starting "Case Study House #21 was designed for Dr. & Mrs. Walter C. Bailey . . . ," n.d., PKPD, box 1, folder 13.
88. Jeffrey Wells, "All That's Left," *Hollywood Elsewhere, (*column), *Movie Poop Shoot: All the News That's Shit to Print,* 18 June 2004, https://web.archive .org/web/20040622000449/http://moviepoopshoot.com:80/elsewhere /index.html.
89. All quotations in this paragraph up to note 90 are from the following source: Cynthia Riebe to Pierre Koenig, 17 September 1989, quoting a letter from Garrett Eckbo dated 9 September 1989, PKPD, box 10, folder 6.
90. Michael LaFetra sold the house to Mark Haddawy in 2002.
91. See Jackson, "Case Study House 21: The (Re)making of a Collector's Item," 62, 64.
92. The area of the house is 1,330 square feet.
93. Giovannini, "A Modernist Jewel Rescued from Disgrace," F8.

## CHAPTER 13

1. See chapter 12, this volume, and "Interview Questions, Andrea Truppin, Ed. *Modernism* 01/09/07," 2, Pierre Koenig papers and drawings, 1925–2007 (hereafter PKPD), 2006.M.30, box 10, folder 4.
2. Now the Geffen Contemporary at 152 North Central Avenue, Los Angeles.
3. Elizabeth A. T. Smith to Pierre Koenig, 28 March 1985, PKPD, box 49, folder 1.
4. Richard Koshalek to Pierre Koenig, 29 July 1985, PKPD, box 49, folder 1.
5. Elizabeth A. T. Smith to Pierre Koenig, 8 August 1988, PKPD, box 49, folder 1.
6. MOCA, Los Angeles, "The Museum of Contemporary Art Presents Major Architecture Exhibition Examining the Case Study Houses," press release, 8 August 1989, 1, PKPD, box 49, folder 1.
7. MOCA, Los Angeles, "The Museum of Contemporary Art Presents Major Architecture Exhibition Examining the Case Study Houses," 3.
8. Cynthia Campoy, MOCA press officer, to Pierre Koenig, 18 October 1989, PKPD, box 49, folder 1. Pierre Koenig to Cynthia Campoy, fax, 30 October 1989, PKPD, box 49, folder 1.
9. Sherri Geldin to Pierre Koenig, 27 October 1989, PKPD, box 49, folder 1.
10. Elizabeth A. T. Smith to Pierre Koenig, 21 February 1990, PKPD, box 49, folder 1.
11. For papers relating to Koenig's sabbatical in 1988, see PKPD, box 30, folder 4A.
12. Geldin to Koenig, 27 October 1989.
13. Katherine W. Rinne to Pierre Koenig, 22 November 1989, PKPD, box 49, folder 2.

14. Art Seidenbaum had been the art and architecture editor for the *Los Angeles Times* during the late 1950s and early 1960s.

15. Architecture and Design Council of MOCA, Los Angeles, "Blueprints for Modern Living: History and Legacy of the Case Study Houses (1954–1966)," typescript of program, 21 October 1989, PKPD, box 49, folder 2.

16. James Tyler to Pierre Koenig, 4 November 1989, PKPD, box 49, folder 2.

17. Koenig spoke on "The Future of the Case Study House Today" on 19 November 1989. See advertisement for *Art Talks,* MOCA at the Temporary Contemporary, PKPD, box 49, folder 3.

18. Paul Goldberger, "When Modernism Kissed the Land of Golden Dreams," *New York Times,* 10 December 1989, 42, PKPD, box 49, folder 4.

19. Goldberger, "When Modernism Kissed the Land of Golden Dreams."

20. Allen Temko, "Blueprints for Beauty," *San Francisco Chronicle,* 10 December 1989, PKPD, box 49, folder 4. The date on the cutting is handwritten by Koenig; however, on Sundays, the San Francisco paper was the *Examiner.*

21. Cynthia Riebe to Pierre Koenig, 17 September 1989, PKPD, box 10, folder 6.

22. "Interview Questions, Andrea Truppin," 4.

23. The first meeting had been on or about 9 August 1990. See Koenig client index cards, PKPD, box 36.

24. Martin Schwartz to Pierre Koenig, 17 August 1990, PKPD, box 12, folder 3.

25. AIA Standard Form of Agreement between Architect and Owner, signed by Martin Schwartz and Pierre Koenig, 4 September, PKPD, box 12, folder 3.

26. See Koenig client index cards.

27. Martin Schwartz, Preliminary Specifications—Schwartz Residence, August 1990, PKPD, box 12, folder 3.

28. Martin Schwartz to Pierre Koenig, 22 October 1990, 1, PKPD, box 12, folder 3.

29. Schwartz to Koenig, 22 October 1990, 2.

30. Schwartz to Koenig, 22 October 1990, 3.

31. Schwartz to Koenig, 22 October 1990, 1, 2.

32. Schwartz to Koenig, 22 October 1990, 2.

33. Martin Schwartz to Pierre Koenig, fax, 23 October 1990, PKPD, box 12, folder 3.

34. Pierre Koenig to Martin Schwartz, fax, 24 October 1990, PKPD, box 12, folder 3.

35. Pierre Koenig to Martin Schwartz, fax, 30 October 1990, PKPD, box 12, folder 3.

36. Schwartz to Koenig, 22 October 1990, 1.

37. Schwartz to Koenig, 22 October 1990, 2.

38. Koenig offered Schwartz either a spiral stair or a square newel stair with landings. Schwartz chose the spiral version. Martin Schwartz, email to the author, 16 January 2017.

39. Pierre Koenig to Martin Schwartz, fax, 16 November 1990, PKPD, box 12, folder 3.

40. Martin Schwartz to Pierre Koenig, fax, 21 November 1990, PKPD, box 12, folder 3.

41. Koenig to Schwartz, fax, 16 November 1990.

42. Koenig to Schwartz, fax, 16 November 1990.

43. Koenig to Schwartz, fax, 16 November 1990.

44. Martin Schwartz to Pierre Koenig, fax, 16 November 1990, PKPD, box 12, folder 3.

45. See photographs of house model, PKPD, box 27, folder 1, and box 92, folder 2.

46. Martin Schwartz to Pierre Koenig, 14 January 1991, PKPD, box 12, folder 8. The fee sum was $3,750.00.

47. The following drawings labeled "Mr. Martin Schwartz" have revisions dated 1 September 1991: sections, sheet 3; elevations, sheet 4; spiral stair, sheet 10, PKPD, flat files (respectively) 161, 160, and 171.

48. See Martin Schwartz to Pierre Koenig, fax, 11 September 1991, PKPD, box 14, folder 7. For the full-cost estimate, including architectural fees, see California Federal Estimated Cost Breakdown, 5 September 1991, PKPD, box 12, folder 5. For Koenig's $400,000 "second" cost estimate, see Bid Comparison–Spot Items 444 Sycamore Rd., Plan "A," 27 January 1992, PKPD, box 13, folder 1.

49. Schwartz to Koenig, fax, 11 September 1991.

50. Schwartz to Koenig, fax, 11 September 1991. Emphasis Schwartz.

51. Martin Schwartz to Pierre Koenig, regarding 4 November 1991 meeting, n.d., PKPD, box 12, folder 14.

52. See Pierre Koenig to Martin Schwartz, fax, 12 November 1991, 3, PKPD, box 12, folder 14.

53. Koenig to Schwartz, fax, 12 November 1991, 3.

54. Martin Schwartz to Pierre Koenig, fax, 13 November 1991, PKPD, box 12, folder 14.

55. See Bid Comparison–Spot Items 444 Sycamore Rd., plan "A," 27 January 1992.

56. Martin Schwartz to Pierre Koenig, fax, 28 January 1992, PKPD, box 13, folder 1.

57. Martin Schwartz to Frank Kamel, memo, 2 February 1992, PKPD, box 13, folder 1.

58. See Estimated Cost Breakdown, 5 September 1991 and 21 February 1992, PKPD, box 13, folder 1.

59. Kemal Ramezani of R. G. West Corporation to Martin Schwartz, 3 June 1992, PKPD, box 13, folder 5.

60. AIA Standard Form of Agreement between Owner and Contractor, between Martin Schwartz and R. G. West Corporation, fax, 17 June 1992, PKPD, box 13, folder 5.

61. Pierre Koenig to Martin Schwartz, Kemal Ramezani, and Joe Bavaro, fax, 30 June 1992, PKPD, box 13, folder 5.

62. Martin Schwartz to Pierre Koenig, fax, 1 July 1992, 1–2, PKPD, box 13, folder 7. Emphasis Schwartz.

63. Pierre Koenig to Kemal Ramezani, 7 July 1992, PKPD, box 13, folder 7.

64. Martin Schwartz to Kemal Ramezani, fax, 7 July 1992, PKPD, box 13, folder 7.

65. Cayetano Cardenas of F. B. Fabricators to Martin Schwartz, 17 December 1992, PKPD, box 13, folder 10.

66. Martin Schwartz to Kemal Ramezani, fax, 21 December 1992, PKPD, box 13, folder 10.

67. Kemal Ramezani to Martin Schwartz, 28 December 1992, 2, PKPD, box 13, folder 10.

68. Ramezani to Schwartz, 28 December 1992, 2.

69. Pierre Koenig to Kemal Ramezani, fax, 29 December 1992, PKPD, box 13, folder 10. Emphasis Koenig.

70. Martin Schwartz to Pierre Koenig, fax, 5 January 1993, PKPD, box 13, folder 1. This copy is incorrectly date-stamped by Koenig with "JAN–6 1992."

71. Martin Schwartz to Pierre Koenig, fax, 12 October 1992, PKPD, box 13, folder 9. Emphasis Schwartz.

72. Kemal Ramezani to Martin Schwartz, fax, 21 January 1993, PKPD, box 13, folder 12.

73. See Pierre Koenig to Martin Schwartz, fax, 27 March 1993, PKPD, box 13, folder 12.
74. Kemal Ramezani to Mohamad Farrohki, fax, 30 March 1993, PKPD, box 13, folder 12.
75. Martin Schwartz to Kemal Ramezani, fax, 23 April 1993, PKPD, box 14, folder 1. Emphasis Schwartz.
76. Kemal Ramezani to Pierre Koenig, fax, 23 April 1993, PKPD, box 14, folder 1.
77. Pierre Koenig to Kemal Ramezani, fax, 23 April 1993, PKPD, box 14, folder 1. Emphasis Koenig.
78. Ramezani to Koenig, fax, 23 April 1993.
79. See Martin Schwartz to Kemal Ramezani, fax, 10 May 1993, PKPD, box 14, folder 3.
80. Schwartz to Ramezani, fax, 10 May 1993.
81. Schwartz to Ramezani, fax, 10 May 1993. Emphasis Schwartz.
82. Schwartz to Ramezani, fax, 10 May 1993.
83. See Martin Schwartz to Kemal Ramezani, fax, 1 July 1993, PKPD, box 14, folder 5.
84. Kemal Ramezani to Pierre Koenig, fax, 1 July 1992, PKPD, box 14, folder 5.
85. Kemal Ramezani to Pierre Koenig, fax, 2 July 1992, PKPD, box 14, folder 5.
86. Martin Schwartz to Kemal Ramezani, fax, 17 August 1993, PKPD, box 14, folder 6. Emphasis Schwartz.
87. The deposit, representing about 40 percent of the quoted sum of $29,671.16, was paid to Design Supply, who, in turn, ordered the windows from Fleetwood Aluminum Products Inc.
88. See Martin Schwartz to Jerry Peryman, 4 October 1993, PKPD, box 14, folder 8.
89. Schwartz to Peryman, 4 October 1993, 2.
90. Schwartz to Peryman, 4 October 1993, 2.
91. For correspondence relating to the BBC Education television program *Forging Ahead,* part of the *Wall to Wall* series produced by Dr. Dick Foster, see PKPD, box 49, folder 19. The program was first broadcast in the United Kingdom on 14 August 1994.
92. See 35 mm color slide, October 1993, PKPD, box 92, folder 2.
93. City of Los Angeles Department of Building and Safety Inspection Record, PKPD, box 14, folder 10.
94. Schwartz, email to the author, 16 January 2017.
95. Exemption Letter, California Coastal Commission to Martin Schwartz, 28 July 1995, PKPD, box 15, folder 11.
96. See Martin Schwartz to Kamel Ramezani, fax, 9 November 1995, PKPD, box 15, folder 11.
97. Kamel Ramezani to Pierre Koenig, fax, 4 January 1996, PKPD, box 15, folder 11.
98. Schwartz, email to the author, 16 January 2017.
99. AIA Standard Form of Agreement between Owner and Architect, between Jrffrey [sic] Ressner and Pierre Koenig, January 2000, PKPD, box 17, folder 1A.
100. See Koenig client index cards.
101. See Koenig client index cards.
102. See Ressner modular addition, elevations, 2001, PKPD, box 17, folder 7.
103. See Ressner modular addition, elevations and sections, 27 March 2000, sheet 2, PKPD, flat file 193.
104. See Ressner modular addition, elevations and sections, 29 June 2000, sheet 2, PKPD, flat file 192.
105. Kemal Ramezani to Pierre Koenig, 31 May 2000, PKPD, box 17, folder 2.
106. Kausen Associates, Proposal, Ressner Res. Addition, 25 May 2000, PKPD, box 17, folder 2.
107. AIA Abbreviated Standard Form of Agreement between Owner and Contractor for a Small Project, signed by Jeffery [sic] Ressner and Kausen Construction Company, 10 July 2000, PKPD, box 17, folder 2.
108. Statement issued to Jeffrey Ressner, 20 July 2001, PKPD, box 17, folder 2.
109. AIA Abbreviated Standard Form of Agreement between Owner and Architect, between William Koppany and Pierre Koenig, 17 July 1999, PKPD, box 18, folder 3.
110. See Mark Yamashita of Becker & Miyamoto to Bill Koppany, 10 August 1999, PKPD, box 18, folder 5. See Richard Garcia to Pierre Koenig, 6 November 1999, PKPD, box 18, folder 5. See William H. Koh to Pierre Koenig, 28 December 2000, PKPD, box 18, folder 5. It was, however, Ficcadenti & Waggoner who were employed as consulting structural engineers.
111. Richard Garcia to Pierre Koenig, fax, 20 June 2000, PKPD, box 18, folder 5.
112. William John Koppany to Randall Akers, 14 August 2000, PKPD, box 18, folder 5.
113. Richard Garcia to Pierre Koenig, fax, 17 October 2000, PKPD, box 18, folder 5.
114. Notice of Public Hearing to Property Owners, Case no. CA 2002-1845(ZAA), Randall Akers applicant, Office of Zoning Administration, City of Los Angeles, n.d., PKPD, box 18, folder 8.
115. Pierre Koenig to Wayne Shick [sic], fax, 25 September 2001, PKPD, box 18, folder 8. The fax says, "Attached are the soils corrections."
116. The construction details, Mr. & Mrs. Koppany, sheet 8, are signed and dated 3 September (no year) and date-stamped 7 October 2002. See PKPD, flat file 197.
117. For the undated working drawings, see PKPD, flat file 198.

CHAPTER 14

1. Information Sheet, The Laguna Project, n.d., 1, Pierre Koenig papers and drawing, 1925–2007 (hereafter PKPD), 2006.M.30, box 16, folder 1, Getty Research Institute, Los Angeles. This statement can be dated to no later than 19 December 1996, when he sent it by fax to *Global Architecture* in Tokyo. See Pierre Koenig to GA/A.D.A. Edita Tokyo Co., fax, 19 December 1996, PKPD, box 16, folder 1.
2. Information Sheet, The Laguna Project, n.d., 2.
3. Information Sheet, The Laguna Project, n.d., 1.
4. AIA Standard Form of Agreement between Owner and Architect, between Vida Tarassoly and Mohsen Mehran and Pierre Koenig, July 2000, PKPD, box 19, folder 1. Koenig client index card, PKPD, box 36.
5. See Proposed Schedule, 7 August 2000, PKPD, box 19, folder 7.
6. See Tarassoly & Mehran plans, sheets 1 and 2, 6 September 2000, PKPD, flat file 214.
7. Vida Tarassoly to Pierre Koenig, fax, 20 September 2000, PKPD, box 19, folder 7.
8. See Tarassoly to Koenig, fax, 20 September 2000.
9. Tarassoly to Koenig, fax, 20 September 2000.
10. Pierre Koenig to Vida and Mehren [sic], fax, 22 March 2001, PKPD, box 19, folder 7.

11. Statement, 6 November 2001, PKPD, box 19, folder 7.

12. Plan, lower floor, scheme 103B, revised 15 September 2001, PKPD, box 19, folder 15.

13. This is shown in an elevation prepared on 27 February 2002 and revised twice subsequently. See Residence for Tarassoly & Mehran, elevation at C-C, sheet 8, 27 February 2002, PKPD, flat file 218.

14. See Tarassoly and Mehran House, plan, top floor, sheet 4, 28 June 2008, overwritten 13 July 2002, PKPD, flat file 218.

15. See plans, elevations, sections, and details, dated 10 December 2003, some revised 9 March 2004, and some undated, PKPD, box 19, folder 11.

16. See Jan Ipach to Vida Tarassoly, fax, 9 March 2004, PKPD, box 19, folder 7.

17. Jan Ipach to Vida Tarassoly, fax, 18 March 2004, PKPD, box 19, folder 7.

18. Jan Ipach to Vida Tarassoly, fax, 21 April 2004, PKPD, box 19, folder 7.

19. Vida Tarassoly, email to the author, 23 July 2006. Quoted in Neil Jackson, *Pierre Koenig* (Cologne: Taschen, 2007), 14.

20. Michael LaFetra to Pierre Koenig, 21 March 2002, PKPD, box 18, folder 11A.

21. LaFetra to Koenig, 21 March 2002.

22. Professional Construction Analysts Inc., Malibu, Demolition Plan, 1st and 2nd Floor, and Demolition Plan, 3rd Floor, Michael LaFetra Residence, sheets 3 and 4, 1 February 2001, PKPD, flat file 209.

23. AIA Standard Form of Agreement between Owner and Architect, between Michael LaFetra and Pierre Koenig, 16 April 2001, PKPD, box 18, folder 12.

24. Statement, 1 October 2001, PKPD, box 18, folder 12.

25. For revisions dated variously 3 July 2001 and 12 March, 1 June, 24 July, 25 July, and 18 September 2003, see PKPD, flat files 207 and 210. See also flat file 211 for undated but revised drawings.

26. See Koenig client index card, PKPD, box 36.

27. Hilre Hunt to Pierre Koenig, 23 June 2000, PKPD, box 17, folder 1.

28. See Mrs. Henry Frost to Mr. and Mrs. Koening [*sic*], 21 April 1999, PKPD, box 17, folder 1.

29. Mrs. Henry Frost to Pierre Koenig, email, 15 May 2000, PKPD, box 17, folder 1.

30. See Koenig client index card. Koenig misspelled her first name as "Hilri."

31. See Legend Airlines ticket stubs and ticket wallets, 27 and 28 June 2000, PKPD, box 17, folder 1.

32. See guest receipt, folio number 12062, Guest Lodge at the Cooper Aerobics Center, 20 June 2000, PKPD, box 17, folder 1.

33. AIA Abbreviated Standard Form of Agreement between Owner and Architect, between Henry Frost and Hilri [*sic*] Hunt and Pierre Koenig, July 2000, PKPD, box 17, folder 1.

34. Pierre Koenig to Hilre Frost, memo, 31 July 2000, PKPD, box 17, folder 1.

35. See Frost/Hunt House, untitled perspective drawing, n.d., PKPD, box 17, folder 1.

36. See Survey of Property Situated at Shelter Island, n.d., PKPD, box 16, folder 14.

37. Koenig added Stuart Parr's name to a client index card on 25 January 2001.

38. Neither Nick Sands nor Kerri Scharlin is listed on Koenig's client index cards. This suggests that no retainer was paid and no contract entered into.

39. Nick Sands to Pierre Koenig, December 1997, envelope postmarked Orlando, Florida, 29 December 1997, PKPD, box 16, folder 7A.

40. See Nick Sands to Pierre Koenig, email, 11 July 1998 (dated 12 July 1998), PKPD, box 16, folder 7A.

41. See Nick Sands to Pierre Koenig, fax, 9 October 1998, PKPD, box 16, folder 7A.

42. Sands to Koenig, fax, 9 October 1998.

43. Sands to Koenig, fax, 9 October 1998.

44. Nick Sands to Pierre Koenig, fax, 23 August 1999, PKPD, box 16, folder 7A.

45. Sands to Koenig, fax, 23 August 1999. Emphasis Sands.

46. See Nick Sands to Pierre Koenig, 23 August 1999, PKPD, box 16, folder 7A. James Steele and David Jenkins, *Pierre Koenig* (London: Phaidon, 1998).

47. Sands to Koenig, 23 August 1999.

48. Kerri Scharlin to Pierre Koenig, 21 November 1999, PKPD, box 16, folder 11.

49. Pierre Koenig to Kerri Scharlin, 23 November 1999, fax, PKPD, box 16, folder 11.

50. Pierre Koenig to Kerri Scharlin, fax, 29 November 1999, PKPD, box 16, folder 11.

51. Nadir Safai to Pierre Koenig, email, 14 August 1999, PKPD, box 16, folder 9A.

52. Pierre Koenig to Tony Merchell, fax, 31 August 1999, PKPD, box 16, folder 9A.

53. Dr. J. W. Colin to Pierre Koenig, email, 14 April 2000, PKPD, box 16, folder 12.

54. Alan Steinberger to Pierre Koenig, email, 30 September 1999, PKPD, box 16, folder 10.

55. Alan Steinberger to Pierre Koenig, email, 10 December 1999, PKPD, box 16, folder 10.

56. Steinberger to Koenig, email, 10 December 1999.

57. AIA Abbreviated Standard Form of Agreement between Owner and Architect, between Mr. and Mrs. Jeff Levy and Pierre Koenig, 9 October 1999, PKPD, box 16, folder 8.

58. Agreement between Joe Bavaro and Pierre Koenig, 25 November 1999, PKPD, box 16, folder 8.

59. See Joe Bavaro to Pierre Koenig, fax, 4 December 1999, PKPD, box 16, folder 8.

60. Handwritten notes, headed "Pamela Jeff Levy," probably made by Pierre Koenig during a telephone conversation, n.d., PKPD, box 16, folder 8.

61. Jan Ipach in an email to the author, 9 January 2017. Ipach cites Doug Noble and Karen Kensek, "both excellent teachers in that field," as Koenig's instructors. The software Koenig used was MiniCAD, later known as Vectorworks.

## CHAPTER 15

1. Proposed Piano Factory, n.d., Pierre Koenig papers and drawing, 1925–2007 (hereafter PKPD), 2006.M.30, flat file 225B, Getty Research Institute, Los Angeles.

2. Proposed Piano Factory, PKPD, flat file 225B.

3. Preliminary Study, plan, section, sheet 1, 13 September 1966, PKPD, flat file 53.

4. James Steele and David Jenkins, *Pierre Koenig* (London: Phaidon, 1998), 117.

5. See Koenig client index cards, PKPD, box 36. Robert Alan Franklyn, *On Developing Bosom Beauty* (New York: F. Fell, 1959). Robert Alan Franklyn and Helen Gould, *The Art of Staying Young* (New York: F. Fell, 1964).

6. Franklyn Building promotional statement, n.d., PKPD, box 2, folder 19.

7. Although these drawings, which are held in the archive, are dated 1 February 1963, the building was eventually completed to a revised design in 1967. See PKPD, flat file 241.

8. Cabana for Dr. and Mrs. Robert A. Franklyn, 1 July 1964, PKPD, flat file 50.

9. For the site survey drawings dated 23 October 1969, see PKPD, flat file 102.

10. Restaurant for Apryl Franklyn, 2 January 1977, PKPD, flat file 101.

11. See Steele and Jenkins, *Pierre Koenig*, 101. The British protectorate of Kuwait ended in 1961.

12. Undated notes starting "Clients—," 1, PKPD, box 48, folder 1. Emphasis Koenig.

13. Pierre Koenig, "The Way We Were USC Architecture in the 40's," lecture typescript, 10 April 1995, PKPD, box 48, folder 2.

14. Undated notes starting "What I am doing…," PKPD, box 48, folder 2.

15. Undated notes starting "Clients—."

16. Undated notes headed "Pierre Koenig," PKPD, box 48, folder 1. In this one-page statement, he describes the Iwata House, referring to it as "my latest work."

17. Undated notes starting "Although we have been…," PKPD, box 48, folder 1. On page 5 of this paper, Koenig refers to "a psychologist-client living in one of my houses."

18. Undated notes headed "Pierre Koenig."

19. Undated notes starting "Clients—," 2.

20. Undated notes starting "Clients—," 3.

21. Undated notes starting "Although we have been…," 3.

22. Undated notes starting "Clients—," 2–3.

23. Undated notes headed "Pierre Koenig." Emphasis Koenig.

24. Undated notes headed "Pierre Koenig."

25. This meeting on 11 June 1963 could have been arranged to coincide with the Construction Industries Exposition and Home Show held in Los Angeles on 19–30 June.

26. Pierre Koenig, "Talk at AIA Meeting June 11, 1963," lecture typescript, 1, PKPD, box 48, folder 1.

27. See press release from Dave Wood, Press Relations Department, Bethlehem Steel Company, 18 April 1963, PKPD, box 2, folder 4. See also J. B. Warner, Bethlehem Steel Company, "Circulating Exhibitions—The American Federation of the Arts," memo, 3 June 1963, and accompanying schedule of display locations from August 1962 to September 1964, titled "The Architecture of Steel," PKPD, box 2, folder 4.

28. Pierre Koenig, "Commercial Exhibit for Bethlehem Steel Company," statement, 1, PKPD, box 2, folder 4.

29. Pierre Koenig, "Commercial Exhibit for Bethlehem Steel Company," 1.

30. Bethlehem Steel Company Pavilion, Steel Erection Order, n.d., PKPD, box 2, folder 7.

31. Undated notes starting "Although we have been…," 2–3, PKPD, box 48, folder 1.

32. Untitled lecture given at Harvard University, lecture typescript, 30 October 1991, 2, PKPD, box 147, folder 14.

33. "Interview Questions, Andrea Truppin, Ed. *Modernism* 01/09/07," 2, PKPD, box 10, folder 4.

34. See Koenig client index cards.

35. Addition for Jeffrey Klawans, n.d., PKPD, flat file 139. The survey and preliminary sketches are dated January and February 1986. See PKPD, flat file 139.

36. See Addition for Jeffrey Klawans, plans, sections, elevation, n.d., PKPD, flat file 139.

37. See bibliography for Case Study House Number 21, 13 May 1997, PKPD, box 1, folder 13.

38. Richard J. Neutra to Pierre Koenig, 19 April 1962, PKPD, box 34, folder 10. The letter is incorrectly addressed to "12221 Dorsey."

39. Richard J. Neutra to Pierre Koenig, 15 April 1963, PKPD, box 34, folder 10.

40. Pierre Koenig to John Entenza, 18 April 1963, PKPD, box 34, folder 10.

41. John Entenza to Pierre Koenig, 25 April 1963, PKPD, box 34, folder 10. Emphasis and strike-through by Entenza.

42. The drawings for the Beagles House are dated 2 November 1962, with revisions extending through April and June 1963, PKPD, flat file 48.

43. The author gives the date for Koenig joining the Department of Architecture at USC as 1961. This is based on his Individual Teacher's record, which lists him as "age 45" (1970–71) and in which he says he has nine years teaching experience at USC; see Neil Jackson, *Pierre Koenig* (Cologne: Taschen, 2007), 93. In an untitled lecture retained in the archive, Koenig says that he "came to the Dept. of Arch. in 1962" (PKPD, box 48, folder 1). Koenig's curriculum vitae dated 28 March 1995 says he was appointed professor of architecture in 1963. Steele and Jenkins give the date as 1964; see Steele and Jenkins, *Pierre Koenig,* 17. The first USC staff card to show Koenig as an assistant professor is for 1964–65. In 1962–63 and 1963–64, his staff card shows him as an instructor. See PKPD, box 31a, folder 5. There is also a USC Bookstore identification card for Koenig with an expiration date of 30 September 1961, suggesting that, possibly as an alumnus, he began using the bookstore regularly in 1960–61, after he had moved his office to Dorothy Street. PKPD, box 31a, folder 3.

44. Undated notes headed "When I came to the Dept. of Arch…., " 1. PKPD, box 48, folder 1.

45. Pierre Koenig, "Historic Building Analysis," course assignment for Building Science 205, 14 November 1995, 1, PKPD, box 28, folder 1.

46. Pierre Koenig, "Historic Building Analysis," 1.

47. See Pierre Koenig, "Final Presentation Schedule," Building Science 205, 10 April 1996, PKPD, box 28, folder 1.

48. See Pierre Koenig, "Arch 211 Outline & Schedule," Materials and Methods of Building Construction—Architecture 211, Spring 1996, PKPD, box 28, folder 1a.

49. Pierre Koenig, "Course Syllabus for Arch 499: Graphic Communication," Lesson 2, Visual Graphics 3D, Notes on problem 2, 1977, PKPD, box 30, folder 1.

50. Undated notes headed, "When I came to the Dept. of Arch….," 1.

51. Undated notes headed, "When I came to the Dept. of Arch…., " 1.

52. Undated notes headed, "When I came to the Dept. of Arch….," 2.

53. See Pierre Koenig, "Suggested Reading List," Natural Forces Design 418, 307, 199, 599, 14 December 1992, box 28, folder 5.

54. See Request for Leave of Absence, 5 June 1980; and Pierre Koenig to Panos Koulermos, 3 March 1980, PKPD, box 30, folder 4a. "Summary of Proposed Project during Sabbatical Leave for Pierre Koenig, Spring 1981," 3 March 1980, PKPD, box 30, folder 4A.

55. See Panos Koulermos to Pierre Koenig, 14 June 1980, PKPD, box 30, folder 4A.

56. "Summary of Proposed Project during Sabbatical for Pierre Koenig, Fall 1996," n.d., PKPD, box 30, folder 4A.

57. Pierre Koenig to Julius Shulman, fax, 4 August 1998, PKPD, box 28, folder 6.

58. See Pierre Koenig, "Revised Course Outline," History of Modern Architecture in Southern California, 19 January 1999, 2, PKPD, box 28, folder 6.

59. Elaine Sewell to Pierre Koenig, 14 March 1999, PKPD, box 28, folder 6.

60. Pierre Koenig, *Modern Architecture in Southern California,* vols. 1 and 2, CD-ROM, 1998, PKPD, box 28, folder 11.

61. For annual records, see PKPD, box 30, folder 5.

62. See Lloyd Armstrong to Robert Timme, memo, 16 January 1997, PKPD, box 31, folder 1.

63. Dean Robert H. Timme to the author, 29 July 1996, author's collection.

64. Lloyd Armstrong to Pierre Koenig, 29 June 1998, PKPD, box 31, folder 1.

65. Barry Wasserman to Pierre Koenig, 19 October 1989, PKPD, box 147, folder 11.

66. San Francisco Museum of Modern Art to Pierre Koenig, 20 June 1990, PKPD, box 147, folder 12.

67. For papers relating to *Los Angeles—City on the Move,* see PKPD, box 148, folder 1. A letter of 4 November 1991 from Francesca Garcia-Marques thanks Koenig for participating in the Salon international de l'architecture, where their exhibit was "given a prominent position adjacent to the conference center in the Triennale Hall." See PKPD, box 148, folder 1.

68. For papers relating to *100 Projects/100 Years,* see PKPD, box 148, folder 5.

69. For papers relating to *Steel Houses,* see PKPD, box 148, folder 4.

70. For papers relating to *Architects' Own Homes Tour,* see PKPD, box 148, folder 3.

71. Pierre Koenig to the author, fax, 2 August 1995, PKPD, box 148, folder 4.

72. For the University of Texas lecture, see Kevin Alter to Pierre Koenig, 11 July 1997, PKPD, box 148, folder 9. For the 1997 lecture at Cal Poly Pomona, see Sigrid Miller Pollin to Pierre Koenig, 5 March 1997, PKPD, box 148, folder 10. For Arizona State, see Darren Petrucci to Pierre Koenig, 23 August 1999, PKPD, box 149, folder 2. For the 1999 lecture at Cal Poly Pomona, see William Adams to Pierre Koenig, 23 September 1999, PKPD, box 149, folder 4. For the AIA Student Forum, see Anne Marie Taheny to Pierre Koenig, email, 8 November 2000, PKPD, box 150, folder 5.

73. For *Architecture L.A. at the Hammer,* see Ann Philbin to Pierre Koenig, email, 27 October 2000, PKPD, box 150, folder 1.

74. Ann Philbin to Pierre Koenig, 27 October 2000, PKPD, box 150, folder 1.

75. See Bob Pool, "Thoroughly Beguiled by Modernist House," *Los Angeles Times,* 5 November 2000, n.p., PKPD, box 150, folder 2. Steele and Jenkins, *Pierre Koenig.*

76. See Renée Harrison to Pierre Koenig, 18 December 2000, PKPD, box 150, folder 2.

77. See AIA California Council, Monterey Design Conference Faculty, 3 April 2001, PKPD, box 150, folder 9.

78. Amy Eliot to Pierre Koenig, 26 April 2001, PKPD, box 150, folder 9.

79. Pierre Koenig, AIA California Council Continuing Education Credit, 23 April 2001, PKPD, box 150, folder 9.

80. For awards, see Design Awards 1956–2001, PKPD, box 32, folder 3.

81. Martin Gelber to Pierre Koenig, 26 March 1984, PKPD, box 33, folder 13.

82. Maybeck Award certificate, 1996, PKPD, box 35, folder 15.

83. Nicci Solomons to Pierre Koenig, 2 June 1999, PKPD, box 33, folder 17.

84. The author to Alex Reid, 17 October 1996, PKPD, box 33, folder 18A.

85. See Julie Grover to the author, 29 January 1997, PKPD, box 33, folder 18A.

86. Sir Norman Foster to the author, 30 January 1998, PKPD, box 33, folder 18A.

87. See the author to Alex Reid, 4 February 1999, PKPD, box 33, folder 18A.

88. Julie Grover to the author, 26 February 1999, PKPD, box 33, folder 18A.

89. Alex Reid to Pierre Koenig, 6 April 2000, PKPD, box 33, folder 18A.

90. Alex Reid to Pierre Koenig, 18 May 2000, PKPD, box 33, folder 18A.

91. Draft copy of acceptance letter with the handwritten heading "I regret . . . ," n.d., PKPD, box 33, folder 18A.

92. Pierre Koenig to the author, fax, 3 June 2000, PKPD, box 33, folder 18A.

93. Press release from RIBA Head of Awards Tony Chapman, RIBA Press & TV Services, 19 May 2000, 1, PKPD, box 33, folder 18A.

94. For papers relating to the National Design Awards, see PKPD, box 33, folder 20.

95. Remarks by Mrs. Bush at National Design Awards, transcription, 10 July 2002, PKPD, box 33, folder 20.

96. Sir Norman Foster to the author, 30 January 1998, PKPD, box 33, folder 18A.

97. Dan Cray and Jeffrey Ressner, "Back to the '50s," *Time,* 16 November 1998, 103.

98. Pierre Koenig, interview by Mohamed Sharif, Los Angeles, January–November 2003, QuickTime movie, © 2016 by in-D media.

99. Pierre Koenig, "Talk at AIA Meeting June 11, 1963," lecture typescript, 2, PKPD, box 48, folder 1.

100. "Low-Cost Production House," *Arts & Architecture* (March 1957): 24–25.

101. Pierre Koenig, "The Modern Southern California House," typescript, 2, PKPD, box 48, folder 1.

102. Pierre Koenig, interview by Mohamed Sharif.

103. Unsigned contract between Pierre Koenig, Bethlehem Steel Company, and "the owners" of Case Study House 22, n.d., PKPD, box 1A, folder 1.

104. Pierre Koenig, interview by Mohamed Sharif.

105. Edward Allen to Pierre Koenig, 14 March 1999, 1–2, PKPD, box 35, folder 6.

106. Hassam Cham to Pierre Koenig, fax, 26 December 1999, PKPD, box 35, folder 6.

107. See assorted membership cards, dated 1966 to 1969, PKPD, box 57, folder 8.

108. United States passports issued to Pierre Koenig on 26 March 1968 and 25 October 2000, and United States International Driving Permit issued to Pierre Koenig on 18 June 1968, PKPD, box 57, folder 8.

109. See California Council of Diving Clubs Membership Card for 1969 and California Sports Fishing License for 1959, PKPD, box 57, folder 1.

110. Santa Monica Sea Lancers hand-drawn advertisements, 21 March, 16 April, 18 April, 7 May, 16 May, 3 and 4 June, and 18 July 1961, PKPD, box 57, folder 2.

111. R. R. "Dick" Schreiber to Pierre Koenig, 13 March 2003, PKPD, box 57, folder 3.

112. UCLA Extension Program and Instructor Evaluation, "Railroads: The Romance and the Reality," 26 October 1976. See also UCLA Extension lecture program, "Railroads: The Romance and the Reality," and annotated bibliography, September–November 1976, PKPD, box 57, folder 4.

113. Undated receipt for $15 from the National Railroad Museum, Washington, D.C., with peel-off address labels, PKPD, box 57, folder 4.

114. He bought track and rolling stock from Allied Model Trains in Culver City, the Brass Locomotive Co. in San Diego, and Model Expo Inc. in Hollywood, Florida. See receipts in PKPD, box 57, folder 4.

115. Pierre Koenig, interview by Mohamed Sharif.

116. Pierre Koenig, interview by Mohamed Sharif.

117. Pierre Koenig, interview by Mohamed Sharif.

118. Gloria Koenig continued to live at 12221 Dorothy Street until she died there on 2 September 2014, aged 89. Her sons, Barry and Tom Kaufman, restored the house, which was thirty years old at the time, and put it on the market for $3,795,000. It was sold for $3,460,000.

# INDEX

Note: page numbers in italics refer to figures; those followed by *t* refer to tables; those followed by *n* refer to notes, with note number.

All buildings, restorations, additions, remodels, designs, drawings, lectures, and written documents listed below are by Pierre Koenig unless otherwise attributed.

## ABOUT THE AUTHOR

NEIL JACKSON is a British architect and architectural historian who first met Pierre Koenig while teaching architecture in Los Angeles in the 1980s. His subsequent publications on midcentury California architecture include *The Modern Steel House* (1996) and the award-winning *Craig Ellwood* (2002). The present book, which builds on his earlier writings on Pierre Koenig, developed from a guest scholar residency at the Getty Conservation Institute in 2013. Jackson currently holds the Charles Reilly Chair of Architecture at the University of Liverpool and is president of the Society of Architectural Historians of Great Britain.

**The Getty Research Institute Publications Program**
Thomas W. Gaehtgens, *Director, Getty Research Institute*
Gail Feigenbaum, *Associate Director*

**Published by the Getty Research Institute, Los Angeles**
Getty Publications
1200 Getty Center Drive, Suite 500
Los Angeles, California  90049-1682
www.getty.edu/publications

Lauren Edson, *Manuscript Editor*
Catherine Lorenz, *Designer*
Victoria Gallina, *Production*
Diane Franco, *Typesetter*

Type composed in Suisse Int'l Condensed

Distributed in the United States and Canada by the University of Chicago Press
Distributed outside the United States and Canada by Yale University Press, London

Printed in China

Library of Congress Cataloging-in-Publication Data

Names: Jackson, N. (Neil), author.
Title: Pierre Koenig : a view from the archive / Neil Jackson.
Description: Los Angeles : Getty Research Institute, [2019] | Includes bibliographical
    references and index.
Identifiers: LCCN 2018028173 | ISBN 9781606065778
Subjects: LCSH: Koenig, Pierre, 1925-2004. | Architect-designed houses—California—
    Los Angeles County. | Architecture—California—Los Angeles County—History—
    20th century.
Classification: LCC NA737.K63 J33 2019 | DDC 720.9794/94—dc23
LC record available at https://lccn.loc.gov/2018028173

Front cover: The Oberman House with Catalina Island in the distance, 1962. Los Angeles,
    Getty Research Institute. Photo by Leland. Y. Lee. Courtesy the Leland Y. Lee Estate. See
    page 57, fig. 6.8.
Back cover and pages 172–73: Riebe Addition to Johnson House, elevations (detail),
    ca. 2002. See page 212, pl. 61.
Page i: Chemehuevi Housing Project, axonometric drawing of sixteen house types,
    18 July 1976. See page 235, pl. 97.